# Proportionality in International Humanitarian Law

The Lieber Studies is one of the two flagship publications of the Lieber Institute for Law and Land Warfare. It is designed to provide scholars, practitioners, and students with in-depth and critical analysis of the most challenging legal issues related to warfare in the 21st Century. Established by the Department of Law of the United States Military Academy at West Point, the mission of the Lieber Institute is to foster a deeper understanding of the complex and evolving relationship between law and land warfare in order to educate and empower current and future combat leaders. It does so through global academic engagement and advanced interdisciplinary research. As such, it lies at the crossroads of scholarship and practice by bringing together scholars, military officers, government legal advisors, and members of civil society from around the world to collaboratively examine the role and application of the law of armed conflict in current and future armed conflicts, as well as that of other regimes of international law in situations threatening international peace and security.

Lieber Institute for Law and Land Warfare
The Lieber Studies

VOLUME 6

# Proportionality in International Humanitarian Law

## *Consequences, Precautions, and Procedures*

---


**General Editor**

PROFESSOR MICHAEL N. SCHMITT

**Managing Editors**

COLONEL SHANE R. REEVES

COLONEL WINSTON S. WILLIAMS

DR. SASHA RADIN

**Authors**

AMICHAI COHEN

DAVID ZLOTOGORSKI



OXFORD
UNIVERSITY PRESS

OXFORD
UNIVERSITY PRESS

Oxford University Press is a department of the University of Oxford. It furthers the University's objective of excellence in research, scholarship, and education by publishing worldwide. Oxford is a registered trade mark of Oxford University Press in the UK and certain other countries.

Published in the United States of America by Oxford University Press
198 Madison Avenue, New York, NY 10016, United States of America.



Library of Congress Cataloging-in-Publication Data
Names: Cohen, Amichai, author. | Zlotogorski, David, author.
Title: Proportionality in international humanitarian law : consequences,
precautions, and procedures / Amichai Cohen & David Zlotogorski.
Description: New York, NY : Oxford University Press, [2020] |
Includesbibliographical references and index.
Identifiers: LCCN 2020044178 | ISBN 9780197556726 (hardcover) |
ISBN 9780197556740 (epub) | ISBN 9780197556733 (updf) | ISBN 9780197556757 (online)
Subjects: LCSH: Humanitarian law. | Proportionality in law.
Classification: LCC KZ6471 .C64 2020 | DDC 341.6/7—dc23
LC record available at https://lccn.loc.gov/2020044178

DOI: 10.1093/oso/9780197556726.001.0001

# CONTENTS

# PREFACE

This book aims to clarify the current debates regarding the concept of proportionality in international humanitarian law (IHL).

Almost all states involved in armed conflicts recognize the principle of proportionality in IHL as a legal and ethical restraint on their military activities. Specifically, it is broadly accepted that an attacking party cannot justify collateral damage to civilians if the harm caused is expected to be excessive with regard to the concrete military advantage gained. However, the precise meaning of this principle is frequently disputed. There are debates over many issues, including the degree to which force-protection measures can justify extensive collateral damage; the obligation to employ accurate but expensive weaponry; and the impact of using voluntary and non-voluntary human shields. There are also disagreements concerning the parameters that are supposed to be used in assessing such a case: What exactly is a "military advantage," and what does it mean for the harm caused to "exceed" such an advantage?

Controversy is especially rife regarding asymmetrical conflicts. Many states, among them many democracies, are engaged in armed conflicts against non-state actors, some of them terrorist organizations. In these situations, questions relating to the correct interpretation and effective implementation of the principle of proportionality have arisen, for example, in connection with targeted killings and military operations in civilian areas.

The goal of this book is to shine a light on these controversies; to clarify the areas in which there is disagreement; and in some cases, to offer unorthodox points of view on these debates.

The background for the book is an international conference entitled "Proportionality and Civilian Casualties in Asymmetrical Armed Conflicts: An Interdisciplinary Approach." The conference was convened by the National Security and Democracy Center at the Israel Democracy Institute and by the Konrad-Adenauer-Stiftung, and took place at the Israel Democracy Institute in Jerusalem in May 2016.

The purpose of the conference was to evaluate the applicability and parameters of the principle of proportionality with regard to liberal states involved in asymmetrical conflicts. The premise was that a full understanding of the proportionality principle cannot be gained through exclusive use of a legal perspective. The principle of proportionality is at once a **philosophical principle, a political necessity, and a restriction on military operations**; thus, it is both a **theoretical concept** and a **practical tool**. As a result, a worthwhile discussion of the underlying reasoning, effects, and parameters of the proportionality principle must be multidisciplinary in character. Hence, the conference included scholars from diverse academic fields, such as law, philosophy, and political science, as well as varied practitioners: current and former military commanders, representatives of NGOs, and civilians.

The discussions held at the conference gave us the initial impetus to embark on this book project, and the conference participants provided us with many interesting and novel points of view on the subject. Most of the material in the book is based on research undertaken by the authors following the conference. However, there are a few cases in which an original position was presented at the conference, without it being based on a publicly available source. On these rare occasions, we simply cite it as an "opinion presented at the Proportionality Conference."

The result is a book that aims to present many, perhaps most, of the current positions and debates regarding the application of the principle of proportionality. We believe that this work will be of use both to academics with an interest in these issues, and to practitioners, such as military legal advisers and judges. We believe that there are, in David Luban's terms, at least two "cultures" of proportionality: that of the academics, and that of the practitioners.[1] An important goal of this work is to bridge this gap, at least to some degree.

We would like to thank the Israel Democracy Institute's National Security and Democracy Center and the Konrad-Adenauer-Stiftung for their generous financial support, both for the conference and for further work on this book. Dr. Michael Borchard of the Konrad-Adenauer-Stiftung and Professor Mordechai Kremnitzer, then vice president of the Israel Democracy Institute (IDI), were a constant source of support and wisdom. Professor Yuval Shany, current vice president of IDI, provided many important comments on earlier drafts. Mr. Yochanan Plesner, IDI president, supported the project from beginning to end. Special thanks to Dr. Dina Wyshogrod for tireless hours of help and support in her work on the various drafts of this book. We are especially grateful to all the participants in the conference, who invested much time and effort in clarifying concepts and in debating the issues covered in this book.

David Zlotogorski would particularly like to thank Mr. Tal Mimran for all his valuable guidance and advice throughout the journey and Mr. Ori Pomson for his expertise and unflagging assistance.

Amichai Cohen would also like to thank the Faculty of Law at the Ono Academic College, and especially Deans Yuval Elbashan and Elad Finkelstein for their support and encouragement during the work on this book.

Financial support for this book was provided by ERC Grant No. 324182.

1. David Luban, *Military Necessity and the Cultures of Military Law*, 26(2) Leiden J. Int'l L. 315 (2013).

# TABLE OF TREATIES AND CASES

## CONVENTIONS AND TREATIES

## NATIONAL LEGISLATION



## INTERNATIONAL COURT OF JUSTICE - CONTENTIOUS CASES AND ADVISORY OPINIONS



## INTERNATIONAL CRIMINAL TRIBUNAL FOR FORMER YUGOSLAVIA (ICTY)

## EUROPEAN COURT OF HUMAN RIGHTS



## US MILITARY TRIBUNAL NUREMBERG

## INTER-AMERICAN COURT OF HUMAN RIGHTS



## SPECIAL COURT FOR SIERRA LEONE



## ETHIOPIA-ERITREA CLAIMS COMMISSION



## JUDGMENTS OF NATIONAL COURTS

### *Colombia*



### *Germany*



### *Israel*

### *Japan*



### *United Kingdom*

PART I

# General Concepts

This part of the book presents the general concept of proportionality in IHL. We begin this section with two chapters in which the general principle of proportionality is explained, and the historical and legal development of this principle is reviewed.

# 1

# An Introduction to Proportionality

## A. GENERAL CONCEPTS

There are few concepts in international law that both captivate the mind and stir bitter debates as much as the application of the principle of proportionality in contemporary armed conflict. As conflicts are increasingly fought in urban settings, the concept of proportionality plays a crucial role in the protection of civilians from the horrors of war. This book is a study of proportionality as it is currently understood in the laws of armed conflict—also known as international humanitarian law (IHL).[1]

The principle of proportionality is one of the cornerstones of IHL together with the other basic principles of: distinction between civilians and combatants, the prohibition of inflicting unnecessary suffering, the notion of military necessity, and the principle of humanity.[2] Although proportionality is notoriously opaque and can seem a topic for theoreticians, the real-world impact of this principle and its interpretation is very concrete. States, and their armed forces, treat it as a serious limitation on their military activity.[3] There are many reasons for the

1. Proportionality is an important principle not only in IHL, but also in the law that governs the conditions under which states may go to war—*jus ad bellum*. Although contemporary international law contains a broad prohibition on the use of force (United Nations (UN), Charter of the United Nations, Oct. 24, 1945, art. 2(4) 1 U.N.T.S. XVI), the primary, if not sole, exception to this prohibition is self-defense (*Id.*, art. 51). In the simplest terms, in order for use of force in self-defense to be lawful, a state must have been the target of an armed attack, and its resort to force must be proportionate, immediate, and used only when necessary—as a last resort. A discussion of *jus ad bellum* proportionality, which in general terms determine whether the use of force is proportionate to the cause of war, is beyond the scope of this book. See generally *Case Concerning Oil Platforms (Iran v. U.S.A), Merits*, I.C.J. 161, paras. 51, 76–77 (2003); *Case Concerning Military and Paramilitary Activities in and against Nicaragua (Nicar. v. U.S.A), Merits*, I.C.J. 14, para. 194 (1986); *Case Concerning Armed Activities on the Territory of the Congo (Dem. Rep. Congo v. Uganda), Judgment*, I.C.J. 168, para. 147 (2005); Yoram Dinstein, War, Aggression and Self-Defence 230–33 (5th ed., 2011); David Kretzmer, *The Inherent Right to Self Defence and Proportionality in Jus Ad Bellum*, 24 Eur. J. Int'l L. 235 (2013).

2. There is some disagreement as to what are the basic principles of IHL. We adopt here the list proposed by the ICRC in Marco Sassoli et al., How Does Law Protect in War? Vol. 1, 161–62 (I.C.R.C., 3rd ed., 2011).

3. Jack M. Beard, *Law and War in the Virtual Era*, 103 A.J.I.L. 409, 427 (2009).

*Proportionality in International Humanitarian Law.* Amichai Cohen & David Zlotogorski, Oxford University Press.
 DOI: 10.1093/oso/9780197556726.003.0001

prominence of the principle of proportionality, especially, its hold on the "imagination of the epistemic community in which it is used as the prism for viewing, arguing, and ultimately resolving disputes."[4]

It is, perhaps, useful to present the principle of proportionality in the context of two other cardinal principles of IHL: the principles of necessity and of distinction.[5] According to these, only combatants and military objectives may be targeted during armed conflicts. The attacking party must ascertain whether a given target is military or civilian, and refrain from attacking the latter. The principle of proportionality adds a further constraint to the principle of distinction. Even if the target is a military objective, attacking it is prohibited if it is expected to cause incidental harm to civilians "which would be excessive in relation to the concrete and direct military advantage anticipated."[6]

For example, while civilian buildings cannot be attacked during a military operation, a civilian building housing a group of soldiers can be attacked, because its use makes it a military objective. However, the principle of proportionality places limits on how and when this building may be attacked. It is prohibited to attack the building if it is known that a large number of civilians either in the building or in its vicinity would be harmed, even if unintentionally, to an extent that this harm ("collateral damage") would be excessive relative to the military advantage gained by the attack. Thus, distinction and proportionality impose two cumulative conditions that must both be fulfilled in order for an attack to be lawful. Both principles limit the freedom of operation and the discretion of the belligerent parties, and thereby play an important role in protecting civilians from the vicissitudes of armed conflict.[7]

The principle of proportionality is perhaps one of the clearest examples of the balance struck in IHL[8] between the two conflicting interests of military

4. Thomas M. Franck, *On Proportionality of Countermeasures in International Law*, 102 A.J.I.L. 715, 718 (2008).

5. *Legality of the Threat or Use of Nuclear Weapons*, Advisory Opinion, I.C.J. 8, 587, para. 78 (1996) [Nuclear Weapons Case]: "The cardinal principles contained in the texts constituting the fabric of humanitarian law are the following. The first is aimed at the protection of the civilian population and civilian objects and establishes the distinction between combatants and non-combatants."

6. Protocol Additional to the Geneva Conventions of August 12, 1949, and Relating to the Protection of Victims of International Armed Conflicts (Protocol I), June 8, 1977, arts. 51(5)(b), 57(2)(a)(iii), 1125 U.N.T.S. 3 [AP-I].

7. Yoram Dinstein, The Conduct of Hostilities under the Law of International Armed Conflict 130 (2nd ed., 2010).

8. Michael N. Schmitt, *Military Necessity and Humanity in International Humanitarian Law: Preserving the Delicate Balance*, 50 Va. J. Int'l L. 795, 798 (2010). Another clear example is the obligation to avoid causing unnecessary suffering (AP-I, *supra* note 6, art. 35(2)).

necessity and humanity.[9] This balance is meted out in the different treaties and their provisions as well as in the customary law of IHL. Proportionality—in general, and in IHL specifically—represents a social convention that certain societal values must only be achieved at reasonable cost.[10] Proportionality is different from other principles of IHL in that it balances military necessity against humanitarian interests "horizontally" rather than "vertically." That is, rather than allowing for military necessity to justify any harm to civilians, or allowing the principle of distinction to completely prohibit any attacks involving collateral damage, proportionality instead requires the attackers to review their planned operation, weighing the foreseeable damage to the civilian population against the anticipated military advantage. If the harm resulting from the attack is expected to be excessive in relation to the military advantage that is anticipated, then proportionality requires that the attack be canceled or suspended.

Although it is one of the core principles of IHL, the term "proportionality" does not appear in any IHL treaty.[11] As the principle of proportionality clearly limits the freedom of action that armed forces have during armed conflicts, states have been reluctant to limit themselves by adopting an explicit prohibition on the use of disproportionate force.[12]

There seems to be no broad agreement on what constitutes a proportionate attack as opposed to a disproportionate one. It is generally accepted that an attack on a whole battalion, justified from a military perspective, is proportionate when the expected collateral damage is the death of one civilian. It also seems uncontroversial that killing an entire village during an attack on one soldier, even if killing this soldier provides a military advantage, is disproportionate. However, there is

9. Commentary on the Additional Protocols of 8 June 1977 to the Geneva Conventions of 12 August 1949, para. 2206 (ICRC, Yves Sandoz, Christophe Swinarki, & Bruno Zimmerman eds., 1987) [AP-I Commentary].

10. Yuval Shany, The Principle of Proportionality under International Law 13 (2009) (Heb.).

11. This omission is not one of mere happenstance. There was an attempt to include the term proportionality in the First Additional Protocol to the Geneva Conventions (AP-I), though this attempt failed. See Amichai Cohen, *The Principle of Proportionality in the Context of Operation Cast Lead: Institutional Perspectives*, 35 Rutgers L. Record 23, 27 n.37 (2009); W.J. Fenrick, *The Rule of Proportionality and Protocol I in Conventional Warfare*, 98 Mil. L. Rev. 91, 102–07 (1982). Prior to AP-I, the principle itself was not even stipulated in any treaty; see William J. Fenrick, *Applying IHL Targeting Rules to Practical Situations: Proportionality and Military Objectives*, 27 Windsor Y.B. Access Just. 271, 277 (2009). The use of the term "excessive," rather than "disproportionate," in AP-I stems from a concern raised by its framers that the use of the term "proportionality" could result in a standard that would excessively constrain states' abilities to engage in combat. See Shany, *Id.*, at 59.

12. Amichai Cohen, Proportionality in Modern Asymmetrical Wars, 8 (2010), *available at:* din-online.info/pdf/jc2.pdf.

a vast grey area between these two extremes that remains contentious.[13] Almost three decades ago, W. Hays Parks, an expert in IHL who invested significant time studying the issue of proportionality, concluded that "there remains a substantial lack of agreement as to the meaning of the provisions in Protocol I relating to proportionality."[14] In the decades since, the principle still remains contested.[15]

At the outset, it might be useful to set out areas of agreement. Almost everyone agrees that proportionality in IHL is not a matter of the number of combatants or soldiers killed during a single attack or during the entire armed conflict.[16] From the standpoint of IHL proportionality, it is lawful for one state to suffer no military casualties whatsoever while killing thousands of enemy soldiers. Furthermore, according to most scholars, proportionality in IHL does not concern itself with equality or equity in the means or methods of warfare that states employ:[17] it does not prohibit a state from using overwhelming force to subdue the military of the adverse party,[18] and it is lawful for a modern state

13. The latter part of this example is presented by Dinstein (DINSTEIN, *supra* note 7, at 134). This issue was also raised by the Israeli High Court of Justice. See HCJ 769/02, Public Committee against Torture v. The State of Israel, PD 62(1) 507, para. 46 (2006) [Isr.] [*Targeted Killings* Case]. Recently, an empirical study examined how 331 lawyers and legal academics (LLM students) conducted proportionality analyses in different scenarios. The study found that ideology (being a hawk or a dove) is strongly associated with proportionality analysis, as are changes to the facts and circumstances in the scenarios that were presented to the respondents in the survey. In the scenarios presented before the respondents, 90.9% of the "hawks" approved a given attack, as opposed to only 52.1% of "doves." See Raanan Sulitzeanu-Kenan, Mordechai Kremnitzer, & Sharon Alon, *Facts, Preferences, and Doctrine: An Empirical Analysis of Proportionality Judgment*, 50 L. & SOC'Y REV. 348, 366–72 (2016).

14. W. Hays Parks, *Air War and the Law of War*, 32 AIR FORCE L. REV. 1, 175 (1990).

15. COHEN, *supra* note 12, at 13.

16. Gabriella Blum claims that the lives of soldiers should be protected in specific cases, but focuses on the principle of distinction and the principle of necessity. Gabriella Blum, *The Dispensable Lives of Soldiers*, 2 J. LEGAL ANALYSIS 115, 158 (2010). Ido Rozenzweig does suggest that lives of soldiers should be protected under the principle of proportionality, though his opinion seems to be somewhat singular in that respect. See: "Rethinking the Basic Principles of IHL and their Application to Combatants' Lives" (draft article, on file with the authors).

17. Adam Roberts, *The Equal Application of the Law of War: A Principle Under Pressure*, 872 INT'L REV. RED CROSS 931, 932 (2008): "Under this principle, the laws of war . . . apply equally to all those who are entitled to participate directly in hostilities . . . it is not relevant whether a belligerent force represents an autocracy or a democracy, nor is it relevant whether it represents the government of a single country or the will of the international community." However, see also Gabriella Blum, *On a Differential Law of War*, 52 HARV. J. INT'L L. 164, 194 (2011), who suggests that "a common-but-differentiated principle of proportionality and the duty to take precautions in attack might impose substantially higher degrees of responsibility on richer or more technologically advanced countries than on poorer ones."

18. Parks, *supra* note 14, at 170; Fenrick, *supra* note 11, at 277. While proportionality in IHL does not concern itself with the relation between the harm caused to each one of the parties, determining proportionality in *jus ad bellum* does involve a discussion of whether the use of force

to use tanks and airplanes against an adversary that only has poorly equipped infantry soldiers.[19] Proportionality concerns only expected harm to civilians and civilian objects.[20]

Yet even with regard to civilians, proportionality does not require parity between the number of casualties—those killed or injured—on both sides of the conflict. We might imagine a specific scenario in which there will be a direct causal connection between saving the lives of a number of civilians at a cost of the lives of other civilians—for example, in an operation aimed at preventing a specific terrorist attack. But this is not the usual case, or even a very realistic one. In most cases, determining whether an attack is proportionate or not is not simply a matter of crunching numbers.[21] Rather, proportionality is an intricate evaluation of completely different sets of values—on the one hand, the harm to civilians and civilian objects, and on the other, the anticipated military advantage. Most commentators agree that these two values cannot be compared through the simple use of a formula, because they have no common denominator.[22] Proportionality analysis has therefore been called a "value judgment."[23]

and harm committed to the opposing party was proportionate to the justification of the use of force. For more on this matter, see Chapter 7.

19. Such an action *might* be questionable under proportionality in *jus ad bellum*, which is not the subject of this work. See: Kretzmer, *The Inherent Right to Self Defense and Proportionality in Jus Ad Bellum*, *supra* note 1.

20. Dinstein, *supra* note 7, at 129.

21. *Id.*, at 130. One example of this misconstrued application of proportionality analysis can be found in the United Nations Human Rights Council, *Report of the United Nations Fact-Finding Mission on the Gaza Conflict*, U.N. Doc. A/HRC/12/48 (Sept. 25, 2009) [The Goldstone Report]. Robert Sloane writes that: "Many critics of the IDF's conduct in the 2008–09 campaign Operation Cast Lead, including prominent international lawyers on the Goldstone Commission, seized upon the numerical disparity between people (civilians and combatants) killed by Hamas's forces (13) and people killed by the IDF (estimates vary, but likely more than 1,100), as decisive evidence of disproportionate force—without considering the anticipated military objective or *ex ante* context. The IDF might well be culpable for using disproportionate force. But the foregoing would be an indefensible application of AP-I's definition" (Robert D. Sloane, *Puzzles of Proportion and the 'Reasonable Military Commander': Reflections on the Law, Ethics, and Geopolitics of Proportionality*, 6 Harv. Nat'l Sec. J. 299, 317 (2015)).

22. For a view that proportionality can be assessed by using a specific equation tailored to include the different considerations that must be examined in the analysis, see Boaz Ganor, Global Alert: The Rationality of Modern Islamist Terrorism and the Challenge to the Liberal Democratic World (2015). This suggestion will be discussed in some detail in Chapter 11.

23. Dinstein, *supra* note 7, at 132; International Criminal Court, Elements of Crimes, 19 n.37 (2011), *available at:* www.icc-cpi.int/NR/rdonlyres/336923D8-A6AD-40EC-AD7B-45BF9DE73D56/0/ElementsOfCrimesEng.pdf.

## B. LEGAL SOURCES

Today the principle of proportionality is stipulated primarily, but not exclusively, in two separate articles of the First Additional Protocol to the Geneva Conventions (AP-I).[24] Article 51(5)(b) of AP-I proscribes attacks that cause disproportionate damage:

> 51(5): Among others, the following types of attacks are to be considered as indiscriminate: . . . (b) an attack which may be expected to cause incidental loss of civilian life, injury to civilians, damage to civilian objects, or a combination thereof, which would be excessive in relation to the concrete and direct military advantage anticipated.

Article 57(2) of AP-I further requires attackers to take precautions prior to an attack and refrain from launching an attack that is expected to cause disproportionate harm,[25] and to cancel or suspend the attack if it becomes apparent that the attack will cause disproportionate harm.[26] Launching a disproportionate attack, that causes "death or serious injury to body or health," is a grave breach of AP-I.[27]

The prohibition on disproportionate attacks also appears in Protocol II to the Certain Conventional Weapons Treaty of 1980,[28] and in its amended version of 1996.[29]

24. AP-I, *supra* note 6.

25. AP-I, *Id.*, note 6, art. 57(2)(a)(iii): "With respect to attacks, the following precautions shall be taken: (a) those who plan or decide upon an attack shall: . . . (iii) refrain from deciding to launch any attack which may be expected to cause incidental loss of civilian life, injury to civilians, damage to civilian objects, or a combination thereof, which would be excessive in relation to the concrete and direct military advantage anticipated."

26. AP-I, *Id.*, art. 57(2)(b): "With respect to attacks, the following precautions shall be taken: . . . (b) an attack shall be cancelled or suspended if it becomes apparent that the objective is not a military one or is subject to special protection or that the attack may be expected to cause incidental loss of civilian life, injury to civilians, damage to civilian objects, or a combination thereof, which would be excessive in relation to the concrete and direct military advantage anticipated."

27. AP-I, *Id.*, art. 85(3): "In addition to the grave breaches defined in Article 11, the following acts shall be regarded as grave breaches of this Protocol, when committed wilfully, in violation of the relevant provisions of this Protocol, and causing death or serious injury to body or health: . . . (b) launching an indiscriminate attack affecting the civilian population or civilian objects in the knowledge that such attack will cause excessive loss of life, injury to civilians or damage to civilian objects, as defined in Article 57, paragraph 2 a) iii)."

28. Convention on Prohibitions or Restrictions on the Use of Certain Conventional Weapons Which May be Deemed to be Excessively Injurious or to have Indiscriminate Effects, Oct. 10, 1980, 1342 U.N.T.S. 137 [CCW]: Protocol on Prohibitions or Restrictions on the Use of Mines, Booby-Traps and Other Devices (Protocol II), Geneva, Oct. 10, 1980, art. 3(3), 1342 U.N.T.S. 168.

29. CCW, *Id.*; Protocol on Prohibitions or Restrictions on the Use of Mines, Booby Traps and Other Devices (Protocol II), as amended, May 3, 1996, art. 3(8), 35 I.L.M. 1206.

The Rome Statute classifies disproportionate attacks as a war crime, if committed during an international armed conflict, and prohibits

> intentionally launching an attack in the knowledge that such attack will cause incidental loss of life or injury to civilians or damage to civilian objects . . . which would be clearly excessive in relation to the concrete and direct overall military advantage anticipated.[30]

Altogether, the principle of proportionality is widely understood to constitute part of customary international law.[31]

## C. THE STRUCTURE OF THE BOOK

Chapters 2 and 3 lay out a theoretical and historical framework for the principle of proportionality as formulated in IHL. The second chapter presents the theoretical framework from its religious and ethical sources through to its application in IHL, and discusses how the sub-tests found in general proportionality theory find their way into IHL and into the principle of proportionality as articulated in AP-I. The third chapter begins with a description of how proportionality developed in contemporary IHL, from the Lieber Code of 1863 to AP-I in 1977. It then discusses the changing nature of armed conflicts and the prevalence of international human rights law (HRL), and examines how these relate to IHL proportionality.

In Part II, the first two chapters (4 and 5) delve into how the principle of proportionality is applied in practice. Chapter 4 describes the first side of the equation: the concept of military advantage, and how it is analyzed. Chapter 5 presents the second side of the equation: incidental harm, and reviews issues such as the definition of civilians, the assessment of environmental harm, and the required level of certainty.

The next five chapters (6–10) explore more specific aspects of proportionality, which can be discussed following the analysis in the fourth and fifth chapters. Chapters 6 and 7 discuss issues pertaining to the military advantage that is anticipated from an attack. Specifically, Chapter 6 examines whether force protection—protecting the lives of soldiers serving in the military forces that are planning or executing a military operation—can be considered part of the military advantage. This question concerns the level and extent of risk of harm to which states must expose their own soldiers in order to reduce the risk of harm to civilians. Chapter 7 evaluates whether broader strategic considerations can be

30. Rome Statute of the International Criminal Court, Jul. 17, 1998, art. 8.2(b)(iv), 2187 U.N.T.S. 90 (1998).

31. Jean-Marie Henckaerts & Louise Doswald-Beck, Customary International Humanitarian Law, Vol. 1, rule 14 (2005), *available at:* ihl-databases.icrc.org/customary-ihl/eng/docs/v1_rul. Prosecutor v. Kupreskić, ICTY Trials Chamber, IT-95-16, *Judgment*, para. 524 (Jan. 14, 2000); *Targeted Killings* Case, *supra* note 13, paras. 40–43.

included in proportionality analysis, and whether specific cultural sensitivities can be taken into account when examining the military advantage anticipated from an attack. The chapter reviews the different interpretations that states, organizations, and scholars have offered on this matter.

The subsequent three chapters (8–10) discuss how different aspects of the principle of distinction affect the proportionality analysis. Chapters 8 and 9 look at how the principle of distinction applies to persons, and how this affects proportionality. Chapter 8 tackles the notion of "direct participation in hostilities," referring to civilians who, by actively taking part in hostilities, lose their protection from direct attack and from incidental harm. Chapter 9 deals with a correlating situation: the deployment of voluntary and involuntary human shields in armed conflicts, and the ensuing risk of harm to the civilian population. Chapter 10 analyzes how the definitions of military objectives, dual-use targets, and indiscriminate attacks affect the proportionality analysis.

Part III of the book moves to an analysis of what we believe to be the crux of proportionality analysis: the procedural aspects of proportionality.

Chapter 11 considers whether the vague notion of proportionality can be simplified, by using either a mathematical formula or the experiences and practical tools of practitioners in the field. The chapter lays out the significant barriers facing such efforts.

Chapter 12 explores the more procedural aspects of proportionality, examining such questions as these: Who is responsible for assuring that attacks are proportionate? what is the role of legal advisors in proportionality analysis? and what level of information is required prior to attack? The chapter also discusses whether establishing a proper procedure for proportionality can help improve the protection of civilians during armed conflict.

Chapter 13 discusses the role of investigations in ensuring the protection of civilians and the efficacy of proportionality, asking whether criminal or other forms of investigation are most effective in ensuring respect for the principle of proportionality.

The final chapter of the book takes a look at the future, with a brief exploration of the implications of image-fare, cyber warfare, and autonomous weapon systems for the issue of proportionality.

2

# Ethical and Constitutional Foundations

## A. THE POSSIBLE SOURCES FOR PROPORTIONALITY

We begin by providing a concise background on the various theories justifying IHL in general terms, and explain how these can also be applied to the principle of proportionality.

Intuitively, IHL is meant to regulate interstate conflicts. As such, its very existence is puzzling: Why would opponents bent on destroying each other commit to and obey rules designed to limit their choice of targets, weapons, and tactics?

Traditionally, two kinds of answers have been provided to this question. On the one hand, moralists regard IHL as being inspired by morality.[1] For those supporting this view, IHL in general, and any specific rule in particular, must be justified as a result of some moral principle. Much work in this area is based on ideas of the "just war," which have their roots in past centuries, but have been revived in the 20th century by the influential work of Michael Walzer. On the other hand, realists explain the evolution of IHL on utilitarian grounds, viewing the threat of reciprocal retaliation as the main reason for compliance with it.[2]

Below, we offer a short introduction to the concept of proportionality from each of these viewpoints.

1. The question of the morality of the laws of war is most intimately connected with the "just war" theory; see Michael Walzer, Just and Unjust Wars 127–33 (4th ed., 2006); Larry May, War Crimes and Just War 3–8 (2007). On moral approaches to law, see Gabriella Blum, *The Laws of War and the "Lesser Evil,"* 35 Yale J. Int'l L. 1, 39 (2010) ("From a deontological stance, the actions proscribed by strict IHL rules . . . are inherently repugnant, a violation of a moral imperative in the Kantian sense, independent of any cost-benefit calculation in any particular instance.").

2. Eric A. Posner & Alan O. Sykes, Economic Foundations of International Law 190–95 (2013) (suggesting that laws of war are possible in the first place and would be respected only under conditions of *symmetry* (namely, when the rules give advantage to neither side) and *reciprocity* (namely, the ability of the opponent to retaliate to prior violations)); Eric A. Posner, *Human Rights, the Laws of War, and Reciprocity*, 6 L. & Ethics Hum. Rts. 147, 150, 170–71 (2012); Eric A. Posner, Centennial Tribute Essay, *A Theory of the Laws of War*, 70 U. Chi. L. Rev. 297, 297 (2003).

*Proportionality in International Humanitarian Law.* Amichai Cohen & David Zlotogorski, Oxford University Press.
 DOI: 10.1093/oso/9780197556726.003.0002

## B. A PHILOSOPHICAL AND RELIGIOUS PRISM OF PROPORTIONALITY

### Premodern Views of Proportionality

Imagine a town somewhere in the Levant whose entire population is comprised of ISIS fighters, with the exception of only 10 civilians.[3] Under IHL, attacking such a town in its entirety would presumably not raise any questions of legality. The terrorists and the buildings they use are lawful targets. Few would argue that carpet bombing the town would present a difficult question of proportionality: the unfortunate loss of 10 civilian lives is clearly not excessive in relation to the anticipated military advantage of destroying an ISIS stronghold and such a large group of fighters.

It may seem surprising, but there is a well-known parallel example with identical parameters in which a court of higher instance "held" that an attack against such a town would be unlawful due to the expected collateral damage. This example, possibly the earliest discussion relevant to the concept of proportionality, is the story of Sodom and Gomorrah and Abraham's debate with God (substituting evildoers for terrorists and the righteous few for civilians).[4]

The book of Genesis tells the story of Abraham challenging God's decision to destroy the twin city of Sodom and Gomorrah, whose inhabitants were evildoers.[5] Faced with the complete destruction of these cities, Abraham asks God, "Wilt thou also destroy the righteous with the wicked?,"[6] and enquires whether God would deign to destroy the city if there were 50 righteous people within it, stating: "Far be it from You! Shall not the Judge of all the earth deal justly?"[7] When God responds that he would spare the city if 50 righteous people were present, Abraham continues his challenge, presenting steadily diminishing numbers of potentially affected righteous persons, until God confirms that he will not destroy the city even if there are only 10 righteous people within.[8]

This early discussion of the question of causing incidental harm to the innocents when attempting to harm evildoers is not the only such discussion in premodern times. Philo of Alexandria wrote that the Jewish law of warfare "distinguishes between those whose life is one of hostility and the reverse. For to breathe slaughter against all, even those who have done very little or nothing amiss, shows what we should call a savage and brutal soul."[9] Early Muslim thought was also cognizant of

3. For the sake of this discussion we are assuming that an armed conflict, whether international or non-international, exists with ISIS in this scenario.

4. We wish to thank Dr. Dina Wyshogrod for her reference to the story of Sodom and Gomorrah.

5. Genesis 18:16; Walzer, *supra* note 1, at 133.

6. Genesis 18:23.

7. Genesis 18:25.

8. Genesis 18:32.

9. Michael Newton & Larry May, Proportionality in International Law 29 (2014).

the need to preserve the lives of the innocent: "Umar wrote to the commanders to fight in the way of Allah and to fight only those who fight against them, and not to kill women or minors, or to kill those who do not use a razor."[10]

It has been claimed that the principle of proportionality was already extant in the "just war theory" of early Christendom.[11] According to this theory, war could only be deemed just if the resulting good exceeded the ills and horrors caused.[12] However, the main consideration here was not overall proportionality, but rather the existence of a just cause, and although there existed a requirement for just means during armed conflict, there was no distinction, as exists today, between *jus ad bellum* and *jus in bello*. St. Augustine of Hippo, for example, was of the opinion that once a just cause existed for the war, the ends justified any means.[13]

St. Augustine's positions did not remain unchallenged. Writing nearly a millennium later, in the 13th century, Thomas Aquinas noted that "If a man in self-defense uses *more than necessary* violence, it will be unlawful, whereas if he repels force with *moderation*, his defense will be lawful."[14] While this does not allude directly to *jus in bello* proportionality, the core concept of proportionality when using force does exist.

Later philosophers and theologians did require proportionality during times of war, though their concepts remain distinct from contemporary understandings of proportionality. Writing in the 16th century, Francisco Vitoria wrote that "When war for a just cause has broken out, it must not be waged so as to ruin people against whom it is directed, but only so as to obtain one's rights . . . When victory has been won and the war is over the victory should be utilized with moderation

10. *Id.*, at 29.

11. Mark Totten, *Using Force First: Moral Tradition and the Case for Revision*, 43 STAN. J. INT'L L. 95, n.36 (2007). ". . . [t]he historical antecedents of necessity and proportionality lie at least as far back as the Roman law concepts of *incontinenti* and *modernamen inculpatae tutelage* in the context of individual self-defense . . ." The latter relates to the principle of proportionality and requires moderation in a forceful response relative to the circumstances. Both norms appear in this passage from the Digest of Justinian: "Those who do damage because they cannot otherwise defend themselves are blameless . . . It is permitted only to use force against an attacker, and even then only so far as is necessary for self-defense." THE DIGEST OF JUSTINIAN 291 (Alan Watson ed. & trans., 1998); Noam Lubell & Amichai Cohen, *Strategic Proportionality: Limitations on the Use of Force in Modern Armed Conflicts*, 96 INT'L L. STUD. 159, 164, n.11 (2020). These ideas appear throughout the writings of the canonists.

12. Gary D. Brown, *Proportionality and Just War*, 2 J. MILITARY ETHICS 171 (2003). Amichai Cohen, *The Principle of Proportionality in the Context of Operation Cast Lead: Institutional Perspectives*, 35 RUTGERS L. RECORD 23, 28, n.38 (2009); Judith G. Gardam, *Proportionality and Force in International Law*, 87 AM. J. INT'L L. 391 (1993) [Gardam, *Proportionality and Force in International Law*].

13. Gardam, *Proportionality and Force in International Law*, *Id.*, at 395.

14. Thomas Aquinas, *From Summa Theologiae, in* INTERNATIONAL RELATIONS IN POLITICAL THOUGHT: TEXTS FROM THE ANCIENT GREEKS TO THE FIRST WORLD WAR 213, 218 (Chris Brown et al. eds., 2002) (emphasis added).

and Christian humility."[15] Francisco Suarez, in the 17th century, also explicitly presented considerations of proportionality during times of armed conflict, writing, "Due proportion must be observed in its beginning, during its prosecution, and after victory."[16]

## The Philosophical Background

The philosophical background for the principle of proportionality in general, and in IHL in particular, can be found in two distinct sources. The first is the Catholic idea of double effect, which ties in with the "just war" tradition. The second is the principle of humanity, as developed by modern scholars.

The principle of double effect has a long history. Basically, it assumes that an action that has harmful effects is legitimate if the goal was good, and that the good results outweigh the bad. Walzer summarizes the four conditions of the modern formulation of double effect:

(1) The act in itself is good or at least indifferent (in armed conflicts, this means a legitimate act of war).
(2) The direct effect is morally acceptable (e.g., the destruction of military supplies).
(3) The actor's intentions are good (the attacking force aims to achieve only the acceptable effects).
(4) The good effect is sufficiently good to compensate for the evil effect.[17]

If all these conditions are met, then an act which has undesirable consequences can be seen as justified.[18] The fact that the bad result was not intended strips it

15. Newton & May, *supra* note 9, at 62.

16. *Id.*

17. Michael Walzer, Just and Unjust War 153 (5th ed., 2015). See also Joseph M. Boyle, *Towards Understanding the Principle of Double Effect, in* The Morality of War, 164 (Larry May ed., 2006). David Lefkowitz defined the term a little differently, specifically concerning the use of proportionality in armed conflicts:

(1) The combatant intends to attack a legitimate target of war, and to do so in a manner that conforms to the moral constraints on such acts.
(2) The combatant does not intend to cause harm to noncombatants as a means to achieving his intended goal. Rather, the combatant merely foresees that his attack on a legitimate target of war will cause harm to illegitimate targets of war as a side effect.
(3) There is sufficient reason to warrant the combatants' acting in a way that can be reasonably expected to cause harm to noncombatants (or illegitimate targets of war, more broadly).

David Lefkowitz, *Collateral Damage, in* War: Essays in Political Philosophy 145, 147 (Larry May ed., 2008).

18. And not only as "excused." Boyle, *supra* note 17.

of its moral wrongfulness.[19] Hence, proportionality is a situation where the bad effects outweigh the good effects, and then the fourth condition is not met. In Henry Sidgwisk's terms, "the conduciveness to the end is slight in comparison with the amount of the mischief."[20]

As Larry May notes, proportionality seen in these terms might lead to a consequentialist perception of what is permissible and prohibited in war. If good effects trump bad effects, then many acts could be "whitewashed" through justifying them as having contributed to a just cause.[21] The easiest answer to this claim is that proportionality is only one of the limitations on human action in war. Proportionality operates alongside the requirements of the principle of distinction and military necessity, and the prohibition on the use of force found in the UN Charter.

May, however, does not settle for this "technical" explanation. Instead, he proposes that the source of the principle of proportionality is the idea of humane treatment—namely, that the harm caused by war should be minimized.[22] May's view of proportionality is very different from the double-effect doctrine. Therefore, a disproportional act, according to May, is not merely a justified act that fails to meet one condition. Rather, it is an inhumane act, violating the limitations on acts of war, limitations stemming from humanitarian considerations.

There is a major difference between these two understandings of the principle of proportionality. As Walzer points out, the double-effect analysis does not give *full* protection to any specific group. At the most, it confers the right to be considered as deserving protection, a right that is relatively easy to lose—for example, by soldiers. Based on the principle of double effect, Walzer seems to suggest that once a war has started, the killing of all soldiers is allowed, with no need to assess the specific threat that every single soldier poses.[23] By contrast, a view of proportionality based on humane treatment might suggest otherwise. Indeed, Gabriella Blum, adopting May's position, rejects the "category-based" view that soldiers are always legitimate targets, and views the principle of proportionality as applying to soldiers too.[24]

May's position seems to us to be of significant value in the context of proportionality in IHL. The main goal of IHL is to lessen the suffering of humans. Philosophical consistency aside, it seems to us that this humanitarian approach should guide the analysis of the principle of proportionality.

19. For a criticism of this position on the basis of inability to differentiate between intended and unintended consequences, see Lefkowitz, *supra* note 17.

20. Henry Sidgwick, Elements of Politics 263–65 (London, 1891).

21. Larry May, War Crimes and Just Cause 221 (2007).

22. *Id.*, at 222.

23. Walzer, *supra* note 17, at 145.

24. Gabriela Blum, *The Dispensable Lives of Soldiers*, 2(1) J. Legal Anal. 69 (2010).

## C. THE RATIONAL ANALYSIS OF PROPORTIONALITY

There is no shortage of discussion over the principle of proportionality from a moralist point of view, and above we provided only a brief survey of this issue. Contrary to this, a realist or utilitarian analysis of proportionality in IHL is almost nonexistent. There is very scarce literature explaining IHL *in general* from a utilitarian point of view in any detail. Those that exist either offer only a general overviews and explanation of the matter, or reject the efficacy of IHL altogether.[25] Thus, our following proposal for how the principle of proportionality can be based on the self-interest of the state, rather than on some moral edict, represents an initial attempt to break new ground.

### Rational Reciprocal Explanation

One possible rational explanation for IHL is the implied "agreement" between the parties to a conflict to limit the effects of war.[26] States agree in advance on a reciprocal understanding, which is rationally beneficial to all parties to the conflict. The rule of proportionality is certainly an attempt to limit the impact of armed conflicts on civilians. From this perspective, proportionality is one of a series of rules, like the principle of military necessity and the principle of distinction, which provide the basis of this "contract" between parties to the conflict.

The goals of this contract are both external and internal. Externally, the rules of proportionality and distinction limit the destruction caused by war. Since all parties know that they will have to live together after the war ends, it is in both their interests to limit the deadweight loss caused by armed conflict. This is even truer if one party to the conflict aims to take control of a territory controlled by the other party. There is little sense in completely destroying a civilian area that one aims to control, as this would unnecessarily expose one to even greater animosity from the civilian population.[27]

Internally, limiting the suffering of the civilian population provides the government with more flexibility for conducting its operations, as large numbers of

25. E.g., Eric A. Posner, *Human Rights, the Laws of War, and Reciprocity*, 6 L. & Ethics of Human Rights 148 (2012) (claiming that reciprocity explains why states follow IHL); James D. Morrow, *When Do States Follow the Laws of War?*, 101 Amer. Pol. Sci. Rev. 559 (2007) (claiming that IHL provides a solution to Prisoner's Dilemma of states). But see: Chris af Jochnick & Roger Normand, *The Legitimation of Violence: A Critical History of the Laws of War*, 35 Harv. J. Int'l L. 49 (1994) (claiming that IHL serves to legitimize violence); and Posner, *A Theory of the Laws of War*, *supra* note 2 (arguing that the influence of IHL is limited because of differences between states, and may even make going to war easier for some states).

26. Yitzhak Benbaji & Daniel Statman, War by Agreement: A Contractarian Ethics of War (2019).

27. Not creating animosity within the civilian population is an overt goal of counterinsurgency operations. See, e.g., U.S. Army Field Manual 3–24 *Insurgencies and Countering Insurgencies* (May 2014):

civilian casualties can lead to public uproar. In turn, public pressure can push the government to act in ways that it considers less than optimal, including ending the conflict before it is ready to do so or accepting terms for concluding the conflict that it would not have otherwise entertained.

Limiting civilian casualties also allows the state to garner international support. In modern armed conflicts, international support is based upon how the acts of the parties to the conflict are perceived by a global audience. A larger number of civilian casualties usually means less international support.

All these factors support the relevance of IHL in general and the principle of proportionality in particular. But even in classic conflicts, traditional rationalist explanations can be clouded by doubt. To be effective, reciprocity requires that each side has ample information confirming its opponent's intention and ability to comply with the law indefinitely. This condition is rarely met during combat, as the noise of the battlefield typically induces adversaries to interpret their enemy's mistakes as intentional violations of the law, and prompts them to retaliate in kind.

In modern armed conflicts, there are even stronger factors that bring the rationality of IHL and of the principle of proportionality into question. First among these is the fact that parties to conflicts, usually non-state actors (NSAs), often manipulate the principle of proportionality. Knowing that the other party to the conflict (usually the state) will attempt to limit civilian casualties, these NSAs deliberately act from within civilian population centers, making collateral damage almost unavoidable, and often large scale. Second, some parties to a conflict, once again especially NSAs, direct their fire against civilians. This mode of activity runs against the contractual explanation for IHL, explained before.

Naturally, states that face these acts by NSAs see less utility in following the principle of proportionality. Any state adopting a realist position with regard to respecting IHL might abandon the principles of distinction and proportionality altogether. Other armed forces might come to see it as a serious, unjustified limitation on their ability to act. As will be shown later in this book, these approaches can find expression in the way that states interpret the principle of proportionality—specifically, how they weigh the opposing values of military advantage and cost to civilian life.

> 1-37. Soldiers and Marines are not permitted to use force disproportionately or indiscriminately. Typically, more force reduces tactical risk in the short term. But in counterinsurgency, the more force that is used, the less effective it can be. It is more likely that counterinsurgents will achieve an end state by protecting a population, not the counterinsurgency force. When military forces remain in secure compounds, they lose touch with the situation, appear to be indifferent to the population, simplify enemy intelligence operations, or appear afraid to engage the insurgents. In effect, they concede the initiative to the insurgents. To be successful, counterinsurgency forces must work with and share risks with the host-nation forces and the population. Soldiers and Marines must accept some risk to minimize harm to noncombatants. Accepting prudent risk is an essential part of the warrior ethos and an obligation of honorable service.

We believe that most liberal democracies would never abandon the principle of distinction, and would reject directing fire at civilians under almost any circumstances. The resulting internal and international public outcry would delegitimize any justification for the armed conflict itself. However, a decline in the state's interest to apply IHL when facing an enemy that itself does not respect IHL could certainly be reflected in the application of the principle of proportionality. The attacking party may be more willing to cause collateral civilian damage when fighting an enemy that endangers its own civilians. As we will discuss, some differences in the interpretation of the principle of proportionality, such as regarding the use of "human shields," can be explained in this manner.[28]

## D. PROPORTIONALITY AS A MODE OF CONTROL

In recent years, another rational explanation has emerged for the growing prominence and respect afforded IHL: viewing IHL as a means for the principals in a conflict to exert control over their own *domestic* agents.[29]

According to this approach, the traditional moral and rational explanations fail to grasp a crucial factor in the dynamics of modern warfare: the need for each side to control its own forces. The leaderships of contending armies may indeed be motivated by moral concerns or locked in a reciprocal relationship, but this is not why they are willing to adopt IHL. For this they need no formal law, just as the princes and kings in earlier times could rely on their shared understandings about the law. Rather, modern militaries and their civilian leaderships need IHL—specifically, a form of IHL that is tailored to control their own agents—because they collectively face a daunting challenge of reigning in their respective troops, whose interests may diverge from their own. During war, each decision-maker has a different future to consider: the state's president will have a long-term vision, contemplating the transition to peace, while the military commanders will focus more concretely on the greater scope of the war. But the foot soldiers who serve them both have far more immediate concerns—surviving the current assault on enemy positions while effectively fulfilling their orders and attaining their objectives effectively. The need for laws that maintain discipline within the fighting forces rises in direct relation to the growing disparity between the different "futures" that shape each actor's preferences.

To explain this counterintuitive hypothesis, we must begin by prying open the black box of "the state" and examining the complex interactions between the civilian and military apparatuses that take place behind the veil of sovereignty.[30] Doing so reveals that the prevalent assumption that IHL is designed only to regulate interstate conflicts is too simplistic. The map of the battlefield may show one

28. See our discussion in Chapter 9.

29. Eyal Benvenisti & Amichai Cohen, *War Is Governance: Explaining the Laws of War from a Principal-Agent Perspective*, 112 Mich. L. Rev. 1363 (2014).

30. This is true not only in the context of IHL. Like any complex organization, states promote policies preferred by those domestic actors who are more politically effective than their

state fighting another, but there are other less visible and more complex intrastate battles raging simultaneously between different domestic actors, each seeking to control the conduct of the army and shape the war's outcome. As scholars of political science have long observed, controlling the armed forces, especially during war, is one of the most acute challenges faced by any government. In democracies, one of the "most basic of political questions" is how to "reconcile a military strong enough to do anything the civilians ask, with a military subordinate enough to do only what civilians authorize."[31] This question leads to

> an ineluctable and potentially dangerous tension between military force and constitutional government [which] makes for a vexing dilemma. Although raising and deploying armed forces may be indispensable for sustaining a secure environment for constitutionalist politics, creating a safe place . . . for military institutions [is] among the most troublesome challenges of a constitutionalist order.[32]

There is conflict not only between the high command of the armed forces and the civilian government that seeks to control it. Recourse to force also creates conflicts between civil society and elected officials, between elected officials and military commanders, and between military commanders and combat soldiers. IHL is an external tool designed to address many of these internal conflicts.

These diverse conflicts can all be framed as principal-agent conflicts, situations in which each "principal" (the public, elected officials, and military commanders) necessarily employs an "agent" (elected officials, military commanders, and combat soldiers, respectively) to further its goals and secure its interests. The delegation of authority to engage in combat exposes the principal to the risk that agents might act in their own interests rather than in those of the principal.[33] "Agency costs" tend to be high during war.[34] The principals want to win the war, but they are also aware that it will be necessary to re-establish peace afterward. The

competitors. Hence, theories that are based on the assumption that somehow "the state" can have unitary preferences risk being unrealistic. Compare with Eyal Benvenisti, *Exit and Voice in the Age of Globalization*, 98 Mich. L. Rev. 167 (1999) (focusing on the influence of interest groups on the shaping of international norms); Jack L. Goldsmith & Eric A. Posner, The Limits of International Law 4–5, 7 (2005) ("We give the state the starring role in our drama. . . . Our theory of international law assumes that states act rationally to maximize their interests."); Andrew T. Guzman, How International Law Works 121 (2008) ("Our basic rational choice assumptions imply that states will only enter into agreements when doing so makes them (or, at least, their policymakers) better off").

31. Peter D. Feaver, Armed Servants: Agency, Oversight, and Civil-Military Relations 1–2 (2003).

32. Mark E. Brandon, *War and the American Constitutional Order*, *in* The Constitution in Wartime: Beyond Alarmism and Complacency 11, 13 (Mark Tushnet ed., 2005).

33. In this context, the military is no different from any other bureaucracy that may be framed as an agent of political principals. See generally Kenneth A. Shepsle & Mark S.

principals therefore fear that their agents might act too aggressively, undermining the principals' long-term goals. Conversely, the military may have similar concerns when it is the civilian government that weighs only short-term interests at the expense of long-term ones, while soldiers are primarily concerned about their own survival during each engagement. "Agency slack" is high due to the opportunities for the agents to shirk their obligations during combat with impunity.

Reliance on IHL and IHL-based institutions can reduce the agency costs prevalent in war. IHL provides several benefits over purely domestic rules, such as military manuals and various legal regulations. First, by committing to international norms, domestic principals can tie their own hands in domestic bargaining and thereby preempt domestic opposition, such as from a politically powerful military. Second, IHL can overcome monitoring and enforcement difficulties because the law is interpreted and enforced by actors other than national principals. If a military agent breaches IHL, the victims (civilians and combatants on the enemy side), as well as neutral third countries and actors such as the International Committee of the Red Cross (ICRC), can invoke the shared system of norms and bring violations to the attention of the principals.[35] The principals can then use this "fire alarm" mechanism to restrain their agents.[36] Finally, third-party enforcement can prove an effective and credible threat to agents who might otherwise disregard their principals' commands.

As will be explained in detail in later chapters of this book, this principle-agent concept of IHL supports a specific interpretation of the principle of proportionality. If the principle of proportionality is indeed intended to provide control over the actions of the military, it should be interpreted in a more procedural and bureaucratic manner. The more procedures required to apply the principle, the easier it will be to control.[37]

Bonchek, Analyzing Politics: Rationality, Behavior, and Institutions 360–70 (1997) (discussing how bureaucratic policies drift toward an agency's ideal); Mathew D. McCubbins et al., *Structure and Process, Politics and Policy: Administrative Arrangements and the Political Control of Agencies*, 75 Va. L. Rev. 431, 433–35 (1989) (discussing problems in limiting the discretion of agencies).

34. See Feaver, *supra* note 31, at 4, 68; Brandon, *supra* note 32, at 20–22.

35. Indeed, one of the ICRC's major tasks, for example, is codifying and creating a shared interpretation of IHL, as evidenced in Int'l Comm. of the Red Cross, Commentary on the Additional Protocols of 8 June 1977 to the Geneva Conventions of 12 August 1949 (Yves Sandoz et al. eds., 1987), as well as the restatement of customary law in Jean-Marie Henckaerts & Louise Doswald-Beck, Customary International Humanitarian Law, Vol. 1 (2005).

36. See Mathew D. McCubbins et al., *The Political Origins of the Administrative Procedure Act*, 15 J. Law Econ. & Org. 180, 198–99 (1999) (discussing the role of administrative law as providing a fire alarm to the legislature when the executive deviates from its mandate).

The principal-agent explanation provided earlier has a distinct advantage over other explanations of IHL. On the one hand, it provides an incentive for states to follow the principle of proportionality in IHL. On the other, it is not dependent on the actions of other parties to the conflict. For those interested in promoting compliance with IHL in modern armed conflicts, this explanation seems to hold a significant advantage.

## E. THE CONSTITUTIONAL AND ADMINISTRATIVE BACKGROUND TO PROPORTIONALITY ANALYSIS

The contemporary principle of proportionality in legal jurisprudence in general can be traced back to German law in the 19th century. From there, it spread to many other states and jurisdictions over the course of the 20th century, including Canada, South Africa, New Zealand, Israel, the European Union, the European Convention on Human Rights, and even the World Trade Organization.[38]

In domestic jurisdictions, proportionality analysis includes several preliminary elements and sub-tests. The two preliminary elements are, first, that proportionality is examined only if a policy infringes upon a person's rights; and second, the infringement can only be justified as long as the policy is adopted for a worthy purpose.

There are three sub-tests of proportionality:

(1) There is a rational connection between the means and the policy objective. This is referred to as the *suitability test*.
(2) The goal cannot be achieved by less harmful means. If there are other means by which the same policy objective can be achieved while causing less harm, then the policy is not proportionate. This is called the *least harmful means test*.
(3) Using utilitarian analysis, it can be determined that the action's benefit outweighs the harm it caused. This is called *strict-sense proportionality*.[39]

Proportionality, as just described, is a legal tool whose essence is to enable society to make moral decisions by employing a legal instrument that incorporates both deontological and consequentialist elements. The first sub-test, suitability, guarantees that only relevant measures are used to achieve goals. In addition to the rational means-end test, there are instances where certain means might be

37. On procedures, bureaucracy, and administrative law as modes of control see "McNollgast": Mathew D. McCubbins, Roger G. Noll, & Barry R. Weingast, *Administrative Procedures as Instruments of Political Control*, 3 J. L. Econ. & Org. 243 (1987).

38. Raanan Sulitzeanu-Kenan, Mordechai Kremnitzer, & Sharon Alon, *Facts, Preferences, and Doctrine: An Empirical Analysis of Proportionality Judgment*, 50 L. & Soc'y Rev. 348, 350 (2016).

39. *Id.*, at 351–52.

effective for achieving a desired societal policy, but their use would otherwise be unjust. An example of this is punishing an innocent person for a crime he or she did not commit in order to successfully deter other serious crimes in the future. Even if this policy succeeded, there is something manifestly unjust about punishing an innocent person for something he or she did not do so as to achieve a wider goal. The suitability sub-test has its roots in deontological ethics; some actions are forbidden even if they cause more good than harm.

The second sub-test, the least harmful means test, is rooted in consequentialist ethics. Consequentialism defines moral acts as those which result in the best possible result (such as the highest total utility, usually happiness or pleasure) from all alternative acts.[40] If the same policy goal can be achieved through an alternative measure to the one planned, which would cause less harm, then from a moral (consequentialist) standpoint there is no justification for choosing the more harmful measure rather than the less harmful one.

The third sub-test, strict-sense proportionality, is also a manifestation of consequentialist ethics. If the action causes more harm than good there is no justification for it. This legal instrument for performing assessments of moral actions on a societal level is crucial, as it permits the public to establish and maintain a just society by comparatively examining the costs and benefits of governing norms.

The use of proportionality in constitutional and administrative settings, as well as in the IHL context, relies on this third meaning of proportionality. The two first sub-tests can be presented as simple logic, or at least, as common-sense claims that are not objectionable. The third sub-test, however, is of a different nature. It requires the decision-maker to balance good and bad effects, and sometimes to make decisions that will mean giving up or compromising on some important social goal or interest. This inevitably invites argument regarding the suitability of the decision-maker, relative moral claims, and other factors affecting the weighting of competing values. It is exactly because of this complex nature that proportionality is interesting, and it is why most of the following discussions focus on this meaning of proportionality.

40. SHELLEY KAGAN, NORMATIVE ETHICS 25–48 (1998); Phillip Petit, *Consequentialism*, *in* A COMPANION TO ETHICS 230 (Peter Singer ed., 1991).

# 3

# A General Overview of Proportionality in IHL

## A. THE HISTORY AND DEVELOPMENT OF IHL PROPORTIONALITY

Compared with other branches of international humanitarian law, regulations respecting the protection of civilians in armed conflicts were a relatively late development. This is probably due to the fact that traditional weapons and means and methods of warfare were intended to destroy the enemy's armed forces, and not its property or matériel.[1] For example, as the technology of incendiary bombs developed, legal scholars were still of the opinion that there were no legal limitations on the use of projectiles against civilians.[2]

Even when the protection of civilians in armed conflict began to be codified, during the 19th century, no constraints existed on causing incidental collateral harm to civilians—as long as an attack was directed against a military objective, it was considered to be lawful.[3] For example, the Lieber Code of 1863,[4] the first modern codification of the laws of armed conflict, contains the requirement that

1. Alexander Gillespie, A History of the Laws of War: Volume 2, The Customs and Laws of War with Regards to Civilians in Times of Conflict (Hart, Oxford, 2011), 13.

2. *Id.*, at 14.

3. Yoram Dinstein, The Conduct of Hostilities under the Law of International Armed Conflict 129 (2nd ed., 2010). For a detailed description of the development and attitudes toward the principle of proportionality see A. P. V. Rogers, *The Principle of Proportionality, in* The Legitimate Use of Military Force: The Just War Tradition and the Customary Law of Armed Conflict 189, 190–205 (Howard M. Hensel ed., 2007) [Rogers, *The Principle of Proportionality*]; Judith G. Gardam, *Proportionality and Force in International Law*, 87 Am. J. Int'l L. 391, 397–403 (1993); W.J. Fenrick, *The Rule of Proportionality and Protocol I in Conventional Warfare*, 98 Mil. L. Rev. 91, 95–8 (1982).

4. The Lieber Code was promulgated in 1863, during the American Civil War. It was the result of a request from the general-in-chief of the Union Armies, Henry Wager Halleck, to Dr. Francis Lieber of Harvard College, to prepare a code of law for the Union Armies. The reason for this request was the problem of guerilla warfare faced by the Union. This code was adopted by the Union Army and became the first statement of the law of war during contemporary times, and was the basis for much of that law until as recently as World War II. W. Hays Parks, *Air War and the Law of War*, 32 Air Force L. Rev. 1, 7 (1990).

*Proportionality in International Humanitarian Law.* Amichai Cohen & David Zlotogorski, Oxford University Press.
 DOI: 10.1093/oso/9780197556726.003.0003

"commanders, whenever admissible, inform the enemy of their intention to bombard a place, so that the non-combatants and especially the women and children may be removed."[5] Nevertheless, the Code contained no prohibition on causing excessive damage to civilians. Indeed, article 15 stipulated: "Military necessity admits of all direct destruction of life or limb of armed enemies, *and of other persons whose destruction is incidentally unavoidable in the armed contests of the war*."[6]

Article 22 of the Lieber Code limited the harm that could be caused to civilians, albeit only so far as there was no military necessity for causing the harm. The Code still does not concern itself with the need to strike a balance between the harm and the gain achieved from military action:

> Nevertheless, as civilization has advanced during the last centuries, so has likewise steadily advanced, especially in war on land, the distinction between the private individual belonging to a hostile country and the hostile country itself, with its men in arms. *The principle has been more and more acknowledged that the unarmed citizen is to be spared in person, property, and honor as much as the exigencies of war will admit.*[7]

The need to balance the two interests of humanity and military necessity was raised in the St. Petersburg Declaration of 1868, which was an important step forward in the understanding that the horrors of war should be limited. The preamble of the Declaration recognized a need to "fix . . . the technical limits at which the necessities of war ought to yield to the requirements of humanity,"[8] and further stipulated that

> the only legitimate object which States should endeavor to accomplish during war is to weaken the military forces of the enemy; that for this purpose it is sufficient to disable the greatest possible number of men; that this object would be exceeded by the employment of arms which uselessly aggravate the sufferings of disabled men, or render their death inevitable.[9]

5. Adjutant Gen.'s Office, U.S. War Dep't, Instructions for the Government of Armies of the United States in the Field, Gen. Ord. No. 100, Apr. 24, 1863, *available at:* ihl-databases.icrc.org/ihl/INTRO/110 [Lieber Code].

6. *Id.*, at art. 15. (emphasis added). This might be a reflection of what we described as the second sub-test of proportionality.

7. *Id.*, at art. 22 (emphasis added).

8. St. Petersburg Declaration Renouncing the Use in Time of War of Explosive Projectiles under 400 Grammes Weight, Dec. 11, 1868, 138 C.T.S. 297 [St. Petersburg Declaration], preamble; Michael N. Schmitt, *Military Necessity and Humanity in International Humanitarian Law: Preserving the Delicate Balance*, 50 VA. J. INT'L L. 795, 799 (2010).

9. St. Petersburg Declaration, *supra* note 8, preamble. See also, for example, The Hague Convention (IV) Respecting the Laws and Customs of War on Land, Annexed Regulations, 1907, art. 25, 205 C.T.S. 277 [Hague Regulations]: "The attack or bombardment, by whatever means, of towns, villages, dwellings, or buildings which are undefended is prohibited". The very

Nonetheless, the Declaration still did not limit the extent of hostilities with regard to collateral damage, or allude to such a need.

The Hague Regulations signed in 1907, included a provision regulating the destruction or seizure of enemy property, prohibiting such actions unless "imperatively demanded by the necessities of war."[10] Frits Kalshoven sees this as an early expression of the principle of proportionality.[11] Article 27 of the Hague Regulations refers to the special protection of certain civilian objects, and requires belligerents to take

> all necessary steps . . . to spare, as far as possible, buildings dedicated to religion, art, science, or charitable purposes, historic monuments, hospitals, and places where the sick and wounded are collected, provided they are not being used at the time for military purposes.[12]

This article does not obligate an attack to be proportionate in the strict sense; however, it does seem to allude to an obligation to minimize collateral harm to certain types of civilian structures.[13]

Following World War I, which saw the first use of aerial warfare, a commission of jurists met and drafted the "Rules of Air Warfare." These Rules were never adopted and were therefore not binding,[14] but they did include one of the first formulations of proportionality in modern IHL:[15]

> In the immediate vicinity of the operations of the land forces, the bombardment of cities, towns, villages, habitations and buildings is legitimate, *provided there is a reasonable presumption that the military concentration is important*

restriction of war to military targets is an important step in protecting civilians from attacks directed at targets that may have a strategic value, but are still not military targets. The concept that "the only legitimate object which States should endeavour to accomplish during war is to weaken the military forces of the enemy" (quoted from St. Petersburg Declaration, *supra* note 8, preamble) is the basis for the prohibitions in IHL prohibiting weapons that cause unnecessary suffering and also for the provisions forbidding the denial of quarter. Gardam, *supra* note 3, at 397.

10. Hague Regulations, *supra* note 9, art. 23(g).

11. Frits Kalshoven, *Remarks by Frits Kalshoven*, 86 Am. Soc'y Int'l L. Proc. 40, 41 (1992).

12. Hague Regulations, *supra* note 9, art. 27.

13. Kalshoven, *supra* note 11, at 42. Causing the least harm possible is a sub-test of proportionality in general, and its existence in the *jus in bello* principle of proportionality is contested. For further reading, see Chapter 2.

14. These rules were later held to be "authoritative of the law of air warfare," and the rules, along with (uncited) state practice, form the basis for the determination that the use of nuclear weapons on the cities of Hiroshima and Nagasaki in August 1945 had been in violation of international law. Shimoda v. The State, 8 Jap. Ann. Intl L. 212 (1964) [Jap.].

15. Rogers, *supra* note 3, at 194.

*enough to justify the bombardment, taking into account the danger to which the civil population will thus be exposed.*[16]

Indeed, it was the advent of aerial warfare and bombing that brought a considerably greater risk of harm to civilians than had existed previously.[17] The non-binding 1938 Resolution of the League of Nations Assembly Concerning Protection of Civilian Population against Bombing from the Air in Case of War was also intended to protect civilians from the effects of aerial warfare, though it is unclear if its provisions contained an absolute prohibition on civilian casualties or were simply an attempt to minimize them:[18]

> (1) The intentional bombing of civilian populations is illegal;
> (2) Objectives aimed at from the air must be legitimate military objectives and must be identifiable;
> (3) Any attack on legitimate military objectives must be carried out in such a way that civilian populations in the neighborhood are not bombed through negligence . . .[19]

Regardless of the concerns regarding incidental civilian casualties that had arisen in prior years, during World War II it was understood that "collateral injury to the civilian population or damage to civilian objects was the 'price of doing business.'"[20] The war resulted in vast numbers of collateral civilian casualties. For

16. Article 24(4) Hague Rules concerning the Control of Wireless Telegraphy in Time of War and Air Warfare, The Hague, December 1922–February 1923, *available at:* ihl-databases.icrc.org/applic/ihl/ihl.nsf/Article.xsp?action=openDocument&documentId=8F0205182641A279C12563CD00518530 (emphasis added); Gardam, *supra* note 3, at 400–01.

17. Gardam, *supra* note 3, at 397. One should not mistakenly infer from this that civilians had been spared the ravages of war before the invention of the aerial bombardment. It is clear that siege warfare affected civilians as well as fighters, and civilians were also clearly the victims of repeated violations outside of sieges as well. One example of the severe suffering of civilians during war is the Crusader conquest of Jerusalem in 1099, which saw the wholesale slaughter of the non-Christian civilians and fighters of the city (Muslims and Jews). One description of the event relates that "Citizens and soldiers fled to the Temple Mount, pursued by Tancred [de Hauteville] and his men. . . . In the Temple Mount, . . . they rode in blood up to their bridles. Indeed, it is a just and splendid judgment of God that this place should be filled with the blood of unbelievers." SIMON SEBAG MONTEFIORE, JERUSALEM: THE BIOGRAPHY 221–22 (2011) .

18. Fenrick, *supra* note 3, at 96.

19. Protection of Civilian Populations against Bombing from the Air in Case of War, September 30, 1938, Resolution of the League of Nations Assembly, O.J. Spec. Supp. 182, at 16; Fenrick, *supra* note 3, at 96.

20. Parks, *supra* note 4, at 56 (cited in W.J. Fenrick, *Targeting and Proportionality during the NATO Bombing Campaign against Yugoslavia,* 12 EJIL 489, 494 (2001)). For example, Parks notes that though estimates vary, the number of German civilian deaths caused by Allied bombing between 1943 and 1945 is high, ranging from some 250,253 civilians to 600,000. Those numbers, however, account for only some 20–40% of German civilian casualties during the war

example, the bombing of Dresden on February 14–15, 1945, by both the US Air Force and the British Royal Air Force appears to have killed at least 25,000 people and injured around 30,000;[21] the bombing of Pforzheim resulted in the deaths of 20,000 civilians;[22] and a vast number of civilian deaths were caused by the use of two atomic bombs on the Japanese cities of Hiroshima and Nagasaki.[23] Even if we accept that the attacks in these cases were *not* directed against civilians,[24] the number of civilian casualties was immense.

The question of incidental harm to civilians was, however, a consideration that was raised by commanders during World War II, albeit primarily concerning civilians of occupied nations.[25] For example, in February 1945, General Douglas McArthur was asked for permission to bomb the heavily defended city of Manila, Philippines. McArthur refused, saying, "You would probably kill off the Japanese all right, but there are several thousand Filipino civilians in there who would be killed too. The world would hold up its hands in horror if we did anything like that."[26] However, to maintain that these considerations were paramount, or even

(Parks, *supra* note 4, at 1–2, n. 1). The issue of incidental harm to civilians aside, there is a consensus among scholars that *deliberate* attacks targeted at the civilian population for the purpose of terrorizing them were unlawful during the war (Gardam, *supra* note 3, at 401).

21. Dresden was bombed on February 14–15, 1945, by both the US Air Force and the RAF. It appears that at least 25,000 people were killed and 30,000 injured in the attack, in which some 7,100 tons of bombs were dropped on the city. Though the city did contain some military objectives, which were damaged in the attack, even Winston Churchill, a supporter of the bomber offensive, felt distaste about the attack. There are suggestions, however, that the military advantage to be gained from the attack on Dresden was not only anticipated from the destruction of the military objectives in the city, but rather also possibly "provide[d] support for the advance of Soviet forces into eastern Germany, destruction of the lines of communication at a critical chokepoint in order to prevent German reinforcement in opposition to the Soviet advance, and possible hastening of the end of the war." See Parks, *supra* note 4, at 154 n. 459, and at 176–77; Fenrick, *supra* note 3, at 127.

22. Pforzheim was a small industrial town in Germany that was attacked by the RAF on February 23–24, 1945. The town produced precision instruments for the *Wehrmacht* (which may have been used in the V2 rockets) and served as a communications hub for the Western Front. After 22 minutes of bombing some 20,000 civilians had been killed and 90% of the town had been destroyed. See Rogers, *supra* note 3, at 190, 210 note 8.

23. Estimates of the number of people killed in the two nuclear attacks range from just under 100,000 to some 300,000. See Gabriella Blum, *The Laws of War and the "Lesser Evil,"* 35 Yale J. Int'l L. 1, 24–25 (2010).

24. Jorg Friedrich, The Fire: The Bombing of Germany 1940–1945 (2008).

25. Fenrick, *supra* note 3, at 118.

26. Gary Solis, The Law of Armed Conflict: International Humanitarian Law in War 276 (2010) [Solis (2010)]. The city of Manila was eventually conquered by the Allies in March 1945, at the end of a month-long brutal urban battle. The Battle of Manila resulted not only in the deaths of some 1,000 American soldiers and 16,000 Japanese soldiers, but also of

widespread, would appear to be an overstatement, especially when one considers the extent of incidental civilian casualties inflicted during the war.[27]

Following World War II, and once the horrors of the war had been widely publicized, it was understood that a change in international law was required, offering more comprehensive protection for civilians from incidental harm. In spite of this, the first major codification of IHL after the war—the four Geneva Conventions adopted in 1949—did not address the protection of civilians from the effects of armed conflict, but focussed rather on the protection of victims of war who found themselves in the hands of the enemy (including interned civilians).[28]

The 1956 Draft Rules for the Limitation of the Dangers Incurred by the Civilian Population in Time of War, which constituted a stage toward the drafting of the First Additional Protocol to the Geneva Conventions, contained a provision that explicitly prohibited attacks expected to cause damage "disproportionate to the military advantage anticipated."[29] In the same year, the United States published an

100,000 Filipino civilians, who were, for the most part, killed incidentally during the battle. See Fenrick, *supra* note 3, at 91–92.

27. Despite the initial decision not to bomb the city of Manila in order to avoid Filipino civilian casualties, and despite corresponding strict limitations on the use of artillery, when faced with the fierce street-to-street battle put up by the Japanese and the prospect of the destruction of 37th and 1st cavalry divisions, the American forces removed certain restrictions, "pounded" the city with artillery, and reduced much of "southern Manila into shambles." Nonetheless, the restriction regarding the use of dive-bombers and napalm strikes against Japanese in the city was not lifted out of the concern of causing high incidental harm to civilians, due to the inaccurate nature of these means of warfare (Fenrick, *supra* note 3, at 120–21).

28. Frits Kalshoven & Liesbeth Zegveld, Constraints on the Waging of War: An Introduction to International Humanitarian Law 3–4, 16–20 (4th ed., 2011).

29. "Art. 8. The person responsible for ordering or launching an attack shall, first of all: . . . (b) take into account the loss and destruction which the attack, even if carried out with the precautions prescribed under Article 9, is able to inflict upon the civilian population. *He is required to refrain from the attack if, after due consideration, it is apparent that the loss and destruction would be disproportionate to the military advantage anticipated.*

Art. 9. All possible precautions shall be taken, both in the choice of the weapons and methods to be used, and in the carrying out of an attack, to ensure that no losses or damage are caused to the civilian population in the vicinity of the objective, or to its dwellings, *or that such losses or damage are at least reduced to a minimum*. In particular, in towns and other places with a large civilian population, which are not in the vicinity of military or naval operations, the attack shall be conducted with the greatest degree of precision. It must not cause losses or destruction beyond the immediate surroundings of the objective attacked. The person responsible for carrying out the attack must abandon or break off the operation if he perceives that the conditions set forth above cannot be respected."

Int'l Comm. of the Red Cross, Draft Rules for the Limitation of the Dangers incurred by the Civilian Population in Time of War (1956), *available at:* ihl-databases.icrc.org/applic/ihl/ihl.nsf/Article.xsp?action=openDocument&documentId=5968DF93FC478018C12563CD0051D111.

Fenrick, *supra* note 3, at 97.

official manual on the law of land warfare that included a reference to proportionality.[30] By 1972, the conduct of the United States in armed conflict included proportionality considerations, at least before conducting significant aerial strikes.[31]

In 1973, the ICRC produced drafts of the First Additional Protocol to the Geneva Conventions (AP-I) that referred to the principle of proportionality.[32] The final version was adopted on June 8, 1977, and included articles 51(5)(b) and 57(2)(a)(iii), reflecting the modern proportionality rule.

## B. CONTEMPORARY IHL AND PROPORTIONALITY

IHL proportionality, as described in articles 51 and 57 of AP-I, is quite different from proportionality in domestic, constitutional, and municipal law.[33] Traditionally, proportionality under IHL includes only the third sub-test—strict-sense proportionality.[34] This is arguably still the law, though there are several indications that the legal situation might be in the process of changing. As we shall explain in detail in later sections of this book, the focus on procedural safeguards regarding the application of the principle of proportionality seems to suggest that

30. Rogers, *supra* note 3, at 203.

31. For example, in 1972, during the Vietnam War, the United States considered striking the Lang Chi hydroelectric facility in North Vietnam as part of Operation Linebacker I. Breaching the dam was expected to result in 23,000 civilian casualties, despite a significant military advantage that was anticipated from destroying the power plant itself. President Nixon approved the attack based on an assurance of a 90% chance of a successful mission against the facility without the dam being breached. See Rogers, *supra* note 3, at 204; Parks, *supra* note 4, at 168–69. For further discussion of this example see Chapter 5, note 78 and the accompanying text.

32. The draft included the term "disproportionate," however, this term was later replaced with "excessive" over the course of the drafting process (Rogers, *supra* note 3, at 204). For a discussion of the drafting process of these articles during the Diplomatic Conference on the Reaffirmation and Development of International Humanitarian Law Applicable in Armed Conflicts, see Fenrick, *supra* note 3, at 102–106.

33. There is a debate as to whether proportionality is a general principle in IHL or even in all of international law. The Israeli High Court of Justice in the *Beit Surik* case opined that "proportionality is recognized today as a general principle of international law" (HCJ 2056/04, Beit Sourik Village Council v. The Government of Israel, 58(5) PD 807, para.37 (2004) [Isr.] [Beit Surik case]). However, this view seems to be far from the consensus. Dame Rosalyn Higgins for one has written that: "the critical point is this: the rules on armed conflict fully subsume the doctrine of proportionality [ . . . ] By contrast [ . . . ] the substantive obligations of human rights law do not subsume proportionality: it is said to exist over and above the provisions specified" (ROSALYN HIGGINS, PROBLEMS & PROCESS: INTERNATIONAL LAW AND HOW WE USE IT 234 (1994)). For a discussion of this issue see YUVAL SHANY, THE PRINCIPLE OF PROPORTIONALITY UNDER INTERNATIONAL LAW 86–103 (2009) (Heb.).

34. Raanan Sulitzeanu-Kenan, Mordechai Kremnitzer, & Sharon Alon, *Facts, Preferences, and Doctrine: An Empirical Analysis of Proportionality Judgment*, 50 L. & SOC'Y REV. 348, 352 (2016).

the first two facets of proportionality (a rational connection and the least harmful means) form a major part of proportionality analysis.[35]

Nonetheless, even if the specific provisions of proportionality in IHL do not include the three sub-tests, these sub-tests are expressed by other specific provisions of IHL and by its other main principles.[36] The prohibition on all attacks against civilians and civilian objects[37] can be seen as an expression of the suitability test: there must be a rational connection between the means (the attack) and the goal (the planned military advantage). The prohibition on directly attacking civilians can also be viewed as an embodiment of the second sub-test, as it reduces the suffering of civilians, as long as there is an alternative that causes less harm. It therefore reflects a facet of the least harmful means test.

An aspect of the second sub-test is explicitly mentioned in AP-I article 57(3). Under this provision, if there are several, each offering the same military advantage, parties must attack the objective that is expected to result in the least amount of harm to civilians and civilian objects.[38] However, this article only refers to choosing between several targets, and does not discuss choosing different courses of action relating to the same target. Some scholars are of the opinion that IHL does indeed contain a general obligation to opt for the least amount of collateral damage possible, and an attack causing avoidable damage is a violation of the principle of proportionality.[39] The ICRC's *Commentary on AP-I* seems to support this position as well: ". . . so as to prevent loss or damage to the population . . . When a well-placed 500kg projectile is sufficient to render a military objective useless, there is no reason to use a 10-ton bomb or a series of projectiles aimed without

35. See Chapter 12.

36. SHANY, *supra* note 33, at 56–57.

37. Protocol Additional to the Geneva Conventions of August 12, 1949, and Relating to the Protection of Victims of International Armed Conflicts (Protocol I), June 8, 1977, arts. 48, 52, 1125 U.N.T.S. 3 [AP-I]. This principle is also articulated in the preamble of the St. Petersburg Declaration *supra* note 8: "The only legitimate object which States should endeavour to accomplish during war is to weaken the military forces of the enemy."

38. "When a choice is possible between several military objectives for obtaining a similar military advantage, the objective to be selected shall be that the attack on which may be expected to cause the least danger to civilian lives and to civilian objects." AP-I, *supra* note 37, art. 57(3).

It should be noted that the obligation to limit the harm caused to certain civilian objects is contained in other provisions of IHL, such as in article 27 of the Hague Regulations, *supra* note 9: "In sieges and bombardments *all necessary steps must be taken to spare, as far as possible*, buildings dedicated to religion, art, science, or charitable purposes, historic monuments, hospitals, and places where the sick and wounded are collected, provided they are not being used at the time for military purposes" (emphasis added).

39. IAN HENDERSON, THE CONTEMPORARY LAW OF TARGETING: MILITARY OBJECTIVES, PROPORTIONALITY AND PRECAUTIONS IN ATTACK UNDER ADDITIONAL PROTOCOL I 198 (2009).

sufficient precision."[40] This position is also supported by the practices of certain states. For example, the United Kingdom maintains that proportionality requires commanders to choose the means and methods of warfare that would cause the least amount of collateral damage.[41]

There is also some support for this in case law. For example, in the *Galić* case, the International Criminal Tribunal for the former Yugoslavia (ICTY) Trial Chamber discussed the relationship between the obligation to take precautions and the obligation to cause the least amount of harm, stating that "the basic obligation to spare civilians and civilian objects as much as possible must guide the attacking party when considering the proportionality of an attack."[42] This coupling of the principles of precautions and proportionality can be construed as an obligation to cause the least amount of damage in an attack.[43] For example, attacking a military objective during daytime might be disproportionate if an attack during the night would be expected to result in fewer civilian casualties.[44]

In fact, there seems to be a basis for a broader interpretation of the second subtest: The ICTY Appeals Chamber in *Kordić and Cerkez* appears to have adopted the least harmful means test, even with regard to soldiers, meaning that it is prohibited to cause unnecessary damage to soldiers.[45] However, there are those who

40. Commentary on the Additional Protocols of 8 June 1977 to the Geneva Conventions of 12 August 1949, para. 2200 (ICRC, Yves Sandoz, Christophe Swinarki, & Bruno Zimmerman eds., 1987) [AP-I Commentary].

41. "Modern, smart weaponry has increased the options available to the military planner. He needs not only to assess what feasible precautions can be taken to minimize incidental loss but also to make a comparison between different methods of conducting operations, so as to be able to choose the least damaging method compatible with military success. . . . It will be a question of fact whether alternative, practically possible methods of attack would reduce the collateral risks. If they would, the attacker may have to accept the increased risk as being the only way of pursuing an attack in a proportionate way." United Kingdom Ministry of Defence, Joint Service Publication 383, The Joint Service Manual of the Law of Armed Conflict, paras. 2.7–2.7.1 (2004) [UK 2004 LOAC Manual].

42. Prosecutor v. Galić, ICTY Trial Chamber, IT-98-29, *Judgment*, para. 58 (Dec. 5, 2003) [Galić, TC].

43. The position of the U.S. is that a commander must choose the form of attack that causes the least amount of harm to civilians only if all other things are equal. However, if an attack that is expected to cause more harm to civilians is also anticipated to yield a greater military advantage, the commander possesses full discretion to choose this more harmful means. US Department of Defense, Law of War Manual paras. 5.11.7–7.1 (2015, updated Dec. 2016) [DoD Manual].

44. Shany, *supra* note 33, at 69.

45. "The Appeals Chamber notes that, in principle, international humanitarian law allows for acts of war to be directed against military objectives, e.g., enemy soldiers. However, the general lawfulness of destroying the life or limb of an enemy combatant is restricted by the principles of necessity and proportionality. . . . It follows that the unnecessary or wanton application of force is prohibited and that "a belligerent may apply only that amount and kind of force necessary to defeat the enemy." This principle is, e.g., the basis for the prohibition on employing arms, projectiles, or material calculated to cause unnecessary suffering" (Prosecutor v. Kordić &

argue that the Appeal Chamber's position was ambiguous, and did not pose this requirement.[46]

An opinion voiced by some practitioners, especially those in the armed forces, is that proportionality in IHL is not a general principle from which legal obligations directly emanate, but rather a policy rationale underlying specific rules.[47] According to this position, the state's obligations to IHL are limited only to those expressly stated in AP-I. This opinion is driven by several considerations: First, many lawyers in the armed forces prefer a narrower interpretation of the limitations imposed on military activity by IHL.[48] Second, many legal practitioners, especially in the armed forces, prefer clear rules to general standards.[49] Even as expressly stated in articles 51 and 57 of AP-I, proportionality is an opaque rule. Once interpreted as a general principle, its interpretation becomes even broader and less certain.

Some argue that this limited application of the principle of proportionality in IHL is wrong as a matter of positive law. The principle of proportionality is embedded in several other areas of IHL, in addition to its obvious application in articles 51 and 57 of AP-I. An example of the application of the principle can be seen in the rulings of the Israeli High Court of Justice (HCJ) regarding the route of the separation barrier in the West Bank.[50] The HCJ, led by Justice Aharon Barak, then president of the Israel Supreme Court, based its view of the legality of the barrier on the principle of proportionality. Barak applied proportionality as a general principle of international law, and especially IHL. As a result, he approved

Čerkez, ICTY Appeals Chamber, IT-95-14/2, *Judgment*, para. 686 (Dec. 17, 2004)). One should not infer from this that proportionality in general applies to soldiers, but rather, that an argument can be made that there is a need not to cause more harm to soldiers than necessary. If there are two ways of achieving a specific military advantage, one of which is expected to harm five soldiers and the other, to harm 10, then according to this interpretation, the first way must be chosen. For a discussion regarding the obligation to protect the lives of enemy combatants during armed conflict, see Chapter 6.

46. Yuval Shany suggests that the meaning of the Appeals Chamber's statement remains unclear and also that it might relate to *jus ad bellum* rather than to *jus in bello*. SHANY, *supra* note 33, 101–102.

47. This appears to be the position of the U.S. In its 2016 Law of War Manual, the U.S. provides examples where proportionality is reflected in IHL, such as in the prohibition on using weapons that would cause unnecessary injury. However, that document does not state that proportionality binds states beyond the specific obligations. DoD Manual, *supra* note 43, para.2.4.2.

48. Amichai Cohen, *Legal Operational Advice in the Israeli Defense Forces: The International Law Department and the Changing Nature of International Law*, 26 CONN. J. INT'L L. 402–03 (2011).

49. Amichai Cohen, *Rules and Standards in the Application of IHL*, 41 ISR. L. REV. 41 (2008).

50. HCJ 2056/04, Beit Sourik Village Council v. The Government of Israel, 58(5) PD 807, para.37 (2004) [Isr.]; HCJ 7957/04, Mara'abe v. The Prime Minister of Israel, PD 60(2) 477 (2005) [Isr.] [English translation available at: https://versa.cardozo.yu.edu/opinions/mara%E2%80%99abe-v-prime-minister-israel].

or disapproved various sections of the planned route based on a balance between security needs and the infringement upon the rights of Palestinians caused by construction of the fence. Following this view, some claim that customary IHL might include a principle of proportionality that encapsulates more than the specific articles in AP-I suggest.[51] According to this view, proportionality would require taking into account the collateral damage to all protected persons, not only to civilians—also soldiers and combatants who are out of combat.

More important, however, is the normative point. Proportionality is a tool that enables placing limits on military actions. Not only should it be embodied in the concrete application of articles 51 and 57, but should have a wider impact on the behavior of the armed forces of parties to armed conflicts. It should serve as paradigm influencing military commanders in all their actions.

We shall devote more attention to the procedures that can give a practical structure to this paradigm later. Here, it is sufficient to note that viewing proportionality as a general principle in the application of force would require every soldier, commander, and statesperson to autonomously consider the damage that may be inflicted by a military operation, and to weigh the military advantages against these consequences. In our view, only by instilling routine attention to this principle in the armed forces can a real reduction in the suffering caused by armed conflicts be achieved.

## C. THE CHANGING NATURE OF ARMED CONFLICT AND PROPORTIONALITY

In recent times, increasing attention has been paid to the changing nature of armed conflicts. Many recent conflicts have followed a pattern in which a sovereign state engages in armed conflict with a non-state actor (NSA), whether a terrorist organization, a militia, or an organized armed group such as ISIS, FARC, Hezbollah, Boko Haram, the Taliban, or Hamas.

Conflicts in this category vary. The spectrum ranges from high-intensity interstate armed conflicts[52] to protracted low-intensity armed conflicts between a state and a non-state actor. Other instances include conflicts involving multiple NSAs, trans-border conflicts involving NSAs and states,[53] situations of relatively peaceful belligerent occupation,[54] and targeted killing operations undertaken

51. Jan Kleffner, *Military Collaterals and Ius in Bello Proportionality*, 48 Isr. YB Human Rights 43 (2018).

52. Such as World War II.

53. A good illustration is the situation prevailing in Syria in 2017, when multiple states (such as Russia, the United States, France, Germany, Turkey, etc.) fought multiple factions (such as ISIS, Peshmerga, and the Free Syrian Army).

54. IHL applies during all situations of occupation. Common Article 2 of the Geneva Conventions stipulates that: "(2) The Convention shall also apply to all cases of partial or total occupation of the territory of a High Contracting Party, even if the said occupation meets with no armed resistance." For a discussion regarding the conditions for occupation, and the beginning

away from the battlefield. Such conflicts may be classified either as international armed conflicts (IACs), as non-international armed conflicts (NIACs), or alternatively, they may not be classified as armed conflicts at all (if they do not meet the conditions that define when an "armed conflict" exists legally).[55] IHL applies to all armed conflicts.[56]

Formally, there is no explicit rule of proportionality in non-international conflicts; there is no provision in treaty law relating to NIACs that is parallel to articles 51 and 57 of AP-I. For example, the Second Additional Protocol to the Geneva Conventions (AP-II), the treaty that regulates non-international armed conflicts, contains the principle of distinction. Article 13(2) of AP-II stipulates that "the civilian population as such, as well as individual civilians, shall not be the object of attack." Proportionality and excessive harm to civilians, however, are not expressly mentioned in AP-II.[57] In other words, AP-II only prohibits

and end of an occupation, see INT'L COMM. OF THE RED CROSS, COMMENTARY ON THE SECOND GENEVA CONVENTION: CONVENTION (II) FOR THE AMELIORATION OF THE CONDITION OF THE WOUNDED, SICK AND SHIPWRECKED MEMBERS OF ARMED FORCES AT SEA, paras. 307-63 (2nd ed., 2017), *available at:* ihl-databases.icrc.org/applic/ihl/ihl.nsf/Comment.xsp?action=openDocument&documentId=1A35EE65211A18AEC12581150044243A [GC-II COMMENTARY].

55. An international armed conflict is defined in Common Article 2 of the Geneva Conventions as any situation of hostilities between two or more states. Determining that a non-international armed conflict exists is more complicated. The minimal conditions for a non-international armed conflict appear in Common Article 3 of the Geneva Conventions. The ICTY has, according to the formula set out in the *Tadic* case, determined that the existence of a non-international armed conflict rests upon assessing two criteria: "(i) the intensity of the conflict and (ii) the organisation of the parties" (Prosecutor v. Dusko Tadić, ICTY Appeals Chamber, IT-94-1-AR72, *Decision on the Defence Motion for Interlocutory Appeal on Jurisdiction*, para. 70 (Oct. 2, 1995)). See also Prosecutor v. Boškoski, ICTY Trial Chamber II, IT-04-82-T, *Judgment*, para. 175 (Jul. 10, 2008); Prosecutor v. Limaj, ICTY Trial Chamber II, IT-03-66, *Judgment*, para. 84 (Nov. 30, 2005). The holding in *Tadić* was that: "an armed conflict exists whenever there is a resort to armed force between States or protracted armed violence between governmental authorities and organized armed groups or between such groups within a State" (Tadić, *Id.*, para. 70). The conditions set out by the ICTY differ from the higher threshold of application found in the Protocol Additional to the Geneva Conventions of 12 August 1949, and Relating to the Protection of Victims of Non–International Armed Conflicts (Protocol II), June 8, 1977, art. 1, 1125 U.N.T.S. 609. For a thorough discussion of issues relating to the classification of conflicts, see GC-II COMMENTARY, *Id.*, paras. 223–363, at 406–525; Marko Milanovic & Vidan zi-Vidanovic, *A Taxonomy of Armed Conflict, in* RESEARCH HANDBOOK ON INTERNATIONAL CONFLICT AND SECURITY LAW 256 (Nigel D. White & Christian Henderson eds., 2013); Andreas Paulus & Mindia Vashakmadze, *Asymmetrical War and the Notion of Armed Conflict—A Tentative Conceptualization*, 873 INT'L REV. RED CROSS 95 (2009).

56. However, there may be differences in the laws which apply during different conflicts, and especially in international armed conflicts as opposed to non-international armed conflicts. See Dieter Fleck, *The Law of Non-International Armed Conflicts, in* THE HANDBOOK OF INTERNATIONAL HUMANITARIAN LAW 605, 605–634 (2nd ed., 2008).

57. The principle is mentioned in one multi-lateral treaty which applied to non-international armed conflicts: Convention on Prohibitions or Restrictions on the Use of Certain Conventional

indiscriminate attacks *directed* at civilians. Still, it is widely understood that according to customary international law the principle of proportionality applies in non-international armed conflicts as well.[58] In fact, no state has declared the principle of proportionality to be inapplicable during an armed conflict.

And yet, while states profess loyalty to the principle of IHL, the application of the principle in modern armed conflict is somewhat different in non-international armed conflicts, and when states fight NSAs.

At this stage of the present volume, it is possible to consider different applications of proportionality in practice, and the dilemmas that decision-makers involved in modern armed conflicts face. Below, we shall describe several cases in which the question of proportionality has arisen. Using these examples, we shall try to flesh out the dilemmas confronted by decision-makers, and the different ways in which they approached them.

## Applying Proportionality: Examples and Dilemmas

On March 24, 1999, NATO forces began bombing Serbia in an attempt to halt the atrocities committed by Serbia in the region of Kosovo.[59] Several of the attacks caused civilian deaths. One of these was the air attack on the main studios of the state-owned broadcasting corporation (RTS) in Belgrade, discussed in the Final Report (NATO Bombing Report) of the Committee Established to Review the NATO Bombing Campaign ("the Committee").[60] This attack, carried out on April 23, 1999, resulted in the deaths of between 10 and 17 people. NATO claimed that the RTS studio was a military objective because it was a part of the Yugoslav C3 (command, control, and communications) system and thus a part of the war effort.[61]

In its analysis of the incident, the Committee tried to apply the basic components of the proportionality formula presented in this chapter. The Committee asked whether the target was indeed a military objective (it was), and whether bombing it did, in fact, give the attackers a concrete military advantage. Next, the committee

Weapons Which May be Deemed to be Excessively Injurious or to Have Indiscriminate Effects, Oct. 10, 1980, 1342 U.N.T.S. 137 [CCW]: Protocol on Prohibitions or Restrictions on the Use of Mines, Booby-Traps and Other Devices (Protocol II), Geneva, Oct. 10, 1980, art. 3(8)(c), 1342 U.N.T.S. 168.

58. Jean-Marie Henckaerts & Louise Doswald-Beck, Customary International Humanitarian Law, Vol. 1 48 (2005) [Henckaerts & Doswald-Beck, ICRC Study].

59. Tim Judah, Kosovo: What Everyone Needs to Know 75–93 (2008).

60. ICTY, *Final Report to the Prosecutor by the Committee Established to Review the NATO Bombing Campaign Against the Federal Republic of Yugoslavia* (2000), *available at:* http://www.icty.org/en/press/final-report-prosecutor-committee-established-review-nato-bombing-campaign-against-federal.

61. *Id.*, para. 55.

asked whether adequate warning had been given to civilians, and whether the death toll of civilians was disproportionate.

The Committee concluded that there was no need for the ICTY to investigate the incident.[62] We shall discuss this conclusion later in the book. At this point, we will simply say that the questions that the committee raised seem to be completely in line with those expected in analyses of the formula of proportionality. There is a military target, there are civilians, and the question is whether the collateral damage was excessive with regards to the military advantage attained.

In his classic book *Just and Unjust War*, Michael Walzer uses the destruction of the Norse Hydro power plant in Vermork, in Nazi-occupied Norway during World War II, as an example of the application of the principle of proportionality.[63] The plant produced heavy water, essential for the German effort to win the race to create an atomic bomb. Hence, from the Allied perspective it had to be destroyed. In 1942, the United Kingdom decided not to bomb the plant from the air, for fear of causing heavy civilian casualties. Instead, the British Special Operations Executive (SOE) despatched a commando unit to destroy the plant. A first raid failed in November 1942, and 34 soldiers died. A second attempt, in February 1943 was more successful, and the commandos caused considerable damage to the plant. However, the Germans were able to repair the damage. In February 1944, when a sufficient quantity of heavy water was accumulated, the Germans loaded it on a ferry, on the way to Germany. The Norwegian resistance, acting under the direction of the British SOE managed to sink the ferry, causing the deaths of 14 civilians, and thus ending the German effort to create an atomic bomb.

The Vermork raid, and the subsequent sinking of the ferry carrying the heavy water, are presented by Walzer as a classical application of the principle of proportionality. The UK was willing to risk the lives of soldiers in order to achieve an important military target, but tried to attain the objective without causing the loss of civilian lives. However, later it became evident that achieving the military target necessitated some collateral damage to civilians. This damage, claims Walzer, is justified by the principle of proportionality because the real intent was to achieve the military advantage.

Walzer's example, of course, is different in practice from the way we usually think about proportionality, since the persons who concerned the UK authorities were Norwegian civilians, not German civilians. Walzer probably uses this example deliberately. According to the traditional application of proportionality in an armed conflict between two states, no differences should exist between the

62. *Id.*, para. 79.

63. Michael Walzer, Just And Unjust War 158 (5th ed., 2015), Walzer's description of the incident is not historically accurate, although this has no bearing on his legal and philosophical discussion. Our own account derives from Anthony Beevor, The Second World War 523–24 (2012).

protection afforded to enemy civilians and those of the attacking state, or, in this specific cases, to those of allies.[64]

### Fighting Non-State Actors: American Operations in Fallujah: Operation Vigilant Resolve (April 2004) and Operation Phantom Fury/Al-Fajr (November–December 2004)

In March 2003 a US coalition invaded Iraq, and after just over five weeks managed to take control of most of Iraq. However, starting in May 2003, Iraqis began mounting insurgency operations in various regions. One of the centers of this insurgency was the city of Fallujah, home to approximately 300,000 inhabitants, most of them Sunni Muslims. Over the course of 2003 and early 2004 it became clear to US commanders that Fallujah had to be retaken in order to restore stability to the region.

The first attempt to take Fallujah, Operation Vigilant Resolve (also known as the First Battle of Fallujah), commenced in April 2004, but was soon halted due to a lack of planning and concerns over potentially large numbers of civilian casualties.[65]

In November 2004, US and Iraqi forces launched a new attempt to conquer Fallujah.[66] Most reports agree that the majority of the city's inhabitants—perhaps as many as 270,000 out of 300,000—had fled, and many of those who remained were combatants. The number of people killed was never verified, with reports ranging from a few hundred to several thousand.[67] The tactics adopted by US forces in this operation included ground raids and the use of air power and white phosphorous shells. Most importantly, a vast amount of firepower was employed in an urban setting known to house civilians, in order to protect the lives of American soldiers.

The battle of Fallujah is an example of an armed conflict very different from those presented earlier in this book. Also different are the issues requiring examination. For example: What degree of responsibility for the civilian casualties should be placed on the Iraqi insurgents, who chose to operate from within the civilian population, thus endangering them? Should all Iraqis who were not members of any rebel NSA be considered civilians? Or perhaps, should all those

64. Norway was occupied throughout World War II by Germany. However, the allies operated in Norway in cooperation with the Norwegian government in exile, and domestic resistance forces.

65. Ahmed S. Hashim, Insurgency and Counter-insurgency in Iraq 31–46 (2006); Carter Malkasian, *The First Battle for Fallujah*, *in* War in Iraq: Planning and Execution 163 (T. G. Mahnken and T. A. Keaney Eds., Routledge 2007).

66. The facts here are based on: Operation Al-Fajr, *in*: www.globalsecurity.com; Hashim, *supra* note 65.

67. The website *Iraq Bodycount*, which keeps track of all databases regarding civilian casualties, puts the number at a few hundred. *Available at:* http://www.iraqbodycount.org/.

who stayed in Fallujah once fighting broke out be counted as combatants, and not civilians, for the purpose of analyzing proportionality?

What is the level of intelligence that military commanders need to have at their disposal before deciding to launch an attack?

### Proportionality in Targeted Killing Operations under the Obama Administration

In August 2017, the US administration declassified and released a "presidential policy guidance" document, authored in 2013, in which the Obama administration articulated a series of rules and procedures governing the use of drones in targeted killings operations.[68] The *Playbook*, as it became known, includes a specific ruling according to which targeted killing operations are not to be undertaken unless there is near certainty that *no civilian* will be killed.[69]

Whether or not this is actually the way in which the United States executed targeted killing operations is debatable.[70] Indeed, there are accounts of US attacks being undertaken with the full knowledge that civilians will be killed,[71] and even formally, the *Playbook* explicitly states that the president may deviate from the policies it describes. The point is, however, that the formal position of the US administration seems to create a much stricter prohibition than the principle of proportionality requires. The idea that civilians enjoy complete, or nearly complete, protection during attacks on legitimate military targets deviates from all traditional rules.[72]

And yet, the standard laid down by the Obama administration should not be entirely unexpected, as it is in line with the declared positions of numerous human rights organizations and scholars. There appears to be growing unease at the prospect of any civilian casualties resulting from targeted killing operations against terrorists, and from operations in which the attacking force enjoys significant technological advantages.

68. Procedures for Approving Direct Action against Terrorist Targets Located Outside the United States and Areas of Active Hostilities (May 22, 2013), *available at:* https://www.justice.gov/oip/foia-library/procedures_for_approving_direct_action_against_terrorist_targets/download.

69. *Id.*, at 15. New York Times reporter Charlie Savage revealed the existence of the document and its contents before it was declassified. Charlie Savage, Power Wars: Inside Obama's Post-9/11 Presidency 283–84 (New York, 2015).

70. See e.g., "Get the Data: Drone Wars," *The Bureau of Investigative Journalism, available at*: https://www.thebureauinvestigates.com/category/projects/drones/drones-graphs/.

71. Ryan Devereaux, "Manhunting in the Hindu-Kush: Civilian Casualties and Strategic Failures in America's Longest War", (article no. 5 of the "Drone Papers") The Intercept (Oct. 15, 2015) *available at:* https://theintercept.com/drone-papers/manhunting-in-the-hindu-kush/.

72. Alexander Gillespie, A History of the Laws of War: Volume 2, The Customs and Laws of War with Regards to Civilians in Times of Conflict 39–51 (Hart, Oxford, 2011).

The reasoning behind the difference between these cases is the changing nature of warfare. As we shall discuss below, new circumstances require states to reevaluate the way in which they confront the question of proportionality. We shall first discuss the practical and realist questions that these new kinds of conflicts raise. Then, we shall discuss a more legal doctrinal issue—the parallel application of IHL and International Human Rights Law in modern armed conflicts.

## Fighting NSAs and the Application of the Principle of Proportionality

The claim that the application and interpretation of the principle of proportionality should change in modern armed conflicts is based on several factors that differentiate classic conflicts, where two professional armies fight each other, from contemporary armed conflicts, where states are mostly fighting NSAs—or which involve failed states, where the armed forces behave similarly to NSAs.[73]

First, the NSA embeds itself and operates from within the civilian population: its fighters dress as civilians, hide their weapons and equipment in civilian houses and places of worship, and even conduct hostilities from within these civilian locations.

Should the principle of proportionality apply in the same manner when the NSAs regularly use the civilian population as a shield? We shall discuss the issues of the definition of a combatant and the use of human shields in Chapters 8 and 9 respectively. At this stage, suffice it to say that while the legal principle of proportionality does not change when states engage NSAs, the application of the principle should, and does, take the unique characteristics of modern armed conflicts into account. There is more flexibility in the application of the rule when the non-state party intentionally manipulates the battlefield in order to involve civilians in the armed conflict.

Second, modern conflicts are often prolonged, at times raging for years at high or low levels of intensity.[74] If a state of armed conflict becomes the norm, rather than an exceptional situation within a limited time frame, should the law not

73. For one discussion of the nature of the "new wars" and armed conflicts, see Cherif M. Bassiouni, *The New Wars and the Crisis of Compliance with the Law of Armed Conflict by Non-State Actors*, 98 J. CRIM. L. & CRIMINOLOGY 711, 759–770 (2008).

74. A few illustrative examples which may serve are:

(1) The civil war in Somalia from 1991 to the present (Roland Adjovi, *Introductory Note to United Nations Security Council Resolution 2093 on the Situation in Somalia*, 52 INT'L LEGAL MATERIALS 1185, 1185 (2013);

(2) The war in Afghanistan, where a conflict still rages despite fact that the official US and NATO operations within the state (that commenced in 2001), ended in 2014. As recently as May 31, 2017, over 90 people were killed and 400 wounded in a suicide bombing in Kabul near the German embassy (Ehsan Popalzai et al., *Kabul blast: Attack kills 90 near diplomatic area in Afghanistan*, CNN, June 1, 2017, *available at:* https://edition.cnn.com/2017/05/31/asia/kabul-explosion-hits-diplomatic-area/index.html); and

(3) The Syrian Civil War, which has lasted for nearly a decade; An armed conflict has also been in progress in Iraq since 2003, when Operation Iraqi Freedom began,

evolve to reflect this reality?[75] For example, should states take into account not only the immediate effects of a specific action, but the cumulative effects, physical and mental, of the armed conflict on civilian populations? We shall discuss these differences throughout the book.

A third difference, and one which deserves more attention at this stage, is the proliferation of digital technology, particularly cameras and social media. For example, these developments enabled the dissemination of live updates the operation in which Osama Bin Laden was killed.[76] Until recently, images and pictures from the battlefield took relatively long periods of time to reach audiences at home. The advent of modern technology services such as Twitter, Facebook Live, and Periscope allows images from conflict zones to be shared in real time, giving the public a greater sense of involvement and engagement in conflicts than ever before.[77]

> through December 2011, when US forces completed their withdrawal from the country, to the present day and the 2017 Battle of Mosul (*Mosul battle: Iraqi forces attack IS-held Old City*, BBC, June 18, 2017, *available at:* www.bbc.com/news/world-middle-east-40317917).

However, it should be noted that this distinction between contemporary and traditional conflicts is not entirely coherent or obvious, as throughout history there have been extended conflicts which were marked by scattered battles spread over several years. One well-known example is the so-called Hundred Years War between France and England, which lasted for more than a century, from 1337 to 1453.

75. When examining whether conflicts today are completely different from previous armed conflicts, it has been asked whether the laws of armed conflict should be treated differently, tweaked or altered, so as to better conform to reality. For one way of dealing with this problem (and for a general discussion regarding the issue of compliance in the new wars), see Bassiouni, *supra* note 73, at 714 n.6.

76. Anne Herzberg & Gerald M. Steinberg, *IHL 2.0: Is There a Role for Social Media in Monitoring and Enforcement*, 45 Isr. L. Rev. 493, 493–94 (2012).

The dissonance between the law and reality raises concerns regarding the legitimacy of the law. This is due to the asymmetry in the application and the creation of the law. For more on this issue, see Michael N. Schmitt, *Asymmetrical Warfare and International Humanitarian Law*, 62 A.F. L. Rev. 1, 33–38 (2008). Legitimacy of the rule of law involves two components: one substantive and the other procedural. The substantive component asks whether the rule itself is legitimate. The procedural component examines whether the party which must comply with the law had a role in its creation or implementation. One of the problems with IHL today is that it is phrased in an ambiguous manner which permits several contradictory interpretations. A second problem is that IHL suffers from a lack of coherence and equality in application, as it appears to be more strictly applied to some states than others. Finally, IHL seems to permit terrorists and non-state entities to flout the law while at the same time denying states the capability to defend themselves. Cohen, *supra* note 48, at 402–03.

77. A point worth noting is that not all conflicts are created equal, and while the law applicable to all conflicts might be the same, the focus of public and international attention and consternation on different conflicts is often unequal. That is, the public may not feel a sense of involvement and engagement in *all* conflicts to the same degree. This has a significant effect on the implementation and enforcement of IHL. US Supreme Court Justice, Louis Brandeis has written

This virtual proximity to the conflict brings to light an important distinction between law, morality, and public perception. The three may lead to the same conclusion or attitude on certain issues and occurrences, but this is not necessarily the case. Indeed, inconsistencies between the three different frameworks for judging human activity—public opinion, what is moral, and what is lawful—coupled with easy, real-time access to information, make conducting wars today more complicated than in the past.

One example of the three frameworks leading to different results during armed conflicts is evident in the attitude toward incidental harm caused to children in attacks. The formal rule of proportionality in IHL does not distinguish between different types of civilians; the value of the life of a young man or an old man is no different from the value of the life of a woman or a child.[78] However, public perception and moral intuition attribute different value to the lives of different civilians, and tend to view child casualties as more heinous than others.

At times, the extralegal consideration of public perception, as well as the moral sensitivities of states themselves, result in stricter constraints being placed on military operations than required by law, in order to lower the collateral damage.[79]

that "sunlight is . . . the best of disinfectants." Similarly, scrutiny and public attention can act as the guarantors of human rights. Conflicts which the public follows will presumably be ones in which there is more compliance than other conflicts, or than would exist without the public scrutiny. (The full quote of Justice Brandeis reads: "Publicity is justly commended as a remedy for social and industrial diseases. Sunlight is said to be the best of disinfectants; electric light the most efficient policeman.") For a discussion of the role of social media as a tool which promotes compliance with IHL, see Herzberg & Steinberg, *supra* note 76.

78. There are certain protections which apply specifically and exclusively to children in armed conflicts, such as the proscription regarding child conscription, limitations on detention, and rules concerning evacuation of children (AP-I, *supra* note 37, art. 77–78; Convention Relative to the Protection of Civilian Persons in Time of War, Aug. 12, 1949, art. 24, 6 U.S.T. 3516, 75 U.N.T.S. 287 [GC-IV]; Protocol on the Involvement of Children in Armed Conflict, May 25, 2000, G.A. Res. 263, U.N. GAOR, 54th sess., annex I, U.N. Doc. A/54/263). For example, AP-I, *Id.*, art. 77(1) stipulates that "Children shall be the object of special respect and shall be protected against any form of indecent assault." However, there are no norms which require the life of a child to be weighed differently than the life of an adult when considering proportionality. It is possible (though it is not clear from the wording) that the special protection referred to in article 77 means that the lives of children would be protected more than adults.

The same ambiguity exists in the Convention of the Right of the Child, Nov. 20, 1989, 1577 U.N.T.S. 3. Article 38(4) of the convention states that: "In accordance with their obligations under international humanitarian law to protect the civilian population in armed conflicts, States Parties shall take all feasible measures to ensure protection and care of children who are affected by an armed conflict." It is unclear whether this article requires the state parties to protect children *more* than any other civilians.

79. Henderson, *supra* note 39, at 206; Michael N. Schmitt & John J. Merriam, *The Tyranny of Context: Israeli Targeting Practices in Legal Perspective*, 37 U. Pa. J. Int'l L. 53, 81 (2015). Public perception, the mass media and even social media can all serve as significant contributing factors in enhancing compliance with IHL. Voeneky, *Implementation and Enforcement of International Humanitarian Law*, *in* The Handbook of International Humanitarian Law 647, 652–53 (3rd ed., Dieter Fleck ed., 2013). Generally, on the role and effect of media coverage on military

The contemporary prevalence in all battlefields of cameras that can instantly relay images and videos to people around the globe via social media appears to be having an effect on armed conflicts and the use of force. The result is that even relatively small and tactical operations with limited military significance can have strategic effects if captured by the lens.

In recent years, states have been paying increasing attention to considerations that go beyond legal constraints in order to attain their tactical and strategic goals. For example, in 2004, the US Military published a field manual outlining its doctrine on counterinsurgency operations. The manual specifies rules of conduct and engagement, some of which are not based on legal sources. These rules take into account considerations aimed at attaining the ultimate goals of military actions, such as securing the trust of the local populace. When discussing the destruction of the insurgent party's infrastructure, the manual requires commanders to examine (alongside the principle of proportionality) whether the planned attack and destruction of infrastructure could possibly contribute to the recruitment of insurgent fighters.[80] Indeed, states are willing to make various concessions in order to secure public and international legitimacy and support. This makes good sense, as states understand that "legitimacy is the main objective [of counter insurgency operations]."[81]

Legitimacy, therefore, is the reasons that all states involved in armed conflicts claim that they are acting legally and that their actions are legitimate, while often also claiming that the actions of their adversary are illegitimate and unlawful.[82]

Possibly, Obama's administration *Playbook* was influenced by such legitimacy concerns. The administration's policy of using targeted killing was legitimized by the claim that these operations would cause *less* collateral damage to civilians than any other method of fighting terrorism.[83] It was therefore extremely important to verify that this policy would reduce civilian casualties to a minimum.

operations and the effect of questions of legitimacy in armed conflicts, see Laurie R. Blank, *Military Operations and Media Coverage: The Interplay of Law and Legitimacy, in* ROUTLEDGE HANDBOOK ON MILITARY ETHICS 348 (George Lucas ed., 2015).

80. HEADQUARTERS, DEPARTMENT OF THE ARMY, FIELD MANUAL 3-24/MCWP 3-33.5, INSURGENCIES AND COUNTERING INSURGENCIES, paras. 9-44 (Washington, D.C., 2 June 2014), *available at:* fas.org/irp/doddir/army/fm3-24.pdf.

81. *Id.*, at 1–19, paras. 1–78.

82. Bassiouni, *supra* note 73, at 781–82. Of course, in practice states do not always follow the laws of war. In fact, Morrow concludes that the protection of civilians in times of war, which is the main subject of this work, is the areas in which states *least* comply with international law. JAMES MORROW, ORDER WITHIN ANARCHY: THE LAWS OF WAR AS AN INTERNATIONAL INSTITUTION (2014).

83. In May 2013 Obama gave a speech at the National Defense University in which he said: "So it is false to assert that putting boots on the ground is less likely to result in civilian deaths or less likely to create enemies in the Muslim world. The results would be more U.S. deaths, more Black Hawks down, more confrontations with local populations, and an inevitable mission creep in support of such raids that could easily escalate into new wars." *Remarks by the President at the National*

The final factor in the application of the principle of legitimacy to modern armed conflicts is the issue of reciprocity in the application of IHL. Many current conflicts between liberal democracies and non-state actors are characterized by the fact that at least one of the parties, usually the NSA, disregards IHL. The literature advances two reasons for the violation of IHL by NSAs: first, they have not played a role in the formation of IHL and the shaping of its rules;[84] and second, due to the asymmetry of strength between states and NSAs, the latter parties would be disadvantaged were they to comply with IHL.

If one state or party to the conflict violates its obligations regarding civilians—whether its own or the adversary's—is the other party free to violate its obligations in turn? There are two contexts in which this question may arise: The first is when the civilians of one party are attacked, and there is public pressure to respond by attacking the civilians of the other party. The second is when NSAs do not comply with the rules of international law and fail to distinguish their own fighters from civilians.[85] In these cases, the state party is under pressure from its own public not to afford more protection to enemy civilians than the enemy itself is prepared to extend its own people.

Reciprocity is thus an important element when it comes to states' compliance with international law; one party's violation of international law provides a strong disincentive to the other party to comply with the law.[86]

Nonetheless, it is understood today that the core obligations of IHL are not couched in terms of reciprocity. That is, although one of the bases for the rule of law is reciprocity and equality between sovereigns and belligerents in terms of their legal obligations, the duty to comply with these obligations is not dependent on the opposing party's fulfilment or violation of its obligations. One party's violation does not validate an opposing party's violation.[87]

*Defense University*, The White House (May 23, 2013), *available at:* https://obamawhitehouse.archives.gov/the-press-office/2013/05/23/remarks-president-national-defense-university.

84. Treaties are uniformly negotiated by states, as states are normally their primary parties. See generally, Malcolm N. Shaw, International Law 93–98 (6th ed., 2008).

85. This failure to distinguish combatants from civilians is subject to varied academic discussion which pertains to various questions, including those combatants' status and what protections such combatants are entitled to upon their capture. See generally, Yoram Dinstein, *Unlawful Combatancy, in* International Law and the War on Terror, 151 (Fred L. Borch & Paul S. Wilson eds., 2003); Knut Dormann, *The Legal Situation of Unlawful/Unprivileged Combatants*, 849 Int'l Rev. Red Cross 45 (2003); Knut Ipsen, *Combatants and Non-Combatants, in* The Handbook of International Humanitarian Law 80, 89–92 (3rd ed., Dieter Fleck ed., 2013).

86. Voeneky, *supra* note 79, at 653. Morrow, *supra* note 82.

87. The ICRC maintains there is a customary rule of international law according to which "the obligation to respect and ensure respect for international humanitarian law does not depend on reciprocity." See Henckaerts & Doswald-Beck, ICRC Study, *supra* note 58, rule 146. For

As stated by the ICTY Trial Chamber in the *Kupreskić* case, "the bulk of this body of law lays down absolute obligations, namely obligations that are unconditional or in other words not based on reciprocity."[88]

Keeping this in mind, it should be noted that reprisals and countermeasures do exist in international law. Though treaty law prohibits reprisals against civilians,[89] and reciprocal violations of the protections for civilians,[90] it has been questioned whether the prohibition on reprisals against the civilian population constitutes customary international law.[91]

These considerations lead states in different directions. Whether, and how, states apply proportionality differently in modern armed conflict than in classic conflicts very much depends on the context of the specific conflict. In some conflicts, policy calculations (such as winning the hearts and minds of the civilian population) would cause the state to apply the principle more strictly. In other contexts, when there is public pressure to deter the enemy from using civilians as shields, states might apply the principle with more flexibility. The Fallujah case, may serve as an example where the overriding consideration prompting US troops to apply proportionality in a flexible manner was the fact that Iraqi insurgents were embedding themselves within the civilian population.

As we shall reiterate throughout this book, policy considerations certainly constitute an important basis for understanding the real-life application of the principle of proportionality. However, this factor does not seem to fully explain the Obama administration's attempt to avoid *any* civilian casualties. In order to fully understand this policy, we need to look at another relevant legal issue: the relationship between the principle of proportionality based on IHL, and the right to life in international human rights law (HRL). In the next part of the chapter we will discuss this subject.

## Parallel Application of IHL and International Human Rights Law

There is a fundamental distinction between the law that applies during armed conflicts and the law that applies during times of peace. In the latter case, HRL

a utilitarian explanation which detaches IHL from reciprocity see: Eyal Benvenisti & Amichai Cohen, *War is Governance: Explaining the Logic of the Laws of War from a Principal- Agent Perspective,* 111 MICH. L. REV. 1363 (2014).

88. Prosecutor v. Kupreskić, ICTY Trial Chamber, IT-95-16, *Judgment*, para. 517 (Jan. 14, 2000) (See also para. 125: "The fact that the adversary engages in unlawful behaviour and persecutes or kills civilians cannot be a justification for similar and reciprocal conduct").

89. AP-I, *supra* note 37, art. 51(6).

90. *Id.*, art. 51(8).

91. The ICRC, in its study of customary international law, does not go as far as stating that reprisals against the civilian population are prohibited by customary law. There is contrary state practice and *opinio juris* in this regard, including that of the United States, the United Kingdom

is the body of international law that governs the use of force by states against individuals. During armed conflicts, however, the legal situation is less clear.

Some states maintain that IHL is the sole body of law that applies during armed conflict—i.e., HRL does not apply.[92] This position is also based on the fact that although the two bodies of law were largely developed after World War II, it was not initially understood that the Universal Declaration of Human Rights and the 1949 Geneva Conventions would both apply at the same time.[93]

To modern scholars, human rights activists, and large parts of the public, all this seems to be incredibly wrong. In their view, the right to life, protected by international human rights law, does not simply disappear in armed conflicts.[94] Indeed, most states and scholars reject the dichotomous approach—applying HRL during peace and IHL during armed conflict. The prevailing position is that HRL continues to apply during times of armed conflict, unless circumstances permit impinging on these rights.[95] However, there are disagreements on how exactly the two bodies of law interrelate.

and France. DoD Manual, *supra* note 43, para. 18.18.3.4; Henckaerts & Doswald-Beck, ICRC Study, *supra* note 58, rule 146.

92. This remains the position of some states, such as the United States and Israel, that human rights law applies during times of peace, but not during armed conflicts, or at least, that in situations of conflict between the two bodies of law, IHL always perseveres. DoD Manual, *supra* note 43, para. 1.6.3.1 ("the law of war is the *lex specialis* during situations of armed conflict, and, as such, is the controlling body of law with regard to the conduct of hostilities and the protection of war victims."); The State of Israel, Ministry of Foreign Affairs, The Operation in Gaza 27 December 2008 – 18 January 2009: Factual and Legal Aspects, para. 28 (July 2009) ("the applicable legal framework for assessing the recent operations in Gaza is the 'Law of Armed Conflict,' also known as 'International Humanitarian Law.'"); Human Rights Committee, *Consideration of Reports Submitted by States Parties under Article 40 of the Covenant Pursuant to the Optional Reporting Procedure: Fourth periodic reports of states parties due in 2013—Israel*, para. 47 (Oct. 14, 2013).

93. Cordula Droege, *The Interplay between International Humanitarian Law and International Human Rights Law in Situations of Armed Conflict*, 40 Isr. L. Rev.310, 313–14 (2007).

94. As Marko Milanovic claimed: "If human rights accrue to human beings solely by virtue of their humanity, why should these rights evaporate merely because two states, or a state and a non-state actor, have engaged in armed conflict? More limited these rights may be, but they cannot be completely extinguished or displaced if their basic universality premise, that they are immanent in the human dignity of every individual, is accepted." Marko Milanovic, *Norm Conflicts, International Humanitarian Law, and Human Rights, in* International Humanitarian Law and International Human Rights Law 95, 101 (Orna Ban-Naftali ed. 2011).

95. Certain HRL treaties permit states to derogate from their obligations in times of public emergency. The International Covenant on Civil and Political Rights, Dec. 19, 1966, art. 4, 999 U.N.T.S. 171 [ICCPR], for example, stipulates that: "In time of public emergency which threatens the life of the nation and the existence of which is officially proclaimed, the States Parties to the present Covenant may take measures derogating from their obligations under the present Covenant to the extent strictly required by the exigencies of the situation, provided that such measures are not inconsistent with their other obligations under international law

The Human Rights Committee has opined that both bodies of law continue to apply during armed conflict, and while IHL might contain more specific rules on certain issues, the two bodies should be applied in a complementary fashion, rather than in a mutually exclusive manner.[96] Others have argued that the two bodies can be applied in parallel only when they can truly complement one another in a harmonious fashion. This is true primarily regarding judicial guarantees, the treatment of persons, economic and social rights, and persons in the power of the state. However, when there is no way to harmonize the two bodies of law, the *lex specialis*—IHL—will prevail; i.e., the closer the situation is to combat.[97] The International Court of Justice, in its Advisory Opinion Regarding the Legality of the Threat or Use of Nuclear Weapons, expressed the position that while HRL still applies during armed conflicts, it will be interpreted in light of the *lex specialis*:

> The Court observes that the protection of the International Covenant of Civil and Political Rights does not cease in times of war, except by operation of Article 4 of the Covenant whereby certain provisions may be derogated from in a time of national emergency. Respect for the right to life is not, however, such a provision. In principle, the right not arbitrarily to be deprived of one's life applies also in hostilities. The test of what is an arbitrary deprivation of life, however, then falls to be determined by the applicable *lex specialis*, namely, the law applicable in armed conflict which is designed to regulate the conduct of

and do not involve discrimination solely on the ground of race, colour, sex, language, religion or social origin." For further discussion of the conditions under which states may derogate from their obligations, and examination of which situations merit such derogation, see e.g., Lawless v. Ireland, E.Ct.H.R., App. No. 332/57, para.28 (1961); A. v. U.K., E.Ct.H.R., App. No. 3455/05, paras.176-181 (2009); Evan J. Criddle & Evan Fox-Decent, *Human Rights, Emergencies, and the Rule of Law*, 34 HUM. RTS. Q. 39, 48 (2012); Joan F. Hartman, *Working Paper for the Committee of Experts on the Article 4 Derogation Provision*, 7 HUM. RTS. Q. 89, 91 (1985); Richard B. Lillich, *The Paris Minimum Standards of Human Rights Norms in a State of Emergency*, 79 AM. J. INT'L L. 1072 (1985); SARAH JOSEPH ET AL., THE INTERNATIONAL COVENANT ON CIVIL AND POLITICAL RIGHTS: CASES, MATERIALS, AND COMMENTARY 825 (2004); David Zlotogorski, *Derogation from the Obligations under the Refugee Convention in Times of Emergency in Israel*, 18 HAMISHPAT ONLINE: HUMAN RIGHTS 25, 35 n.67–68 (2013) (Heb.). It is important to note that not all derogations may be justified in all armed conflicts, as the "Covenant requires that even during an armed conflict measures derogating from the Covenant are allowed only if and to the extent that the situation constitutes a threat to the life of the nation." (Human Rights Committee, *General Comment 29*, U.N. Doc. CCPR/C/21/Rev.1/Add.11, para. 3 (2001); Zlotogorski, *Id.*, at 36).

96. Human Rights Committee, *General Comment 31*, U.N. Doc.CCPR/C/21/Rev.1/Add.13, para.11, (2004) ("The [International Covenant on Civil and Political Rights] applies also in situations of armed conflict to which the rules of international humanitarian law are applicable. While, in respect of certain Covenant rights, more specific rules of international humanitarian law may be especially relevant for the purposes of the interpretation of Covenant rights, both spheres of law are complementary, not mutually exclusive").

97. Droege, *supra* note 93.

> hostilities. Thus, whether a particular loss of life, through the use of a certain weapon in warfare, is to be considered an arbitrary deprivation of life contrary to Article 6 of the Covenant, can only be decided by reference to the law applicable in armed conflict and not deduced from the terms of the Covenant itself.[98]

The Court voiced a slightly different opinion in the *Wall* Advisory Opinion, delivered eight years later. Maintaining that HRL continues to apply during armed conflicts, the Court discussed the relationship between the two bodies of law, stating that:

> There are thus three possible situations: some rights may be exclusively matters of international humanitarian law; others may be exclusively matters of human rights law; yet others may be matters of both these branches of international law. In order to answer the question put to it, the Court will have to take into consideration both these branches of international law, namely human rights law and, as *lex specialis*, international humanitarian law.[99]

The difference between these two positions of the Court can be significant. According to the 1996 Advisory Opinion, in situations of a clash between the two bodies of law, IHL would always trump the rights of the individuals under HRL. This rule offers clearer guidance to states regarding how they should conduct themselves. However, it also results in greater infringement upon individuals' rights and gives states more discretion due to the fact that, in most cases, HRL grants more significant protections to civilians than IHL. Contrary to this, the Advisory Opinion of 2004 states that during armed conflict, the applicable law might be one of three: solely HRL; solely IHL; or both IHL and HRL. This might result in greater civilian protection during armed conflict; however, it offers no clear guidance on which of the two bodies of law apply in any given situation, leaving the normative framework murky.[100]

Thus, the interplay between the two bodies of law remains unclear to this day, despite the fact that the differences between them can be significant, particularly when concerning issues such as the right to life and proportionality. Below we aim to clarify two issues. First, how the right to life—an essential part of HRL—applies during armed conflict, according to the view that there is parallel application of

98. *Legality of the Threat or Use of Nuclear Weapons*, Advisory Opinion, I.C.J. 8, 587, para. 25 (1996).

99. *Legal Consequences of the Construction of a Wall in the Occupied Palestinian Territory*, Advisory Opinion, I.C.J. 136, para. 106 (2004).

100. It may be claimed that the difference is not conceptual. The 1996 opinion relates to issues of overlap, as the discussion relates to the use of nuclear weapons. The 2004 opinion refers to occupied territories, where there is also a possibility of an exclusive human rights regime, where the law of occupation gives no concrete answers.

IHL and HRL. Second, we suggest that some state's actions can be understood as attempts to balance the principle of proportionality against the principle of the right to life.

## The Right to Life During Armed Conflicts

Article 6 of the International Covenant on Civil and Political Rights enshrines the right to life.[101] The article stipulates that "Every human being has the inherent right to life. This right shall be protected by law. No one shall be arbitrarily deprived of his life." The protection from arbitrary deprivation of life is also enshrined in other human rights treaties.[102]

There are substantial discrepancies between IHL and HRL with regard to the use of force by state agents, even in combat situations. Under IHL, combatants may be killed almost without question solely by virtue of their being combatants. The primary constraint in most cases is proportionality—the need to assess incidental harm to civilians. Under HRL, however, the situation is very different. Most importantly, under HRL, the right to life and the need to justify depriving life under the principle of proportionality apply not only to civilians, but also to the combatants themselves. There are controls governing the use of force against those who are directly participating in the hostilities. Force, even if used against combatants, must only be used when it is "absolutely necessary."[103]

In *Khatsiyeva and Others v. Russia*, the European Court of Human Rights held that there are very strict limits on the ability to lawfully infringe upon the right to life, even during times of armed conflict.[104] The Court ruled that:

The use of force which may result in the deprivation of life must be no more than "absolutely necessary" for the achievement of one of the purposes set out in Article 2 § 2 (a), (b) and (c). This term indicates that a stricter and more compelling test

101. ICCPR, *supra* note 95.

102. For example, see the European Convention for the Protection of Human Rights and Fundamental Freedoms, Nov. 4, 1950, art.2, 213 U.N.T.S. 221: "Article 2. (1) Everyone's right to life shall be protected by law. No one shall be deprived of his life intentionally save in the execution of a sentence of a court following his conviction of a crime for which this penalty is provided by law. (2) Deprivation of life shall not be regarded as inflicted in contravention of this Article when it results from the use of force which is no more than absolutely necessary: (a) in defence of any person from unlawful violence; (b) in order to effect a lawful arrest or to prevent the escape of a person lawfully detained; (c) in action lawfully taken for the purpose of quelling a riot or insurrection."

103. McCann v. United Kingdom, E.Ct.H.R., App. No. 18984/91, paras. 147–49 (1995).

104. The case concerned the killing of individuals by Russian helicopters near the Chechen border, as part of the Russian counter-terrorist operation within the territory of the Chechen Republic. Russia alleged that the men who were killed had been armed, but the Court, making no finding on that question, found no evidence to support this claim.

of necessity must be employed than that normally applicable when determining whether State action is "necessary in a democratic society" . . . Consequently, the force used must be strictly proportionate to the achievement of the permitted aims.[105] The Court held that this obligation exists even if the individuals are armed.[106]

The UN Human Rights Committee General Comment no. 36 attempts to introduce greater clarity to the matter:[107]

> Like the rest of the Covenant, article 6 continues to apply also in situations of armed conflict to which the rules of international humanitarian law are applicable, including to the conduct of hostilities. While rules of international humanitarian law may be relevant for the interpretation and application of article 6 when the situation calls for their application, both spheres of law are complementary, not mutually exclusive. Use of lethal force consistent with international humanitarian law and other applicable international law norms is, in general, not arbitrary.
>
> By contrast, practices inconsistent with international humanitarian law, entailing a risk to the lives of civilians and other persons protected by international humanitarian law, including the targeting of civilians, civilian objects and objects indispensable to the survival of the civilian population, indiscriminate attacks, failure to apply the principles of precaution and proportionality, and the use of human shields, would also violate article 6 of the Covenant.
>
> States parties should, in general, disclose the criteria for attacking with lethal force individuals or objects whose targeting is expected to result in deprivation of life, including the legal basis for specific attacks, the process of identification of military targets and combatants or persons taking a direct part in hostilities, the circumstances in which relevant means and methods of warfare have been used, and whether less harmful alternatives were considered. They must also investigate alleged or suspected violations of article 6 in situations of armed conflict in accordance with the relevant international standards.

This general comment indeed brings these two bodies of law—IHL and HRL—closer together. With regard to the implementation of proportionality, the Committee seems to adopt the position that the principle of proportionality in IHL is also part of HRL. As a result, civilian deaths caused by an attack that was

105. Khatsiyeva v. Russia, E.Ct.H.R., App. No. 5108/02, para. 129 (2008).

106. "Having regard to the above, the Court is not persuaded that the killing of Khalid Khatsiyev and Kazbek Akiyev, even assuming that they were armed, constituted a use of force which was no more than absolutely necessary in pursuit of the aims provided for in Article 2 § 2 (a) and (b) of the Convention." *Id.*, para. 138.

107. Human Rights Committee, *General Comment No. 36 (2018) on article 6 of the International Covenant on Civil and Political Rights, on the Right to Life*, para. 64 (Oct. 31, 2018), *available at:* www.tbinternet.ohchr.org/Treaties/CCPR/Shared%20Documents/1_Global/CCPR_C_GC_36_8785_E.pdf (footnotes omitted).

conducted according to the principle of proportionality will not be in violation of HRL.

The question of collateral damage to civilians seems, indeed, to be the most problematic part of IHL from the point of view of human rights principles. The idea that the attacking party can legitimately use lethal force knowing that civilians would be killed contravenes the most basic principles of human rights. A relevant example is the decision of the German Constitutional Court in the Federal Aviation Law case.[108] In this case, the Federal Constitutional Court found that certain articles of the Federal Aviation Law of 2005 were incompatible with the right to human dignity under German Basic Law. The law allowed the federal government to deploy armed forces to shoot down a hijacked civilian airplane that is about to be used by terrorists to cause significant damage, as in the attacks of September 11, 2001. The court held that the law treated individual humans as objects, and it therefore did not respect the right to life and the right to human dignity.

There may be some practical implications resulting from these somewhat abstract discussions. There is no disagreement that during armed conflict, causing *some* collateral damage, even lethal, is not illegal per se. However, as human rights law becomes more influential in armed conflict, it should only be expected that the limits deriving from the principle of proportionality will be interpreted more strictly. As we stated earlier, in these situations it should also be expected that the right to life of both combatants and civilians directly participating in hostilities would also be protected, and be taken into consideration in the proportionality analysis.

## Different Balances of IHL/HRL in Different Types of Armed Conflicts?

One way to reconcile the differences between IHL and HRL is to suggest that the law governing armed conflicts should apply differently in different situations or different types of conflicts.

The pronouncement of the ICJ, quoted earlier, suggests that the relationship between IHL and HRL, however interpreted, is the same in all kinds of armed conflict. Yet this position seems problematic. Surely, there is a spectrum of possible balances between the two bodies of law. The more the situation resembles a classical armed conflict, the greater the reason to adopt the more permissive IHL standard. The more the situation resembles a peacetime operation, the more we would turn to the more restrictive HRL standard. This is the position promoted by Michael Newton and Larry May,[109] who suggest a scale of application of the principal of proportionality. They identify five thresholds of application, in each of which the balance between IHL and HRL is different. The first threshold is

108. 1 BvR 357/07 Dr. H v. §14.3. of the Aviation Security Act (Feb. 15, 2006).

109. MICHAEL NEWTON & LARRY MAY, PROPORTIONALITY IN INTERNATIONAL LAW 290 (2014).

defined by cases of a war between two states that field professional armed forces. In this category of cases, the principle of proportionality should be the most lenient, allowing the state considerable flexibility in its application. There are practical reasons, such as professionalism and reciprocity for the opposing parties to respect the principle of proportionality. Therefore, there is no reason to turn to the more restrictive HRL standard.

The next threshold suggested by May and Newton regards cases in which a unit is under specific attack, and acts in self-defence, even if the conflict is asymmetric. May and Newton suggest that the proportionality standard that should be used in this case is similar to that applied in classic armed conflict.[110] Soldiers facing a real threat to their lives and acting in self-defence, are likely to be more prone to use force in order to save themselves. Hence a stricter application of the principle may be warranted.

The Battle of Mogadishu provides a possible instance of this category.[111] In October 1993, when a force of US troops was pinned down under enemy fire in the streets of Mogadishu, Somalia, the United States deployed relatively large numbers of troops and massive firepower in a rescue effort. Eighteen American soldiers were killed during the operation. According to the testimony of Ambassador Robert Oakley, the US special representative to Somalia:

> My own personal estimate is that there must have been 1,500 to 2,000 Somalis killed and wounded that day, because that battle was a true battle. And the Americans and those who came to their rescue, were being shot at from all sides . . . a deliberate war battle, if you will, on the part of the Somalis. And women and children were being used as shields and in some cases women and children were actually firing weapons, and were coming from all sides. Sort of a rabbit warren of huts, houses, alleys, and twisting and turning streets, so those who were trying to defend themselves were shooting back in all directions. Helicopter gunships were being used as well as all sorts of automatic weapons on the ground by the U.S. and the United Nations. The Somalis, by and large, were using automatic rifles and grenade launchers and it was a very nasty fight, as intense as almost any battle you would find.[112]

Other accounts of the operation report a lower number of casualties than Ambassador Oakley. *The Washington Post*, reported that the Somali leaders put their casualties at 312 dead and 815 wounded.[113]

110. *Id.*, at 291.

111. The following description is based on: Mark Bowden, Black Hawk Down: A Story of Modern War (1999); George J. Church, *Somalia: Anatomy of Disaster*, Time Magazine (Oct. 18, 1993).

112. "Ambush in Mogadishu" Interview with Ambassador Robert Oakley," Frontline, *available at:* https://www.pbs.org/wgbh/pages/frontline/shows/ambush/interviews/oakley.html.

113. Ron Atkinson, *Night of a Thousand Fires*, Washington Post (Jan. 31, 1994).

It is hard to verify how many of the Somali dead were civilians, and how many were Somali militiamen operating under the instructions of Rebel Leader, General Aidid. The International Committee of the Red Cross estimated that 200 Somali civilians were killed and several hundred were wounded in the fighting.[114]

Absent an in-depth study, it is o impossible to assess whether the principle of proportionality was observed in all stages of the battle. However, the high discrepancy between the proportion of Somali civilian fatalities and that of US soldiers may indicate the emphasis the United States put on preserving the life of its own soldiers, an issue we shall return to in later chapters.

The third threshold of Newton and May's proposed scale of application of the principal of proportionality concerns scenarios in which states act in order to prevent large-scale terrorist attacks against civilians. In these cases, provided that the attacking state can demonstrate that the threat is indeed very serious, it is deemed to be justified in resorting to force that might cause incidental harm to civilians. However, since such actions are invariably likely to take place outside a specific battlefield, against terrorists who are embedded in a civilian population, proportionality should be applied more strictly than usual.[115]

The fourth threshold is marked by actions that, although intended to prevent terrorist operations, are not undertaken to halt a specific large-scale terrorist attack, but as part of the ongoing war on terror. Targeted killing operations usually fall within this category. In those cases, Newton and May suggest, HRL, that is, the right to life, should almost always prevail, except in some very narrowly crafted exceptions.[116]

The Obama administration's *Playbook* is relevant to this category. Although Newton and May do not discuss this text, their conclusion seems to support its position: a targeted killing operation likely to cause collateral civilian fatalities would never be sanctioned, unless personally approved by the president. This position, which tilts the balance towards the HRL standard of the right to life, is not universally accepted. The background for this discussion is a major and unresolved doctrinal question, regarding the use of targeted killing operations outside actual battlefields. It is clear that when a battle erupts, and the state chooses to attack a specific individual, the applicable law is IHL. Many scholars and practitioners agree that in this case, IHL allows the targeting of individuals, and hence targeted killings are allowed.[117] However, few targeted killings take place on a conventional battlefield, where they are usually less effective. Rather, they are directed against targets not actually fighting or personally involved in an ongoing battle, but engaged in ordinary daily activities. Which legal paradigm is applicable under those circumstances? As mentioned, the governments of the United States and Israel

114. Church, *supra* note 111.

115. Newton and May *supra* note 109, at 292.

116. *Id.*, at 294.

117. E.g., David Kretzmer, *Targeted Killing of Suspected Terrorists: Extra-Judicial Executions or Legitimate Means of Defense?* 16 EJIL 171 (2005).

have long held the view that since the *general* context is still that of armed conflict, IHL remains the applicable law. After all, the person targeted is part of an organized group participating in an armed conflict.[118]

An alternative view is that the situation in these cases no longer corresponds to that of armed conflict. Rather, it must be classified as a law enforcement operation in which (absent an actual battle) terrorists are merely criminals. In law enforcement operations, as previously explained, IHL does not apply. Rather, the applicable governing law is HRL, as is the case in any other state action.[119] An attack carried out against a target in the knowledge that it will cause the deaths of innocent civilians, not inadvertently, but as a foreseen result of the operation, presumably constitutes a violation of the right to life.[120]

The *Playbook* is an attempt to adopt a middle ground between these conflicting views. It reflects an attempt to avoid any civilian death, unless the circumstances are extreme. However, this position is not accepted by all states. Israel, for example, as we will see throughout the book, believes that the principle of proportionality is indeed applicable to targeted killing operations, but does not accept the "almost no civilian deaths" formula. A similar position was adopted in the German Kunduz case.[121] The case concerned an attack by US planes on fuel tanks taken over by Taliban insurgents during the armed conflict in Afghanistan in 2009, which caused the death of approximately 90 civilians. Since the US planes were called in by German forces, the incident was also investigated by the German Federal Prosecutor. The position adopted by the latter was that even if the German forces were aware of the presence of civilians in the area of operations, provided that they had made an effort to minimize civilian casualties, the incidental killing of civilians was not a violation of international law.[122]

We discuss this debate here, but it may actually be the underlying reason for many of the disagreements discussed throughout this book. Clearly, if the activities of the attacking army are judged under the principle of the right to life, especially with regard to collateral civilian death, then the questions of force protection, human shields, and other similar issues should also be discussed in this light, even if, as according to most scholars, some degree of civilian collateral damage is allowed.

The fifth, and last, threshold suggested by Newton and May is the one in which states act to confront a threat from areas under the state's control, such as occupied

118. Yoram Dinstein, Non-International Armed Conflicts in International Law 224–230 (Cambridge, Cambridge UP, 2014).

119. Nils Melzer, Interpretative Guidance on the Notion of Direct Participation in Hostilities Under International Humanitarian Law (ICRC, 2009).

120. Brian Orend, The Morality of War 124 (2nd ed., 2013).

121. Chapter 5, n. 86–88 and accompanying text.

122. For a summary for the decision of the Federal Prosecutor see: Constantin von der Groeben, *German Federal Prosecutor Terminates Investigation Against German Soldiers With Respect to NATO Air Strike in Afghanistan*, EJIL:Talk! (April 29, 2010).

territory. Newton and May suggest that in these cases, HRL is the only relevant legal norm, and incidental civilian deaths should never be sanctioned.

This position, too, is contested by some states. Arguably, this was the case in the Gaza Strip in the spring of 2018, when Palestinians began holding a series of large demonstrations near the border fence with Israel. The official Israeli position, as presented to the Israeli High Court of Justice, was that there is an ongoing armed conflict between Israel and the Hamas, which controls the Gaza Strip. However, the demonstrations were not part of this armed conflict, and thus Israel's response to them might properly be viewed as "law enforcement."[123] Which body of law applies to this situation?

Most scholars support the position that HRL is the sole applicable body of law,[124] but the official Israeli position was that this situation falls under IHL, and that HRL does not apply. The Israeli position was apparently based on a principled legal position that HRL does not apply extraterritorially, and hence is not relevant, as well as on the legal position that HRL does not apply concurrently with IHL. The Israeli claim was that IHL actually includes a separate framework for law enforcement situations, one that is not specified in any treaty, but exists in customary international law.[125] The content of this elusive body of law is not completely clear, but it seems to be closely correlated, though not identical, with HRL.[126] Neither the position submitted by the state nor the judgment of the court specify whether collateral damage to civilians is allowed under this legal framework.

It seems that the position of the Israeli government was taken, inter alia, in order to allow the government greater flexibility for using lethal force. For example, the Israeli government adopted a position according to which "instigators" of demonstrations could be shot using non-lethal ammunition (a method which has caused some deaths, even if by mistake).[127]

It is unclear whether the position of the Israeli government was also intended to allow Israeli armed forces more flexibility in the application of the principle of

123. HCJ 3003/18, Yesh Din—Volunteers for Human Rights v. The IDF Chief of Staff (Published in Nevo, May 24, 2018) [Isr.]. For an analysis of the decision see: Amichai Cohen, *Analysis of Israel's Supreme Court Decision Allowing Lethal Force in Gaza*, Just Security (May 27, 2018), *available at:* https://www.justsecurity.org/57033/analysis-israels-supreme-court-decision-allowing-lethal-force-gaza/.

124. Eliav Lieblich, *Collectivizing Threat: An Analysis of Israel's Legal Claims for Resort to Force on the Gaza Border*, Just Security (May 16, 2018), *available at:* https://www.justsecurity.org/56346/collectivizing-threat-analysis-israels-legal-claims-resort-force-gaza-border/.

125. *Id.*

126. See Cohen, *supra* note 123. Elena Chechko & Yuval Shany, *The Supreme Court of Israel Dismisses a Petition Against Gaza Rules of Engagement*, Lawfare (May 26, 2018), *available at:* https://www.lawfareblog.com/supreme-court-israel-dismisses-petition-against-gaza-rules-engagement.

127. The government's position was that this was allowed even under HRL, but this position can be seen as problematic. Lieblich, *supra* note 124; Cehchko & Shany, *Id.*

proportionality, and correspondingly, less protection to the lives of civilians in a situation outside Israel's borders with characteristics of law enforcement.

## D. CONCLUSION

The framework suggested by Newton and May for applying proportionality in different categories of conflicts is not a formula that can be applied simply. As will be discussed in the following chapters, and especially in Chapter 11, proportionality is a vague concept, shrouded in disagreements regarding almost every aspect of its application. The thresholds suggested by Newton and May do not resolve these disagreements. Moreover, where Newton and May state their position most clearly—in thresholds 4 and 5, where they posit that almost no incidental death would be allowed—not all states concur that their stance truly reflects the law as it is.

That said, we conclude that Newton and May's framework is extremely helpful in highlighting that the application of proportionality cannot be assumed to be identical in all cases. This insight will be utilized in various contexts in the following chapters of the book.

PART II

# The Practical Application of Proportionality

This second section forms the backbone of this book. It discusses the major questions, disagreements, and opinions that have been raised in the literature regarding the actual implementation of the principle of proportionality in modern IHL. In general, we analyze the principle of proportionality through an intuitive model of analysis, relating to direct military advantage, incidental harm, and the "excessiveness" of the latter relative to the former.

However, many of the issues dealt with in this section do not fall easily into this tripartite division. Hence, our choice was first (in Chapters 4 and 5) to introduce an overview of the issues of military advantage and incidental civilian harm. The subsequent five chapters (6–10) address specific topics that require special attention due to their effect on proportionality. We begin with a discussion of issues relating to military advantage (namely, whether and how force protection and strategic considerations can be weighed in the "military advantage" of an attack), and progress to issues that relate to the incidental harm of an attack (direct participation, human shields, and distinction and dual-use targets).

# 4

# Military Advantage

Previous chapters have provided some theoretical background to proportionality in IHL. But what, exactly, is proportionality?

At the outset, it should be noted that, until recently, the principle of proportionality in IHL was the subject of very limited jurisprudence.[1] This affects the extent to which the principle has been developed and clarified, making the task of determining what proportionality is all the more challenging.

As previously stated, the common view is that proportionality cannot be measured simply by crunching numbers and comparing the losses of one side to the losses of the other. Rather, proportionality is based on a complex, fact-based, case-by-case assessment that depends on the information reasonably available to the military commanders with a view to evaluating the military advantage anticipated prior to the attack, relative to the expected harm to civilians.[2] Proportionality is an attempt to balance incommensurable values and interests: on the one hand, the harm to civilians and civilian objects; and on the other, the anticipated military advantage. According to most commentators, these two values cannot be compared through the simple use of a formula, as there is no common denominator between them.[3] Parks has said of proportionality that "by American domestic law

1. Yuval Shany, The Principle of Proportionality under International Law 75 (2009); Robert D. Sloane, *Puzzles of Proportion and the "Reasonable Military Commander": Reflections on the Law, Ethics, and Geopolitics of Proportionality*, 6 Harv. Nat'l Sec. J. 299, 303 (2015). For a discussion of the challenges of prosecuting perpetrators of disproportionate attacks, see Rogier Bartels, *Dealing with the Principle of Proportionality in Armed Conflict in Retrospect: The Application of the Principle in International Criminal Trials*, 46 Isr. L. Rev. 271 (2013). In recent years the situation has changed. Works quoted throughout this book have assisted in clarifying the concept.

2. Yoram Dinstein, The Conduct of Hostilities under the Law of International Armed Conflict 130–32 (2nd ed., 2010); The State of Israel, Ministry of Foreign Affairs, The 2014 Gaza Conflict: 7 July–26 August 2014: Factual and Legal Aspects, para. 330 (May 2015) [MoFA 2015 Report].

3. Dinstein, *Id.*, at 132. For this reason, Michael Newton and Larry May call upon military commanders to attempt to find a common denominator when examining the proportionality of an attack, as a rule of thumb. This would require, at times, understanding the broader goals that a specific attack aims to achieve, which could possibly facilitate a better balance between the

*Proportionality in International Humanitarian Law.* Amichai Cohen & David Zlotogorski, Oxford University Press.
 DOI: 10.1093/oso/9780197556726.003.0004

standards, the concept of proportionality . . . would be constitutionally void for vagueness."[4]

As noted in earlier chapters, the principle of proportionality is referenced in AP-I articles 51(5)(b) and 57(2)(a)(iii). The language of these articles leaves much room for discussion regarding the application of the balance between direct military advantage and incidental damage to civilians. Specifically, several obvious questions arise:

> What counts as a concrete and direct military advantage? What is an attack, and how is military advantage assessed? What forms of incidental harm are to be included in the analysis? How are the military advantage and the incidental civilian harm weighed against one another? And from whose perspective is proportionality to be examined?

These questions will now be examined in order, beginning in this chapter with what counts as a military advantage and a military attack, followed by a discussion of incidental civilian harm in Chapter 5.

## A. WHAT CONSTITUTES A MILITARY ADVANTAGE?

There are diverse views regarding the question of what constitutes a military advantage. The ICRC's *Commentary on AP-I* gives a narrow interpretation of the term, stating that "military advantage can only consist in *ground gained* and in *annihilating or weakening the enemy armed forces*."[5]

States take the view that a wider range of operational considerations and developments can provide a military advantage to the attacker. These include those cited by the ICRC—gaining ground and weakening the enemy's military forces—but also encompass many others, such as disrupting enemy activities,[6] diverting an enemy force's resources and attention,[7] denying the enemy the ability

military advantage and collateral damage. One example of this could be a comparison between how many lives are expected to be lost and how many are likely to be saved as a result of an operation. Michael Newton & Larry May, Proportionality in International Law 285 (2014). This may be possible at times; however, there may be instances in which taking a look at the bigger picture and goal of an operation will draw the commander into examining strategic considerations as part of the military advantage. It also risks conflating *jus in bello* proportionality with *jus ad bellum* proportionality. For more on this issue, see Chapter 7.

4. W. Hays Parks, *Air War and the Law of War*, 32 Air Force L. Rev. 1, 273 (1990).

5. Commentary on the Additional Protocols of 8 June 1977 to the Geneva Conventions of 12 August 1949, para. 2218 (ICRC, Yves Sandoz, Christophe Swinarki & Bruno Zimmerman eds., 1987) [AP-I Commentary] (emphasis added).

6. MoFA 2015 Report, *supra* note 2, at 181.

7. US Department of Defense, Law of War Manual, para. 5.12.2. (2015, updated Dec. 2016) [DoD Manual].

to benefit from the military objective's effective contribution to its military action (e.g., by using this object in its military operations),[8] improving the security of the attacking force,[9] as well as lowering the morale of enemy forces.[10] To summarize, according to this broader approach, a military advantage is "any consequence of an attack which directly enhances friendly military operations or hinders those of the enemy."[11] It is clear, however, that damaging the morale of the enemy state and its population, or inflicting political, psychological, social, or economic harm are not included in the definition of military advantage.[12] Moreover, military advantage should be clearly separated from political or economic advantage. Recently, the ICRC published a report of an expert meeting, held in 2016 in Quebec (hereinafter, "the ICRC Proportionality Report"),[13] which notes that

> despite the fact that the use of military force is often a means for a political end, the military advantage has to be articulated separately from the political or economic context of the conflict. The advantage cannot be considered military if it materializes only at the political level.[14]

It is also worth noting, in this regard, that at times it might be very hard for an observer outside the military to assess the military advantage of an attack. As stated by the guidance given by the US Department of Defense,

8. *Id.*, para. 5.12.5. One example of this could be "the blocking of an important line of communication." Program on Humanitarian Policy and Conflict Research (HPCR) at Harvard University, *Commentary on the HPCR Manual on International Law Applicable to Air and Missile Warfare* 45 (2010) [HPCR].

9. DoD Manual, *supra* note 7, para. 5.6.7.3; MoFA 2015 Report, *supra* note 2, at 181; Australia, *Statement on Ratification of AP-I*, Jun. 21, 1991, 1642 U.N.T.S. 473, *available at:* ihl-databases.icrc.org/applic/ihl/ihl.nsf/Notification.xsp?action=openDocument&documentId=10312B4E9047086EC1256402003FB253 [Australia, *Statement on Ratification of AP-I*]; New Zealand, *Statement on Ratification of AP-I*, Feb. 8, 1988, 1499 U.N.T.S. 358, *available at:* ihl-databases.icrc.org/applic/ihl/ihl.nsf/Notification.xsp?action=openDocument&documentId=8FEC3861203ABE21C1256402003FB53B [New Zealand, *Statement on Ratification of AP-I*]; This was also the position of the international Group of Experts who authored the HPCR Manual on International Law Applicable to Air and Missile Warfare. HPCR, *Id.*, at 92. The contentious issue of the inclusion of the interest in protecting one's own troops in proportionality analysis is examined at length in Chapter 6.

10. DoD Manual, *supra* note 7, para. 5.6.7.3 (It should be noted that lowering the morale of *enemy forces* provide a military advantage, whereas lowering the morale of civilians does not).

11. HPCR, *supra* note 8, at 45.

12. Michael N. Schmitt, *Targeting and International Humanitarian Law in Afghanistan, in* The War in Afghanistan: A Legal Analysis, 85 Int'l Law Stud. 307, 323 (2009).

13. *The Principle of Proportionality in the Rules Governing the Conduct of Hostilities Under International Humanitarian Law*, International Expert Meeting June 22–23, 2016, Quebec (Univesité Laval and ICRC, September 2018) [ICRC Proportionality Report].

14. ICRC Proportionality Report, *Id.*, at 16.

> the military advantage expected to be gained from an attack might not be readily apparent to the enemy or to outside observers because, for example, the expected military advantage might depend on the commander's strategy or assessments of classified information.[15]

Attaining a military advantage is not necessarily dependent upon the destruction of military objectives, and the definition of the term "military advantage" as regards proportionality is not necessarily the same as the way in which this term is used in connection with military objectives, which are the legitimate targets for attacks.[16] For example, decoding enemy communications offers a significant military advantage, but does not necessarily involve the "destruction, capture, or neutralization" of a military objective.[17] There are questions as to whether broader strategic or cultural considerations can also be seen as part of the military advantage of an attack. These questions are explored in Chapter 7.

Proportionality does not merely compare *any* military advantage with the incidental harm caused. Rather, proportionality requires that the military advantage be "concrete and direct." There are different opinions as to what these terms actually mean. The ICRC, for one, expressed the view that "the words 'concrete and direct' impose stricter conditions on the attacker than those implied by the criteria defining military objectives in Article 52."[18]

Other than this, the ICRC *Commentary* offers little guidance on the matter: "The expression 'concrete and direct' was intended to show that the advantage concerned should be substantial and relatively close, and that advantages which are hardly perceptible and those which would only appear in the long term should be disregarded."[19] Judith Gardam interprets the ICRC's position as

15. DoD Manual, *supra* note 7, para. 5.6.7.3.

16. Military objectives are defined in Protocol Additional to the Geneva Conventions of August 12, 1949, and Relating to the Protection of Victims of International Armed Conflicts (Protocol I), June 8, 1977, arts. 52(2), 1125 U.N.T.S. 3 [AP-I]): ". . . military objectives are limited to those objects which by their nature, location, purpose or use make an effective contribution to military action and whose total or partial destruction, capture or neutralization, in the circumstances ruling at the time, offers a definite military advantage." Further discussion regarding the effects of the definition of military objectives and its effect on proportionality can be found in Chapter 10. But also see a different opinion of an unnamed expert in the ICRC Proportionality Report *supra* note 13, at 16. While this approach makes sense from the point of view of harmonization of IHL, we do not see why it is necessary to limit the attainment of military advantage. Of course, any specific attack on an object can only be justified if the object is a legitimate target.

17. Sloane, *Puzzles of Proportion*, *supra* note 1, at 321.

18. AP-I Commentary, *supra* note 5, para. 2218. Article 52(2) of AP-I defines a military objective as one "whose total or partial destruction . . . offers a definite *military advantage*."

19. AP-I Commentary, *Id.*, para. 2209.

follows: "'Concrete' means specific as opposed to general, and 'direct' relates to causation, in that the advantage must not be too remote from the attack itself."[20]

What can be gleaned from the *Commentary* is that the military advantage must meet two cumulative criteria: first, the advantage must not appear only in the long term, but rather be relatively close in time to the attack; and second, it should be substantial rather than barely perceptible. In other words, it should not be just one small element in a long chain of causation.

The ICRC's position regarding the time element has been criticized by some. Dinstein, for instance, points out that military advantage does not necessarily have to occur in close temporal proximity, as suggested by the ICRC.[21] The Elements of Crimes of the Rome Statute, for example, accepts that any military advantage that was *foreseeable* by the attacker "at the relevant time" is considered concrete, even if it was not "temporally or geographically related to the object of the attack."[22] Several experts quoted in the ICRC Proportionality Report also support the view that long-term military advantage can be considered an advantage. The example given is that of an attack on military assets, such as weapons, that will incrementally degrade the military strength of the enemy.[23]

Judith Gardam supports a middle ground regarding the temporal scope of the anticipated military advantage, stating that

> the Protocol rule, therefore, is designed to ensure that the assessment of the military advantage is in the relatively short term rather than to allow for the inclusion of the long-term cumulative impact of the attacks. However, this is not to suggest that the military advantage must be assessed on a narrow case-by-case basis in relation to each distinct target. . . . The military advantage for the purposes of the proportionality rule is to be determined on the basis of "the advantage anticipated from the attack as a whole and not only from isolated or particular parts of the attack," and this appears a workable interpretation of the rule.[24]

Regarding the second element of the military advantage—that it be substantial rather than hardly perceptible, there are those who give states more leeway. They understand "concrete and direct" to mean that the military advantage cannot

20. Judith Gardam, Necessity, Proportionality and the Use of Force by States 101 (2004) [Gardam, Necessity, Proportionality and the Use of Force by States].

21. Dinstein, *supra* note 2, at 133–34. Henderson holds this view as well; see Ian Henderson, The Contemporary Law of Targeting: Military Objectives, Proportionality and Precautions in Attack under Additional Protocol I 200 (2009).

22. International Criminal Court, Elements of Crime, 19 n.36 (2011).

23. ICRC Proportionality Report, *supra* note 13, at 19.

24. Gardam, Necessity, Proportionality and the Use of Force by States, *supra* note 20, at 102.

be "merely hypothetical or speculative," though it need not be immediate.[25] The United Kingdom requires that the military advantage be "identifiable and quantifiable and one that flows directly from the attack, not some pious hope that it might improve the military situation in the long term."[26] Similarly, the Tallinn Manual 2.0, which applies the principle of proportionality to military cyber operations, maintains that the military advantage must be real and quantifiable, and not solely of speculative value.[27] By the same token, it has been stated that the military advantage must be "clearly identifiable and, in many cases, quantifiable,"[28] or "readily apparent and tangible."[29] Australia and New Zealand have made identical declarations, according to which the term "concrete and direct" military advantage "means a bona fide expectation that the attack will make a relevant and proportionate contribution to the objective of the military attack involved."[30]

One primary problem with the term "military advantage" is that it is not easy to assess, and does not necessarily have clear instrumental value. Destroying an enemy tank, plane, radar installation, or logistical base clearly gives a military advantage under the current rule of proportionality. However, it might not be apparent to observers that such an attack *caused* a *tangible* contribution to the overall military operation.

An example of this is the famous "highway of death" incident during the 1991 Gulf War. This occurred on the night of February 26–27, 1991, and involved coalition airplanes attacking and destroying an Iraqi convoy on Highway 80, which leads from Kuwait City to the city of Basra in Iraq. Coalition officials contended that the Iraqis were merely conducting a tactical retreat, while others argued that the soldiers were trying to flee the combat.[31] If the latter were true, then it would beg the question of whether killing fleeing soldiers (who are not set to regroup and attack), or killing soldiers far removed from the fighting, provides any real "concrete and direct" military advantage. Would the military advantage from their deaths justify the incidental killing of one civilian?[32] While some hold that

25. DoD Manual, *supra* note 7, paras. 5.6.7.3, 5.12.2.

26. United Kingdom Ministry of Defence, Joint Service Publication 383, The Joint Service Manual of the Law of Armed Conflict, para. 5.33.3 (2004) [UK 2004 LOAC Manual].

27. Tallinn Manual 2.0 on the International Law Applicable to Cyber Operations, 473 (Michael N. Schmitt ed., 2017).

28. HPCR, *supra* note 8, at 92.

29. Henderson, *supra* note 21, at 200.

30. Australia, *Statement on Ratification of AP-I*, *supra* note 9; New Zealand, *Statement on Ratification of AP-I*, *supra* note 9.

31. Gabriella Blum, *The Dispensable Lives of Soldiers*, 2 J. Legal Analysis 115, 158 (2010).

32. There are times when it clearly could provide a significant military advantage, such as when those troops could regroup, or their deaths would require the adverse party to divert vital resources from combat.

destroying enemy weaponry, for example, is inherently valuable,[33] the military advantage that can be gained from attacks might be context-specific and dependent on the circumstances.[34]

## B. MILITARY ADVANTAGE OF AN ATTACK

AP-I requires that proportionality be examined prior to an attack, with article 57(2)(a)(iii) referring to "any attack." This leads to the following questions: What constitutes an "attack" for the sake of proportionality? And when should proportionality be examined?

The term "attack" is defined in article 49(1) of AP-I as an "[act] of violence against the adversary, whether in offence or in defense."[35] The ICRC's commentary on article 49(1) clarifies that "attack" means simply "combat action."[36] But should proportionality be assessed before every single shot fired, or every missile launched?

Arguably, article 52(2) requires that "attacks shall be limited strictly to military objectives." Clearly, this refers to every single attack, down to a single missile, artillery shell, or bullet. It can be argued that the term "attack" should be interpreted in the same manner when assessing proportionality under article 57(2)(a)(iii). Indeed, some commentators hold the position that proportionality should be assessed for each individual strike.[37]

However, the use of the term "military advantage" in article 52(2) may lead to a different conclusion. Article 52(2) defines a military objective as one "whose total or partial destruction . . . offers a definite *military advantage*."[38] In article 52(2), the military advantage must result from the specific individual "attack," otherwise

33. See, for example, the position cited in Michael N. Schmitt & John J. Merriam, *The Tyranny of Context: Israeli Targeting Practices in Legal Perspective*, 37 U. Pa. J. Int'l L. 53, 127 (2015).

34. "Disparity also aggravates the application of the proportionality principle by distorting its various valuation paradigms. . . . Because of the disadvantages, the calculation of military advantage likely to result from an operation will be greater, for the issue is not the objective value of a target, but rather the target's subjective value to the attacker. To an attacker facing impending defeat, the destruction of any of the enemy's capability is invaluable; to one certain of victory, there may be very little value added in the destruction of further targets, at least relative to the likelihood of civilian loss." Michael N. Schmitt, *The Principle of Discrimination in 21 Century Warfare*, 2 Yale Hum. Rts. & Dev. L.J. 143, 157 (1999).

35. AP-I, *supra* note 16, art. 49(1).

36. AP-I Commentary, *supra* note 5, at para. 1880.

37. Philip Alston, *Report of the Special Rapporteur on Extrajudicial, Summary or Arbitrary Executions*, UN Human Rights Council, U.N. Doc. A/HRC/14/24/Add.6 (2010), para. 89.

38. AP-I, *supra* note 16, art. 52(2) (emphasis added). The full article reads: "2. Attacks shall be limited strictly to military objectives. In so far as objects are concerned, military objectives are limited to those objects which by their nature, location, purpose or use make an effective contribution to military action and whose total or partial destruction, capture or neutralization, in the circumstances ruling at the time, offers a definite military advantage." For the impact of the definition of military objectives on proportionality, see Chapter 10.

there would be no value to the principle of distinction. However, the state practice and *opinio juris* on the question of the military advantage in the application of *proportionality* seems to be different.

The more broadly accepted interpretation is that assessments of proportionality, or of the military advantage anticipated, should not be made on the basis of isolated or specific parts of more comprehensive attacks—the dropping of a particular bomb, or an attack on a particular building—but rather in view of the *attack as a whole*. This stems from an interpretation of the terms of articles 51 and 57 concerning proportionality. These articles require attackers to gather and analyze information prior to an attack and make an assessment regarding the proportionality of each and every attack.[39]

Regarding the practice of states, many countries have made declarations upon ratification of AP-I that the military advantage means "the advantage anticipated from the military attack *considered as a whole* and not only from isolated or particular parts of that attack."[40] These states include Canada,[41] Côte d'Ivoire,[42] France,[43] Germany,[44] Italy,[45] New Zealand,[46] Nigeria,[47]

39. W.J. Fenrick, *The Rule of Proportionality and Protocol I in Conventional Warfare*, 98 Mil. L. Rev. 91, 102 (1982).

40. Australia, *Statement on Ratification of AP-I*, *supra* note 9 (emphasis added); Andreas Zimmerman, *The Second Lebanon War: Jus ad Bellum, Jus in Bello and the Issue of Proportionality*, 11 Max Planck UNYB 99, 131 (2007).

41. Canada, *Statement on Ratification of AP-I*, Nov. 20, 1990, 1591 U.N.T.S. 462, *available at:* ihl-databases.icrc.org/applic/ihl/ihl.nsf/Notification.xsp?action=openDocument&documentId =172FFEC04ADC80F2C1256402003FB314 [Canada, *Statement on Ratification of AP-I*] ("the advantage anticipated from the attack considered as a whole and not from isolated or particular parts of the attack").

42. Int'l Comm. of the Red Cross, *Customary IHL, "Practice Relating to Rule 14. Proportionality in Attack"*, *available at:* ihl-databases.icrc.org/customary-ihl/eng/docs/v2_cha_chapter4_rule14 [ICRC, *Practice Relating to Rule 14*].

43. France, *Statement on Ratification of AP-I*, Apr. 11, 2001, *available at:* ihl-databases.icrc.org/applic/ihl/ihl.nsf/Notification.xsp?action=openDocument&documentId=D8041036B40EBC44C1256A34004897B2.

44. Germany, *Statement on Ratification of AP-I*, Feb. 14, 1991, 1607 U.N.T.S. 526, *available at:* ihl-databases.icrc.org/applic/ihl/ihl.nsf/Notification.xsp?action=openDocument&documentId =3F4D8706B6B7EA40C1256402003FB3C7.

45. Italy, *Statement on Ratification of AP-I*, Feb. 27, 1986, 1425 U.N.T.S. 438, *available at:* ihl-databases.icrc.org/applic/ihl/ihl.nsf/Notification.xsp?action=openDocument&documentId=E2F248CE54CF09B5C1256402003FB443.

46. New Zealand, *Statement on Ratification of AP-I*, *supra* note 9.

47. ICRC, *Practice Relating to Rule 14*, *supra* note 42.

Spain,[48] and the United Kingdom.[49] The government of Belgium declared that military advantage would be "from an attack considered in its totality."[50] This is also the position of the United States[51] and Israel,[52] which are not parties to the protocol but do apply many of its provisions, because they view them as part of customary international law.

This broad interpretation is also supported by the definition of the crime of disproportionate attacks under the Rome Statute (article 8(2)(b)(iv)), which mentions the "*overall* military advantage anticipated."[53] The formulation of proportionality as contained in the Rome Statute is considered by some to be the closest reflection of the customary rule of proportionality in IHL, notwithstanding the stricter requirements of the Rome Statute due to its criminal nature.[54] In addition, the ICRC apparently accepts this broader interpretation, noting however, that the consideration of an attack as a whole should not be construed as

48. Spain, *Statement on Ratification of AP-I,* Apr. 21, 1989, 1537 U.N.T.S. 390, *available at:* ihl-databases.icrc.org/applic/ihl/ihl.nsf/Notification.xsp?action=openDocument&documentId=FC622F31C9E2236EC1256402003FB660.

49. United Kingdom of Great Britain and Northern Ireland, *Reservation*, July 2, 2002, *available at:* ihl-databases.icrc.org/applic/ihl/ihl.nsf/Notification.xsp?action=openDocument&documentId=0A9E03F0F2EE757CC1256402003FB6D2; UK 2004 LOAC MANUAL, *supra* note 26, para. 5.33.5.

50. Belgium, *Statement on Ratification of AP-I,* May 20, 1986, 1435 U.N.T.S. 367, *available at:* ihl-databases.icrc.org/applic/ihl/ihl.nsf/Notification.xsp?action=openDocument&documentId=EA2560B9B790488EC1256402003FB2BC.

51. DoD Manual, *supra* note 7, paras. 5.6.7.3, 5.12.2.1.

52. MoFA 2015 Report, *supra* note 2, para. 318; THE STATE OF ISRAEL, MINISTRY OF FOREIGN AFFAIRS, THE OPERATION IN GAZA 27 DECEMBER 2008—18 JANUARY 2009: FACTUAL AND LEGAL ASPECTS, para. 123, 126 (July 2009) ("considering the military advantage of the attack as a whole. . . . the 'military advantage anticipated' from a particular targeting decision must be considered from the standpoint of the overall objective of the mission.").

53. Rome Statute of the International Criminal Court, Jul. 17, 1998, art. 8.2(b)(iv), 2187 U.N.T.S. 90 (1998) (emphasis added). It is worthwhile noting, however, that the definition of proportionality in the Rome Statute concerns individual criminal responsibility, as opposed to proportionality in AP-I, which concerns the obligations of states. The threshold of individual criminal responsibility could very well require a more stringent threshold than IHL proportionality. It is therefore not clear that one can interpret proportionality in IHL in light of the definition of proportionality in International Criminal Law as adopted by the state parties to the Rome Statute. As noted by Gardam, "this addition is intended to indicate to the Court that only obvious cases of disproportionate attacks should be punished." GARDAM, NECESSITY, PROPORTIONALITY AND THE USE OF FORCE BY STATES, *supra* note 20.

54. A. P. V. Rogers, *The Principle of Proportionality, in* THE LEGITIMATE USE OF MILITARY FORCE: THE JUST WAR TRADITION AND THE CUSTOMARY LAW OF ARMED CONFLICT 189, 208 (Howard M. Hensel ed., 2007); Sloane, *Puzzles of Proportion*, *supra* note 1, at 311.

permitting disproportionate harm or neglecting other obligations such as the principle of distinction.[55]

The rationale for this broader interpretation is that single attacks are often only part of a broader operation that offers a greater military advantage. For example, attacking a single radio tower might not significantly diminish the command, control, and communications network of the enemy; however, disabling many towers would cumulatively produce a considerable military advantage, much greater than the sum of each individual attack's military advantage, when viewed separately.

Additionally, states sometimes engage in ruses of war.[56] They attack certain military objectives not so much to disable them specifically, but rather in order to trick or confuse the enemy about the true location and nature of the main thrust of the attack. One famous example of such a ruse was Operation Fortitude during World War II, an operation intended to deceive Nazi Germany into believing that the Allied invasion of Europe (Operation Overlord) would be launched at any location other than the beaches of Normandy, France. This encompassed Operation Fortitude North aimed at Norway,[57] and Operation Fortitude South aimed at Pas de Calais, France. Part of this latter operation included bombing raids against targets in Pas de Calais whose purpose was to shift General Rommel's attention from the true landing sites.[58] A bombing raid against a military objective offering limited intrinsic military advantage might justify a greater (and otherwise excessive) amount of collateral damage if its true purpose is to serve as a ruse for another, much larger operation.

One case in which the assessment of the proportionality of a specific strike reviewed the anticipated military advantage from the attack as a whole was the air attack on the RTS studio, discussed in the Final Report (NATO Bombing Report)

55. AP-I Commentary, *supra* note 5, para. 2218 ("It goes without saying that an attack carried out in a concerted manner in numerous places can only be judged in its entirety. However, this does not mean that during such an attack, actions may be undertaken which would lead to severe losses among the civilian population or to extensive destruction of civilian objects").

56. AP-I, *supra* note 16, art. 37(2) permits the use of ruses of war: "Ruses of war are not prohibited. Such ruses are acts which are intended to mislead an adversary or to induce him to act recklessly but which infringe no rule of international law applicable in armed conflict and which are not perfidious because they do not invite the confidence of an adversary with respect to protection under that law. The following are examples of such ruses: the use of camouflage, decoys, mock operations and misinformation."

57. The operation paid off, as on D-Day there were 13 *Wehrmacht* divisions in Norway, along with 90,000 naval and 60,000 *Luftwaffe* personnel. General Rommel had convinced Hitler in late May to move 5 infantry divisions to France, but actions taken during the continuing Operation Fortitude North led Hitler to cancel the order. With 50 German infantry divisions already in France, there is no telling how a 10% increase in German infantry units might have affected the success of Operation Overlord. Stephen E. Ambrose, D-Day June 6, 1944: The Climactic Battle of World War II, 50, 80–82 (1994).

58. *Id.*, 80–86; Parks, *Air Warfare and the Law of War*, *supra* note 4, at 176.

of the Committee Established to Review the NATO Bombing Campaign ("the Committee").[59] In 1999, NATO bombed the main studios of the state-owned broadcasting corporation (RTS) in Belgrade, in what was then Yugoslavia, killing between 10 and 17 people. NATO claimed that the RTS studio was a military objective because it was a part of the Yugoslav C3 (command, control, and communications) system and thus a part of the war effort.[60]

In its proportionality analysis, when assessing the military advantage anticipated from the attack, the Committee found that NATO had known in advance that attacking the studio would interrupt broadcasts only for a brief period (which was indeed the end result of the attack), and that the RTS studio was just one part of the Yugoslav command and control network. It was clear that this network could not be dismantled or halted by a single attack. The Committee thus determined that proportionality should not be assessed by focusing exclusively on one specific instance, such as the RTS studio attack, but rather, it should be assessed on a broader level—the overall attack against the Yugoslav command and control network. In this regard, the RTS attack should be seen as part of an operation aimed at targets that were essential to Yugoslavia's ability to direct and control troops, as well as at key elements of the Yugoslav air defense.[61] Based on this analysis, the Committee found that the attack did "not appear to be clearly disproportionate."[62]

The Committee's assessment appears to be ambiguous from a methodological standpoint. The Committee assessed the military advantage of the attack as part of the military advantage anticipated from the broader operation. However, with regard to the harm to civilians and civilian objects, the Committee was not so clear as to which civilian casualties should be taken into consideration. In its final report, it merely stated that the deaths of the 10–17 civilians killed in the specific RTS attack did not appear to be disproportionate. This accounting is not in line with the analysis of the law of proportionality made by the Committee itself, according to which there was a need to conduct "an overall assessment of the totality of civilian victims as against the goals of the military campaign."[63]

There are several possible ways of interpreting this statement, but the most obvious is that the Committee held that if the military advantage being considered is that of a broader operation, then the incidental civilian damage considered should also be that of the entire operation. Say, for example, that taking out the entire Yugoslav command and control infrastructure would require 10 attacks on 10

59. ICTY, *Final Report to the Prosecutor by the Committee Established to Review the NATO Bombing Campaign Against the Federal Republic of Yugoslavia*, (2000), *available at:* http://www.icty.org/en/press/final-report-prosecutor-committee-established-review-nato-bombing-campaign-against-federal.

60. *Id.*, para. 55.

61. *Id.*, para. 78.

62. *Id.*, para. 77.

63. *Id.*, para. 52.

different locations, and that in each attack 15 civilians would be killed. The question that should then be asked is whether the deaths of 150 civilians is excessive with regard to the anticipated concrete military advantage of the destruction of the command and control infrastructure.

At any rate, current IHL does not require an assessment of civilian casualties of the *entire campaign* with *jus in bello.* Arguably, there is a need for such an assessment within *jus ad bellum,* and perhaps this is what the Committee was referring to. In a later statement regarding criminal responsibility, the Committee stressed that:

> It is the Committee's view that where individual (and legitimate) attacks on military objectives are concerned, the mere cumulation of such instances, all of which are deemed to have been lawful, cannot ipso facto be said to amount to a crime.[64]

Indeed, we do not believe that the current state of IHL requires an assessment of the accumulation of the victims of the entire campaign. As will be discussed later, however, we do suggest that in some cases, this should be taken into account, in connection with the repeated use of problematic practices.[65]

Notwithstanding this comment, we agree with the approach of the Committee regarding the fact that the attack should be viewed as a whole. The question of proportionality in armed conflict should be assessed at the operational level, and not every single shot needs to be justified. Similarly, it seems to us that an attack directed at several military objects at once cannot be judged as several different attacks if there is a sufficient link of context, time, and place between these targets.[66]

64. *Id.*

65. See our discussion in Chapter 5, notes 95–96 and the accompanying text.

66. We are aware of the ambiguity on this subject in AP-I COMMENTARY, *supra* note 5, at 685, para. 2218 (commentary on article 57(a)(iii)), which states:

> it goes without saying that an attack carried out in a concerted manner in numerous places can only be judged in its entirety. However, this does not mean that during such an attack actions may be undertaken which would lead to severe losses among the civilian population or to extensive destruction of civilian objects. Nor does it mean that several clearly distinct military objectives within an urban area may be considered as a single objective.

The second sentence of this paragraph is clearly correct. Every target of the operation must by identified separately as a military objective. If the first sentence quoted earlier suggests that collateral civilian damage must be evaluated under the principle of proportionality separately for every target, and not as a whole, we think this statement does not represent the law as it stands today. Nor do we believe this to be the correct norm. If a specific operation achieves its military goal, which is direct and concrete, by attacking several different targets, it seems to us that

Let us explain what we mean by this.

It is lawful to target a rocket launching site or stockpile even if the attack could result in civilian casualties, provided the attack is proportionate. However, if the adverse party has such a large stockpile of rockets that no matter how many rockets were destroyed, other rockets would be available, then from a strategic point of view, attacking each and every single rocket is close to pointless. In such a case, it can be argued that each individual rocket has little military significance. Attacking one rocket, out of many, would give the attacker—at best—a small, possibly even negligible, military advantage. Naturally, if the attack is a "one-off" operation, in which the entire operation consists of attacking this one rocket, then the answer seems to be that the military advantage gained by this one operation is miniscule compared to human lives.

However, this is probably atypical. Attacking any particular missile is usually part of an ongoing operation, in which many missile launchers are attacked. Thus, attacking the single missile cannot be judged out of context. This question is similar to that of targeted killings of the leaders of terrorist organizations, where there is almost always someone who is willing and able to fill the position that is "vacated." If strategic considerations of this type were included in the proportionality analysis, then perhaps conducting attacks against one target that is only a small cog in a larger system would not be permissible if incidental civilian harm was expected. It seems to us that taking into account such strategic consequences strays from the currently predominant interpretation of IHL.[67]

This discussion should not be conflated with another one, regarding the overall effect of the actions of a specific unit. There are cases in which the decision regarding proportionality cannot be taken by an individual commander in the field, because his activities are part of a larger operation. In these cases, as we said earlier, the decision regarding the targeting of specific military targets is made by the overall commander of the operation, and not by the commander in the field. In such circumstances, the commander in the field may be required to provide information regarding the presence of civilians, as part of the requirement for precautions, in order to allow the commander of the operation to conduct a fully informed proportionality analysis.[68]

In other cases, however, the field commander may face a situation that was not foreseen in the planning stage, such as shots suddenly being fired at his unit from a house that is occupied both by enemy forces and civilians. In this case, even

there is no reason not to evaluate the collateral damage *as a whole* against this concrete military advantage.

67. E.g., ICRC Proportionality Report *supra* note 13, para. 77. For a discussion of strategic considerations, see the discussion in Chapter 7.

68. AP-I *supra* note 16, art. 57; and see AP-I Commentary, *supra* note 5, at 680, para. 2197 (discussing the relative responsibility of high command and commanders on the ground for taking precautions in attack under article 57).

though the unit is part of a larger operation, the unit commander himself is responsible for the evaluation of the proportionality of attacking the specific target, based on the information at his disposal.

The position that an attack should be considered as a whole seems to us to be sensible from an additional perspective, as well. To further the goals of the principle of proportionality, commanders should be encouraged to look at the big picture in order to assess alternative attacks that might cause less harm to civilians. Directing the attention of commanders only to smaller, specific targets undermines this important purpose of IHL.

# 5

# Incidental Harm and the Analysis of Proportionality

## A. CIVILIANS OR ALL PERSONS PROTECTED FROM ATTACK

The principle of proportionality requires weighing the expected harm to military objectives against the anticipated harm to civilians and civilian objects. IHL defines a civilian as:

> [a]ny person who does not belong to one of the categories of persons referred to in Article 4 A 1), 2), 3) and 6) of the Third Convention and in Article 43 of this Protocol. In case of doubt whether a person is a civilian, that person shall be considered to be a civilian.[1]

1. Protocol Additional to the Geneva Conventions of August 12, 1949, and Relating to the Protection of Victims of International Armed Conflicts (Protocol I), June 8, 1977, art. 50(1), 1125 U.N.T.S. 3 [AP-I]. This article excludes from the category of civilians all those who are referred to in the following articles:

Convention Relative to the Treatment of Prisoners of war, Aug. 12, 1949, art. 4(A), 75 U.N.T.S. 135 [GC-III]:

"(1) Members of the armed forces of a Party to the conflict as well as members of militias or volunteer corps forming part of such armed forces.
(2) Members of other militias and members of other volunteer corps, including those of organized resistance movements, belonging to a Party to the conflict and operating in or outside their own territory, even if this territory is occupied, provided that such militias or volunteer corps, including such organized resistance movements, fulfil the following conditions: (a) that of being commanded by a person responsible for his subordinates; (b) that of having a fixed distinctive sign recognizable at a distance; (c) that of carrying arms openly; (d) that of conducting their operations in accordance with the laws and customs of war.
(3) Members of regular armed forces who profess allegiance to a government or an authority not recognized by the Detaining Power.
(6) Inhabitants of a non-occupied territory, who on the approach of the enemy spontaneously take up arms to resist the invading forces, without having had time to form

*Proportionality in International Humanitarian Law.* Amichai Cohen & David Zlotogorski, Oxford University Press.
 DOI: 10.1093/oso/9780197556726.003.0005

This is a negative definition, meaning "that the civilian population is made up of persons who are not members of the armed forces."[2] Therefore, according to the language of AP-I, military personnel are not included in the assessment of collateral damage from an attack. However, in recent years some have claimed that members of the armed forces should be included.

The ICTY Trial Chamber in *Blagojević and Jokić* advanced this position, and offered a broader definition of the term civilian, stating that it also refers to *combatants* who have been removed from combat because they surrendered, are sick or wounded.[3] This position has also been promoted by the ICRC, which submits that proportionality must be applied to excessive harm to military medical personnel and objects, and to sick and wounded members of the military, and to the shipwrecked. According to the ICRC, this rule stems from the obligation to respect and protect wounded and sick members of the military under all circumstances, as stipulated in article 12 of the First Geneva Convention.[4] The ICRC argues that if a party to an armed conflict is barred from attacking wounded and injured members of the military, and must respect and protect them, then it must also not attack objectives if the incidental harm to the wounded or injured members of the military is likely to be excessive.[5] The ICRC has also opined that this applies to members of the armed forces who are at sea and who are wounded,

themselves into regular armed units, provided they carry arms openly and respect the laws and customs of war."

AP-I, *Id.*, art. 43: "1. The armed forces of a Party to a conflict consist of all organized armed forces, groups and units which are under a command responsible to that Party for the conduct of its subordinates, even if that Party is represented by a government or an authority not recognized by an adverse Party. Such armed forces shall be subject to an internal disciplinary system which, "inter alia," shall enforce compliance with the rules of international law applicable in armed conflict.

2. Members of the armed forces of a party to a conflict (other than medical personnel and chaplains covered by Article 33 of the Third Convention) are combatants, that is to say, they have the right to participate directly in hostilities.
3. Whenever a Party to a conflict incorporates a paramilitary or armed law enforcement agency into its armed forces it shall so notify the other Parties to the conflict."

2. Commentary on the Additional Protocols of 8 June 1977 to the Geneva Conventions of 12 August 1949, para. 1913 (ICRC, Yves Sandoz, Christophe Swinarki, & Bruno Zimmerman eds., 1987) [AP-I Commentary].

3. Prosecutor v. Blagojević, ICTY Trial Chamber, IT-02-60-T, *Judgment*, para.544 (Jan. 17, 2005) ("The term 'civilian' refers to persons not taking part in hostilities, including members of armed forces who have laid down their arms and those placed hors de combat by sickness, wounds detention or any other cause.").

4. Convention for the Amelioration of the Condition of the Wounded and Sick in Armed Forces in the Field, Aug. 12, 1949, art. 12, 75 U.N.T.S. 31.

5. Int'l Comm. of the Red Cross, Commentary on the First Geneva Convention (I) for the Amelioration of the Condition of the Wounded and Sick in the Field, para. 1357 (2nd ed., 2016); Int'l Comm. of the Red Cross, *32nd International Conference of the Red Cross*

sick or shipwrecked members of the military, under article 12 of the Second Geneva Convention.[6]

It appears that the ICRC did not adopt the same position regarding prisoners of war. In the recently published updated commentary of the ICRC to the Third Geneva Convention, regarding protection of Prisoners of War,[7] no mention is made of a requirement to protect prisoners of war from disproportionate attacks.[8] This might stem from the fact that the Third Convention obligates the Detaining Power, and not the party that is likely to be attacking—i.e., the party whose forces are detained.[9]

Including members of the armed forces who are out of combat in the proportionality analysis seems to run contrary to certain indications of state practice as well as the specific language of the articles on proportionality in AP-I and their use of the term "civilian" as understood in contemporary IHL.[10] For example, one can imagine a situation during an armed conflict in which a state bombs a military fortification in order to make it easier to capture the position. Even if most of

*and Red Crescent: International Humanitarian Law and the Challenges of Contemporary Armed Conflicts* 31–32 (Oct. 2015) [ICRC Challenges Report].

6. Int'l Comm. of the Red Cross, Commentary on the Second Geneva Convention (II) for the Amelioration of the Condition of Wounded, Sick and Shipwrecked Members of Armed Forces at Sea, paras. 1401–03 (2nd ed., 2017), *available at*: https://ihl-databases.icrc.org/ihl/full/GCII-commentary.

7. The first version of the commentary to the Third Geneva Convention is from 1960, included no discussion of the principle of proportionality.

8. Int'l Comm. of the Red Cross, Commentary on the Third Geneva Convention (III) relative to the Treatment of Prisoners of War (2nd ed., 2020), *available at*: https://ihl-databases.icrc.org/ihl/full/GCIII-commentary [GC-III Commentary].

9. The Commentary does mention the obligation of the Detaining Power to protect prisoners of war from attack by distancing them from attacks and avoiding using prisoners of war as human shields (GC-III Commentary, *Id.*, paras. 1880, 2025–32). These obligations in IHL are often seen as the correlating obligation to proportionality. Whereas the attackers are obligated to limit the incidental harm to civilians caused by their attacks, defenders are under an obligation to "avoid locating military objectives within or near densely populated areas" (article 58 of AP-I, *supra* note 1). For more discussion of human shields see Chapter 9.

10. US Department of Defense, Law of War Manual paras.3.5.1, 5.10.1.2, 7.3.3.1 (2015, updated Dec. 2016) [DoD Manual] (stating that *jus ad bellum* proportionality does not consider harm suffered by military forces). See also: John Merriam, *Must Military Medical and Religious Personnel Be Accounted for in a Proportionality Analysis?*, Just Security (July 8, 2016), *available at:* www.justsecurity.org/31905/military-medical-religious-personnel-accounted-proportionality-analysis/; Marty Lederman, *A quick response to John Merriam on proportionality and military medical personnel*, Just Security (July 9, 2016), *available at:* www.justsecurity.org/31909/quick-response-john-merriam-proportionality-military-medical-personnel/; Geoffrey S. Corn, *Transatlantic Workshop on International Law and Armed Conflict: Wounded and Sick, Proportionality, and Armaments*, Lawfare (Oct. 10, 2017), *available at:* www.lawfareblog.com/transatlantic-workshop-international-law-and-armed-conflict-wounded-and-sick-proportionality-and.

the enemy combatants are incapacitated in the first salvo, it might still be necessary to continue shelling the position in order to further "soften" the opposition. If the wounded military combatants are taken into account during assessment of proportionality, it might be unlawful to continue shelling the enemy fortification because the harm to the wounded soldiers might be excessive in relation to the anticipated military advantage from the prolonged bombardment. However, such a conclusion seems to run contrary to all state practice.[11]

It is nevertheless, important to note that in the 2016 edition of the DoD manual, after taking the position that protected persons other than civilians are not protected by the principle of proportionality, the United States stipulated that feasible precautions must be taken to reduce the harm expected to soldiers who are protected from direct attack, such as the wounded, sick, or shipwrecked.[12] As noted by Corn and Culliver, this interpretation is also congruent with the language of article 57 of the First Additional Protocol, which requires the attacking party to "do everything feasible to verify that the objectives to be attacked . . . are not subject to special protection."[13] It seems, therefore, that there is a textual basis for applying the precautions before attacks under article 57 to protected soldiers, even if the principle of proportionality applies only to collateral damage to civilians.[14]

As will be discussed in more detail below, we believe that the precautions noted above are an important part of modern proportionality.[15] Therefore, in practical terms, the positions adopted by the ICRC and the United States are not as far apart as they seem at first glance. Were states to adopt precautions with regard

11. Geoffrey Corn & Andrew Culliver, *Wounded Combatants, Military Medical Personnel, and the Dilemma of Collateral Risk,* 45 Georgia J. of Int'l & Comp. L 445, 456–57 (2017).

12. DoD Manual, *supra* note 10, 5.10.1.2, 7.3.3.1.

13. AP-I, *supra* note 1, article 57(2)(a)(i).

14. Geoffrey Corn & Andrew Culliver, *Wounded Combatants, Military Medical Personnel, and the Dilemma of Collateral Risk*, 45 Georgia J. of Int'l & Comp. L 445, 468–70 (2017). Corn and Culliver had previously suggested that the obligation to take precautions regarding wounded and injured members of the military prior to an attack was based on the *Martens clause* first included in the Hague convention of 1899 which, in its most modern form in AP-I, *supra* note 1, art. 1(2) reads:

> "In cases not covered by this Protocol or by other international agreements, civilians and combatants remain under the protection and authority of the principles of international law derived from established custom, from the principles of humanity and from the dictates of public conscience."
>
> *The Martens Clause* was included in the additional protocol to the Geneva conventions and indeed was used to develop IHL in matters not expressly included in the conventions. See: Theodor Meron, *The Martens Clause, Principles of Humanity, and Dictates of Public Conscience*, 94 AM. J. INT'L L. 78 (2000).

15. Chapter 12.

to attacks on protected categories of soldiers, this would go a long way toward applying proportionality toward them.

Beyond the protected members of the military, *all* civilians—not only the citizens of the adverse party—must be taken into account in the proportionality analysis.[16] This rule is commonly understood to mean that harm to a state's own civilians, as well as civilians of third parties, must be examined in the proportionality analysis.[17] This situation could arise, for example, if a state attempts to reconquer its own territory that had been captured or occupied by the belligerent party. A similar situation could arise when a state conducts hostilities on the territory of an ally, and there is a risk of collateral damage to the allied state's civilians.[18]

One clarification regarding incidental harm to civilians is that not all civilian loss of life is counted in the proportionality analysis, though this may be hard to ascertain. For example, harm to civilians that is caused by defensive measures taken by the attacked party (such as use of anti-aircraft fire that incidentally kills civilians) is not attributed to the attacking party.[19] By the same token, it should be noted that some of the actions taken by a belligerent party are intended to diminish the capacity of the adverse party to hit and engage their targets. These actions could include the use of anti-aircraft

16. As opposed to the definition of "Protected Persons" contained in the Geneva Conventions (Convention Relative to the Protection of Civilian Persons in Time of War, Aug. 12, 1949, art. 4, 6 U.S.T. 3516, 75 U.N.T.S. 287 [GC-IV]) under which a state's own nationals do not deserve protection, the definition of civilians under the Additional Protocols does not explicitly limit itself to the civilians of the opposing party.

17. The ICRC, in the *Commentary on AP-I*, writes: "In protecting civilians against the dangers of war, the important aspect is not so much their nationality as the inoffensive character of the persons to be spared and the situation in which they find themselves." AP-I Commentary, *supra* note 2, para.1909. Contrast the AP-I definition of "civilian," and the customary norm of proportionality in non-international armed conflict, with the definition of "protected person" in the Fourth Geneva Convention. GC-IV, *Id.*, art. 4.

18. Ian Henderson, The Contemporary Law of Targeting: Military Objectives, Proportionality and Precautions in Attack under Additional Protocol I 228 (2009). This was the case in in the Battle of Manila and in France during the allied invasion of 1944, when American and British bombers were attacking German military objectives in French territory. The question of the extent of French civilian casualties was discussed by the Allies at the highest levels during the months prior to the invasion of France on Jun. 6, 1944, including by Prime Minister Winston Churchill and President Franklin D. Roosevelt. See W. J. Fenrick, *The Rule of Proportionality and Protocol I in Conventional Warfare*, 98 Mil. L. Rev. 91, 118–20 (1982). For a description of the Battle of Manila, see Chapter 3, notes 26–27.

19. W. Hays Parks, *Air War and the Law of War*, 32 Air Force L. Rev. 1, 174 (1990). This is also the position of the United States, that harm caused to civilians from projectiles that were launched but did not reach their target and harmed civilians due to enemy deception activities (such as smoke or chaff) are not included in the proportionality analysis of the attacker, though the defending side should consider them when they take feasible precautions in defense. DoD Manual, *supra* note 10, para. 5.12.1.4.

fire,[20] electronic warfare,[21] and other defensive measures, or be simply due to the fog of war.[22] The effects of all these on the civilians of the party that employs them does not factor into the proportionality analysis.

## B. WHAT CONSTITUTES HARM?

It is clear from the language of the AP-I articles themselves that damage includes physical harm to civilians and civilian objects, including "loss of civilian life, injury to civilians, damage to civilian objects."[23]

### Harm to the Person

Under AP-I, loss of civilian life is certainly taken into account when assessing proportionality. It is also clear that serious injuries must be considered as well.

Treaties, commentaries, and manuals usually limit discussions of harm to physical harm,[24] and there is less clarity regarding mental harm and disease caused by an attack. The Tallinn Manual 2.0 seems to accept that it is "reasonable to extend the definition to serious illness and severe mental suffering that are tantamount to injury."[25] Similarly, the ICTY Trial Chamber, in the *Prlić* case, examined the psychological damage as well as the physical harm caused to civilians when it assessed the issue of proportionality.[26] As Emanuela-Chiara Gillard notes, in view

20. Which might precipitate the jettisoning of armaments or otherwise inaccurate fire. Parks, *supra* note 19, at 190–91.

21. Effects of electronic warfare can be indiscernible, as jamming might cause munitions to hit civilian targets without leaving a forensic trace. Parks, *Id.*, at 191–92.

22. Parks surveys a series of strikes which hit unintended targets due to the use of smoke to shield targets, or obscuring of the target due to the effects of previous strikes against the target. Parks, *Id.*, at 193–94.

23. AP-I, *supra* note 1, art. 51(5)(b), 57(2)(a)(iii).

24. Emanuela-Chiara Gillard, Proportionality in the Conduct of Hostilities: The Incidental Harm Side of the Assessment 32 (Chatham House International Law Programme, 2018).

25. Tallinn Manual 2.0 on the International Law Applicable to Cyber Operations 417 (Michael N. Schmitt ed., 2017) [Tallinn Manual 2.0]. The passage discusses the definition of a "cyber-attack." Isable Robinson & Ellen Nohle, *Proportionality and Precautions in Attack: The Reverberating Effects of Using Explosive Weapons in Populated Areas*, 98 Int'l Rev. Red Cross 107, 130 (2016).

26. Prior to ruling that the destruction of the bridge was disproportionate, the Trial Chamber also noted that destroying the bridge had a "very significant psychological impact on the Muslim population of Mostar." Prosecutor v. Prlić, ICTY Trial Chamber III, IT-04-74-T, *Judgment*, Vol. III, paras. 1582–84 (May 9, 2013) [Prlić, Trial Chamber]. The Appeals Chamber has since overturned the Trial Chamber's ruling that the attack on the bridge was disproportionate. Noting that the Trial Chamber had determined that the bridge was a military objective, the Appeals Chamber dismissed the assertion that the destruction of the bridge, in and of itself,

of the increased medical understanding of the mental health problems caused to civilians by armed conflicts, such as post-traumatic stress disorder, there is no reason *in principle* to exclude mental harm from proportionality assessments.[27] However, as noted by experts quoted in the ICRC Proportionality Report, applying this principle may be extremely problematic.[28] First, it is difficult to assess in advance what effect attacks might have on the mental health of civilians. Second, intuitively, it appears that different people have very different mental responses to attacks, whereas it is far easier to assess what physical harm will be suffered because of to attacks.

With rare exceptions, state practice does not seem to support taking mental harm into account.[29] As a practical matter, it seems that doing so could only be part of a proportionality estimation if the attack is preplanned, and if specific mental harm is expected. One example that has been suggested would be an attack on a military target stationed near a kindergarten.[30]

The modern world's reliance on cyber technologies requires some adaptations and clarifications of this rule. Some of the effects of cyberattacks on infrastructure will be discussed in section C below, under the heading of "indirect and reverberating effects." But even prior to the issue of cyber infrastructure, there is a question as to whether humanity's reliance on the internet and cyber technologies should not change the way we think about damage. For people in many modern societies, being connected to the internet is not only essential as a tool, but also forms part of their identity. Certainly, losing a limb is still considered more severe than losing one's internet connection (though some today might argue with this point), however, at least for some people, the loss of their virtual identity might be more sorely felt than, say, losing their house. So, should these effects be considered too?

We believe that while the law currently does not seem to encompass damage to civilians' virtual identities and other damage caused by cyberattacks, this may change in the future. Within a few decades, life without cyber technologies will be inconceivable to large parts of humanity, or at least would be considered a significant handicap. In the more distant future, suggests Harari, the physical attributes

could amount to a violation of the crime of wanton destruction not justified by military necessity. The Appeals Chamber found that as no other property had been destroyed, the elements of the crime has not been satisfied and overturned the Trial Chamber's judgment on this count. Despite this, the Appeals Chamber did not criticize the statements of the Trail Chamber regarding the psychological damage caused to civilians. Prlić, ICTY Appeals Chamber, IT-04-74-A, *Judgment*, Vol. I, para. 411 (Nov. 29, 2017) [Prlić, Appeals Chamber].

27. Gillard, *supra* note 24, at 32.

28. *The Principle of Proportionality in the Rules Governing the Conduct of Hostilities Under International Humanitarian Law*, International Expert Meeting June 22–23, 2016, Quebec 35-6 (Univesité Laval and ICRC, September 2018) [ICRC Proportionality Report].

29. Gillard, *supra* note 24, at 33.

30. ICRC Proportionality Report, *supra* note 28, at 36.

of humanity might change to include cyber components.[31] It is possible that proportionality should be adapted to reflect these changes.

## Economic Damage

Armed conflict inevitably and unfortunately disrupts the lives of civilians. This disruption may include, for example, shortages of food, basic goods and services, and blackouts.[32] Shortages of this nature are generally not counted as "incidental harm" in terms of proportionality. First, these types of damage are very difficult to compute. Furthermore, their attribution to the actions of one of the parties is almost always disputed. It can be hard to track the source of damage solely to the actions of one party or the other, as parties to the conflict often take actions to limit such shortages suffered by their own people. In fact, it can be claimed that no war may be fought without some economic harm to civilians.

This does not mean that economic loss is never to be considered. While the US position is that economic hardship and harm to the economy are not to be examined as part of the proportionality of an attack,[33] the ICRC Proportionality Report recounts an agreement among experts that *direct* economic harm from the attack is part of the proportionality equation, especially if it involves long-term loss or damage to infrastructure.[34] In fact, several articles in AP-I could possibly be interpreted as stating that damaging objects essential to the survival of the civilian population could be considered "excessive" compared to almost any military advantage, though this is understood more often as stemming from the principle of distinction than proportionality.[35]

31. Yuval Noah Harari, Homo Deus: A Brief History of Tomorrow (2017).

32. Yoram Dinstein, The Conduct of Hostilities under the Law of International Armed Conflict 135 (2nd ed., 2010).

33. DoD Manual, *supra* note 10, para. 5.12.1.3 ("the attacker would not be required to consider the economic harm that the death of an enemy combatant would cause to his or her family, or the loss of jobs due to the destruction of a tank factory."). This position is in line with the position we supported *supra.*

34. ICRC Proportionality Report *supra* note 28, at 42. See also ICTY, *Final Report to the Prosecutor by the Committee Established to Review the NATO Bombing Campaign Against the Federal Republic of Yugoslavia*, para. 18 (2000) [NATO Bombing Report] (stating that there is a need to avoid excessive long-term damage to economic infrastructure).

35. E.g. AP-I, *supra* note 1, arts. 54, 56(1): 56(1).

> "Works or installations containing dangerous forces, namely dams, dykes and nuclear electrical generating stations, shall not be made the object of attack, even where these objects are military objectives, if such attack may cause the release of dangerous forces and consequent severe losses among the civilian population."

A more controversial issue is whether "displacement" should be viewed as a form of collateral damage and taken into account in proportionality analysis. It is clear that "forced displacement" intended by one party as a way of applying pressure to the civilian population of the other party is prohibited. But almost any attack taking place within or near a civilian population might cause displacement of civilians from the area of the attack. One view quoted by the ICRC Proportionality Report is that such displacement should be taken into account in proportionality analysis. Others have rejected this view.[36]

One area in which this discussion is relevant concerns warnings given to civilians in war zones to evacuate their houses. An argument has been made that if displacement itself is considered a civilian damage, then the warning that preceded the attack caused the displacement. As will be discussed below, we see warnings as one of the basic duties of an attacking party in modern conflicts. It is therefore in the interest of IHL to motivate attackers to warn civilians in advance. Claiming that issuing warnings causes displacement and is therefore sometimes itself prohibited, would undermine the efforts to incentivize armies to use warnings *more* extensively.

At any rate, we know of no state practice supporting the claim that the civilian evacuation of homes in response to nothing other than issuing warnings to do so constitutes "damage to civilians." In fact, and as will be discussed later in this book, quite the contrary is the case.[37]

## Civilian Objects

IHL includes also civilian objects in the proportionality analysis, and rules out damage to civilian objects that is excessive relative to the military objective. Civilian objects are all objects that are not considered military targets. The definition of these objects, and the problem of dual-use objects, will be discussed in Chapter 10.

## Damage to the Natural Environment

The provisions of AP-I discuss "widespread, long-term and severe damage" to the natural environment.[38] Furthermore, the Rome Statute explicitly binds together the long-term effects of an attack with damage to the environment: "Intentionally launching an attack in the knowledge that such attack will cause . . . widespread, long-term and severe damage to the natural environment which would be

36. ICRC Proportionality Report, *supra* note 28, at p. 41.

37. Chapter 12E.

38. AP-I, *supra* note 1, art. 35(3), 55(1).

clearly excessive in relation to the concrete and direct overall military advantage anticipated" is a war crime within the jurisdiction of the Court.[39]

There are diverging views regarding the extent of protection to the natural environment. Gillard supports the view that the protected environment consists of every part of the environment that has some intrinsic value, and not only the environment that has value to humans.[40] According to this stance, almost any military activity would have some effect on the natural environment. As Gillard correctly notes, current scientific knowledge may not even recognize some of the harm caused to the natural environment by military activity.[41] While war is, at least theoretically, possible without incidental damage to civilians, it is quite impossible to fight without causing at least some damage to the environment.

It seems to us that while any damage to the environment *should* be considered in the proportionality analysis, only especially severe environmental damage (causing "widespread, long-term and severe damage") might rise to the level of a prohibited attack. Of course, destruction of an environmental resource important to the survival of mankind might be illegal, but this is because of the long-term effects on humans rather than the intrinsic nature of the environment.[42] In the future, perhaps, the rights of animals will also be taken into account in proportionality analysis. In current law, however, there is very little protection afforded the rights of animals as such.[43] Perhaps the complete extinction of a species would, in some circumstances, be considered severe enough environmental damage to make an attack illegal.

Recent years have witnessed significant developments in international law with regard to the protection of the environment, especially in the context of climate change.[44] We have become more sensitive than ever before to the negative effects of human activity on the environment, and to the implications of damage on the future of the environment. It seems to us that this understanding would surely affect the law with regard to the protection of the environment in armed conflict. Consequently, damage to the environment would be recognized by states as deserving the protection afforded by the principle of proportionality.

39. Rome Statute of the International Criminal Court, Jul. 17, 1998, art. 8.2(b)(iv), 2187 U.N.T.S. 90 (1998).

40. Gillard, *supra* note 24, at 37.

41. *Id.*

42. See our discussion below on long term effects.

43. Anne Peters, *Global Animal Law: What is It, and Why We Need It,* 5 TRANSNAT'L ENVIRON. L. 9, 13 (2016).

44. Cinnamon P. Carlarne et. al., *International Climate Change Law: Mapping the Field, in* THE OXFORD HANDBOOK ON INTERNATIONAL CLIMATE CHANGE 3 (Carlarne et. al. Eds., Oxford UP, 2016).

## Benefitting from Proportional Harm

One point also worth noting is that according to some, as long as the collateral damage to civilians is not excessive and the attacker has taken all feasible precautions to minimize the collateral damage, there is nothing in IHL that prohibits the attacker from benefitting from the collateral damage or from *desiring* the lawful collateral damage,[45] so long as the attack is proportionate and fulfils the other obligations under IHL. For example, if attacking a particular military objective were to cause lawful collateral damage to civilian infrastructure that would demoralize the civilians of the country, the attacking state can lawfully *desire* that civilian damage. An important opposing view was expressed by Judge Rosalyn Higgins, who wrote in the Nuclear Weapons Advisory Opinion that "it is said that collateral damage to civilians, even if proportionate to the importance of the military target, must never be intended."[46]

This latter view seems to us to be the correct one. The moral justification for incidental harm is that it was not intended nor desired.[47] If the attacking party desires harm to civilians, even if it does not intend to inflict it—that is, it does not take deliberate measures to achieve this outcome—the discussion becomes one of "hairsplitting" the difference between desire and intent. Furthermore, an approach allowing the attacking party to desire a result (rather than intending it) seems to blur the clear line distinguishing between civilians and combatants as objects of attacks. We therefore reject this view.

## C. INDIRECT AND REVERBERATING EFFECTS

The expected harm caused to civilians from attacks must be balanced against the anticipated military advantage. The term "expected harm" includes civilian casualties caused incidentally by explosions and shrapnel from the bombing of military objectives. However, to what extent, if at all, must the reverberating effects—the secondary, tertiary effects, and so on—be factored into proportionality analysis?

For example, a power plant that supplies both military and civilian purposes is a lawful target and can be destroyed. However, the loss of power can cause further harm to civilians. Destroying the electric power system and network can disable water, sewage, and drainage systems to the detriment of civilian welfare and survival.[48] Is such harm, and any ensuing public health risks such as the spread of illness and disease, included in the expected damage to civilians?

45. Henderson, *supra* note 18, at 198–99.

46. *Legality of the Threat or Use of Nuclear Weapons*, Advisory Opinion, I.C.J. 8, 266, para. 22 Diss. Op.) (J. Higgins) (1996) [Nuclear Weapons Case].

47. See Chapter 2, note 17 and text accompanying.

48. Judith Gardam, Necessity, Proportionality and the Use of Force by States 119 (2004).

Reverberating effects can be wide ranging and diverse: unemployment caused by the destruction of munitions factories and industrial plants; harm to civilians who could not flee conflict zones because of harm to roads systems and bridges or diminished supply of humanitarian aid;[49] civilian displacement due to loss of housing when homes that are used as military objectives are attacked; disruption of medical services when hospitals are attacked or power grids harmed; and the possible spread of disease from the loss of potable water, sewage systems, and medical facilities.[50]

Civilian casualties from reverberating effects can sometimes be more significant than the casualties suffered directly from attacks. There are estimates that the attacks on Iraq's power system in 1991 resulted in a lack of access to water that caused the deaths of between 40,000 and 110,000 civilians.[51]

Gillard suggests that when assessing reverberating effects, there are two main issues that should be discussed: foreseeability and causality.[52]

## Foreseeable Harm

The ICRC's position is that reverberating effects should be included in proportionality analysis as long as they are foreseeable, yet the ICRC questions whether these effects are taken into consideration by states when conducting their proportionality assessments.[53] The ICRC's position is supported by several scholars[54] as well as the recent Tallinn Manual 2.0, which considers that proportionality

49. In *Prlić*, prior to holding that the destruction of the old bridge of Mostar was disproportionate, the Trial Chamber noted that destruction of the bridge put civilians on one of its banks in nearly total isolation, making it nearly impossible to get food and medical supplies. Prlić, Judgement of the Trial Chamber, *supra* note 26, Vol. III, paras. 1582–1584.

50. For a discussion of the effects of reverberating attacks see: ICRC Challenges Report, *supra* note 5, at 52.

51. Marco Sassoli & Lindsey Cameron, *The Protection of Civilian Objects – Current State of Law and Issues de lege ferenda, in* THE LAW OF AIR WARFARE: CONTEMPORARY ISSUES, 35, 65 (Natalino Ronzitti & Gabriella Venturini eds., 2006). There are some that estimate this number at 70,000 civilian deaths. Robinson & Nohle, *supra* note 25, at 123.

52. Gillard, *supra* note 24, at 13.

53. ICRC Challenges Report, *supra* note 5, at 52.

54. Michael Schmitt also suggests that "reverberating effects were theoretically always calculated when assessing proportionality." MICHAEL N. SCHMITT, ESSAYS ON LAW AND WAR AT THE FAULT LINES, 156 (2011); Marco Sassoli and Lindsey Cameron are of the opinion that foreseeable reverberating effects must be included in the proportionality analysis. Sassoli & Cameron, *supra* note 51, at 65; see also Cordula Droege, *Get Off My Cloud: Cyber Warfare, International Humanitarian Law, and the Protection of Civilians*, 886 INT'L REV. RED CROSS 533, 572–73 (2012).

includes both the direct and indirect effects that can be anticipated as resulting from an attack.[55]

To some extent, reverberating effects are dealt with in AP-I itself. Article 54, for example, prohibits attacking sources of food, even if they are used for military purposes, if their attack "may be expected to leave the civilian population with such inadequate food or water as to cause its starvation or force its movement."[56] Similarly, article 56 gives special protection to "works or installations containing dangerous forces, namely dams, dykes, and nuclear electrical generating stations" if attacking them "may cause the release of dangerous forces and consequent severe losses among the civilian population."[57]

These specific prohibitions could be seen as a reflection of a more general rule of proportionality—taking into account foreseeable severe reverberating effects on the civilian population. We do not think that the fact that AP-I chooses to mention only these specific prohibitions precludes taking into account other foreseeable severe reverberating effects.

Certain state practice also supports some consideration of reverberating effects.[58] The United Kingdom, for example, holds that "the foreseeable effects of the attack" must be regarded in proportionality analysis, and gives the following example:

> If, for example, a precision bombing attack of a military fuel storage depot is planned but there is a foreseeable risk of the burning fuel flowing into a civilian residential area and causing injury to the civilian population which would be excessive in relation to the military advantage anticipated, that bombardment

55. Tallinn Manual 2.0, *supra* note 25, at 472. Direct effects are defined in the Manual as "the immediate, first order consequences [of a cyber-attack], unaltered by intervening events or mechanisms." Indirect effects are defined as "the delayed and/or displaced second-, third-, and higher-order consequences of action, created through intermediate events or mechanisms."

56. AP-I, *supra* note 1, art. 54(3)(b).

57. AP-I, *Id.*, art. 56(1).

58. It is also worth mentioning a position mentioned by the Committee in the NATO Bombing Report, which appears to accept that long-term effects must be included in the proportionality analysis, at least when discussing damage to the environment: "Even when targeting admittedly legitimate military objectives, there is a need to avoid excessive long-term damage to the economic infrastructure and natural environment with a consequential adverse effect on the civilian population. Indeed, military objectives should not be targeted if the attack is likely to cause collateral environmental damage which would be excessive in relation to the direct military advantage which the attack is expected to produce" (NATO Bombing Report, *supra* note 34, para. 18).

It is important to note, however, that long-term effects are included in the provisions regarding the protection of the environment during armed conflict. Therefore, it is unclear whether the position regarding long-term effects and the collateral harm caused in relation to damage to the environment can be illustrative regarding the inclusion of reverberating effects in proportionality in general.

> would be indiscriminate and unlawful, owing to the excessive collateral damage.[59]

Though the United Kingdom does take certain reverberating effects into consideration, it is unclear whether the example presented, which involves physical damage to civilian objects rather than the long-term repercussions on civilians from the loss of fuel and displacement, can serve as a basis for the broader position posited by the ICRC.

In a similar vein, certain states maintain that the long-term effects of cluster bombs on civilians are included in proportionality analysis.[60] Cluster bombs disperse small explosive munitions over an area. They are used to destroy power grids, runways, and military personnel. The problem is that many of the individual munitions often do not detonate upon impact, and remain on the ground in areas where civilians can inadvertently set them off.

Other states seem to hold the contrary position, namely, that indirect damage should be discounted when assessing proportionality.[61] Referring to the "considerable effects on the conditions of life [in Baghdad] that persist or even emerge long after termination of the hostilities," Kalshoven wrote that "it would be wonderful" if the law included such reverberating effects, "but I am not convinced that it does so."[62]

This is, for example, the position of the United States, according to whose practice "remote harms" are not seen as "expected" when assessing proportionality, rather only "immediate or direct harms foreseeably resulting from the attack." Therefore, while the death of civilians in a hospital "very soon after" the attack that cut off its power supply would be considered foreseeable, "remote harm" would not. This could include economic hardship resulting from attacks, or the risk that munitions might not detonate immediately, but would result in harm to civilians "much later after the attack."[63]

59. United Kingdom Ministry of Defence, Joint Service Publication 383, The Joint Service Manual of the Law of Armed Conflict, para. 5.33.4. (2004). Others take the position that reverberating effects are part of the proportionality analysis: "It is by now largely undisputed that reverberating effects—that is, indirect second- or third-tier effects from an attack—must be taken into account, there remains some discussion as to how far this obligation goes."

60. This includes the position of Brazil, Ireland, and Switzerland. Robinson & Nohle, *supra* note 25, at 115, 126–27.

61. Gardam, Necessity, Proportionality and the Use of Force by States, *supra* note 48, at 119.

62. Frits Kalshoven, *Remarks by Frits Kalshoven*, 86 Am. Soc'y Int'l L. Proc. 40, 45 (1992); Henderson, *supra* note 18, at 208.

63. DoD Manual, *supra* note 10, para. 5.12.1.3 ("Similarly, in determining the expected loss of civilian life, injury to civilians, and damage to civilian objects, the attacker would not be required to consider the possibility that a munition might not detonate as intended and might injure civilians much later after the attack. This is due to the difficulty in assessing such risks and the responsibility of the party controlling the territory and the civilian population to take steps

Overall, it seems to us that for many states, the problem lies not so much with the concept of "indirect damage," but rather with the issue of causality.

## Causality

In the example of the damage to power plants, discussed before, the causality is straightforward. The question becomes more complicated when there is a third party that affects the result. Gillard suggests that even when a third party intervenes, there is a causal connection if the *physical actions* of the attacking party caused the harm. For example, if an attack on a power plant causes the water supply to become contaminated, the attacking party is considered to have caused the damage, even if the actions of a third party denied the attacked party the means to purify its water (for example, if a third state imposed sanctions on trade with the attacked party). Another example is harm caused to involuntary human shields. The attacking party is considered to have caused the damage even though the human shields are only in place because a third party forced them to be there.[64]

Greenwood's position is different. He notes that when cluster munitions are used in areas where civilians are known to be, then proportionality may have to include "the risk from unexploded sub-munitions in the hours immediately after the attack," in addition to the risk to civilians from exploding munitions during the attack itself. However, the long-term risks of cluster munitions, subsequent to the hours immediately after the attack, cannot be taken into account when analyzing the proportionality of the attack, as there are too many factors affecting the risk to civilians that cannot be assessed at the time of the attack. Such factors can include "when and whether civilians will be permitted to return to an area, what steps the party controlling that area will have taken to clear unexploded ord nance, what priority that party gives to the protection of civilians, and so forth."[65]

Similarly, Henderson is of the opinion that certain long-term effects must be included in the proportionality assessment. There are attacks that will almost inevitably lead to civilian casualties in the long run. For example, the use of a nuclear weapon near an urban area can clearly be expected to result in long-term civilian harm as a result of exposure to radiation. However, Henderson also argues that casualties that may be averted through choices of the adverse party should not be included in the proportionality assessment. For instance, the proportionality

with regard to the protection of the civilian population from unexploded ordnance.") (citations omitted).

64. Gillard, *supra* note 24, at 15.

65. Christopher Greenwood, *Legal Issues Regarding Explosive Remnants Of War*, Group of Government Experts of States Parties to the Convention on Prohibitions or Restrictions on the Use of Certain Conventional Weapons, U.N. Doc. CCW/GGE/I/WP.10, 8 (2002) (cited in DoD Manual, *supra* note 10, para. 5.12.1.4, n.388).

analysis prior to attacking a power plant should not include expected casualties that could result from disease if sewage pumps or hospitals might be cut off. This is because the attacked party could choose to allocate the requisite power supply to the crucial civilian infrastructure, and the attacker should not have to take responsibility for the choices of the attacked party.[66]

A. P. V. Rogers presents an interesting middle viewpoint, according to which the long-term effects of attacks can be included in proportionality analysis as long as both the long-term effects of both the military advantage and civilian harm are examined.[67] This proposal has been criticized, as the military advantage anticipated from an attack must be "direct and concrete," whereas there is no caveat relating to the expected damage to civilians.[68]

The approach supported by the Tallinn Manual seems to us to be the preferred one. As long as the indirect effects are a reasonable, and natural, result of the operation they should be taken into account. This means that possible consequences that a reasonable person would not consider should not be taken into account. This includes when the consequences would only happen in the far future. This also means that if the defending party can reasonably prevent the damage (such as in the cluster munition example), the attacking party may rely on the reasonableness of the defending party in protecting its own civilians, and these effects should not be taken into account.

## D. THE LEVEL OF EXPECTATION/ANTICIPATION

Proportionality is prospective: it is analyzed prior to an attack, based on the facts known at the time, and not on facts that may come to light afterward. The *ex ante* assessment of the facts balances the *expected* risk to civilians with the *anticipated* military advantage, as both are foreseen prior to the attack.[69] For example, the NATO Bombing Report examined the attack in which a civilian passenger train was hit during a bombing run on a bridge at the Grdelica Gorge, killing at least 10 civilians and injuring 15 more. The Committee did not initiate an investigation as the train had not been targeted and harm to the civilians had not been anticipated.[70] The same is true regarding the attack on the Korisa village, in which

66. Henderson, *supra* note 18, at 210.

67. A.P.V. Rogers, Law on the Battlefield 22 (2nd ed., 2004).

68. Robinson & Nohle, *supra* note 25, at 128.

69. "The consequences that actually flow from an attack come into play in the course of an ex post facto evaluation of whether the attacker ought reasonably to have expected the resulting collateral damage." (Program on Humanitarian Policy and Conflict Research (HPCR) at Harvard University, *Commentary on the HPCR Manual on International Law Applicable to Air and Missile Warfare* 91 (2010) [HPCR].)

70. NATO Bombing Report, *supra* note 34, paras. 58–62. While it is true that the Committee focused on the issue of distinction, whether the civilian train had intentionally been targeted,

as many as 87 civilians were killed.[71] By contrast, when the Committee examined the proportionality of the attack against the RTS studio,[72] it discussed the actual harm to the 10–17 civilians who had been killed, and did not try to assess the expected harm to civilians.[73]

In other words, an attack that was not expected to cause any harm to civilians would be considered proportionate even if dozens of civilians were killed, while an attack that does not result in a single civilian casualty but was expected to cause tens of deaths might be disproportionate.[74] Naturally, a result in which dozens of civilians were "unexpectedly" killed is problematic, and should be investigated to verify whether all precautions were indeed taken,[75] but the mere results of the attack cannot establish the wrongfulness of the act. Similarly, an attack that was expected to result in excessive harm to civilians would still be disproportionate if the military advantage actually achieved was higher than that anticipated prior to the attack. This could occur, for instance, if it turned out that the enemy army's chief of staff was unexpectedly in a building under attack.

What is the requisite level of expectation? Additionally, to what extent does proportionality recognize or address the probability of anticipated military advantage or the expected harm to civilians? Consider a situation in which a certain weapon system is known to malfunction 10% of the time and miss the military target. However, if it malfunctions it will definitely cause excessive harm to civilians. Is an attack employing this weapons system

its examination and determination are relevant to the question of the proportionality of the attack as well.

71. *Id.*, paras. 86–89.

72. See Chapter 4, notes 60–64 and accompanying text.

73. It should be noted, however, that the Report assesses the question of whether NATO had fulfilled its obligation to warn civilians of the impending attack. This discussion might be related to the question of the anticipated harm to civilians, as the Committee noted that apparently foreign journalists had been warned to stay away from the RTS studio before the attack. This fact could weigh in as part of the proportionality analysis if NATO knew that those journalists were not going to be present at the time of the attack, thus lowering the risk and extent of collateral damage. NATO Bombing Report, *supra* note 34, para. 77.

74. Attacks that were expected to cause disproportionate damage which did not materialize might still be a violation of international law, though they are not grave breaches of AP-I, as grave breaches must actually cause "death or serious injury to body or health." AP-I, *supra* note 1, art. 85(3).

75. This seems to be the position of the Israel High Court of Justice President, Justice Barak in the *Targeted Killings* case, where Barak required an investigation each time civilian casualties happened (HCJ 769/02, Public Committee against Torture v. The State of Israel, PD 62(1) 507, para. 59 (2006)). This suggestion makes sense only if these were unforeseen civilian casualties. See Amichai Cohen & Yuval Shany, *A Development of Modest Proportions: The Application of the Principle of Proportionality in the Targeted Killings Case*, 5 J. Int'l Crim. Jus. 310–321 (2007).

disproportionate? What if the probability of malfunction were 1%? Or alternatively 50%?[76]

Mistakes and malfunctions often occur in battle, resulting, unfortunately, in loss of life. One need only look at the prevalence of incidents of friendly fire. For instance, 58 of the 514 Syrian aircraft lost during the 1973 Yom Kippur War, more than 10%, were shot down by friendly fire.[77] Nonetheless, human error and mechanical malfunction are not assessed as a part of proportionality.[78] This, as with all other aspects of proportionality, is subject to the attacker acting "reasonably and in good faith."[79]

The question of the probabilities in attack is much broader than this. The implication of the "fog of war" is that decisions to attack objectives are always made in situations of doubt. As Clausewitz famously wrote, "War is the realm of uncertainty."[80] This is so even in contemporary armed conflicts, despite the technological advances made since Clausewitz's time. How, for example, should a state's assessment of an 80% certainty that a particular house is being used for a meeting of five senior terrorists affect the proportionality analysis? By the same token, how does the proportionality analysis factor in the probability of 40% that a specific attack will result in 10 civilian casualties, but a 60% chance that the number of civilian casualties will be lower than three?

An interesting illustration of the question of the probabilities of causing damage to civilians can be seen in the 1972 Linebacker I air offensive by the United States against North Vietnam during the Vietnam War. During this operation, the United States considered attacking the Lang Chi hydroelectric facility, which was capable of supplying 75% of Hanoi's industrial and defense requirements. The military advantage anticipated from the attack was substantial. However, it was also estimated that some 23,000 civilians could be killed if the dam was breached as a

76. This example using different probabilities is presented by Robert D. Sloane, *Puzzles of Proportion and the "Reasonable Military Commander": Reflections on the Law, Ethics, and Geopolitics of Proportionality*, 6 HARV. NAT'L SEC. J. 299, 313 (2015).

77. Parks, *supra* note 19, at 198–201.

78. DINSTEIN, *supra* note 32, at 135; Remarks of Yoram Dinstein, *Interpretive Complexity and the International Humanitarian Law Principle of Proportionality*, 108 AM. SOC'Y INT'L L. PROC. 82, 86 (2014).

79. DINSTEIN, *supra* note 32, 132–33; YUVAL SHANY, THE PRINCIPLE OF PROPORTIONALITY UNDER INTERNATIONAL LAW 67 (2009) (Heb.).

If it was known that a certain weapon system malfunctions 95% of the time then, its use might be prohibited as an indiscriminate weapon (AP-I, *supra* note 1, art. 51(4)(b): "Indiscriminate attacks are: (b) those which employ a method or means of combat which cannot be directed at a specific military objective."); or this factor might have to be assessed in proportionality in certain cases. For a related discussion, see the discussion regarding cluster munitions, *supra* notes 57–60 and accompanying text.

80. Cited in Parks, *supra* note 19, at 181.

result of an attack. President Nixon, in reviewing the attack, stated that he would not authorize it unless he could be assured that there was no chance that the dam would be breached. In the end, the president authorized the attack after having been assured by the military that there was a 90% chance the mission could be accomplished without causing a breach of the dam. The mission was carried out and the power plant was destroyed without damaging the dam.[81] During the assessment of the proportionality of the attack, should the 23,000 civilian casualties have been balanced against the anticipated military advantage? Should only 2,300 civilian casualties (10% of 23,000) have been viewed as expected collateral damage?[82] Or conversely, was the probability of failure low enough so that the civilian casualties should have been discounted altogether when performing the proportionality analysis?

There are those who set the level of expectation at that of the "reasonable" information available to the attacker.[83] The experts who authored the Humanitarian Policy and Conflict Research (HPCR) Manual opine that "reasonable" means that the results must be foreseeably "probable, i.e. more likely than not."[84] Some of the experts who participated in the preparation of the Tallinn Manual 2.0 were of the opinion that the degree of certainty of the expected harm should be factored in. In other words, if there was a low probability of collateral damage, a more modest military advantage could warrant an attack. However, the majority of experts expressed the opinion that as long as there was a reasonable, rather than a merely speculative, expectation of damage being caused, the damage should be weighed against the anticipated military advantage.[85]

The terms "expected" and "anticipated" give the attacker a "fairly broad margin of judgment."[86] However "the mere possibility of occurrence" seems to be too low a standard of expectation.[87] Therefore, according to the authors of the Tallinn Manual 2.0, determining whether an attack is proportionate or not depends upon the "reasonable" expectations of the attacker.[88]

81. Parks, *Id.*, at 168–169.

82. The figure 2,300 reflects the expected value of the civilian casualties as a result of the attack against the Lang Chi hydroelectric facility (2,300 is equal to the 23,000 civilian casualties multiplied by the 10% probability of the harm actually occurring).

83. HPCR, *supra* note 69, at 33; Dinstein, *supra* note 32, at 130–132; The State of Israel, Ministry of Foreign Affairs, The 2014 Gaza Conflict: 7 July–26 August 2014: Factual and Legal Aspects, para. 330 (May 2015) [MoFA 2015 Report].

84. HPCR, *supra* note 69, at 92.

85. Tallinn Manual 2.0, *supra* note 25, at 475.

86. *Id.*, at 475 (citing AP-I Commentary, *supra* note 2, para. 2210).

87. Tallinn Manual 2.0, *supra* note 25.

88. *Id.*, at 471.

The standard of reasonableness is supported by some state practice—for example, in the *Fuel Tankers* case. In 2009, near the city of Kunduz, Afghanistan, an American warplane struck two fuel tankers that had been seized by the Taliban. The request for the attack was made by Germans forces who feared the trucks would be used in an attack. The airstrike resulted in the deaths of many civilians, with estimates ranging from dozens to 137 killed. Due to public outcry, the prosecutor-general of the Federal Republic of Germany examined the attack, and on April 16, 2010, dismissed criminal proceedings against the German personnel involved.[89]

The prosecutor-general made two factual determinations. First, that prior to the attack, the commander knew that the trucks were surrounded by some 70 persons believed to be Taliban fighters. Second, that only some 50 people had actually been killed. However, no finding was made regarding the extent of actual civilian harm. Having determined that there had been no grounds to expect civilians to be in the vicinity, the prosecutor-general ruled the attack proportionate, regardless of the result, due to the expectations prior to the attack. He also took his assessment a step further, and, for the sake of argument, determined that even had there been an expectation of a high number of civilian casualties, the attack would not have violated the principle of proportionality.[90] Recently, in the *Fuel Tankers* case, a claim for compensation regarding the 2009 Kunduz incident, the German Federal Court of Justice reinforced the primary finding of the prosecutor-general, holding that no violation of the rule of proportionality had been proven, as under the circumstances the commander *neither knew, nor could have known* about the civilian presence near the trucks.[91]

This view has a lot of merit. Proportionality, as we shall explain, is far from an exact science, and "factoring" of statistical certainties is not realistically possible. Hence, once a reasonable person assumes that collateral damage will happen, this damage should be considered.

## E. A BALANCING ACT: WHAT CONSTITUTES A VIOLATION?

Having discussed what should be considered part of the expected civilian harm on the one hand, and what should be considered as part of the "direct and concrete military advantage" on the other, an important question remains: What is the relation between the two competing sides of the equation? What is the meaning of

89. Wolff Heintschel von Heinegg & Peter Dreist, *The 2009 Kunduz Air Attack: The Decision of the Federal Prosecutor-General on the Dismissal of Criminal Proceedings against Members of the German Armed Forces*, 53 German Y.B. Int'l L. 833 (2010).

90. *Id.*, at 848–49.

91. BGH, Urteil, III ZR 140/15 (Oct. 6, 2016) [Ger.], *available at:* juris.bundesgerichtshof.de/cgi-bin/rechtsprechung/document.py?Gericht=bgh&Art=en&Datum=Aktuell&Sort=12288&Seite=1&nr=76401&pos=35&anz=487.

"excessive?" Is a mere imbalance between the two a violation of the proportionality rule, or is a significant imbalance required?

The drafters of AP-I used the term "excessive" rather than "disproportionate" or "disproportional" out of concern that these alternate terms would too severely curtail states' abilities to conduct hostilities.[92]

There are two different approaches regarding the balance between military advantage and incidental harm to civilians. The first gives more latitude to belligerents, requiring attacks to be clearly disproportionate in order to be ruled out, while the second, which constrains belligerents to a greater degree, views certain grey areas as indicators of violations. State practice seems to support the former approach, while the latter is supported primarily by certain judgments of the ICTY.

In the *Galić* case, the ICTY Trial Chamber appears to favor humanitarian interests to a greater degree, by stating that, in borderline cases, if there is uncertainty as to the proportionality of an attack, the attack must be called off in order to protect interests of civilians.[93] This is also the ICRC's position in the *Commentary on AP-I*. Accordingly, in the grey areas, when the proportionality of an attack is unclear, humanitarian interests must prevail.[94] These positions do not clarify explicitly where the balancing point between the two interests lies, but do serve to infuse the equation with humanitarian concerns.

In the *Kupreskić* case, the ICTY Trial Chamber went further, opining that multiple attacks of questionable legality—attacks "within the grey area between indisputable legality and unlawfulness"—which are legal on an individual basis, and "do not appear on their face to fall foul per se," might be seen cumulatively to violation of IHL.[95]

92. Shany, *supra* note 79, at 59.

93. Prosecutor v. Galić, ICTY Trial Chamber, IT-98-29, *Judgment*, para. 58 (Dec. 5, 2003) [Galić, TC]; Shany, *supra* note 79, at 60.

94. AP-I Commentary, *supra* note 2, para. 1979. In the *Kupreskić* case, the ICTY Trial Chambers held that when multiple attacks "within the grey area between indisputable legality and unlawfulness" occur, interests of humanity might bring the conclusion that the attacks might be a violation of IHL, when viewed in aggregate, even though the individual attacks "do not appear on their face to fall foul per se" (Prosecutor v. Kupreskić, ICTY Trial Chamber, IT-95-16, *Judgment*, para. 526 (Jan. 14, 2000)); Andreas Zimmerman, *The Second Lebanon War: Jus ad Bellum, Jus in Bello and the Issue of Proportionality*, 11 Max Planck UNYB 99, 136 (2007).

95. Kupreskic, *Id.*, para. 526 ("It may happen that single attacks on military objectives causing incidental damage to civilians, although they may raise doubts as to their lawfulness, nevertheless do not appear on their face to fall foul per se of the loose prescriptions of Articles 57 and 58 (or of the corresponding customary rules). However, in case of repeated attacks, all or most of them falling within the grey area between indisputable legality and unlawfulness, it might be warranted to conclude that the cumulative effect of such acts entails that they may not be in keeping with international law. Indeed, this pattern of military conduct may turn out to jeopardise excessively the lives and assets of civilians, contrary to the demands of humanity"); Zimmerman, *supra* note 94, at 136.

This position, which may have far-reaching ramifications, was criticized by the Committee in the NATO Bombing Report, which called it a "progressive statement of the applicable law," and found its practical application "far from clear." The Committee stated that the "mere cumulation of such instances, all of which are deemed to have been lawful, cannot *ipso facto* be said to amount to a crime."[96] The Committee's position seems to us to be especially pertinent because of its focus on the issue of criminal responsibility. Apart from the disagreement detailed earlier regarding the contents of the principle of proportionality, when criminal responsibility is being discussed, we believe that the "clearly excessive" standard is appropriate.

The Committee in the NATO Bombing Report goes on to clarify the "clearly disproportionate" test.[97] If the disproportion of the attack is not "clear," then the attack cannot be deemed to violate the rule of proportionality. Gary Solis presents this perspective concisely: "What is clear is that to violate proportionality, the discrepancy between the loss of civilian life and destruction of civilian objects must be *clearly* disproportionate to the direct military advantage anticipated. 'Close' issues do not rise to a violation."[98] This approach has been echoed by other scholars,[99] such as Dinstein, who maintains that an "excessive" attack is one in which the "disproportion is not in doubt."[100]

Israel seems to have adopted this latter position, namely that disproportionate actions are those in which there is a "*significant imbalance* between the expected collateral damage and the anticipated military advantage."[101] This position is also

96. NATO Bombing Report, *supra* note 34, para.52; Zimmerman, *Id.*, at 137.

97. NATO Bombing Report, *supra* note 34, paras. 50, 77 (emphasis added). For example, in 1999 NATO bombed the central studio of the state-owned broadcasting corporation (RTS) in Belgrade, killing between 10 and 17 people. The Committee conducted an examination of the proportionality of the attack on the RTS studio, finding that "the civilian casualties were unfortunately high but do not appear to be clearly disproportionate" (*Id.*, para. 77). For further discussion regarding this case, see Chapter 10.

98. Gary D. Solis, The Law of Armed Conflict: International Humanitarian Law in War 294 (2nd ed., 2016).

99. Kalshoven and Zegveld similarly write: "A subtle weighing process cannot be expected here: the attacker is obliged to refrain from the attack only if the disproportion between the two sides in the equation '*becomes apparent*.'" Frits Kalshoven & Liesbeth Zegveld, Constraints on the Waging of War: An Introduction to International Humanitarian Law 115 (4th ed., 2011).

100. Dinstein, *supra* note 32, at 131. This position is also supported by others: Michael N. Schmitt & John J. Merriam, *The Tyranny of Context: Israeli Targeting Practices in Legal Perspective*, 37 U. Pa. J. Int'l L. 53, 131 (2015).

101. MoFA 2015 Report, *supra* note 83, para. 330 (emphasis added).

that of the international group of experts who authored the HPCR Manual on International Law Applicable to Air and Missile Warfare.[102]

It is worth recalling that 20 years after AP-I was adopted, the Rome Statute defined the crime of disproportionate attacks as:

> Intentionally launching an attack in the knowledge that such attack will cause incidental loss of life or injury to civilians or damage to civilian objects . . . which would be *clearly excessive* in relation to the concrete and direct overall military advantage anticipated.

Rogers contends that this formulation of proportionality is the closest reflection of the customary rule of proportionality in IHL[103] though it can be argued that the threshold for individual criminal responsibility for the crime of proportionality is higher than that of state responsibility under IHL.[104]

One case that discusses what is "clearly excessive," albeit in significantly different circumstances, is the *Hostages Trials*, held by the Nuremberg Military Tribunal. The trials concerned the killing of hostages in reprisal for the killing of German soldiers. Aside from addressing the main question whether killing hostages could ever be justified, which is a question of distinction, the Tribunal judgment also discussed the definition of what would be considered "clearly excessive," which is a question of proportionality:

> The reprisals taken under the authority of this order were clearly excessive. The shooting of 100 innocent persons for each German soldier killed at Topola, for instance, cannot be justified on any theory by the record. An order to shoot 100 persons for each German soldier killed under such circumstances is not only excessive but wholly unwarranted.[105]

Obviously, a ratio of 100:1 is not the lower limit to what may be "clearly excessive" in the circumstances. Clearly, the Germans did not weigh collateral damage against military advantage. In fact, they killed civilians *because* of their civilian status. In this case, as in other cases purportedly using the term *proportionality*, the court used proportionality analysis to establish the fact that the relevant party had no regard for the civilian status of the victims of its actions.

102. HPCR, *supra* note 69, at 92 ("[The term 'excessive'] applies when there is a significant imbalance between the military advantage anticipated, on the one hand, and the expected collateral damage to civilians and civilian objects, on the other").

103. A. P. V. Rogers, *The Principle of Proportionality*, *in* THE LEGITIMATE USE OF MILITARY FORCE: THE JUST WAR TRADITION AND THE CUSTOMARY LAW OF ARMED CONFLICT 189, 208 (Howard M. Hensel ed., 2007).

104. See discussion in Chapter 4, note 53 and accompanying text.

105. See Fenrick, *supra* note 18, at 117.

Whether proportionality violations must be "clearly excessive" or merely "excessive" is only part of the problem, as the analysis of what may be excessive can vary significantly based on the circumstances.

For example, one examination of the proportionality of a targeted killing can be found in the Report of the Israeli Special Investigatory Commission on the Targeted Killing of Salah Shehadeh.[106] Shehadeh was the commander of Hamas's military wing and was killed in a targeted killing on July 22, 2002, in Gaza City. Unfortunately, in addition to Shehadeh, 14 civilians were also killed, including his wife and his 15-year-old daughter, and dozens of civilians were injured. It is worth noting that previous attempts to kill Shehadeh had been called off for fear of high collateral damage.[107] Following a recommendation of the Israeli Supreme Court, an independent commission was formed to investigate possible violations of law in the incident. The commission was headed by retired Supreme Court justice Tova Strasberg-Cohen. The Commission found that there was no violation of proportionality, as it had not been known that the civilians would be in the target area. However, the Commission declared that had the extent of collateral damage been known in advance, the attack would have been called off.[108]

The Commission's findings seem to differ from the conclusions of the Committee that reviewed the NATO Bombing Campaign.[109] In 1999, NATO bombed the central studio of RTS, the state-owned broadcasting corporation in Belgrade, killing between 10 and 17 people. The Committee examined the proportionality of the attack and found it was not clearly disproportionate. As discussed in Chapter 4, the bombing was part of a wider attack against the Yugoslav command, control, and communications network. The Committee found that the attack was proportionate despite the fact that, prior to the attack, NATO had been aware that attacking the RTS studio would only interrupt broadcasts for a brief period.[110] The divergent conclusions of the two commissions—that one attack with an arguably higher military advantage (killing Shehadeh, the commander of Hamas's military wing) would violate the proportionality rule, whereas a different attack with a seemingly more limited military advantage (a brief interruption of broadcasts) was not disproportionate—can only leave practitioners and scholars perplexed.

106. *Report of the Special Investigatory Commission on the Targeted Killing of Salah Shehadeh* (Feb. 2011) (Heb.), *available at:* https://www.gov.il/BlobFolder/news/spokeshchade270211/he/sitecollectiondocuments_pmo_32communication_spokemes_reportshchade.pdf [Strasberg Cohen Report] (A summary of the report is available in English at: www.mfa.gov.il/mfa/aboutisrael/state/law/pages/salah_shehadeh-special_investigatory_commission_27-feb-2011.aspx).

107. Ariel Meyerstein, *Case Study: The Israeli Strike Against Hamas Leader Salah Shehadeh*, Crimes of War, (Sept. 19, 2002), *available at*: http://www.crimesofwar.org/print/onnews/Shehadeh-print.html.

108. Strasberg Cohen Report, *supra* note 106, at 71–89, 97–98.

109. NATO Bombing Report, *supra* note 34.

110. *Id.*, paras. 77–78.

As previously mentioned, judicial decisions examining proportionality are sparse. One example of the application of proportionality in the jurisprudence of international (albeit criminal) tribunals can be found in the *Galić* case. A majority in the ICTY Trial Chamber found that the firing of two mortars on a crowd watching a soccer match was disproportionate, even though the number of military casualties exceeded the number of civilian casualties. When discussing the attack, the court noted that "the Majority understands the evidence to show that there were soldiers present at the parking lot, who were off-duty, unarmed and not engaged in any military activity." The civilian nature of the activity seems to have weighed on the Trial Chamber's assessment of the military advantage. The Trial Chamber decided that

> though the number of soldiers present at the game was significant, an attack on a crowd of approximately 200 people, including numerous children, would clearly be expected to cause incidental loss of life and injuries to civilians excessive in relation to the direct and concrete military advantage anticipated.

It therefore concluded that this was an example of indiscriminate shelling on a civilian area.[111]

The ICTY Trial Chamber conducted one of the only discussions of the proportionality of an attack in the *Gotovina* case, though the judgment was reversed on appeal.[112] The Trial Chamber examined an attack on the political leader and supreme commander of the Serbian Army of Krajina, Milan Martić. The Chamber determined that "firing at his residence could disrupt his ability to move, communicate, and command and so offered a definite military advantage."[113] The question of the proportionality of the attack arose from the fact that Martić's residence was in a civilian apartment building, which was located in a residential area:

> The Trial Chamber considers that Martić's apartment was located in an otherwise civilian apartment building and that both the apartment and the area marked R on P2337 were in otherwise predominantly civilian residential areas. The Trial Chamber has considered this use of artillery in light of the evidence on the accuracy of artillery weapons reviewed above and the testimony of expert Konings on the blast and fragmentation effects of artillery shells. At the times of firing, namely between 7:30 and 8 a.m. and in the evening on 4 August 1995, civilians could have reasonably been expected to be present on the streets of Knin near Martić's apartment and in the area marked R on

111. Galić, TC, *supra* note 93, para. 387.

112. Prosecutor v. Gotovina, ICTY Trial Chamber I, IT-06-90-T, *Judgment* (Apr. 15, 2011). For further discussion of the proportionality analysis in the *Gotovina* case, see Rogier Bartels, *Dealing with the Principle of Proportionality in Armed Conflict in Retrospect: The Application of the Principle in International Criminal Trials*, 46 Isr. L. Rev. 271, 286–92 (2013).

113. Gotovina, *supra* note 112, para. 1899.

P2337. Firing twelve shells of 130 millimetres at Martić's apartment and an unknown number of shells of the same calibre at the area marked R on P2337, from a distance of approximately 25 kilometres, created a significant risk of a high number of civilian casualties and injuries, as well as of damage to civilian objects. The Trial Chamber considers that this risk was excessive in relation to the anticipated military advantage of firing at the two locations where the HV believed Martić to have been present. This disproportionate attack shows that the HV paid little or no regard to the risk of civilian casualties and injuries and damage to civilian objects when firing artillery at a military target on at least three occasions on 4 August 1995.[114]

As noted, the Appeals Chamber reversed the judgment of the Trial Chamber in *Gotovina* and acquitted the accused. In particular, the Appeals Chamber held that the Trial Chamber's analysis of the attack on Martić "was not based on a concrete assessment of comparative military advantage, and did not make any findings on resulting damages or casualties."[115]

The Appeals Chamber is correct in its critique of the analysis carried out by the Trial Chamber. The latter did not compare the military advantage with the civilian damages, and hence had no basis for deciding that the attack was disproportionate. However, in the context of the case, it seems to us that the Trial Chamber, while purportedly discussing the principle of proportionality, was actually referring to factors more commonly associated with precautions in attack. Specifically, the Trial Chamber was in effect claiming that the attacking force did not do everything it could to minimize civilian casualties. It seems that an alternative way of framing of this claim would have been to cite a violation of article 57(a)(ii) of AP-I, that states that the attacking party should "take all feasible precautions in the choice of means and methods of attack with a view to avoiding, and in any event to minimizing, incidental loss of civilian life, injury to civilians and damage to civilian objects."

We shall discuss the relationship between precautions and proportionality later in this book. At this stage, suffice it to say that neither the Trial Chamber nor the Appeals Chamber in the *Gotovina* case referred to this issue explicitly.

There are other cases in which the ICTY discussed proportionality. In the *Blaskić* case, the Trial Chamber held that the "vigorous" use of heavy weaponry to capture villages that were mostly occupied by civilians was disproportionate. This was deduced from the fact that most of the casualties caused by the attacks were civilian, rather than military.[116] The decision of the Trial Chamber seems

114. *Id.*, para. 1910 (footnotes omitted); Bartels, *supra* note 112, at 290.

115. Prosecutor v. Gotovina, ICTY Appeals Chamber, IT-06-90-A, *Judgment*, para. 82 (Nov. 16, 2012).

116. Prosecutor v. Blaskić, ICTY Trial Chamber, IT-95-14-T, *Judgment*, paras. 507, 512, 651 (Mar. 3, 2000); Amichai Cohen, Proportionality in Modern Asymmetrical Wars 22–3 (2010); Shany, *supra* note 79, at 70; Dinstein, *supra* note 32, at 131–32.

intended to be less a discussion of the allegations of disproportionate attacks, and more a type of counter-argument that the attacks were indiscriminately aimed at civilians, in violation of the principle of distinction.[117] This conclusion seems to be in line with more recent findings of the ICTY in which proportionality was discussed and assessed with direct connection to violation of the principle of distinction, such as the *Prlić* case,[118] and most recently, the *Karadzić* case.[119]

## Different Standards in Different Conflicts?

In Chapter 3 we discussed a framework suggested by Newton and May, according to which different standards of proportionality should be adopted for different kinds of conflicts. A distinction of that sort might provide a rationale for some of the differences between the approaches to balancing. According to Newton and May's framework, the more the conflict resembles classic war, the more flexible the state's interpretation of the principle of proportionality can be. The NATO bombing of Belgrade was part of an attack carried out by military professionals against military professionals from another state. That situation justifies the decision of the NATO bombing committee to grant states flexibility when balancing between military advantage and collateral damage.

However, a stricter balancing act is required in specific instances of targeted killing operations, such as that carried out against Saleh Shehade. Hence, the position of the Israeli committee, which judged 13 casualties to be excessive, makes sense according to this view.

117. Cohen, *supra* note 116, at 23.

118. In *Prlić*, the Trial Chamber examined the heavy shelling of East Mostar, which resulted in the killing and wounding of many people, mostly civilians. The Trial Chamber held that the attacks, which did not properly discriminate between military objectives and civilian objects, caused excessive harm to the civilian population in relation to the anticipated military advantage (Prlić, Trial Chamber, *supra* note 26, Vol. II, para. 1018, Vol. III, paras. 1684–86 (see also Vol. II, paras. 994–1018)). Recently, the Appeals Chamber criticized the Trial Chamber's finding on this matter, maintaining that the Trial Chamber had found the damage to be disproportionate without having determined the military advantage from the attack "and as such erred in law by failing to provide a reasoned opinion." Prlić, Appeals Chamber, *supra* note 26, Vol. I, para. 561.

119. In *Karadzić*, the ICTY Trial Chamber examined the shelling of Sarajevo between the end of the month of May and early June 1992, and held that the shelling of the city, particularly certain neighborhoods therein, was disproportionate. The Trial Chamber decided that although attacks against the city might have been launched by the SRK (Sarajevo-Romanija Corps) in response to Bosnian Muslim attacks from within the city, the attacks against the city as a whole, using various weapons and types of artillery, were indiscriminate and disproportionate. This finding was also based on statements made by commanders who were aware of the civilian nature of the city preceding the attack, including the statement that "Sarajevo will shake" (Prosecutor v. Karadzić, ICTY Trial Chamber, IT-95-5/18-T, *Judgment*, paras. 4052–55, 4497–4502 (Mar. 24, 2016) (see also paras. 4018–4055)).

## Excessive vs. Extensive: An Upper Limit to Civilian Harm?

Can high levels of harm to civilians be justified given a sufficiently large military advantage, or is there an upper limit to the incidental damage that can ever be justified by military necessity? That is, is there a level of civilian harm that can never be justified, no matter how great the anticipated military advantage?

It is widely accepted that the term "excessive" should not be confused with the term "extensive," meaning that there might be circumstances in which even high levels of expected damage to civilians could be justified in light of a sufficiently significant military advantage:

> If the military advantage anticipated is marginal, the collateral damage expected need not be substantial in order to be excessive. Conversely, extensive collateral damage may be legally justified by the military value of the target struck, because of the high military advantage anticipated by the attack.[120]

The issue of extensive harm to civilians was also discussed explicitly by Judge Rosalyn Higgins in her separate opinion in the International Court of Justice's (ICJ) Nuclear Weapons Advisory Opinion, in which she wrote that there may be circumstances in which even the severe collateral damage caused by nuclear weapons could be justified.[121] The Court seemed to be of the same opinion, as can be seen from its *dispositif*.[122]

120. HPCR, *supra* note 69, at 92.

121. Nuclear Weapons Case, *supra* note 46, para. 21 (Diss. Op.) (J. Higgins). Few weapons systems imaginable are capable of causing more incidental civilian harm than nuclear weapons. One seminal case regarding severe *incidental* harm to civilians concerns the use of nuclear bombs on the Japanese cities of Hiroshima and Nagasaki, in the last days of World War II, on Aug. 6 and 9, 1945, respectively. In *Shimoda v. The State*, 8 JAP. ANN. INTL L. 212 (1964) [Jap.]. Several plaintiffs, who were injured in the bombings, sued the Japanese government for injuries they had suffered. The Tokyo District Court rejected the plaintiffs' claim, but decided that the atomic bombings were illegal. The Court ignored the argument made by the defense that the use of the atomic bombs had hastened the end of the war, thus reducing the number of casualties. Instead, the Court held that there were not sufficient military objectives in Hiroshima and Nagasaki that could justify the dropping of the bombs on the cities in their entirety, as opposed to the lawfulness of conducting area bombings against localized and smaller scale industrial zones, which could, as a whole be justified. The decision of the court relied on the indiscriminate nature of the bombing, though the discussion does not appear to be couched in terms of proportionality, rather in the field of distinction. It should be noted that Fenrick has viewed the case as one of the most "useful proceedings" regarding the rule of proportionality. See Fenrick, *The Rule of Proportionality*, *supra* note 18, at 113, 121–22.

122. "In view of the current state of international law, and of the elements of fact at its disposal, the Court cannot conclude definitively whether the threat or use of nuclear weapons would be lawful or unlawful in an extreme circumstance of self-defence, in which the very survival of a State would be at stake." Nuclear Weapons Case, *supra* note 46, at 266.

Meanwhile, the ICRC's *Commentary on AP-I* expresses the reverse position, that *extensive* harm to civilians is disproportionate:

> The idea has also been put forward that even if they are very high, civilian losses and damages may be justified if the military advantage at stake is of great importance. This idea is contrary to the fundamental rules of the Protocol . . . The Protocol does not provide any justification for attacks which cause extensive civilian losses and damages. Incidental losses and damages should never be extensive.[123]

## F. FROM WHOSE PERSPECTIVE SHOULD PROPORTIONALITY BE EXAMINED?

Given that proportionality must be examined *ex ante*, what perspective should be used for such an examination? Using a *subjective* standard—from the perspective of the commander of the attacking party, who must act in good faith or using an *objective* standard—i.e., from the perspective of a theoretical "reasonable military commander?" There is no clear answer to this question in legal doctrine.

Several scholars maintain that proportionality is assessed by a subjective standard, as opposed to an objective one.[124] Dinstein's opinion is that, due to the complexity of the analysis involved, the assessment of proportionality must be subjective and the attacker must act "reasonably and in good faith."[125] Some believe that "objective standards for the appraisal of expected collateral damage and intended military advantage are virtually non-existent."[126] The United States holds the position that the assessment of proportionality is subjective, requiring a good faith assessment, based on the information available to the decision-maker at the time.[127]

123. AP-I Commentary, *supra* note 2, para. 1980.

124. Gardam, Necessity, Proportionality and the Use of Force by States, *supra* note 48, at 105–106 ("There is consensus that although the wording of the prohibition implies an objective standard, the determination of which attacks fall within this prohibition is necessarily a subjective one that must be made in a diligent and honest manner by a competent commander at the appropriate level of command"); Nils Melzer, Targeted Killing in International Law 361 (2009); For more sources, see Jason D. Wright, *"Excessive" Ambiguity: Analysing and Refining the Proportionality Standard*, 886 Int'l Rev. Red Cross 819, 839 (2012).

125. Dinstein, *supra* note 32, at 132–33; Shany, *supra* note 79, at 67.

126. The objective standard was adopted by Oeter in Dieter Fleck's commentary on IHL, in which it is written that the principle "remains loosely defined and is subject to subjective assessment and balancing. . . . Objective standards for the appraisal of expected collateral damage and intended military advantage are virtually non-existent." Stefan Oeter, *Methods and Means of Combat, in* The Handbook of International Humanitarian Law 119, 205 (Terry Gill & Dieter Fleck eds., 2nd ed., 2008).

127. DoD Manual, *supra* note 10, para.5.10.2.3, 5.12.3.

Others, however, hold a different view, and set a semi-objective standard of proportionality: While the information must be based on the information that is actually, *subjectively*, available to the attacker, the assessment of that information must be carried out using an *objective* standard of reasonableness. In other words, determining whether the expected and anticipated harm and advantage from the attack is excessive must be objectively reasonable, but that assessment must be based on the actual information held by the attacker.[128]

This appears to have been the position taken by the ICTY Trial Chamber in the *Galić* case:[129]

> In determining whether an attack was proportionate it is necessary to examine whether a *reasonably well-informed person* in the circumstances of the actual perpetrator, *making reasonable use of the information available to him or her*, could have expected excessive civilian casualties to result from the attack.[130]

Similar views can be found in the NATO Bombing Report[131] and the Elements of Crimes of the Rome Statute,[132] and are reflected in the position of states such as Israel[133] and Ecuador.[134] Strictly concerning the issue of the relevant information, several other states maintain that proportionality is to be assessed based on

128. A.P.V. Rogers and Ian Henderson appear to be proponents of this approach: "A Court has to look at the situation as the accused person saw it and on the basis of the information available to him before making an objective finding about the foreseeability of excessive loss or damage" (Rogers, *supra* note 103, at 207); "An assessment of the proportionality of an attack is based on the circumstances of the commander and the information available to him or her. However, the *conclusions* to be reached on whether collateral damage is *expected* and whether it is *proportional* is then based on what a reasonable person would have concluded from that information" (Henderson, *supra* note 18, at 222 (emphasis in the original)).

129. Henderson, *Id.*

130. Galić, TC, *supra* note 93, para. 58 (citations omitted; emphasis added).

131. "It is suggested that the determination of relative values must be that of the 'reasonable military commander'. Although there will be room for argument in close cases, there will be many cases where reasonable military commanders will agree that the injury to noncombatants or the damage to civilian objects was clearly disproportionate to the military advantage gained" (NATO Bombing Report, *supra* note 34, para. 50; Shany, *supra* note 79, at 67).

132. International Criminal Court, Elements of Crimes 19 n.37 (2011). The Elements of Crime requires that the crime of disproportionate attacks be examined based on the "requisite information available to the perpetrator at the time."

133. "Conduct must be considered from the perspective of the 'reasonable commander' based on the information available at the time, not after the fact." MoFA 2015 Report, *supra* note 83, para. 435.

134. "On the basis of an objective and reasonable estimate of the available information." Int'l Comm. of the Red Cross, *Customary IHL, "Practice Relating to Rule 14. Proportionality in Attack," available at:* ihl-databases.icrc.org/customary-ihl/eng/docs/v2_cha_chapter4_rule14.

the information available at the relevant time. These states include Australia,[135] Austria,[136] France,[137] Italy,[138] and the Netherlands.[139]

Others, however, take the view that the entire analysis must be entirely objective—both the final assessment of proportionality and the information upon which that analysis is based.[140] The international group of experts who authored the HPCR Manual on International Law Applicable to Air and Missile Warfare seem to espouse a fully objective standard for proportionality analysis: the expectations of the attacker regarding the anticipated and expected results of the attack must be reasonable, based on the information reasonably available at the time of the attack.[141] The standard of "reasonableness" is also held by several states with regard to the extent of information on the basis of which proportionality should be assessed. Belgium,[142] Canada,[143] Germany,[144] Ireland,[145] New

135. "The information from all sources, which is available to them at the relevant time." Australia, *Statement on Ratification of AP-I*, Jun. 21, 1991, 1642 U.N.T.S. 473.

136. "Information actually available at the time of the decision is determinative." Austria, *Statement on Ratification of AP-I*, Aug. 13, 1982, 1289 U.N.T.S. 303, *available at:* ihl-databases.icrc.org/applic/ihl/ihl.nsf/Notification.xsp?action=openDocument&documentId=C5CD201B43C3E56AC1256402003FB262.

137. "Sur la base des informations dispose celui qui décide de l'attaque." France, *Statement on Ratification of AP-I*, Apr. 11, 2001.

138. "The information from all sources which is available to them at the relevant time." Italy, *Statement on Ratification of AP-I*, Feb. 27, 1986, 1425 U.N.T.S. 438.

139. "Information from all sources which is *available* to them at the relevant time" (emphasis added). Netherlands, *Statement on Ratification of AP-I*, Jun. 26, 1987, 1477 U.N.T.S. 300, *available at:* ihl-databases.icrc.org/applic/ihl/ihl.nsf/Notification.xsp?action=openDocument&documentId=E6EF925C67966E90C1256402003FB532.

140. Kalshoven seems to be one of these: "Decisive is whether a normally alert attacker who is reasonably well informed and who, moreover, makes reasonable use of the available information could have expected the excessive damage among the civilian population." Kalshoven & Zegveld, *supra* note 99, at 115.

141. HPCR, *supra* note 69, at 91–92. "The standard is objective in that expectations must be reasonable. If the attacker expected, in light of reliable information available at the time, that the collateral damage to civilians or civilians would be excessive relative to the anticipated military advantage, the principle of proportionality will have been violated. . . . They are 'judged in the light of the information reasonably available' at the time."

142. "The only information on which that decision can possibly be taken is such relevant information as is then available and that it has been feasible for him to obtain for that purpose." Belgium, *Statement on Ratification of AP-I*, May 20, 1986, 1435 U.N.T.S. 367.

143. "Information from all sources which is reasonably available to them at the relevant time." Canada, *Statement on Ratification of AP-I*, Nov. 20, 1990, 1591 U.N.T.S. 462.

144. "All information available to him at the relevant time, and not on the basis of hindsight." Germany, *Statement on Ratification of AP-I*, Feb. 14, 1991, 1607 U.N.T.S. 526.

145. "Information from all sources which is reasonably available to them at the relevant time." Ireland, *Statement on Ratification of AP-I*, May 5, 1999, 2073 U.N.T.S. 28, *available at:* ihl-databases.icrc.org/applic/ihl/ihl.nsf/Notification.xsp?action=openDocument&documentId=27BBCD34A4918BFBC1256402003FB43A.

Zealand,[146] Spain,[147] the United Kingdom,[148] and the United States[149] all maintain that the analysis should be based on the information *reasonably* available at the relevant time.

Clearly, then, there is no consensus as to the standard by which proportionality should be examined. Perhaps one of the sources of disagreement lies in the difference between state responsibility and individual criminal responsibility. Arguably, when dealing with criminal responsibility, the primary focus should be on the information that the decision-maker possessed at the time.[150] However, regarding state responsibility for possible violations, a more objective position should be taken, based on the extent of information that can reasonably be expected to have been held.

The objective position seems to us to be also correct as a matter of institutional policy. In trying to deter states from possible violations of international law, we want to incentivize them to base their decisions regarding military operations on the entirety of information available to the state. If a specific commander did not have the relevant information not for lack of resources or time to gather it, but because other state agencies did not share it with him, the state should still be responsible for the violation of the rule. Hence, it seems to us that with regard to state responsibility, the fully objective criterion is a better fit.

We shall return to the attempt to evaluate proportionality in Chapter 11, where we will review various attempts that have been made to inject specific content into the abstract notion of proportionality.

Before concluding this chapter, however, it is worth remembering that trying to determine whether an attack is proportionate—examining the necessary elements, and assigning each the appropriate weight—is a difficult undertaking at the best of times. War is hardly the "best of times." As pointed out by Parks, the

146. "Information from all sources which is reasonably available to them at the relevant time." New Zealand, *Statement on Ratification of AP-I*, Feb. 8, 1988, 1499 U.N.T.S. 358.

147. "The relevant information available at the time and which it has been possible to obtain to that effect." Spain, *Statement on Ratification of AP-I*, Apr. 21, 1989, 1537 U.N.T.S. 390.

148. "Information from all sources which is reasonably available to them at the relevant time." United Kingdom of Great Britain and Northern Ireland, *Reservation*, July 2, 2002, *available at:* ihl-databases.icrc.org/applic/ihl/ihl.nsf/Notification.xsp?action=openDocument&documentId =0A9E03F0F2EE757CC1256402003FB6D2.

149. US, *Statement on Consent to Be Bound by CCW Protocol III on Incendiary Weapons*, Jan. 21, 2009, 2562 U.N.T.S. 36, 37. "Any decision by any military commander, military personnel, or any other person responsible for planning, authorizing or executing military action shall only be judged on the basis of that person's assessment of the information reasonably available to the person at the time the person planned, authorized, or executed the action under review."

150. It is possible to claim that commanders should also be held criminally responsible if they could have obtained the information, so that commanders have an incentive to obtain all possible information. We understand, however, that this criminal standard of "negligence" places a very heavy burden on commanders.

rules governing the conduct of hostilities often seem better suited to academic discussions in the classroom than to the confusion of the battlefield.[151]

However, while Parks's criticism of the rules governing the conduct of hostilities is well justified, there is undoubtedly a crucial need to protect civilians from the vicissitudes of armed conflict. The various component issues presented in this and the previous chapter, as well as the discussions regarding specific applications of proportionality in the following chapters, present the current common understandings of the contours of those protections as they relate to the principle of proportionality. They lay out the protections and shortcomings of proportionality as it currently stands in international law. It is germane to bear in mind the simple words of Union General William Tecumseh Sherman: "War is hell."[152]

151. Parks writes: "A fundamental problem with articles 48 to 58 of Protocol I is that those articles appear to be developed less for combat than for a basketball free-throwing contest in which each opponent obligingly permits the other to shoot his shots. The applicability of the rules to combat would be appropriate if neither opponent had consciously slept for 48 hours; each is ill-fed (if fed at all); the basket is constantly moving, at times obscured by smoke or fog; and the opponent is moving about the court in unknown strength, shooting at the player trying to make his baskets, who may be using a ball that is (perhaps unbeknownst to the shooter) defective or damaged by actions of his opponent. In the midst of this, the non-shooting opponent shifts his basket into the center of the spectator seats, in violation of the rules of the competition." Parks, *supra* note 19, at 182.

152. Michael Newton & Larry May, Proportionality in International Law 91 (2014).

6

# Soldiers vs. Civilians

## A. THE BASIC DILEMMA

Chapter 4 examined the definition of proportionality and discussed what constitutes a military advantage. One aspect of the term "military advantage" merits particular discussion: Should the interest of protecting the lives of soldiers be examined as part of the military advantage anticipated from an attack? To what level of risk should states expose their soldiers in order to minimize harm to civilians? This dilemma, also known as force protection, has been gaining particular prominence in legal discourse and military practice as Western societies have become more averse to suffering casualties of members of their own military.

One paradigmatic example for this dilemma is whether a well-defended military objective within a civilian area should, from a legal perspective, be bombed from the air or attacked by ground troops. Attacking from the air reduces the risk faced by the attacking troops while raising the risk of civilian harm, whereas attacking from the ground arguably lowers the risk of collateral damage but endangers the lives of the attacking soldiers. A second example concerns the altitude from which bombers carry out bombing runs. Bombing military objectives from high altitudes raises the risk of collateral damage, but reduces the risk to the pilots from enemy anti-aircraft fire, while bombing from lower altitudes lowers the risk of mistakenly harming civilians and civilian objects, but raises the risk faced by the pilots.[1]

The stated position of some states is that protecting their own forces constitutes a military advantage and should be considered part of the proportionality analysis.[2]

1. For example, in 1999, NATO airplanes bombed targets in the Federal Republic of Yugoslavia from altitudes above 15,000 feet in order to avoid Yugoslav air defenses. ICTY, *Final Report to the Prosecutor by the Committee Established to Review the NATO Bombing Campaign Against the Federal Republic of Yugoslavia*, para. 64 (2000).

2. This is, for example, the position of the United States, Australia, New Zealand, and Israel. See US Department of Defense, Law of War Manual, para. 5.6.7.3 (2015, updated Dec. 2016); Australia, *Statement on Ratification of AP-I*, Jun. 21, 1991, 1642 U.N.T.S. 473; The State of Israel, Ministry of Foreign Affairs, The 2014 Gaza Conflict: 7 July–26 August 2014: Factual and Legal Aspects 181 (May 2015). This was also the position of the international Group of Experts who authored the HPCR Manual. Program on Humanitarian Policy

*Proportionality in International Humanitarian Law.* Amichai Cohen & David Zlotogorski, Oxford University Press.
 DOI: 10.1093/oso/9780197556726.003.0006

This position is also supported by several scholars.[3] The ICRC, in its *Commentary on AP-I*, takes a different approach and does not consider the protection of one's forces as part of the military advantage in proportionality.[4] There are also scholars who support this latter view.[5]

The issue has become much more important in recent decades, as the value of the lives of soldiers has risen. In the past it could be said that states did not ascribe great value to the lives of their soldiers. In fact, soldiers' lives were open to abuse by their own military and state's chains of command. One has to merely recall such iconic battles as the battle of Verdun during World War I, in which hundreds of thousands of men lost their lives after they were ordered by their own generals to charge enemy trenches with little hope for success.[6]

Over the second half of the 20th century, public opinion has changed significantly in this regard. Opposition to the Vietnam War soared when the media started showing the coffins of dead soldiers being returned to America. In Israel, one of the major factors in the withdrawal from Lebanon in 2000 was the high-profile protests by mothers of soldiers who claimed that their sons' lives were being unnecessarily put at risk.

## B. THE KASHER VS. WALZER DEBATE

The issue of force protection has become the object of heated debate among members of the military and academia. Two opposing sides of the discussion are presented in the opinions of Asa Kasher and Amos Yadlin, on the one hand, and Avishai Margalit and Michael Walzer, on the other.

In 2005, Kasher and Yadlin, an Israeli philosopher and a retired Israeli general, respectively, proposed an ethical code in which they posited that soldiers' lives should have priority over the lives of civilians of the adverse party in cases where

and Conflict Research (HPCR) at Harvard University, *Commentary on the HPCR Manual on International Law Applicable to Air and Missile Warfare*, 92 (2010).

3. See e.g., Yoram Dinstein, The Conduct of Hostilities under the Law of International Armed Conflict 168 (3rd ed., 2016) ("force protection is a valid concern in determining the military advantage of an attack. . . . What is called for is a reasonable 'allocation of risk' between the attacker's military personnel and the collateral damage"); Michael N. Schmitt, *Precision Attack and International Humanitarian Law*, 859 Int'l Rev. Red Cross 445, 462 (2005) ("an attack in which the personnel or equipment are lost is self-evidently not as advantageous as one in which they survive to fight again").

4. According to the Commentary "military advantage can only consist in *ground gained* and in *annihilating or weakening the enemy armed forces*." Commentary on the Additional Protocols of 8 June 1977 to the Geneva Conventions of 12 August 1949, para. 2218 (ICRC, Yves Sandoz, Christophe Swinarki & Bruno Zimmerman eds., 1987) (emphasis added).

5. Gary D. Solis, The Law of Armed Conflict: International Humanitarian Law in War 305 (2nd ed., 2016) ("Force protection does not supersede the requirements of proportionality").

6. Paul Jankowski, Verdun: The Longest Battle of the Great War 117 (2014).

there is a conflict between protecting either the soldiers' or the civilians' lives, as long as the civilians of the adverse party are not under the effective control of one's military.[7] Kasher and Yadlin argued that a state has a duty to protect its own civilians as well as civilians who are under the state's effective control. However, it has no obligation to treat civilians who are not under their control in the same manner. There is no obligation to give such primacy to the lives of those civilians over the lives of one's soldiers. Such an obligation, in their opinion, would practically encourage and enhance terrorism, as it would give non-state armed groups an impetus to embed themselves within the civilian population in order to attain greater protection, thus placing civilians and civilian objects at greater risk.[8]

At the core of this position lies the moral proposition that soldiers are human beings, just like civilians, and that the state's responsibility to protect the lives of its own soldiers supersedes the duty to protect the lives of civilians that are not under that state's control from the risk created by an enemy choosing to conduct its hostilities in their vicinity. Kasher and Yadlin's answer to the examples cited above is that the military is obligated to strike at military targets from the air rather than from the ground, and from higher rather than lower altitudes, in order to minimize harm to soldiers. It should be noted that although the issue of force protection is broader, Kasher and Yadlin limited their discussion and conclusions to a situation of states combatting terror.

Although Kasher and Yadlin seem to propose the preference of the lives of the attacking state's soldiers over those of the enemy's civilians, it seems to us that this claim was made with regard to the specific examples addressed in the article, which require a very complicated balance. We assume that even Kasher and Yadlin would agree that if a very large number of civilian lives can be saved, at the cost of only a small number of soldiers' lives, the preference would be given to the lives of the civilians.

Margalit and Walzer take a different stance on force protection.[9] Part of the criticism leveled at Israel following the 2008–2009 Operation Cast Lead in Gaza, was the allegation that Israel had acted according to Kasher and Yadlin's proposed position, thus causing a high level of casualties among Palestinian civilians.[10] Margalit

7. Asa Kasher & Amos Yadlin, *Military Ethics of Fighting Terror: An Israeli Perspective*, 4 J. Mil. Ethics 3 (2005).

8. Asa Kasher & Amos Yadlin, *Israel & the Rules of War: An Exchange*, The New York Rev. of Books (June 11, 2009), *available at:* www.nybooks.com/articles/2009/06/11/israel-the-rules-of-war-an-exchange/. This discussion is also closely related to the issue of human shields. See Chapter 9.

9. Michael Walzer & Avishai Margalit, *Israel: Civilians & Combatants*, The New York Rev. of Books (May 14, 2009), *available at:* www.nybooks.com/articles/2009/05/14/israel-civilians-combatants/.

10. Ziv Bohrer & Mark J. Osiel, *Proportionality in Military Force at War's Multiple Levels: Averting Civilian Casualties vs. Safeguarding Soldiers*, 46 Vand. J. Transnat'l L. 747, 750 n.5 (2013) (see also the sources cited therein).

and Walzer concluded that states must protect the lives of civilians, regardless of the risk to their own soldiers. In Margalit and Walzer's opinion, soldiers do not enjoy the protection of the right to life during armed conflict. Rather, soldiers become tools of the military and are to be used to achieve military goals. By donning uniforms and training in the use of arms, soldiers impose upon themselves the responsibility to take the risks inherent to soldiering, and the obligation not to shift that risk over to civilians, who are protected under IHL. In the view of Margalit and Walzer, the harm to civilians can be considered incidental to the attack only if the soldiers accept the risk of war in order to reduce the risk to civilians.[11] States are obligated to protect the lives of civilians of the adverse party even if that protection comes at the expense of the lives of their own soldiers. Therefore, in the examples before, Margalit and Walzer's view would require the military to attack the building with ground troops rather than from the air, and where bombing is unavoidable, to do so from low altitudes, in order to avoid or at least limit harm to civilians.

## C. THE LIVES OF SOLDIERS AND PROPORTIONALITY

This issue was extensively discussed at the Proportionality Conference held at the Israel Democracy Institute, where most scholars appeared to take a middle-of-the-road position. On the one hand, almost no one believed that the lives of civilians of the enemy are subordinate to the lives of one's own soldiers, no matter the cost. On the other hand, it seems problematic that no consideration be given to the lives of soldiers compared to the lives of civilians. Consequently, most scholars held that the issue of force protection should be approached as an issue of proportionality. There are several ways in which soldiers' lives can be incorporated into the proportionality analysis.

The first claim is an intuitive one. The idea that the lives of soldiers should not be taken into account at all seems problematic, especially if military service is mandatory. This intuition becomes even stronger when the adverse party to the conflict intentionally violates the principles of IHL by operating from within civilian populations. This intuition, we must stress, is not strictly speaking a legal claim. However, we think it informs much of the discussion regarding force protection. Even if Walzer and Margalit are correct that in armed conflict, soldiers should risk their lives to protect civilians, most people intuitively reject the conclusion that soldiers' lives should not be weighed against those of civilian, particularly when the enemy has no regard to the lives of its own civilian population. This is not to say that soldiers' lives should be given equal importance to the lives of civilians, but they should surely be afforded some consideration.

The second way to present this position is by framing soldiers' lives as part of the military advantage. Soldiers' lives have an instrumental value, whether due to their role in protecting the lives of civilians or as necessary tools for

11. *Id.*, at 747, 773.

carrying out military operations. Consequently, limiting the number of casualties among a state's own soldiers becomes part of the proportionality calculation. According to this view, the lives of soldiers do not supersede the lives of civilians in all circumstances, but rather the lives of soldiers are included as part of the anticipated military advantage in assessing the proportionality of the attack. Thus, force protection is not an end in and of itself, but, rather, is a means of achieving the specific mission or larger strategic military goals. Of course, this argument suffers from an inherent weakness: What if the lives of soldiers do not have instrumental importance for a state's ability to win a battle? In modern conflicts, and particularly in asymmetrical warfare, it is possible that the loss of a single soldier, or even several soldiers, would not diminish the capacity of a modern military to achieve the goals of its mission. If the instrumental value of soldiers was the justification for force protection then it would not carry much weight in some contemporary armed conflicts.

Third, in contemporary armed conflicts, keeping soldiers alive can also be of instrumental value as a means of thwarting the military objectives of some belligerent parties. This argument rests on the assumption that the goal of certain belligerent parties in armed conflicts is to inflict the largest number of casualties on enemy combatants. It can therefore be argued that reducing the number of military casualties suffered becomes part of the military objective of that party.

According to this analysis, however, even if soldiers' lives are included in the military advantage, they should always be balanced against the harm to civilians. In some cases, soldiers will have to take risks in order to protect the enemy's civilian population. In fact, almost all scholars (except Kasher and Yadlin, mentioned before) agree that the lives of civilians, including enemy civilians, should be protected to a greater extent than those of soldiers. This is due to the soldiers' role and their training for armed conflict. Therefore, while soldiers need not bear the risk of preventing *all* harm to enemy civilians, they should still bear the risk inherent in preventing a certain level of harm to enemy civilians.

Regardless of the academic debate, there can be no doubt that throughout history, as well as in contemporary conflicts, the practice of states has consistently been to apply considerations of force protection to their conduct of hostilities. Practical as well as policy considerations are involved in this decision. Not only are militaries averse to endangering members of their own forces—their own people—but practically, one of the few ways of manoeuvring regular ground troops within enemy territory is by using the cover of fire, despite the inherent risks of causing collateral damage. Therefore, in current military doctrine, covering fire—a form of force protection—remains one of the few practical measures by which ground forces can achieve their military goals.

We are aware of only one actual attempt by a quasi-judicial body to claim that a military activity based on "force protection" motivations violate the principle of proportionality. In July 2014, the UN Human Rights Council formed an Independent Commission of Inquiry to look into possible violations of IHL and HRL during the fighting that took place between Israel and Hamas that summer (during the IDF's "Operation Protective Edge").[12] In its report, the Commission referred to the issue of force protection twice. The first time was with regard to the *Shuja'iya* incident, in which significant firepower was used to extract a group of soldiers under fire.[13]

The Commission stated:

> The intense shelling, combined with the use of a large number of one-ton bombs, raise serious concerns about the respect for the principle of proportionality . . . While it is certainly true that the protection of soldiers who are coming under attack represents a concrete and direct military advantage, it is an "undisputed fact that force protection is not an overriding concern that could set aside all other considerations when assessing the proportionality of an attack." . . .
>
> Although the proportionality analysis may properly take into consideration force protection and the neutralization of units of Palestinian armed groups, given the means and methods used by the IDF in Shuja'iya, it is possible to conclude that a reasonable commander would be aware of the potential for such an intense attack to result in the death of a high number of civilians.

The Commission's statement supports the position presented earlier. The real question, however, is *how much* weight should be ascribed to the life of a soldier when assessing the military advantage of an attack.

The Commission also dealt with the issue of force protection in the context of "Black Friday"—a series of events that took place in the city of Rafah in the Gaza Strip on August 1, 2014, when Operation Protective Edge was drawing to a close. Believing that Hamas had succeeded in kidnapping a live Israeli soldier, and in order to prevent them from extracting him from the immediate area, the IDF used immense firepower. Palestinians claimed that dozens of civilians were killed.[14] On this, the Commission said the following:

12. U.N. Human Rights Council, *Report of the Detailed Findings of the Independent Commission of Inquiry Established Pursuant to Human Rights Council Resolution S-21/1.*, U.N. Doc. A/HRC/29/CRP.4. (June 24, 2015), *available at:* https://www.ohchr.org/en/hrbodies/hrc/coigazaconflict/pages/reportcoigaza.aspx [Human Rights Council Report, 2015].

13. *Id.*, para. 296. The Commission based its analysis on the views promoted in Robin Geiss, *The Principle of Proportionality: "Force Protection" as a Military Advantage*, 45 Isr. L. Rev. 74 (2012).

14. On Aug. 1, 2014, IDF soldiers from the Givati paratrooper unit were surveying an area for cross-border tunnels when they were ambushed by Hamas militants. At the time, the area was subject to a humanitarian ceasefire. In the initial exchange of fire, two IDF soldiers were killed. A third soldier, Lt. Hadar Goldin, was kidnapped and dragged inside a nearby tunnel dug by militants. It was subsequently discovered that Lt. Goldin was also killed in the ambush; at the time of this book's writing, his body is still being held by Hamas. At the time of the attack, however, IDF commanders believed Goldin was still alive, and the commanders took decisive

> Preventing the capture [of a soldier] or freeing a soldier from captivity may be conceived as a concrete and direct military advantage, albeit of a limited nature, since the loss of one soldier in a large army such as the IDF does not reduce its military capability.[15]

This blunt statement is somewhat perplexing. The idea that the life of a soldier should be measured only by the reduction in the military force verges on the absurd. The Commission, seemingly aware of this, went on to analyze a different claim regarding the value of the lives of soldiers:

> On the other hand, some have argued that in such a case the proportionality test must take into account the strategic consideration of denying the armed groups the leverage they could obtain over Israel in negotiations for the release of the captured soldier.
>
> The commission considers this an erroneous interpretation of international humanitarian law. The leverage that armed groups may obtain in negotiations does not depend solely on the capture of a soldier, but on how the Government of Israel decides to react to the capture in the aftermath. The strategic military or political advantage sought is therefore not a concrete and direct military advantage as required by international humanitarian law. An assessment of the strategic and political advantage depends on a large number of post facto elements which are merely speculative for the commander on the ground at the moment he decides to launch the attack. Indeed, the proposed interpretation of the anticipated military advantage, which would allow for abstract political and long-term strategic considerations in carrying out the proportionality analysis, would have the consequence of emptying the proportionality principle of any protective element.[16]

The Commission here expressly rejected the third claim made earlier. Prevention of a soldier's kidnapping indeed provides a military advantage. However, the military advantage is limited to the added value of the individual soldier and his contribution to the military force. The Commission maintained that the issue of kidnapping and its effect on military morale could not be considered in the proportionality analysis, which can only consider the damage to the military goal.

As will be explained later,[17] we agree with the committee that strategic goals as such should not enter the calculus of *jus in bello* proportionality. However, we believe that in modern asymmetrical armed conflicts the specific position

actions to attempt a rescue. During the ensuing battle, at least 42 Palestinian militants and 72 civilians were killed.

15. Human Rights Council Report, 2015, *supra* note 12, para. 361.

16. *Id.*, paras. 369–70.

17. See Chapter 7.

of the Commission, as stated earlier, is erroneous. Modern conflicts do not revolve around achieving a "victory" in the traditional sense of crushing the enemy. When a state's armed forces fight an irregular force, to a large extent, the goal of their mission is to complete its operation without a soldier being kidnapped. Kidnapping a state's soldier, much more than killing one, is a specific military objective of the non-state actor. Denying the enemy such an achievement is a legitimate military advantage.

## D. THE CONTEXT OF FORCE PROTECTION

Our position is that the lives of soldiers should be taken into account in proportionality analysis, for legal as well as moral reasons. The only doubt in our minds is the extent to which this should be done and what weight their lives should be given within this analysis.

Regarding force protection, as in other matters, it seems to us that the context of the evaluation is of importance. There are at least three different types of situations in which force protection can be discussed: (1) attacks that are preplanned; (2) situations in which units encounter civilians during an operation; and (3) units that find themselves under attack.

In the first situation, an attack is planned in advance. Here, the extent of the obligation of the attacking army toward the civilians of the other party is at its greatest. As we shall explain later, our view is that precautions in attack, which are the duty of the attacking army during the *planning* of an attack, are the most important part of the implementation of the principle of proportionality. During the planning stage, the attacking army must design the attack in such a way so as to cause the least amount of civilian damage. The relative weight of force protection in these cases is low. Once again, while we believe that some collateral civilian damage is allowed in order to protect soldiers, in the planning stage, the justification for the attacking party to cause civilian deaths due to force protection is at its lowest.[18] The lives of soldiers should be given the least importance in the military advantage part of the proportionality equation.[19]

An example of the extent to which force protection can be taken into account in planning is the NATO bombing campaign in Kosovo in 1999. During that campaign, NATO adopted a 15,000 feet minimum flight altitude for sorties,[20] in

18. For a similar view, see *The Principle of Proportionality in the Rules Governing the Conduct of Hostilities Under International Humanitarian Law*, International Expert Meeting June 22–23, 2016, Quebec 26 (Univesité Laval and ICRC, September 2018) [ICRC Proportionality Report]. At the expert meeting *(Id.)* some raised the idea that when planning, no amount of force protection is allowed at all. This view seems to us to be problematic: clearly, the reasons that force protection is considered a military advantage in the first place are relevant at the planning stage also.

19. The ICRC Proportionality Report *(Id.)* mentions that some states (e.g., Australia, New Zealand) attached a declaration when ratifying AP-I according to which "the term 'military advantage' involves a variety of considerations including the security of the attacking forces."

20. The NATO Bombing Report, *supra* note 1, para. 54.

order to avoid the enemy's air defense. During one sortie, the pilots mistakenly identified a civilian convoy as a military target, an error that resulted in more than 70 civilian fatalities. With respect to this incident, the committee appointed by the ICTY prosecutor for investigating the NATO campaign noted: "it is difficult for any aircrew operating an aircraft flying at several hundred miles an hour and at a substantial height to distinguish between military and civilian vehicles in a convoy." [21] Notwithstanding this comment, the committee found that in this specific instance, no violation of the laws of war had taken place, and that the shooting of the civilian convoy had been an honest mistake.

The second scenario to be considered is when a military force that is already involved in an operation must decide upon the correct way to attack a target or complete a mission. The force realizes that in order to attain the military advantage at minimum cost, there must be some civilian collateral damage. Here the justification for force protection becomes greater. Of course, force protection does not allow an unlimited level of civilian collateral damage, but once a unit is on the ground, the protection of the unit becomes essential. Thus, there is a clear difference between the importance of precautions in attack, during the planning process, and the protection of forces in the ground once an operation is underway. An example of this difference is the decision of the Israeli military advocate-general (MAG) not to launch a criminal investigation into the events of "Black Friday," which occurred during Israel's Operation Protective Edge in the Gaza Strip.[22]

On August 1, 2014, IDF soldiers from the Givati infantry Brigade were surveying an area for cross-border tunnels when they were ambushed by Hamas militia members. At the time, the area was subject to a humanitarian ceasefire. In the initial exchange of fire, two IDF soldiers were killed. A third soldier, Lt. Hadar Goldin, was kidnapped and dragged into a nearby tunnel dug by militants. It was subsequently discovered that Lt. Goldin was also killed in the ambush; at the time of writing, his body is still being held by Hamas. At the time of the attack, however, IDF commanders believed Goldin was still alive, and the commanders took decisive actions to attempt a rescue. During the ensuing battle, at least 42 Palestinian militants and 72 civilians were killed.

21. *Id.*, para. 69.

22. The comments below are based on the Military Advocate General, *Decision of the MAG as to Unusual Events That Occurred during "Operation Protective Edge"—Update No. 6*, IDI (Aug. 15, 2018) (Heb.), *available at:* https://www.idf.il/%D7%90%D7%AA%D7%A8%D7%99%D7%9D/%D7%94%D7%A4%D7%A8%D7%A7%D7%9C%D7%99%D7%98%D7%95%D7%AA-%D7%94%D7%A6%D7%91%D7%90%D7%99%D7%AA/%D7%A2%D7%93%D7%9B%D7%95%D7%A0%D7%99-%D7%A6%D7%95%D7%A7-%D7%90%D7%99%D7%AA%D7%9F/%D7%94%D7%97%D7%9C%D7%98%D7%95%D7%AA-%D7%94%D7%A4%D7%A6%D7%A8-%D7%91%D7%90%D7%A9%D7%A8-%D7%9C%D7%90%D7%99%D7%A8%D7%95%D7%A2%D7%99%D7%9D-%D7%97%D7%A8%D7%99%D7%92%D7%99%D7%9D-%D7%91%D7%9E%D7%A2%D7%A8%D7%9B%D7%AA-%D7%A6%D7%95%D7%A7-%D7%90%D7%99%D7%AA%D7%9F-%D7%A2%D7%93%D7%9B%D7%95%D7%9F-6/.

The MAG was charged with investigating whether the firepower used in response to the ambush was proportional. A disproportionate response would have violated IHL as well as the IDF's own operational directives.

The MAG responded to allegations of disproportionate use of fire by IDF soldiers on a number of levels. Such allegations included claims that the IDF went on a rampage following the abduction of Lt. Goldin; massively and indiscriminately firing artillery, mortars, and tank shells into densely populated Rafah; hitting scores of civilians; and harming numerous civilian objects. Amnesty International, for example, alleged that Israel committed serious violations of IHL, which may amount to war crimes.

The first part of the MAG's report was dedicated to rejecting claims that Israeli forces either directed fire at civilians during the operation or ignored the principle of proportionality altogether because IDF commanders assumed that a soldier had been abducted. According to the MAG, there was no such command or event. With regard to the number of casualties, the MAG asserted that most of the 72 civilians were killed in airstrikes carried out during active combat in the southeastern part of Rafah.

In discussing the proportionality of the firepower used by the IDF during the incident, the MAG's Update No. 6 presents an important analysis of the IDF's military objectives following the ambush, which offers insight into how commanders on the ground would have weighed anticipated harm to civilian lives and objects. According to the MAG, proportionality analysis should not focus on determining whether the significant firepower used by the IDF was justified in order to prevent the abduction of one IDF soldier. Rather, it should focus on whether the use of force was justified in light of the specific combat missions of the IDF forces that responded to the abduction. The ambush directed against the Givati patrol and the subsequent abduction of Lt. Goldin were merely the "trigger" for the collapse of the humanitarian ceasefire and resumption of active hostilities. Thus, IDF forces entered the area in which the ceasefire was violated en masse and attacked legitimate targets in Rafah, including Hamas militants and other military and dual-use targets, such as access roads for potential enemy reinforcement. The MAG concluded that the firepower used in these attacks has to be assessed against the concrete military advantage expected in IDF combat operations against Hamas militants, as well as against the operational need to provide covering fire for the movement of troops in the theatre of hostilities.

Following this proportionality analysis, the document goes on to discuss the application of the proportionality rule to specific IDF military actions. With respect to each of the actions, the MAG found no evidence of a violation of Israeli or international law in light of the IDF's concrete military advantage and the limited anticipated civilian harm.

The assumption of the Israeli MAG in this analysis is clear, and follows the logic presented earlier: once the humanitarian ceasefire collapsed, the forces on the ground were faced with the need to act quickly, and their protection due to this need required more firepower, which could result in more civilian casualties.

One can assume that the MAG is correct in observing that most of the harm to Palestinian civilians occurred during attacks undertaken in connection with the concrete objectives of military operations which resumed after Hamas violated the ceasefire, and not in connection with specific actions taken to recover Lt. Goldin. Yet the MAG admits that had the operation been conducted with more advance planning, rather than as an emergency response to (what was believed to be) the abduction of Lt. Goldin, the safety of manoeuvring forces could have been secured through means requiring less firepower, which might have entailed fewer civilian casualties.[23]

The third situation of force protection is where soldiers find themselves under direct fire, and act in self-defense. The ICRC proportionality report details a disagreement as to whether soldiers can even be expected to apply the principle of proportionality when their lives are at danger.[24] We are of the view that proportionality applies even when a military force is under direct fire. As a practical matter, of course, a unit that comes under surprise attack cannot be expected to gather full information regarding civilians in the area before responding, and will tend to use more aggressive firepower. This, however, is not a reason to disregard proportionality as a guiding principle. Even when coming under direct fire, troops have an obligation to understand that firepower that will cause excessive death of civilians is prohibited.

## E. THE ENEMY'S SOLDIERS

An important twist to the soldier/civilian divide arises in the question whether proportionality takes the lives of the enemy's soldiers into account. According to the classic formulation of IHL, proportionality is a branch of the principle of distinction. The formal definition of the principle of proportionality frames it as an attack that is "indiscriminate," that is, in violation of the principle of distinction. The heading of Article 51 to AP-I, where the definition of the principle of proportionality is found is "protection of the civilian population."

In recent years, however, several IHL scholars have suggested that the principle of proportionality should also protect enemy soldiers, and not just the civilian population.[25] The logic behind this claim is that soldiers are also human beings, and that as much as possible should be done to ensure that their lives are spared.

23. See Amichai Cohen & Yuval Shany, *Israel's Military Advocate General Terminates "Black Friday" and Other Investigations: Initial Observations*, LAWFARE (Aug. 27, 2018), *available at:* www.lawfareblog.com/israels-military-advocate-general-terminates-black-friday-and-other-investigations-initial.

24. ICRC Proportionality Report, *supra* note 18, at 27. Some experts apparently thought that when troops come under surprise attack, they cannot be expected to consider proportionality at all, and act in "self-defense."

25. E.g., MICHAEL NEWTON & LARRY MAY, PROPORTIONALITY IN INTERNATIONAL LAW 287 (2014).

The Kasher vs. Walzer debate regarding force protection is relevant to this issue, too. For Walzer, IHL is about making sure that soldiers kill only each other, and not civilians. Protection of the lives of soldiers, according to this view, lies outside the realm of the principles of proportionality.

As already mentioned, there are those who disagree with this category-based use of the principles of distinction and proportionality.[26] Gabriella Blum, for example, advocates taking the lives of soldiers into account in the application of the principle of proportionality.[27] This view regards the principle of proportionality as an application of the principle of Humanity, a principle that protects all human beings, soldiers and civilians alike. It would seem that Kasher might agree, at least partially, with this view. Kasher bases his position supporting force protection on the idea that the state has a duty to protect its own soldiers. In other words, Kasher finds relevant duties to protect that exist irrespective of the soldier/civilian distinction. If so, the universal duty to protect lives must surely be relevant, especially if we assume the parallel application of HRL and IHL.[28]

Either way, this discussion seems to us to be somewhat hypothetical. We know of no state that takes the lives of enemy soldiers, or combatants, into account in the application of the principle of proportionality.

26. Chapter 2, note 24 and accompanying text.

27. Gabriela Blum, *The Dispensable Lives of Soldiers*, 2(1) J. LEGAL ANAL. 69 (2010).

28. See our discussion in Chapter 3, Section D.

# 7

# Strategic and Cultural Considerations

The previous chapters outlined the general contours of the principle of proportionality as a balancing act between incidental damage to civilians and the military advantage anticipated from an attack. The military advantage discussed is generally understood as referring to a set of narrow, operational, considerations—gaining ground, and harming the enemy and holding them back.[1] We also addressed the question of whether military advantage should only be assessed regarding each individual strike in isolation, or in relation to the attack as a whole.[2]

An additional and related question is whether the proportionality of an attack is affected by broader considerations, such as the context of the conflict and its circumstances. More specifically, can cultural or strategic considerations—such as each party's capabilities, military goals or aims, sensibilities, and vulnerabilities—be weighed as part of the military advantage anticipated from an attack?[3]

This issue recently received attention when Michael Schmitt and John Merriam reviewed the practices of the Israel Defense Forces (IDF) during the 2014 Gaza Conflict, and argued that cultural sensitivities within Israeli society had been taken into account by the IDF as part of the military advantage in its proportionality assessments made during the operation. Schmitt and Merriam referred to

1. For a discussion of what is considered as giving a military advantage, see Chapter 4, notes 5–34 and the accompanying text.

2. See Chapter 4, notes 35–63 and the accompanying text.

3. Even if cultural considerations are not included as a matter of international law, they may still serve to raise the bar of their domestic legal obligations. A case that might illustrate this point occurred in 2008, when German forces in Afghanistan permitted the escape of an important Taliban leader who had links to the killers of British troops, though they had him in their gun sights. The German rules of engagement in Afghanistan, which the British press derided after the incident, permitted use of lethal force only in strict cases of self-defense. For further details regarding the incident, see Michael Newton & Larry May, Proportionality in International Law 27 (2014). Obviously, the reason for a specific regulation in a state's rules of engagement might not necessarily be legal. The rule could be based on broader societal norms or could exist in order to prevent animosity from the local population.

*Proportionality in International Humanitarian Law.* Amichai Cohen & David Zlotogorski, Oxford University Press.
 DOI: 10.1093/oso/9780197556726.003.0007

this as a "contextual application of the rule of proportionality."[4] These sensitivities included the desire to reduce harm to Israeli civilians and soldiers[5] and the perception of being "under siege," due to the threat posed by the large arsenal of cheap rockets possessed by Hamas and Hezbollah:

> The destruction of rockets and rocket-launching infrastructure (often in the form of civilian houses converted to military use in order to deter Israeli attack) has a high degree of "anticipated military advantage," such that it may justify (from the IDF's standpoint) levels of collateral damage that may strike outside observers as potentially excessive.[6]

One of the authors of this book, Amichai Cohen, together with Yuval Shany, criticized Schmitt and Merriam's position. They opined that allowing strategic or cultural considerations into the assessment of proportionality would complicate an already complex equation. According to Cohen and Shany,[7] Schmitt and Merriam's interpretation is contrary to the law and would also make the determination of the proportionality of an attack even more difficult, especially for the commanders in the field who would be tasked with the decision in real time.

This discussion centers upon several concepts. We shall discuss them separately, and will then pull the different threads together and present coherent conclusions.

## A. THE MEANING OF "CONCRETE AND DIRECT MILITARY ADVANTAGE"

The first claim against including strategic and cultural considerations is that these are not included in the definition of military advantage according to IHL.

As far as the definition of proportionality is concerned, it can be argued that cultural and strategic considerations are not included within the "concrete and direct military advantage" that must be anticipated from an attack.[8] The ICRC, in its commentary on article 57 of AP-I, writes that "The expression 'concrete and direct' was intended to show that the advantage concerned should be substantial

4. Michael Schmitt & John Merriam, *A Legal and Operational Assessment of Israel's Targeting Practices,* Just Security (Apr. 24, 2015), *available at:* www.justsecurity.org/22392/legal-operational-assessment-israels-targeting-practices/.

5. Michael N. Schmitt & John J. Merriam, *The Tyranny of Context: Israeli Targeting Practices in Legal Perspective,* 37 U. Pa. J. Int'l L. 53, 127 (2015).

6. *Id.*

7. Amichai Cohen & Yuval Shany, *Contextualizing Proportionality Analysis? A Response to Schmitt and Merriam on Israel's Targeting Practices,* Just Security (May 5, 2015), *available at:* www.justsecurity.org/22786/contextualizing-proportionality-analysis-response-schmitt-merriam/ [Cohen & Shany, *Contextualizing Proportionality Analysis*].

8. For a discussion of the definition of this term, see Chapter 4, notes 18–34 and the accompanying text.

and relatively close, and that advantages which are hardly perceptible and those which would only appear in the long term should be disregarded."[9]

In the Elements of Crime of the Rome Statute, Article 8(2)(b)(iv) interprets the term "concrete and direct overall military advantage" differently, requiring that the military advantage be "foreseeable by the perpetrator at the relevant time. Such advantage may or may not be temporally or geographically related to the object of the attack."[10] The term "foreseeable" seems to relate to proximity in probabilities and causal relations between the attack and the advantage, not some general strategic claim.

An alternative interpretation of the language of the article is also possible: that cultural and strategic considerations should be included, as long as they are "substantial and relatively close," or "foreseeable . . . at the relevant time." The United States' position appears to support the view that strategic considerations are part of the military advantage.[11]

We acknowledge that here, as in many other cases, the language can be interpreted either way. We must, then, consider various policy arguments on the issue.

## B. POLICY ARGUMENTS REGARDING STRATEGIC AND CULTURAL CONSIDERATIONS

### The Divide between IHL and Laws on the Use of Force

One major problem with the inclusion of strategic and cultural considerations within the concept of military advantage is that they seem to have no place in IHL, but rather belong only to the question of the legality of the use of force—*jus ad bellum*. The IHL level of analysis is intended to guide tactical considerations applied by commanders on the field or by the operational command. Strategic considerations are the purview of the military high command and their political superiors.

As Cohen and Shany write:

> Including such considerations—which appear to be neither concrete nor direct, nor strictly military—in the balance between military necessity and humanitarian interests not only renders an already difficult exercise of weighing competing interests hopelessly ambiguous; it also runs the risk of conflating the "big picture" strategic *jus ad bellum* with the "isolated attack" tactical *jus*

9. Commentary on the Additional Protocols of 8 June 1977 to the Geneva Conventions of 12 August 1949, para. 2209 (ICRC, Yves Sandoz, Christophe Swinarki, & Bruno Zimmerman eds., 1987).

10. International Criminal Court, Elements of Crimes, 19 n.36 (2011).

11. US Department of Defense, Law of War Manual, para. 2.2.3.1 (2015, updated Dec. 2016) ("in assessing the military advantage of attacking an object, one may consider the entire war strategy rather than only the potential tactical gains from attacking that object").

> *in bello* proportionality analysis. Furthermore, by referring to broad policy objectives, such as addressing public views, the contextualized approach places a much too heavy burden on soldiers and field commanders, and deprives them of the ability to exercise discretion in relation to the specific attack which they plan to conduct on the basis of more grounded factors, which may be within their professional grasp.[12]

The inclusion of strategic considerations would mean that, in practice, proportionality would not be implemented as part of the operation itself at all. When every target is considered part of a larger scheme of military advantage, no field commander can seriously balance the lives of civilians against such important tasks.

## An Inherent or Tangible Military Advantage?

Another argument against including cultural and strategic considerations in proportionality analysis is that they are not strictly military considerations. For example, casualty aversion—societal reluctance to suffer civilian or military casualties—does not necessarily have a direct correlation with the military advantage of a military operation. A society may, for example, greatly fear the loss of a single soldier's life, even in situations in which each individual soldier, and his life, provides little operational contribution to military activity. For example, contrary to a fighter-pilot, who is directly contributing to the military activity, a soldier holding an administrative job far from the front, might have a very limited contribution to the military activity. If a state has casualty aversion can it take extreme measures to protect the life of that soldiers strictly because of the societal fear of a loss of a single life? It may therefore be argued that there is no justification for including these subjective, societal considerations in the proportionality analysis.

A possible counterargument is that such considerations may have a tangible and detrimental effect on the capacity of certain states to achieve their military goals. For example, if a state has a high aversion to civilian and military casualties, that state could be forced to end an armed conflict prematurely or at a disadvantage, if the number of casualties it suffers becomes too high.[13] It could therefore

12. Cohen & Shany, *Contextualizing Proportionality Analysis*, *supra* note 7.

13. This consideration is known as the "body-bag effect." In democratic societies, military operations require public support in order to continue over time. The body-bag effect is the assumed causal link seen at times in democratic societies between rising casualties in armed conflicts and the ensuing erosion of public support for those same military operations (Ziv Bohrer & Mark Osiel, *Proportionality in War: Protecting Soldiers from Enemy Captivity, and Israel's Operation Cast Lead—"The Soldiers Are Everyone's Children,"* 22 S. Cal. Interdisc. L.J. 637, 666 (2013) [Bohrer & Osiel, *Proportionality in War*]). Bohrer and Osiel also argue that Western societies conduct their hostilities with a view to reducing the casualties that their forces suffer. See: Ziv Bohrer & Mark J. Osiel, *Proportionality in Military Force at War's Multiple Levels: Averting Civilian Casualties vs. Safeguarding Soldiers*, 46 Vand. J. Transnat'l L. 747, 808–809 (2013).

be argued that when interpreting the law, the term "military advantage" should be read in light of the larger societal context.

The problem with this argument is that if the law were based on subjective perceptions, different standards would exist for the different parties to the conflict. Parties to armed conflicts that place value on their soldiers' lives would be permitted to inflict more civilian casualties than parties who attach a lower value to their own soldiers' lives. This seems to us to run counter to the basic goals of IHL as an objective legal framework applicable to all parties to a conflict. Moreover, if the overarching role of IHL, and of the principle of proportionality, is to limit civilian casualties, it makes no sense to allow a state that declares that it is not willing to suffer any, or almost any, military casualties, to protect its soldiers at the price of greater damage to the enemy's civilians.

## Uncertainty and Manipulations

A major problem with the inclusion of strategic considerations is that such considerations are inherently uncertain and open to manipulation. A state may claim that it is especially vulnerable to certain kinds of attack, or that its enemies direct their attacks at specific targets because of their importance, but there is no real way to verify this. Yishai Schwartz explains this problem:

> When we think of the value of taking an enemy position, reasonable observers are likely to come to relative agreement. But when we evaluate the importance of protecting an ancient temple or the impact of a single operation on the enemy's morale, we are in uncharted territory where self-serving evaluations become unacceptably likely. In these situations, it is all too easy (and tempting) to magnify the advantage—and to kill a great number of civilians quite quickly. So even as there is no true conceptual distinction between "broad, strategic" and "concrete and direct," we use the terms as useful stand-ins for distinguishing between military advantages that are more certain (and less susceptible to abuse) and those that are less certain (and more susceptible). There is no firm line here; just varying shades of gray.[14]

A more compelling argument for including strategic and cultural considerations in proportionality analysis is that these represent actual military goals. The parties to the conflict are able to internalize and target each other's strategic and cultural vulnerabilities. At face value, these considerations stem from the parties' subjective perceptions, and do not represent tangible goals. However, it is undeniable

This in turn encourages leaders to protect the lives of the soldiers serving in the armed forces, an issue that is also closely related to the issue of force protection, discussed in Chapter 6.

14. Yishai Schwartz, *Defining Anticipated Military Advantage: The Importance of Certainty*, LAWFARE (May 22, 2015), *available at:* www.lawfareblog.com/defining-anticipated-military-advantage-importance-certainty.

that if one party to the conflict realizes that such vulnerabilities can be used to force concessions from the adverse party, then it could alter its own military policy and operations accordingly, changing its military goals or tactics in order to better exploit the first party's vulnerabilities.[15] In this manner, considerations that might be seen as having only a subjective value could arguably become a tangible military advantage, justifying their inclusion in proportionality analysis.

It can, therefore, be argued that strategic and cultural considerations should be considered in proportionality if they become part of the military advantage sought by the adverse party or are perceived as conferring a military advantage. Adopting this approach may also lessen parties' abilities to manipulate their strategic and cultural vulnerabilities. If the adverse party to the conflict is willing to invest in exploiting certain vulnerabilities, these may be considered "concrete and direct."

For example, on the basis of three decades of experience with Israel, Hezbollah concluded that Israel has an extreme aversion to civilian as well as military casualties. Hezbollah also noted Israeli society's fear of the prospect of captured soldiers. Israel's horror at the thought of a kidnapped soldier rotting in a cell, possibly being tortured, has led to its willingness to go to great lengths obtain the release of captured soldiers.[16] While these considerations are not military in nature, both Hezbollah and Hamas have attempted to exploit Israel's cultural sensitivities and go to great lengths in their attempt to capture Israeli soldiers, and to kill as many civilians and soldiers as possible.[17] Hamas and Hezbollah have framed the successful kidnapping of soldiers as a game-changer; they consider kidnapping a soldier a monumental achievement. These goals therefore become the center of their military plans and operations when they engage in armed conflicts.

It can therefore be argued that Israel, cognizant of these military goals of Hezbollah and Hamas, should be entitled to consider these goals in its proportionality analyses. If so, Israel should be allowed to use more force, and to cause more collateral damage, in order to prevent its adversaries from attaining their military goals.

15. Schwartz, *id.*, assumes that this is actually what Schmitt and Merriam claim, without expressly saying it, and that this is why they focus on the way Hezbollah perceives Israel's vulnerabilities. See: Michael Schmitt, *The Relationship Between Context and Proportionality: A Reply to Cohen and Shany*. Just Security, (May 11, 2015), *available at:* www.justsecurity.org/22948/response-cohen-shany/. This policy would be in tune with the timeless words of Sun Tzu: "If you know the enemy and know yourself, you need not fear the result of a hundred battles." Sun Tzu, The Art of War 51 (Lionel Giles trans., 2002).

16. See the discussion below.

17. Bohrer & Osiel, *Proportionality in War*, *supra* note 13, at 659. For example, Hezbollah captured five Israeli soldiers in two separate incidents on the Lebanese-Israeli border: Adi Avitan, Benyamin Avraham, and Omar Sawaid were kidnapped on Oct. 7, 2000; and Ehud Goldwasser and Eldad Regev were kidnapped on July 12, 2006. A similar attempt to kidnap soldiers on November 21, 2005 failed.

There are some who hold that not taking such considerations into account would lead to a normative framework that is divorced from reality.[18] As discussed earlier, the facts on the ground have made these considerations tangible military goals,[19] and thus it can be claimed that preventing the kidnapping of an Israeli soldier, even at the cost of harming civilians, may prevent harm to other civilians in the future.

## C. WHO BEARS THE BURDEN OF ACCOMMODATING A STATE'S SENSITIVITIES?

The previous argument, while it may seem logical as a matter of realpolitik, should be rejected on normative grounds. The normative question here is this: Who should bear the burden for the vulnerability of a state—the vulnerable state itself, or the civilians of the other party to the conflict? Including subjective cultural and strategic considerations in proportionality analysis places the added costs and risks posed by these considerations on the shoulders of civilians, often those of the opposing party. Should State B's civilians suffer more casualties merely because State A has a more casualty-averse culture?

Some might use the case of the kidnapping of an Israeli soldier to illustrate this point. As discussed in the previous chapter, on August 1, 2014, during that summer's large-scale conflict between Israel and Hamas in Gaza, Israel received information that an officer, Lt. Hadar Goldin, was kidnapped by Hamas in Rafah. In an attempt to stop the kidnappers from escaping the immediate area, Israel engaged in a broad operation involving extensive fire and large numbers of troops, which resulted in many civilian deaths. Schmitt and Merriam seem to ascribe the civilian casualties to the cultural perceptions of Israelis and their fear for kidnapped soldiers.[20] Similar claims may be made regarding the issue of release of terrorists: Israel has the choice whether or not to release terrorists in exchange

18. Some of which were voiced at the Proportionality Conference.

19. One additional argument made in favor of using extreme force to prevent the capture of a soldier is that the unfortunate loss of civilian life now may prevent the deaths of other civilians in the long run. Israeli soldiers captured by the enemy are often returned to Israel as part of extremely large and unbalanced prisoner exchanges. In 2011, Gilad Shalit, an Israeli soldier who had been captured and held by Hamas in Gaza for 5 years, was returned to Israel by Hamas in return for 1,027 prisoners who were collectively responsible for killing 600 Israelis and injuring thousands more. According to various sources, a large number of those released prisoners subsequently returned to committing acts of terror, with recidivism rates ranging from 45% to 80%. The head of the Israeli Mossad has stated that the prisoners released in one of these exchanges have since killed 231 Israelis. Bohrer & Osiel, *Proportionality in War*, *supra* note 13, at 653, n.94.

20. According to Jewish law and culture, every single person is considered to constitute an entire world. This understanding stems back as far as the Mishna and Talmud, compiled around the years 200 and 500 CE, in which it is written: "Whoever saves a life, it is considered as if he saved an entire world" (Mishnah Sanhedrin 4:5; Yerushalmi Talmud 4:9, Babylonian Talmud Sanhedrin 37a). This may explain, at least in part, the Israeli aversion to killed and kidnapped soldiers and civilians.

for captured soldiers; it is under no obligation to release a single terrorist, as long as it is willing to allow its captured soldiers to remain in the hands of Hamas or Hezbollah.[21]

As Cohen and Shany write:

> Even if Israel's military adversaries are keen to exploit Israeli sensitiveness to kidnapped soldiers, it is difficult to accept that this should have any effect on the enemy's civilian population. Put differently, it is not clear to us why the civilian population affected by Israeli military operations should incur the additional burden of a contextualized proportionality analysis and be punished thereby for the culturally based strategic choices of the two clashing militaries and governments, above and beyond the burden associated with a narrower tactical proportionality analysis.[22]

Perhaps this is simply a matter of context.[23]

## A Matter of Context?

Following the events in Rafah described before, Israel came under harsh criticism. It was accused of having violated the principle of proportionality.[24] However, let us ponder a related hypothetical dilemma:[25] What would have happened if Prince Harry, Knight Commander of the Royal Victorian Order and grandson of Queen Elizabeth II, were kidnapped during an operation in Afghanistan? How would the world and the Commonwealth of Nations responded? Is it safe to assume that the international community and NATO would rush in to try to locate and rescue Prince Harry using almost any means at their disposal? How would any other state respond to the abduction of a leader of that state's son or daughter?

This test case refers to an individual who has particular symbolic importance, although from a strict military perspective, he has no more significant than any other individual. Should the response to such a situation be different from the response to the capture of any other soldier or civilian? Perhaps, then, context does matter. Indeed, some societies might ascribe more symbolic weight to their royal

21. This was the position stated in the 2015 Human Rights Council Report. See: U.N. Human Rights Council, *Report of the Detailed Findings of the Independent Commission of Inquiry Established Pursuant to Human Rights Council Resolution S-21/1.*, U.N. Doc. A/HRC/29/CRP.4. (June 24, 2015).

22. Cohen & Shany, *Contextualizing Proportionality Analysis, supra* note 7.

23. This point also concerns the question of the use of human shields and its effect on proportionality. For further discussion, see Chapter 9.

24. Human Rights Council Report, 2015, *supra* note 21, paras. 364–74.

25. Raised by one of the participants at the Proportionality Conference.

families than others. Would this alter the response, and how should that affect the common person?

Let us consider another case: State A is aiming two rockets at two different civilian targets in the United States—the first, at a civilian office building, and the second, at the Statue of Liberty. Both buildings are civilian objects, and for the sake of argument, let us assume that the civilian casualties are expected to be the same. However, it seems intuitive that the United States should be permitted to cause more harm to the civilians surrounding the rocket launcher aimed at the Statue of Liberty than the one targeting the office building. This is due to the relative cultural or strategic significance of the two targets.[26] Destroying or even partially damaging such a symbol, could have a strategic impact on both sides, which might then justify more collateral damage.

## Permitting Less Collateral Damage?

While these considerations could lead to added protection in the case of states that value the lives of their soldiers more highly, it could easily lead to diminished protection afforded to soldiers in the case of states that have little regard for their soldiers' lives. Let us consider an armed conflict between State A, which treats each of its soldiers as a person deserving respect and protection; and State B, which ascribes no value to the lives of its soldiers or civilians and treats them as redundant pawns in a game. In this case, cultural considerations might justify State A causing significant collateral harm to protect its troops, while State B would be practically barred from causing any collateral harm, because the lives' of its citizens and soldiers have no importance in its eyes.

These differences might lead to even more jarring results if different societies place different value on civilian life. Take for example the question of the lives of minorities. Consider the case of a regime that considers the lives of certain individuals to be less valuable than others because of their ethnic origin or religion. Should the opposing state be allowed to cause *more* collateral damage to those civilians because of these discriminatory practices?

Such an interpretation of the principle of proportionality could undermine IHL, which is grounded in the principle of the equal application of the law to all parties to the conflict. Taking cultural differences between adverse parties into account brings the application of IHL close to theories of cultural relativism,[27] and undermines its basic tenet as a universal code. This approach could lead to asymmetry in the application of IHL and also to abuse of the law by one or both

26. Under IHL, cultural property receives special protection from attack. See generally, Roger O'Keefe, *Protection of Cultural Property, in* The Handbook of International Humanitarian Law 425, 425–63 (3rd ed., Dieter Fleck ed., 2013). Nonetheless, this special protection does not alter how the proportionality would change in the scenario described above.

27. Cohen & Shany, *supra* note 7.

of the parties.[28] It introduces highly subjective components into the equation and makes the law less predictable.

It should be noted that the NATO Bombing Report discussed the issue of the subjective effect of the backgrounds and the culture of decision-makers on their decision regarding proportionality. The Committee appears to have rejected this position, noting that:

> The answers may differ depending on the background and values of the decision-maker. It is unlikely that a human rights lawyer and an experienced combat commander would assign the same relative values to military advantage and to injury to noncombatants. Further, it is unlikely that military commanders with different doctrinal backgrounds and differing degrees of combat experience or national military histories would always agree in close cases. It is suggested that the determination of relative values must be that of the "reasonable military commander."[29]

## D. DIFFERENT REQUIREMENTS FOR DIFFERENT STATES?

The position just elaborated—rejecting differences between states according to strategic and cultural considerations—should be distinguished from the position that supports a higher burden on more technologically advanced countries in the application of the principle of proportionality. Such a position was taken, among others, by Professor Gabriella Blum.[30] According to Blum, states with more advanced technological capabilities should be held to higher standards in IHL. Blum makes the point that states that enjoy an objective advantage over other states are able to employ more precautions than states with fewer capabilities.[31] "The application of the principle of proportionality," writes Blum ". . . is susceptible to considerations of relative power, capabilities, and resources, all of which potentially affect the application of the standard to differently situated parties."[32] Hence, the point Blum is making is not about different strategic or cultural considerations, but rather the *different capabilities* of states. One may still reject the position taken by Schmitt and Merriam regarding strategic considerations, and accept that there are cases in which the technological abilities of states mandate that they be held to a higher standard.

28. *Id.* On asymmetry in IHL in general, see Michael N. Schmitt, *Asymmetrical Warfare and International Humanitarian Law*, 62 A.F. L. Rev. 1 (2008).

29. ICTY, *Final Report to the Prosecutor by the Committee Established to Review the NATO Bombing Campaign Against the Federal Republic of Yugoslavia*, para. 50 (2000).

30. Gabriella Blum, *On a Differential Law of War*, 52 Harv. J. Int'l L. 164 (2011).

31. *Id.*, at 192.

32. *Id.*

An example of the possible different technologies available to states as affecting their different obligations are defensive technologies, such as Israel's missile defense shield, Iron Dome.

Iron Dome is a missile defense system deployed by Israel to provide protection from rockets with ranges of up to 70 km. The system is capable of discriminating between dangerous rockets, that is, those likely to hit objectives, and those which will land in open areas or fields, thus posing less harm to civilians and military personnel and hardware. The Iron Dome system has reportedly intercepted 85–90% of the rockets it was activated to intercept.[33]

Prior to the deployment of Iron Dome, Hamas rockets were capable of hitting civilian and military areas in Israel with relative ease. It was therefore clear that there was a military advantage in the destruction of Hamas's rockets. However, after the success of Iron Dome, some argue that while Hamas rockets or rocket launchers still present a legitimate military target, the Iron Dome system may have changed the proportionality analysis. Attacking Hamas's rockets no longer gives the same military advantage, as each rocket now has a very small probability of causing harm to Israel or its civilians. If targeting rockets and rocket launchers gives a smaller military advantage, then, one could argue that such attacks would be unlawful if they were to cause significant collateral civilian damage.

Schmitt and Merriam maintain that defensive capabilities, such as the Iron Dome missile defense system, lower the military advantage obtained from targeting enemy rockets and rocket launchers to a certain degree.[34] Consistent with their general position regarding strategic considerations, as described already, they consider it "appropriate to consider defeat of the enemy's strategic objectives as a factor in calculating the military advantage of an attack, so long as the enemy is seeking to achieve said objectives militarily," as opposed to undermining enemy civilian morale.[35] However, with regard to the operational or tactical proportionality calculus, they agree that the use of defensive weapons makes a difference.

The Israeli Ministry of Foreign Affairs (MoFA) holds a different view. In its report on the 2014 Gaza Conflict, the MoFA opined that the existence of missile defenses, such as Iron Dome, does "not diminish the military value of

33. See: *Iron Dome*, RAFAEL, Advanced Defense Systems Ltd. *available at:* www.rafael.co.il/Marketing/186-1530-en/Marketing.aspx; *Watching Israel's Missile Defense*, CNN (Nov. 20, 2012) security.blogs.cnn.com/2012/11/20/watching-israels-missile-defense/; Steven Erlanger, *A Growing Arsenal of Homegrown Rockets Encounters Israel's Iron Dome*, New York Times (July 9, 2014) www.nytimes.com/2014/07/10/world/middleeast/israel-gaza-missiles-iron-dome.html. For an analysis of the legal aspects of the use of the iron dome system, see Daphne Richmond Barak & Eyal Feinberg, *The Irony of the Iron Dome: Intelligent Defense Systems, Law, and Security*, 7 Harv. Nat'l Sec. J. 469 (2016).

34. Schmitt & Merriam, *supra* note 5, at 128.

35. *Id.*, at 129–30.

IDF offensive operations aimed at curtailing that fire."[36] According to Israel, rockets have intrinsic military value and their firing affected IDF operations and caused deaths and injuries to civilians and soldiers. The high cost of the defense system also needs to be diverted from other sources. Furthermore, this interpretation, according to which deploying defensive military platforms alters the proportionality analysis to the detriment of the defending state, creates a negative incentive that could arguably lower states' investments in the defense of its civilians. This undermines one of the basic humanitarian rationales behind IHL.[37]

Effective defensive weapons, those which can be assumed to block a significant proportion of attacks, are a new phenomenon, and their use in combat was limited until recently, so that discussions regarding the application of IHL toward these weapon systems are still scarce. Thus, the legal position here is open to discussion. Furthermore, we support the view that IHL should generally incentivize the development of such weapon systems, which have the potential to reduce civilian casualties.

However, it also seems to us that, ultimately, the question of how much civilian collateral damage one party to the conflict is allowed to inflict on the other party must be connected to the actual military advantage. A party to the conflict that possesses effective defensive systems cannot calculate the military advantage it attains while ignoring the defensive systems. The incentives to develop such systems are not based on the ability to cause civilian casualties to the enemy, but rather on the desire to protect one's own civilian population, thus allowing the political and military leadership more flexibility in their use of force. An interpretation that allows a state to ignore the defensive system's effect on military advantage, and inflict civilian collateral damage as if the system did not exist, comes very close to intentional cause of damage to civilians and civilian property.

We are not aware of any state that applies a stricter standard of proportionality in its use of force, solely because it possesses a technological advantage, it. However, it might be prudent to differentiate between different kinds of conflicts. In interstate conflicts, the parties indeed do not take technological difference into account. However, in conflicts between states and NSAs, and even more in instances of targeted killing operations, states clearly do take more care than the enemy to protect civilians. This is especially so in asymmetrical conflicts, when the state actor usually possesses a significant technological advantage. It is controversial whether this policy reflects a legal standard, or just a policy decision by states.

36. The State of Israel, Ministry of Foreign Affairs, The 2014 Gaza Conflict: 7 July–26 August 2014: Factual and Legal Aspects, para. 322 (May 2015).

37. *Id.*

## E. THE FUTILITY OF FORCE, DETERRENCE, AND PROPORTIONALITY

An additional issue related to strategic considerations is the question of the futility of engaging in armed conflicts.[38] The question here is whether the odds that the goals of a particular armed conflict will be fulfilled should also be included in the analysis. Some argue that if an armed conflict has little or no chance of succeeding, there can be no justification for harming civilians during that conflict—in effect, in such a scenario, no attack that would harm civilians could be considered proportionate. Others argue further, that if the use of force produces no lasting or significant strategic advantage, then the principle of proportionality should be reconsidered. The justification for harming civilians would be severely reduced if that harm were caused during a futile armed conflict, in an attempt to achieve unattainable military or political goals.

Some, however, claim that, if indeed the possibility of achieving victory should be included in considerations of proportionality, the principle of proportionality might rule out many modern armed conflicts. This is because, in recent decades, Western powers have appeared incapable of achieving "victory" through the use of force. In many asymmetrical armed conflicts, the best result that Western powers could hope to achieve through the use of force was short-term deterrence before the next round of conflict.[39] If this is the case, that single attacks or even entire armed conflicts yield very little strategic significance, could harm to civilians be condoned at all?

It is important to fully understand the strength of this argument. In modern asymmetrical armed conflicts, there is very little strategic advantage to be gained for any state in carrying out any single attack. Conflicts can last for long periods of time, and no single attack against terrorist cells, or even particular operations, can realistically bring one side closer to victory. As some scholars note, this problem becomes compounded by the fact that many conflicts today no longer have clear goals against which *jus ad bellum* and *jus in bello* proportionality can be evaluated. It is possible that none of the parties to the conflict have a clear vision of what they would call a victory.[40] From this viewpoint, because an armed conflict between Israel and Hamas in Gaza or an operation in Afghanistan stands little chance of achieving any lasting political solution or conferring a military advantage, civilians should not be regarded as lawful collateral damage in such a conflict.

38. This issue was discussed at length at the proportionality conference, and views presented here are of participants in that conference.

39. See, for example: RUPERT SMITH, THE UTILITY OF FORCE: THE ART OF WAR IN THE MODERN WORLD (2005) (questioning whether there is a need for a paradigm shift in the conduct of modern warfare and if force alone can be used to achieve political goals).

40. Robert D. Sloane, *Puzzles of Proportion and the "Reasonable Military Commander": Reflections on the Law, Ethics, and Geopolitics of Proportionality*, 6 HARV. NAT'L SEC. J. 299, 307 (2015). Sloane refers to the example of the 2014 Gaza War as an example of this, where neither Hamas nor Israel had a clear vision of what they wanted to achieve in the war.

There are those who reject the factual claim that the use of force or armed conflict is an exercise in futility.[41] Alternatively, some scholars believe that even if all that an armed conflict can attain is deterrence, this is a worthy and valuable achievement that at least extends the periods of quiet between wars, and thus sometimes justifies harming civilians in order to achieve periods of peace.[42]

However, it seems to us that this discussion is somewhat misplaced.

The issue of the futility of an armed conflict relates to a distinction in international law between *jus ad bellum*, the branch of law governing the legality of armed conflict as a whole, and *jus in bello*, the branch of law that governs how armed conflicts are to be fought irrespective of their overall legality. Although one of the criteria for going to war in just war theory is the probability of success (a state may not go to war if it cannot achieve its just goal through the use of force), this is not a criterion in contemporary *jus ad bellum*.[43]

The distinction between *jus ad bellum* and *jus in bello* was introduced in order to guarantee protection regardless of the causes or the justification for the conflict. According to this distinction, irrespective of whether an armed conflict is lawful, the hostilities within that conflict can be conducted lawfully, under a separate set of rules. This guarantees that even if a conflict was initiated in violation of *jus ad bellum*, that original sin does not convert all of the hostile actions of the belligerent parties during the armed conflict into violations of the law. This separation of the two branches of law provides broader protection of civilians and soldiers by granting both parties to the conflict an incentive to fulfil their obligations during an armed conflict, regardless of its causes and context.[44]

Although the two branches of law have been separated so that each applies irrespective of any violation of the other, it seems to us that a proper understanding of *jus ad bellum* would suggest that it continues to apply during times of armed conflict.[45] Proportionality, a form of balancing good against bad results of military activity, is also part of the *jus ad bellum* analysis. A military response, or major

41. Clearly, the use of force can result in political gains in some cases. In Syria, for example, certain factions successfully used force to achieve political results in 2015 and 2016. Similar results were achieved initially by the Coalition forces whose operation led to the toppling of Saddam Hussein's government in Iraq.

42. Cohen and Shany reject the position that general deterrence is an element in the proportionality analysis. Cohen & Shany, *Contextualizing Proportionality Analysis*, *supra* note 7.

43. The conditions for using force in a case of self-defence from an armed attack are proportionality, immediacy, and the force must be used when only necessary, as a last resort. See Chapter 1, note 1.

44. There are those that challenge the extant separation between the two branches of law. For a discussion of this issue, see Robert D. Sloane, *The Cost of Conflation: Preserving the Dualism of Jus in Bello and Jus ad Bellum in the Contemporary Law of War*, 24 YALE J. INT'L L. 47 (2009); Eyal Benvenisti, *Rethinking the Divide Between Jus ad Bellum and Jus in Bello in Warfare Against Nonstate Actors*, 34 YALE J. INT'L L. 541 (2009).

45. This view is also supported by scholars such as Judith Gardam. See: JUDITH GARDAM, NECESSITY, PROPORTIONALITY AND THE USE OF FORCE BY STATES 169 (2004). Perhaps it should

activity, is allowed only if it is necessary and proportional. Naturally, proportionality here means something completely different than IHL proportionality. Proportionality in *jus ad bellum* includes balancing the nature and results of the attack with the nature and result of the force used to thwart the attack.[46]

It is here, in *jus ad bellum* proportionality, that we find the proper venue to address the strategic and cultural questions we discussed earlier. For example, if a single soldier is captured right before the end of an armed conflict, can her army initiate a large-scale military operation in order to protect her, or is it required to act in a manner proportionate to the scale of the attack it suffered? Furthermore, if the operation to rescue this one soldier is expected to result in many deaths, military as well as civilian, is that operation proportionate and therefore lawful?

If *jus ad bellum* continues to apply in this manner, then the strategic considerations of preventing a soldier from being captured could be included in the *ad bellum* proportionality analysis of the operation. This could be one way to resolve the dilemma of whether strategic considerations should be included in proportionality analysis, as these considerations would be weighed solely in the *jus ad bellum* proportionality, leaving the *jus in bello* proportionality to include only narrower elements in the analysis. Similarly, the question of whether victory can be achieved at all should be considered as part of this *jus ad bellum* analysis, and not as a matter of proportionality in IHL.

Because cultural and strategic considerations can act as a double-edged sword, leading to the conclusion that no collateral harm to civilians could be justified, and disrupting the equal application of the law, it seems to us that these considerations should not be included in proportionality analysis in IHL. As far as possible, IHL proportionality should relate to the concrete and direct military advantage, and should not take into account strategic and cultural considerations.

be considered as a third category in between *jus ad bellum* and *jus in bello*. See Noam Lubell & Amichai Cohen, *Strategic Proportionality: Limitations on the Use of Force in Modern Armed Conflicts*, 95 Int'l L. Stud. 159 (2020).

46. David Kretzmer, *The Inherent Right to Self Defence and Proportionality in Jus Ad Bellum*, 24 Eur. J. Int'l L. 235 (2013).

8

# Direct Participation in Hostilities and Its Effect on Proportionality

The principle of distinction, one of the cornerstones of modern IHL, encapsulates the basic tenet of removing the threat to civilians and civilian objects. This is done by distinguishing between civilian objects and military objectives—prohibiting attacks directly targeted at civilian objects and civilians, and permitting attacks to be directed only at combatants and military objectives.

The principle of distinction is directly relevant to proportionality in two primary ways: First, classifying persons and objects as combatants and military objectives rather than civilians and civilian objects directly affects the proportionality of an attack, as the military advantage becomes greater and the collateral damage to civilians is reduced. This relates both to the targeting of human beings and the targeting of objects. Second, indiscriminate attacks—attacks that do not properly distinguish between lawful and unlawful targets—also relate to proportionality.

These issues will be discussed in this chapter and the following chapters. We begin, in this chapter, by discussing what happens when civilians lose their civilian protection. In Chapter 9 we turn to the related question of human shields. Issues relating to the targeting of objects and indiscriminate attacks are discussed in Chapter 10.

## A. THE CONCEPT OF DIRECT PARTICIPATION IN HOSTILITIES

When it comes to humans, the principle of distinction requires that only military targets—combatants—may be targeted during armed conflict.[1] Civilians

1. It is important to note that not all soldiers may be targeted. IHL removes several classes of individuals who are *hors de combat* from the groups of soldiers who may be targeted. These include soldiers who have surrendered (The Hague Convention (IV) Respecting the Laws and Customs of War on Land, Annexed Regulations, 1907, art. 23(c), 205 C.T.S. 277; Protocol Additional to the Geneva Conventions of 12 August 1949, and Relating to the Protection of Victims of International Armed Conflicts (Protocol I), June 8, 1977, art. 41, 1125 U.N.T.S. 3 [AP-I], as well as prisoners of war (see Geneva Convention Relative to the Treatment of

*Proportionality in International Humanitarian Law.* Amichai Cohen & David Zlotogorski, Oxford University Press.
 DOI: 10.1093/oso/9780197556726.003.0008

must not be the object of attack.[2] This rule is customary in international as well in non-international armed conflicts.[3] In AP-I, which reflects customary international law on the matter, the definition of a civilian is a negative one—"[t]he civilian population is made up of persons who are not members of the armed forces:"[4]

> A civilian is any person who does not belong to one of the categories of persons referred to in Article 4 A 1), 2), 3) and 6) of the Third Convention and in Article 43 of this Protocol. In case of doubt whether a person is a civilian, that person shall be considered to be a civilian.[5]

Prisoners of war, Aug. 12, 1949, art. 4(A), 75 U.N.T.S. 135 [GC-III]), the wounded, sick, and the shipwrecked (Geneva Convention for the Amelioration of the Condition of the Wounded and Sick in Armed Forces in the Field, Aug. 12, 1949, art. 12, 75 U.N.T.S. 31; Geneva Convention for the Amelioration of the Condition of the Wounded, Sick and Shipwrecked Members of the Armed Forces at Sea, Aug. 12, 1949, art. 12, 75 U.N.T.S. 85).

2. AP-I, *supra* note 1, art. 51(2). Civilians also "enjoy general protection against dangers arising from military operations." See AP-I, *supra* note 1, art. 51(1).

3. Jean-Marie Henckaerts & Louise Doswald-Beck, Customary International Humanitarian Law, Vol. 1, rule 1 (2005).

4. Commentary on the Additional Protocols of 8 June 1977 to the Geneva Conventions of 12 August 1949, para. 1913 (ICRC, Yves Sandoz, Christophe Swinarki, & Bruno Zimmerman eds., 1987). This should not be taken to mean that all those who are not civilians may be targeted. There are certain members of the military who are protected from direct attack. This includes not only those *hors de combat* but also certain non-combatants, including medical and religious personnel in the military (Henckaerts & Doswald-Beck, *supra* note 3, rule 3).

5. AP-I, *supra* note 1, art. 50(1). This article excludes from the category of civilians all those who are referred to in the following articles:

> GC-III, *supra* note 1, art. 4(A): ". . . (1) Members of the armed forces of a Party to the conflict as well as members of militias or volunteer corps forming part of such armed forces. (2) Members of other militias and members of other volunteer corps, including those of organized resistance movements, belonging to a Party to the conflict and operating in or outside their own territory, even if this territory is occupied, provided that such militias or volunteer corps, including such organized resistance movements, fulfil the following conditions: (a) that of being commanded by a person responsible for his subordinates; (b) that of having a fixed distinctive sign recognizable at a distance; (c) that of carrying arms openly; (d) that of conducting their operations in accordance with the laws and customs of war. (3) Members of regular armed forces who profess allegiance to a government or an authority not recognized by the Detaining Power . . . (6) Inhabitants of a non-occupied territory, who on the approach of the enemy spontaneously take up arms to resist the invading forces, without having had time to form themselves into regular armed units, provided they carry arms openly and respect the laws and customs of war."

Unlike members of the armed forces and combatants who can be targeted,[6] civilians are protected from attack.[7] However, civilians do not enjoy protection at all times and under all circumstances. When civilians take a direct part in the hostilities, such as by taking up arms against the enemy, they lose their civilian protection and can be lawfully targeted. This customary rule is set forth in AP-I: "Civilians shall enjoy the protection afforded by this Section, unless and for such time as they take a direct part in hostilities."[8]

AP-I, *supra* note 1, art. 43: "1. The armed forces of a Party to a conflict consist of all organized armed forces, groups and units which are under a command responsible to that Party for the conduct of its subordinates, even if that Party is represented by a government or an authority not recognized by an adverse Party. Such armed forces shall be subject to an internal disciplinary system which, 'inter alia', shall enforce compliance with the rules of international law applicable in armed conflict. 2. Members of the armed forces of a Party to a conflict (other than medical personnel and chaplains covered by Article 33 of the Third Convention) are combatants, that is to say, they have the right to participate directly in hostilities. 3. Whenever a Party to a conflict incorporates a paramilitary or armed law enforcement agency into its armed forces it shall so notify the other Parties to the conflict."

6. It should be noted that this interpretation of the law is not universally accepted. There are those who argue that not all soldiers or combatants may be killed, and that parties to an armed conflict have an obligation to capture or wound, rather than kill, a combatant in certain situations (e.g., INT'L COMM. OF THE RED CROSS, INTERPRETIVE GUIDANCE ON THE NOTION OF DIRECT PARTICIPATION IN HOSTILITIES UNDER INTERNATIONAL HUMANITARIAN LAW 77–82 (May 2009) [ICRC Interpretive Guidance]; Gabriella Blum, *The Dispensable Lives of Soldiers*, 2 J. LEGAL ANALYSIS 115 (2010); Ryan Goodman, *The Power to Kill or Capture Enemy Combatants*, 24 EJIL 819 (2013)). Jean Pictet has famously written that "if we can put a soldier out of action by capturing him we should not wound him, if we can obtain the same result by wounding him, we must not kill him, if there are two means to achieve the same military advantage we must choose the one which causes the lesser evil". See JEAN PICTET, DEVELOPMENT AND PRINCIPLES OF INTERNATIONAL HUMANITARIAN LAW 75 (1985) (cited in Michael N. Schmitt, *Military Necessity and Humanity in International Humanitarian Law: Preserving the Delicate Balance*, 50 VA. J. INT'L L. 795, 835 (2010)). For an overview of the opposing interpretation of the ruling law, see Michael N. Schmitt, *Wound, Capture, or Kill: A Reply to Ryan Goodman's "The Power to Kill or Capture Enemy Combatants,"* 24 EJIL 855 (2013).

7. For a discussion of whether the anticipated harm from an attack must include non-combatants such as medical forces, see our discussion *supra* Chapter 5A.

8. AP-I, *supra* note 1, art. 51(3). A similar provision regarding non-international armed conflicts exists in Protocol Additional to the Geneva Conventions of 12 August 1949, and Relating to the Protection of Victims of Non-International Armed Conflicts (Protocol II), June 8, 1977, art. 13(3), 1125 U.N.T.S. 609: "Civilians shall enjoy the protection afforded by this Part, unless and for such time as they take a direct part in hostilities." A similar provision is included in Common Article 3 to the Geneva Conventions: "(1) Persons taking no active part in the hostilities . . . shall in all circumstances be treated humanely, without any adverse distinction

The rule, known as direct participation in hostilities (DPH), is customary in international as well as non-international armed conflicts. Therefore, whenever civilians directly participate in hostilities, they lose the protection afforded to them and may be targeted directly.

Classifying a civilian as directly participating in hostilities is relevant to proportionality as well as to the principle of distinction, as it changes the proportionality analysis in two complementary ways. First, if a civilian is taking a direct part in hostilities, an attack on such an individual would arguably augment the expected military advantage of the strike. Second, such civilians are not protected from direct attack and are also not considered civilians in the proportionality assessment. This means that classifying civilians as direct participants in hostilities might make an otherwise disproportionate attack proportionate.

Consider, for example, a situation in which there is an attack on a munitions truck driven by a civilian. The attack is expected to harm a bystander, a second civilian, near the truck. If driving the truck does not qualify as taking a direct part in hostilities, then the driver would still enjoy his civilian protection and the proportionality of the attack must weigh the military advantage from attacking the truck and ammunition against the expected harm to both the civilian driver and the civilian bystander. However, if the act of driving the munitions truck makes the driver a direct participant in hostilities, then the proportionality analysis is different: it is assessed by weighing the military advantage gained from the harm to the truck, the weapons *and the driver* against the expected harm to the single civilian bystander.

Another reason why direct participation is relevant to proportionality has to do with the nature of contemporary armed conflicts, in which the distinction and protection of civilians is increasingly difficult to apply. Today, armed conflicts are less likely to involve battles between armed forces fighting each other on defined battlefields, and more likely to consist of combat taking place within population centers, in which non-state armed groups might not necessarily identify their fighters with distinctive signs or uniforms and may embed their combatants among civilians. The difficulty of defining a civilian as one who is directly participating in hostilities becomes more challenging when civilians intermingle with combatants and might even support the operations of the armed group, whether morally, materially, financially, or otherwise.

We will briefly discuss the primary issues relating to how and when a person is considered to be directly participating in hostilities.

founded on race, colour, religion or faith, sex, birth or wealth, or any other similar criteria. To this end, the following acts are and shall remain prohibited at any time and in any place whatsoever with respect to the above-mentioned persons: (a) violence to life and person, in particular murder of all kinds, mutilation, cruel treatment and torture."

## B. THE DEFINITION OF DIRECT PARTICIPATION IN HOSTILITIES

When are civilians directly participating in hostilities? Direct participation is hard to apply in practice, and the subject has generated considerable disagreement. Views differ on the two cumulative criteria for the loss of civilian protection: First, what counts as direct participation; and second, the period of time during which the protection is lost. These two criteria are stipulated in AP-I article 51(3), as well as AP-II article 13(3): "Civilians shall enjoy the protection afforded by this Section, unless and *for such time* as they take a *direct part in hostilities*."[9] These articles and the norm that they encapsulate raise three primary points of contention: the definition and interpretation of direct participation in hostilities; the temporal element of such participation; and questions of factual doubt.

One interpretation of this definition is offered by the ICRC, which maintains that direct participation in hostilities has three cumulative conditions: a threshold of harm, direct causation, and a belligerent nexus.[10]

The ICRC's first condition, the threshold of harm, means that the civilian's act "must be likely to adversely affect the military operations or military capacity of a party to an armed conflict or, alternatively, to inflict death, injury, or destruction on persons or objects protected against direct attack." The second condition, direct causation, requires that there be a direct single causal link between the specific act, whether an isolated incident or part of a coordinated military operation, and the harm that is expected to result from it. For example, while firing a missile at soldiers counts as direct participation, participating in the research and development of that missile does not, because the causal link is not direct. The third condition is that of the belligerent nexus, according to which the act must be aimed at causing harm in support of one party to the conflict and to the detriment of the opposing belligerent party. For this reason, attacks against soldiers for criminal purposes do not satisfy this condition.[11]

It should be noted, however, that certain states and scholars maintain that the customary definition of direct participation is broader and less restrictive than that presented by the ICRC. Some state practice rejects the authoritative status of the

9. AP-I, *supra* note 1, art. 51(3).

10. In an attempt to delineate the situations in which civilians are direct participants in hostilities, the International Committee of the Red Cross convened a series of meetings of experts from 2003 to 2008 with the goal of clarifying the notion of direct participation in hostilities. Forty experts from around the world participated in the discussions, which were intended to produce a consensus document. However, eventually, due to disagreement, some of the experts requested that their names be removed from the final document. The ICRC Interpretive Guidance, *supra* note 6, thus represents the views of the ICRC alone. See Michael Schmitt, *The Interpretive Guidance on the Notion of Direct Participation in Hostilities: A Critical Analysis*, 1 HARV. NAT'L SEC. J. 6, 6–7 (2010).

11. ICRC Interpretive Guidance, *supra* note 6.

ICRC's three cumulative conditions.[12] The United States, for example, views them merely as factors that *may* be relevant when determining whether a person is directly participating in hostilities.[13] According to the United States, direct participation in hostilities includes not only "actions that are, by their nature and purpose, intended to cause actual harm to the enemy," but also "certain acts that are an integral part of combat operations or that effectively and substantially contribute to an adversary's ability to conduct or sustain combat operations."[14] The United States also cites a source on how civilians in Vietnam served as porters, built fortifications, or placed mines and booby traps, therefore losing their protected status.[15]

It appears that, contrary to the ICRC, states do not possess a specific test for determining who directly participates in hostilities. Rather, they determine the matter on a case-by-case basis, although they do refer to certain considerations that aid them in this determination.[16]

12. For a discussion of the difficulties posed by the three conditions offered by the ICRC and their interpretation, see: Michael N. Schmitt, *Deconstructing Direct Participation in Hostilities: The Constitutive Elements*, 42 N.Y.U. J. INT'L L. & POL. 697, 737–38 (2010).

13. US DEPARTMENT OF DEFENSE, LAW OF WAR MANUAL, paras. 5.8.1.2–5.8.3.2 (2015, updated Dec. 2016) [DoD Manual].

14. *Id.*, para.5.8.3.

15. *Id.*, para.5.8.3, n.240.

16. *Id.*, at para.5.8.3 ("Whether an act by a civilian constitutes taking a direct part in hostilities is likely to depend highly on the context"); Schmitt, *supra* note 10, at 25; HCJ 769/02, Public Committee against Torture v. The State of Israel, PD 62(1) 507, para. 34 (2006) (Isr.) [*Targeted Killings* Case] ("without a comprehensive and agreed upon customary standard, there is no escaping going case by case, while narrowing the area of disagreement"). It should be noted, however, that the Israel HCJ decision in the *Targeted Killings* Case came before the publication of the ICRC Interpretive Guidance. The Israel HCJ did give several examples of acts that would, and would not constitute direct participations in hostilities: "According to the accepted definition, a civilian is taking part in hostilities when using weapons in an armed conflict, while gathering intelligence, or while preparing himself for the hostilities. Regarding taking part in hostilities, there is no condition that the civilian use his weapon, nor is their [*sic*] a condition that he bear arms (openly or concealed). It is possible to take part in hostilities without using weapons at all. . . . Indeed, a civilian bearing arms (openly or concealed) who is on his way to the place where he will use them against the army, at such place, or on his way back from it, is a civilian taking 'an active part' in the hostilities. However, a civilian who generally supports the hostilities against the army is not taking a direct part in the hostilities. Similarly, a civilian who sells food or medicine to unlawful combatants is also taking an indirect part in the hostilities. . . . The following cases should also be included in the definition of taking a 'direct part' in hostilities: a person who collects intelligence on the army, whether on issues regarding the hostilities, or beyond those issues; a person who transports unlawful combatants to or from the place where the hostilities are taking place; a person who operates weapons which unlawful combatants use, or supervises their operation, or provides service to them, be the distance from the battlefield as it may. All those persons are performing the function of combatants. The function determines the directness of the part taken in the hostilities. However, a person who sells food or medicine to an unlawful combatant is not taking a direct part, rather an indirect part in the hostilities. The same is the case regarding a person who aids the unlawful combatants

One practical result of this disagreement regarding the definition is that certain acts, while considered "direct" participation by states, are categorized as only "indirect" participation by the ICRC. For example, the 2016 US DoD Manual cites scholars who write that "repair of a target acquisition or missile guidance equipment in the midst of battle would probably be regarded as direct participation in hostilities."[17] Similarly, according to the same text, in certain circumstances, training and logistical support would be considered direct participation in hostilities. This appears to include individuals who are involved in the preparation and training of the use of improvised explosive devices (IEDs) and in supplying ammunition to the front lines.[18] According to the ICRC, such acts, that are more than one causal link away from the harm caused by the weapon, would probably not constitute direct participation in hostilities.

There is also disagreement as to what passes the threshold of harm criterion. This comes up, for example, in the issue of voluntary human shields, and whether they directly participate in hostilities. We discuss this issue in Chapter 9.

Beyond the differences regarding the interpretation of the term direct participation, there is also disagreement about the length of time for which a person loses his civilian protection. As a rule, the ICRC defines the duration of loss of civilian protection as the length of time of *each specific act* during which the person directly participates in hostilities. According to the ICRC, this time span includes preparing to execute the act, as well as the deployment and return from the action.[19] Otherwise, and notwithstanding thus being involved in hostilities, the civilian participant retains the protections enjoyed by all other civilians.

by general strategic analysis, and grants them logistical, general support, including monetary aid. The same is the case regarding a person who distributes propaganda supporting those unlawful combatants. If such persons are injured, the State is likely not to be liable for it, if it falls into the framework of collateral or incidental damage" (*Targeted Killings* Case, *Id.*, paras. 33–35 (citations omitted)). In 2018, the Israel HCJ seemed to have adopted the tests set by the ICRC in its interpretive guidance, when the court discussed whether certain civilians had directly participated in hostilities, while referring to the ICRC's three conditions. See, HCJ 3003/18, Yesh Din—Volunteers for Human Rights v. The IDF Chief of Staff para. 45 (J. Melcer) (May 24, 2018) [Isr.]. Amichai Cohen, *Analysis of Israel's Supreme Court Decision Allowing Lethal Force in Gaza*, Just Security (May 27, 2018). Others suggest that the reference to the ICRC's tests stems not from the court having adopted them, but rather from the fact that some judges lack expertise in international law. See Yahli Shereshevsky, *HCJ 3003/18 Yesh Din—Volunteers for Human Rights v. Chief of General Staff, Israel Defense Forces (IDF)*, 113 Am. J. Int'l L. 361, 367–68 (2019).

Similar to Israel in the Targeted Killings case, in its 2016 Manual, the United States outlines a set of considerations that may be relevant to determining whether a person is directly participating in hostilities. DoD Manual, *supra* note 13, para.5.8.3.

17. DoD Manual, *supra* note 13, para. 4.15.4, n.318.

18. *Id.*, paras. 5.8.3 n.243, 5.8.3.1.

19. *Id.*, at 65.

This position is known as the "the revolving door" mechanism. Accordingly, a person can theoretically be a "farmer by day and fighter by night"—with different day and night jobs enjoying a clear separation. This is intended to provide civilians with maximum protection and avert attacks on civilians who do not, at a particular time, pose a military threat.[20] It prevents civilians who directly participated in hostilities at one point in time from being the targets of attack for indefinite periods of time. The practical ramification is that a civilian who attacks military targets every few weeks or days might not be a lawful target in between those specific acts of violence.[21]

The ICRC does accept, however, that certain civilians can become lawful targets for longer periods of time than each specific act. Civilians who de facto assume a "continuous combat function" in the armed conflict may be continuously targeted, as they cease to be civilians so long as their combat function persists, thereby losing their civilian protections.[22] This rule applies to persons who continuously engage in acts of direct participation in hostilities.[23]

Some states, however, reject the ICRC'S interpretation of the temporal element. The United States maintains that no "revolving door" exists, and therefore civilians who directly participate in hostilities can be targeted beyond the duration of each specific act, until the point of time when "they have permanently ceased their participation."[24] Israel too, in the *Targeted Killings* case, rejected the notion of a revolving door.[25] Therefore, a person who is a farmer by day but a fighter by night remains a fighter until he or she ceases fighting and clearly disengages from direct participation in hostilities.[26] Furthermore, certain states maintain that members of armed groups can be targeted regardless of whether they assume a continuous combat function. The United States, for example, maintains that civilians who are members of an organized armed group are not classified as civilians and may be continuously targeted solely based upon their membership in an armed group, regardless of their function in the organization.[27] This is also Israel's position.[28] The

20. *Id.*, at 70–73.

21. Naturally, there is also the question of identification: when a civilian is currently involved in a specific military activity, it might be difficult to verify his identity as a past participant in armed activities.

22. ICRC Interpretive Guidance, *supra* note 6, 31–36.

23. *Id.*, at 33.

24. DoD Manual, *supra* note 13, para. 5.8.4.

25. *Targeted Killings* Case, *supra* note 16, paras. 39–40.

26. Schmitt, *supra* note 10, at 37–38.

27. DoD Manual, *supra* note 13, para. 5.8.2.1.

28. The State of Israel, Ministry of Foreign Affairs, The 2014 Gaza Conflict: 7 July–26 August 2014: Factual and Legal Aspects, 156, n.422 (May 2015) ("State practice and *opinio juris* make clear that a member in an organised armed group need not have a 'continuous combat function' in order to be targetable under customary international law").

rationale here is that a different interpretation would create an unjust asymmetry between states and armed groups: All members of state militaries, regardless of function, are lawful targets—even cooks. It is argued that the same standard should apply to organized armed groups.[29]

Beyond the disagreement on the definition and temporal aspects, there is also a debate as to how parties to the armed conflict actually classify persons as directly participating in hostilities. This relates to the issue of doubt, as it might be unclear whether a person is directly participating in hostilities as a matter of fact, rather than as a matter of law.

As stated previously, contemporary armed conflicts raise particular challenges as civilians and combatants often intermingle in populated areas. Actions that can be completely innocuous might appear to be "conspiratorial" and vice versa. For example, a civilian warily observing troop movement from a window while talking on a cellphone could either be a curious civilian conversing with a friend or an enemy scout reporting to his superiors. Similarly, a person carrying a bulky package while running from cover to cover in the rubble of an embattled city, in the direction of might be an enemy combatant likely to attack the soldiers or just an innocent civilian in possession of food or medical supplies, desperately trying to avoid being shot on the way home. How, then, are belligerent parties to act in situations of factual doubt?

The ICRC takes a restrictive approach and maintains that "all feasible precautions must be taken in determining whether a person is a civilian and, if so, whether that civilian is directly participating in hostilities," but that, if doubt remains, that person must be presumed to be a protected civilian.[30] This is based on the ICRC's interpretation of article 50(1) of AP-I, which stipulates that "[i]n

29. Schmitt, *supra* note 10, at 23.

30. ICRC Interpretive Guidance, *supra* note 6, at 74.

When discussing the IDF's Operation Cast Lead in Gaza, the Goldstone Report seems to use this interpretation in determining that an attack against members of the police in Gaza was disproportionate and a violation of international law. Under international law, members of the police force are civilians. They are thus protected unless they directly participate in hostilities or are incorporated in the armed forces (*Report of the United Nations Fact-Finding Mission on the Gaza Conflict*, U.N. Doc. A/HRC/12/48, paras. 428–29 (Sep. 25, 2009) [The Goldstone Report]; The State of Israel, Ministry of Foreign Affairs, The Operation in Gaza 27 December 2008–18 January 2009: Factual and Legal Aspects, para. 238 (July 2009); Prosecutor v. Sesay, Special Court for Sierra Leone Trials Chamber I, SCSL-04-15-T, para. 88 (Mar. 2, 2009)). The Goldstone Committee acknowledged the argument that members of the police may have also been members of the al-Qassam Brigades or other armed groups, thus making them combatants and lawful targets as opposed to civilians. However, the Goldstone Report did not factually assess how many of the policemen were indeed combatants, and therefore failed to analyze whether the harm to civilians was expected to be excessive to the military advantage (The Goldstone Report, *Id.*, para. 434; Amichai Cohen, Proportionality in Modern Asymmetrical Wars, 16–17 (2010); Michael N. Schmitt, *Military Necessity and Humanity in International Humanitarian Law: Preserving the Delicate Balance*, 50 Va. J. Int'l L. 795, 826 (2010). This points to a presumption applied by the Report's authors that when any person who is a civilian is killed during armed conflict, the onus is on the attacker to provide

case of doubt whether a person is a civilian, that person shall be considered to be a civilian."

However, some commentators argue that the ICRC's interpretation misstates the law. In their view, while treaty law contains a presumption that a *person* should be considered a *civilian* in case of doubt,[31] there is no second presumption that a *civilian* should not be considered a *direct participant* when doubt on this point exists.[32] Schmitt opines that when doubt exists as to whether a civilian is directly or indirectly participating in hostilities, that individual should bear the risk that is inherent in the situation of doubt, not the belligerent party.[33]

These differences in interpretation significantly affect the principle of proportionality. For example, consider a case in which an armed combatant is loading arms onto a military truck with the assistance of three unarmed civilians. Can the combatant lawfully be targeted if harm is expected to the three civilians? How must the attacker act if in doubt as to this question? What is the tolerable threat to those civilians and to other civilian bystanders in the vicinity? There would be no real question if the act of loading the truck with arms was itself considered direct participation in hostilities.

To take another hypothetical example: Two armed civilian combatants walk into a building, followed several minutes later by five other unarmed civilians who have participated in hostilities in the past. Are there only two people who can be targeted lawfully, with five civilians as "collateral damage," or are there seven lawful targets? How much additional harm to surrounding buildings is considered justified? All these questions relate directly to issues of proportionality.

Following this discussion, another significant issue concerns how attackers must weigh the lives of human shields—civilians who are intentionally situated near military objectives in order to shield those objects from attack. The following chapter addresses this issue.

clear and unequivocal evidence supporting its position (Cohen, Proportionality in Modern Asymmetrical Wars, *Id.*, at 17).

31. "In case of doubt whether a person is a civilian, that person shall be considered to be a civilian." AP-I, *supra* note 1, art. 50(1). Regarding the presumption in case of doubt in general, see our discussion in Chapter 12, Section C.

32. Bill Boothby, *"And for Such Time as": The Time Dimension to Direct Participation in Hostilities*, 42 N.Y.U. J. Int'l L. & Pol. 741, 766 (2010).

33. Schmitt, *Deconstructing Direct Participation in Hostilities*, *supra* note 12, at 737–38; Boothby also maintains that inferences of present behavior can be made based on information as to previous conduct. See: Boothby, *supra* note 32, at 766.

# 9

# Human Shields and Proportionality

## A. THE PROBLEM OF HUMAN SHIELDS

In contemporary armed conflicts, there is a growing tendency, particularly among certain non-state actors, to operate from within civilian concentrations such as villages, towns, and cities; and to locate military installations in proximity to civilians and civilian objects.[1] This is often due to the asymmetry between the power and military capabilities of many non-state actors as compared with conventional armies. Non-state actors are unable to protect military objectives from their adversaries through conventional methods, "leading" them to resort to other means.

By locating military objectives within civilian concentrations, non-state actors aim to use civilians and civilian objects in a manner that will frustrate their opponents' military activities. This tactic—involving, in effect, the use of human shields—poses two problems to conventional forces. First, it creates a legal barrier, which in certain cases prohibits attacking military objectives if the attack is expected to result in disproportionate harm to civilians. Second, as discussed in previous chapters, inflicting civilian casualties—even when justified by the principle of proportionality—can result in a deleterious loss of both domestic and international legitimacy and public support.[2]

The use of human shields is proscribed in the Geneva Conventions as well as in AP-I.[3] Article 51(7) of AP-I stipulates that:

1. Though prevalent today, this problem is hardly novel, and has existed in many armed conflicts, at least throughout the last century. Michael N. Schmitt, *Human Shields in International Humanitarian Law*, 47 COLUM. J. TRANSNAT'L L. 292, 292–96 (2009) [Schmitt, *Human Shields*].

2. See Chapter 3.

3. Geneva Convention for the Amelioration of the Condition of the Wounded and Sick in Armed Forces in the Field, Aug. 12, 1949, art. 19, 75 U.N.T.S. 31; Geneva Convention Relative to the Treatment of Prisoners of War, Aug. 12, 1949, art. 23(1), 75 U.N.T.S. 135 [GC-III]; Geneva Convention Relative to the Protection of Civilian Persons in Time of War, Aug. 12, 1949, art. 28, 6 U.S.T. 3516, 75 U.N.T.S. 287; Protocol Additional to the Geneva Conventions of 12 August 1949, and Relating to the Protection of Victims of International Armed Conflicts (Protocol I), June 8, 1977, art. 12(4), 51(7), 1125 U.N.T.S. 3 [AP-I].

*Proportionality in International Humanitarian Law*. Amichai Cohen & David Zlotogorski, Oxford University Press.
 DOI: 10.1093/oso/9780197556726.003.0009

> The presence or movements of the civilian population or individual civilians shall not be used to render certain points or areas immune from military operations, in particular in attempts to shield military objectives from attacks or to shield, favor or impede military operations. The Parties to the conflict shall not direct the movement of the civilian population or individual civilians in order to attempt to shield military objectives from attacks or to shield military operations.

The ICRC has defined human shields as "an intentional co-location of military objectives and civilians or persons *hors de combat* with the specific intent of trying to prevent the targeting of those military objectives."[4]

Intent is therefore a critical element when considering if a person constitutes a human shield. It should be noted that belligerents cannot always choose the geographic location in which an armed conflict will take place, and not all hostilities conducted in or near civilian concentrations involve the use of human shields. Nonetheless, parties are obligated by a correlating obligation under article 58 of AP-I to "avoid locating military objectives within or near densely populated areas."

As Newton and May note, the prohibition on using human shields not only forbids the use of civilians as shields, but rather the use of all protected persons, such as prisoners of war.[5] In the *Von Leeb* case (The High Command Trial), the Nuremburg war crimes tribunal expressly stated that "the mere act of forcing prisoners of war to go ahead of advancing enemy troops, thereby acting as a shield to the latter, would itself constitute another type of war crime."[6]

If civilians are placed near military objectives in order to shield those objects, how does this affect the proportionality analysis? The views on this differ. One of the primary questions relating to the status of human shields in this discussion is whether the human shields are voluntary or involuntary: Have these civilians voluntarily chosen to place themselves in harm's way, in order to protect certain military objectives, or are they there involuntarily, either because they were unaware of the objectives' existence or because they were placed there against their will?

4. Jean-Marie Henckaerts & Louise Doswald-Beck, Customary International Humanitarian Law, Vol. 1, rule 97 (2005).

5. GC-III, *supra* note 3, art. 23 states that:

> No prisoner of war may at any time be sent to, or detained in areas where he may be exposed to the fire of the combat zone, nor may his presence be used to render certain points or areas immune from military operations.

6. US Military Tribunal Nuremberg, Judgment of October 27, 1948, in Law Reports of Trials of War Criminals, Selected and Prepared by the United Nations War Crimes Commission, Vol. XII The German High Command Trial, London: United Nations War Crimes Commission, 1949, p. 105.

There are several views as to whether and how involuntary or voluntary human shields should be addressed as part of the proportionality analysis.

## B. INVOLUNTARY HUMAN SHIELDS

Some have suggested that involuntary human shields should not be counted as civilians in proportionality assessments, as the party to the conflict that is using them should not benefit from its own misconduct.[7] This principle can be grounded in the maxim "*Nullus commodum capere potest de sua injuria propria*," which can be translated as "no advantage (may be) gained from one's own wrong."[8] However, this view seems to contrast with the law under which the presence of troops within a civilian population "does not deprive the population of its civilian character,"[9] or remove their civilian status protection.

The prevailing opinion is that reprisals, normally Unlawful actions that are intended to force a party to cease its wrongdoing, are prohibited in IHL as a matter of law,[10] and that obligations under IHL are not dependent on the opposing party fulfilling its IHL obligations, as discussed in Chapter 3.

An opposing view thus calls for treating involuntary human shields just as any other civilians, and therefore includes involuntary human shields in the proportionality assessment. This is grounded in article 51(8) of AP-I, that stipulates that a party's violation of the prohibitions held in article 51, including article 51(7), "shall not release the Parties to the conflict from their legal obligations with respect to the civilian population and civilians."[11]

Another view, which enjoys much support, holds that although involuntary human shields retain their civilian status and protection, the proportionality equation is altered due to the defender's violations of IHL, and the lives of the involuntary human shields count less than they would otherwise.[12] This is the position of the United Kingdom, which maintains that the misconduct of an enemy

7. This position was held by at least one participant in the Proportionality Conference.

8. Ori Pomson & Yonatan Horwitz, *Humanitarian Intervention and the Clean Hands Doctrine in International Law*, 48 Isr. L. Rev. 219, 231 (2015).

9. AP-I, *supra* note 3, art. 50(3).

10. Schmitt, *Human Shields*, *supra* note 1, at 327.

11. *Id.*, at 327–28.

12. *Id.*, at 328–29; "Those carrying out attacks in such circumstances are not relieved of their obligation to attack military objectives only and reduce incidental damage as much as possible, but in considering the rule of proportionality, any tribunal dealing with the matter would be obliged to weigh in the balance in favour of the attackers any such illegal activity by the defenders." A.P.V. Rogers, *Zero-Casualty Warfare*, 837 Int'l Rev. Red Cross 165 (2000), *available at:* www.icrc.org/eng/resources/documents/article/other/57jqcu.htm.

in placing civilians near military objectives should be a mitigating factor, in favor of the proportionality of the attack.[13] Dinstein writes that:

> The principle of proportionality remains prevalent. However, even if that is the case, the actual test of excessive injury to civilians must be relaxed. That is to say, the appraisal whether civilian casualties are excessive in relation to the military advantage anticipated must make allowances for the fact that—if an attempt is made to shield military objectives with civilians—civilian casualties will be higher.[14]

The view of the United States seems to be in line with the United Kingdom's position, though this is not entirely clear. While the United States states clearly that anticipated harm to involuntary human shields must be included in the proportionality assessment, it adds that the party that places civilians near military objectives "assumes responsibility for their injury."[15]

A more nuanced approach has been proposed by Amnon Rubinstein and Yaniv Roznai. They maintain that involuntary human shields retain their protected status and are counted in the proportionality assessment. However, when the use of involuntary human shields becomes widespread and systematic, the weight ascribed to these civilians changes so that they are given less weight than they would be given otherwise. The reason for this is that the interests of protecting civilians and removing them from the cycle of violence justify changing the proportionality equation and creating a disincentive for the party that is violating IHL and placing civilians and their lives at risk by using them as human shields. Therefore, when a party uses involuntary human shields systematically, there is an interest in not rewarding their repeated violations.[16]

The position promoted by Rubinstein and Roznai seems to reflect how states behave in practice. However, it is not certain that it reflects the correct application of the principle of proportionality. It is not clear why civilians, who have become involuntarily "involved" in a conflict, should suffer more through no fault of their

13. "Even where human shields are being used, the proportionality rule must be considered. However, if the defenders put civilians or civilian objects at risk by placing military objectives in their midst or by placing civilians in or near military objectives, this is a factor to be taken into account in favour of the attackers in considering the legality of attacks on those objectives." United Kingdom Ministry of Defence, Joint Service Publication 383, The Joint Service Manual of the Law of Armed Conflict, para. 2.7.2 (2004).

14. Yoram Dinstein, The Conduct of Hostilities Under the Law of International Armed Conflict 127 (2004); Schmitt, *Human Shields*, *supra* note 1, at 330.

15. US Department of Defense, Law of War Manual para. 5.12.3.4 (2015, updated Dec. 2016) [DoD Manual].

16. Amnon Rubinstein & Yaniv Roznai, *Human Shields in Modern Armed Conflicts: The Need for a Proportionate Proportionality*, 22 Stan. L. & Pol'y Rev. 93, 120–23 (2011).

own. Perhaps the opposite is true: when a regime systematically involves civilians in hostilities the civilian population already bears the burden of the conflict.

Perhaps Rubinstein and Roznai's point may be justified as a simple calculus: if the involuntary presence of civilians does not actually serve to protect military targets from attack, their regime may lose the incentive to force them to become human shields. This makes some sense, though it is unclear whether regimes that use their own civilians as human shields would cease to do so just because this was not entirely effective, when they incurred no cost at all by doing so.

Rubinstein and Roznai propose an additional exception to the normal application of the proportionality assessment, when dealing with involuntary human shields who are being used to shield military objectives that present a clear and present danger to the opposing force. In such situations, Rubinstein and Roznai offer an analogy to the self-defense grounds for excluding criminal responsibility in the Rome Statute.[17] In other words, where there is an imminent threat to soldiers' lives the lives of involuntary human shields should be ascribed less weight.[18]

We are not sure that this specific exception is required. When human shields are being used to shield an important military target, whether or not this target presents a clear and present danger, the direct military necessity of the attack soars, and the proportionality analysis allows for more civilian casualties. If, however, Rubinstein and Roznai mean that no protection would be given to civilians in this case, this seems to us to be an incorrect application of the principle of proportionality.

The use of involuntary human shields has become a significant problem in armed conflicts. The main cause for the existence of involuntary human shields is regimes that coerce civilians to be placed near military targets. This regime forces the adverse party to choose between two bad options: shooting at civilians, or forsaking a military advantage.[19]

Indeed, the most important way to prevent the use of human shields is to punish such regimes and leaders through domestic courts and international tribunals.[20]

## C. VOLUNTARY HUMAN SHIELDS

The situation is different when voluntary human shields are involved. Voluntary human shields are people who choose to place themselves near military objectives with the intention of shielding them. Here, there is a greater challenge to the protections afforded by the principle of proportionality, as the discussion centers

17. Rome Statute of the International Criminal Court, Jul. 17, 1998, art. 31(1)(c), 2187 U.N.T.S. 90.

18. Rubinstein & Roznai, *supra* note 16, at 123–26.

19. Michael Newton & Larry May, Proportionality in International Law 204 (2014).

20. *Id.*, at 217.

on the question of whether voluntary human shields—are direct participants in hostilities, thereby forfeit their protection as civilians.[21]

According to the ICRC, even voluntary human shields are not considered direct participants in hostilities unless they create *physical* barrier that impedes enemy attacks, such as by blocking bridges to block advancing ground troops. However, in many instances, such as in attacks from the air, voluntary human shields create only a *legal* barrier, as opposed to physical barriers. According to the ICRC, civilians who pose a legal barrier are not directly participating in hostilities and retain their protection as civilians.[22]

On the opposing side, there are those who posit that voluntary human shields are direct participants in hostilities and thus lose their civilian protection. This was the position of the Israeli High Court of Justice (HCJ) in the *Targeted Killings* case,[23] as well as that of the United States, which maintains that voluntary human shields can be considered civilians directly participating in hostilities, though this should be "[b]ased on the facts and circumstances of a particular case."[24] This position was also adopted by several scholars, such as Michael Schmitt. In Schmitt's opinion, voluntary human shields are taking affirmative steps to frustrate the attacking military's actions, thereby contributing to the opposing military's efforts. Therefore, they qualify as direct participants in hostilities. Schmitt makes the point that if the ICRC's position is accepted, a civilian who is armed and clearly directly participating in hostilities might well be less effective in defending against an attack than a voluntary human shield. Five militants armed with rifles will not be able to prevent a military objective from being bombed; but if voluntary human shields are considered protected civilians, they might succeed in preventing the attack as it might then be considered disproportionate. As a matter of tactics, therefore, voluntary human shields might well provide better protection to a military target than armed militants.[25]

## D. DISCERNING CHOICE

As can be seen, much revolves around whether a human shield is shielding the target voluntarily or involuntarily. However, that question cannot be easily

21. AP-I, *supra* note 3, art. 51(3); Protocol Additional to the Geneva Conventions of 12 August 1949, and Relating to the Protection of Victims of Non-International Armed Conflicts (Protocol II), June 8, 1977, art. 13(3), 1125 U.N.T.S. 609.

22. Int'l Comm. of the Red Cross, Interpretive Guidance on the Notion of Direct Participation in Hostilities under International Humanitarian Law 56–7 (May 2009). For a discussion of the notion of direct participation in hostilities and its effect on proportionality see Chapter 8.

23. HCJ 769/02, Public Committee against Torture v. The State of Israel, PD 62(1) 507, para. 36 (2006) [Isr.].

24. DoD Manual, *supra* note 15, para. 5.12.3.4.

25. Schmitt, *Human Shields*, *supra* note 1, at 318.

determined. How can one know if a person who is standing next to a military objective is there intentionally in order to shield the target, has taken up that position for some other reason entirely, or was forced to do so by a party to the armed conflict?[26] Moreover, one can ask whether there can be a clear epistemic difference between voluntary and involuntary participation when a state is at war, and certainly when that state is controlled by a regime that is clearly willing to use civilians to protect military targets. In such repressive states, it may be difficult to discern when citizens choose to shield targets of their own volition, and when they have been coerced to do so under threat of harm to them or their families.

An illustrative example can found in how civilians react to warnings to evacuate an area prior to its being attacked. IHL obligates parties to a conflict to issue warnings to civilians prior to carrying out attacks, under certain conditions, so that the civilians can flee from danger.[27] However, if an individual does not heed these warnings and chooses to remain in the area of the expected attack, this does not automatically make him a voluntary human shield. There may be many reasons why a person chooses not to leave the area other than the desire to shield a target. These may include a desire to protect possessions or being physically incapable of leaving due to sickness.[28] Civilians near military objectives may also not realize that they are so close to a targeted area or not understand the warnings being issued.[29]

Due to the inherent difficulty in discerning between civilians and human shields, Schmitt, for instance, opines that in cases of doubt, it should be presumed that civilians are not acting as human shields.[30] Similarly, when doubt arises as to whether a civilian is a voluntary or involuntary human shield, Schmitt and others have proposed that there should be a legal presumption that the human shield is involuntary. This is similar to the existing norm in cases of doubt regarding the status of a person as a civilian, as stipulated in article 50(3) of AP-I.[31] This opinion was also held by one of the Proportionality Conference participants, who suggested that only in extreme cases should one assume that an individual is voluntarily shielding a target.

26. During armed conflicts it is difficult to ascertain what a person's *actions* are, not to mention their *intentions*. For example, Ziv Bohrer and Mark Osiel refer to a situation in Iraq in which a helicopter shot at a civilian holding a camera, having mistakenly identified the camera as a gun. See: Ziv Bohrer & Mark J. Osiel, *Proportionality in Military Force at War's Multiple Levels: Averting Civilian Casualties vs. Safeguarding Soldiers*, 46 Vand. J. Transnat'l L. 747, 797 (2013). One can only assume that this was not the first time in the annals of war that such a mistake regarding an action was made. Such mistakes are even likelier when it comes to determining other people's intents.

27. AP-I, *supra* note 3, art. 57.

28. Schmitt, *Human Shields*, *supra* note 1, at 316.

29. Rubinstein & Roznai, *supra* note 16, at 119; Schmitt, *Human Shields*, *supra* note 1, at 327.

30. Schmitt, *Id.*, at 334–35.

31. *Id.*; Rubinstein & Roznai, *supra* note 16, at 112–13.

An example might serve to illustrate this dilemma. In the case of "roof knocking"—the practice of dropping inert or low-impact explosives on the roof of an intended target as a warning for people to flee the building before the attack—it can be argued that a person who then goes onto the roof or into the building is voluntarily shielding the target. In such cases, a civilian running up to the rooftop could certainly be seen as indicating their intention to serve as a voluntary human shield. However, even this is far from clear, as there may be other reasons why a civilian would run up to the roof. They may have been coerced to do so by combatants; have gone to inspect the damage to the roof; or they may be looking for a better vantage point from which to locate and assist others who were wounded by strikes.

It seems, however, that there are two cases in which *voluntary* human shields should be considered *in*voluntary ones, retaining all their civilian protections. First, when the military of a party to the conflict exercises control over civilians—for example, during occupation. In such cases, consent to act as voluntary human shields for the occupier cannot be considered genuinely "voluntary." A civilian facing a hostile army cannot really reject a proposal to act "voluntarily" to assist that army.

This type of situation was addressed in the Israel HCJ's judgment in the *Early Warnings Procedure* case.[32] The court discussed whether the military could use Palestinian civilians to give suspected terrorists, and those in the suspects' houses, an early warning of an impending military operation. This was intended to prevent harm to the soldiers, the suspect, and other people present in the suspect's house. The HCJ held that, due to the inequality between the occupying force and the local residents, true consent to serve in this capacity could not be given.[33] During the Proportionality Conference, it was suggested that civilians under the rule of authoritarian regimes should never be seen as voluntary human shields, as it would be difficult to discern whether their presence was truly voluntary. However, this view was discounted by others as it would lead to a disparity in the law applying to different parties to a conflict.

A second situation in which human shields should not be seen as "voluntary" is that of children serving as human shields, as there is an acute difficulty in determining whether a child is truly acting voluntarily.[34]

Overall, the use of human shields in armed conflicts, and its effects, is a matter for concern. The principle of proportionality was intended to minimize the extent of harm suffered by civilians during armed conflicts. This endeavor to reduce the ravages of war is truly a noteworthy achievement of the international community. However, the modern battlefield, which is often located in populated areas, threatens to frustrate this goal.

32. HCJ 3799/02, Adalah (Legal Center for Arab Minority Rights in Israel) v. IDF Commander of the Central Region, PD 60(3) 67 (2005) [Isr.].

33. *Id.*, para. 13.

34. Schmitt, *Human Shields*, *supra* note 1, at 335–36.

It seems to us that the proper approach to this matter should be to view the "voluntariness" of the participation of civilians as a continuum, rather than a binary issue. At one end of the continuum is the case of the civilian who takes up arms and effectively joins the armed activity. This person should definitely be considered as participating actively in the hostilities, and should receive no special protection. At the other end are the weakest members of society—children and the elderly, who can easily be used by parties to the conflict to protect specific military targets. These should generally be considered civilians, and afforded regular protection. In between are all the cases in which adult civilians take part in the conflict with some degree of consent, as described before. In these cases, a sliding scale of proportionality should be used. The important point is that not all cases in which civilians are involved in armed conflicts are the same.

The use of human shields might affect the application of the principle of proportionality in a further sense: a change in the form of precautions required of the attacking party before launching an attack when faced with human shields, be they voluntary or involuntary.[35] As we shall explain in Chapter 12, we think that precautions are an important part of the application of the principle of proportionality. The attacking party is required to verify, as far as is feasible, that the attack will affect a minimal number of civilians, and, based on that, to choose the least damaging method of attack. However, when the attacking party is faced with human shields, regular precautions may not be relevant. For example, there may be no point in simply changing the route of the attack, as the other party could simply move the civilians to the new chosen alignment. What is needed is more emphasis on giving effective warning to the civilian population, in such a way as to deter the regime from using human shields and encourage civilians not to shield military targets.[36]

35. Newton & May, *supra* note 19, at 227.

36. One such method is the use of warnings. See discussion in Chapter 12E.

# 10

# The Principle of Distinction and Its Relation to Proportionality

## A. THE DEFINITION OF MILITARY OBJECTIVES AND ITS RELATION TO PROPORTIONALITY

Proportionality prohibits causing excessive damage to civilian objects and civilians as compared with the anticipated military advantage when attacking a military objective. The question of which objects are legitimate military objectives, and which are civilian objects, is therefore of great importance.

Civilian objects are defined in AP-I article 52(1) as all objectives that are not military objectives. As stipulated in AP-I article 52(2), the customary definition of military objectives has two elements: first, objectives must make an effective contribution to military action based on their nature, location, use, and purpose; and second, attacking those objectives must offer a definite military advantage to the attacker.[1]

Examples of military objectives by "nature" include military bases, command and control centers, weapon stockpiles, military vehicles, fortifications, military communications centers, and other objectives whose very nature makes an effective contribution to military action.

The situation regarding military objectives by their "location" is a little different. These objectives are not military in and of themselves, but their location makes an effective contribution to the military action of the adverse party. Such targets can include important mountain passes, jungle trails, bridgeheads, and strips of land that offer control over a harbor entrance.[2]

1. "Military objectives are limited to those objectives which by their nature, location, purpose or use make an effective contribution to military action and whose total or partial destruction, capture or neutralization, in the circumstances ruling at the time, offers a definite military advantage" (Protocol Additional to the Geneva Conventions of 12 August 1949, and Relating to the Protection of Victims of International Armed Conflicts (Protocol I), June 8, 1977, art. 52(2), 1125 U.N.T.S. 3 [AP-I]).

2. Yoram Dinstein, The Conduct of Hostilities under the Law of International Armed Conflict 92 (2nd ed., 2010).

*Proportionality in International Humanitarian Law.* Amichai Cohen & David Zlotogorski, Oxford University Press.
 DOI: 10.1093/oso/9780197556726.003.0010

Military objectives by their "use" are normally civilian objects that are used by the adverse party for military purposes. This use turns them into military objectives. This may include civilian houses used as outposts by a party to the conflict, schools from which rockets are fired, bridges over which troops are transported, and places of worship used for firing positions.

Military objectives by their "purpose" are objectives whose intended *future* use is for military purposes. This contrasts with targets by "use," whose current use makes an effective military contribution to the adverse party.

Classifying a target as a military objective is of great importance to the proportionality analysis. If an object is a military objective it can be made the direct target of an attack. Moreover, harming or destroying such a military objective might confer a greater military advantage than if it was not a military objective, thus justifying more collateral harm.

To illustrate this point, consider the following situation: Army A is planning on attacking Army B, which is taking shelter in the outskirts of a town. Army B is using the first line of houses on the outskirts of the town as firing positions. So far, Army B is not using the houses in the second row at all, but plans to do so, as a second line of defense or to mask a route of retreat from Army A.

The first row of civilian houses that Army B is using is a military objective by virtue of its use. The second row of houses is not being used currently by Army B, and therefore does not presently make an effective military contribution. However, its intended purpose as an escape route for Army B future turns the houses into military objectives, as their future use might preserve the lives of Army B soldiers. Therefore, both rows of houses seem to be military objectives.[3]

According to this interpretation, Army A can attack the first row of houses without having to take into account the harm that might be caused to the second row, as both are military objectives. Furthermore, any expected military advantage gained from harming the escape route provided by the second row of houses is added to the military advantage and is weighed against the anticipated harm to civilians or civilian objects, including for example, possible damage to the third or fourth rows of houses.

If this interpretation is incorrect, however, because the possible future use of the houses (their purpose) is deemed too remote to for them to be considered military objectives, then any damage to houses not in the first row is collateral damage.

In this way, a broader definition for "military objectives" can be expected to result in greater harm to civilians and civilian objects, whereas a narrower definition would restrain military operations. This is especially true today, when conflicts are increasingly fought in urban settings, with disturbing consequences for civilians. Yesterday's civilian houses and places of worship become today's

3. We assume that the use of the second row of houses as an escape route is something which has been planned in the immediate future in the context of the ongoing operation.

military objectives. Tomorrow, when the conflict ends and the military forces have gone, so have the civilians' houses.

This relates directly to another characteristic of contemporary armed conflicts that is pertinent to proportionality: "dual-use" objectives. Civilian objects become military objectives when their use makes an effective military contribution. There are, however, instances in which objects are used simultaneously for both military and civilian purposes. These are commonly referred to as "dual-use" objectives. Power grids, industrial facilities, cellphone networks, computer systems, railroad tracks, and highways are some examples of possible dual-use objectives, when they are used concurrently for military and civilian purposes. This military use, even if it is secondary to the primary civilian use, satisfies the conditions of article 52(2) of AP-I, and qualifies the otherwise civilian object as a military objective.[4] The question is whether the civilian elements of the target—either the object itself or the civilians within it—are now all considered part of a legitimate military target, or whether they remain in the civilian category, such that proportionality analysis should be applied.

There is some support in the literature for the first view.[5] According to this position, once an object, dual-use or otherwise, becomes a military objective by its use, it ceases to be a civilian object, and thus harm to that dual-use objective itself is not considered in the proportionality analysis.[6]

Some claim that the Committee in the NATO Bombing Report supported this view in its discussion of the proportionality of an attack on a dual-use target.[7] In 1999, NATO bombed the central studio of the state-owned broadcasting corporation (RTS) in Belgrade, killing between 10 and 17 people. The Committee assessed first whether the RTS studio constituted a military objective, and second, whether the attack was proportionate.

The Committee found that while the broadcasting station was not in and of itself a military objective, "to the extent [that] particular media components are part of the C3 [command, control, and communications] network they are military objectives."[8] Even if a media is not part of the C3 network, it could become

4. Marco Sassoli & Lindsey Cameron, *The Protection of Civilian Objects—Current State of Law and Issues de lege ferenda*, *in* The Law of Air Warfare: Contemporary Issues 35, 57–58 (Natalino Ronzitti & Gabriella Venturini eds., 2006).

5. W. Hays Parks, *Asymmetries and the Identification of Legitimate Military Objectives*, *in* International Humanitarian Law Facing New Challenges 106-7 (Wolff H. von Heinegg ed., Berlin 2007).

6. Ian Henderson, The Contemporary Law of Targeting: Military Objectives, Proportionality and Precautions in Attack under Additional Protocol I 207 (2009).

7. ICTY, *Final Report to the Prosecutor by the Committee Established to Review the NATO Bombing Campaign Against the Federal Republic of Yugoslavia* (2000), *available at:* http://www.icty.org/en/press/final-report-prosecutor-committee-established-review-nato-bombing-campaign-against-federal.

8. *Id.*, para. 55.

a military objective depending upon its use—for example, if it is used to incite crimes,[9] or possibly "if the media is the nerve system that keeps a war-monger in power and thus perpetuates the war effort."[10]

Turning to the issue of proportionality, the Committee decided that "the civilian casualties were unfortunately high but do not appear to be clearly disproportionate."[11] When examining the military advantage anticipated from the attack, the Committee found that NATO had been aware prior to the attack that attacking the studio would only interrupt broadcasts for a brief period (which was indeed the actual result of the attack), and also that the RTS studio was just one part of the Yugoslav command and control network. It had been clear that the command and control network could not be dismantled or stopped by a single attack. The Committee stated that proportionality should not be evaluated by focusing exclusively on one specific attack, such as the attack on the RTS studio, but rather, it should be assessed on a broader level—the overall attack against the Yugoslav command and control network. In this regard, the attack should be seen as part of an operation aimed at targets essential to Yugoslavia's ability to direct and control its troops, as well as at key elements of the Yugoslav air defense.[12] Based on this analysis, the Committee found that the attack did "not appear to be clearly disproportionate."[13]

The Committee's assessment did not include a valuation of the harm expected to civilian objects and civilian infrastructure from the attack on the RTS studio itself.[14] In this specific case, however, this amount of harm to civilians appears to be minor, as the attack on the RTS studio was expected to interrupt the broadcasting only for a brief period of time.

In fact, there are reasons to doubt whether this was actually the position of the Committee. Television and radio broadcasts might not be an essential civilian service, and hence their civilian "value" might be minimal anyway. But even if this is the position of the Committee, there is a strong opposition to this view from academics and practitioners.[15]

The legality of targeting such an objective hinges on the proportionality of the attack on the objective itself, weighing the expected resultant harm to civilians

9. *Id.*, paras. 47, 55.

10. *Id.*, para. 55.

11. *Id.*, para. 77.

12. *Id.*, para. 78.

13. *Id.*, para. 77.

14. *Id.*, para. 78.

15. This latter position was unanimously supported in the ICRC Proportionality Report, see: *The Principle of Proportionality in the Rules Governing the Conduct of Hostilities Under International Humanitarian Law*, International Expert Meeting June 22–23, 2016, Quebec 37–40 (Univesité Laval and ICRC, September 2018).

against the anticipated military advantage.[16] To illustrate this point, when attacking a power station that supplies electricity for both civilian and military purposes, proportionality must also consider the expected damage to civilians resulting from the loss of power, despite the objective being a military one.[17] This appears to be the position of the United States.[18]

When in doubt as to whether a target is a civilian or a military objective, AP-I creates a legal presumption that the objective is a civilian one.[19] The issue of doubt and presumptions will be addressed in detail later in this book.[20]

## B. INDISCRIMINATE ATTACKS

A second element of the principle of distinction is the prohibition against indiscriminate attacks.[21] Indiscriminate attacks are those in which attackers do not

16. Commentary on the Additional Protocols of 8 June 1977 to the Geneva Conventions of 12 August 1949 (ICRC, Yves Sandoz, Christophe Swinarki & Bruno Zimmerman eds., 1987), para. 2023.

17. *Western Front, Aerial Bombardment and Related Claims—Eritrea's Claims 1, 3, 5, 9-13, 14, 21, 25 & 26 (Eritrea v. Ethiopia), Partial Award* (Dec. 19, 2005) (Ethiopia-Eritrea Claims Commission), para.11 (sep. Op.) (J. Van Houte).

18. US Department of Defense, Law of War Manual para. 5.6.1.2 (2015, updated Dec. 2016) [DoD Manual] (Dual use targets "are either military objectives or they are not; there is no intermediate legal category. If an object is a military objective, it is not a civilian object and may be made the object of attack. However, it will be appropriate to consider in applying the principle of proportionality the harm to the civilian population that is expected to result from the attack on such a military objective"). US Joint Chiefs of Staff, Joint Targeting, Joint Publication 3–60, A-5 (Jan. 31, 2013), *available at:* www.cfr.org/content/publications/attachments/Joint_Chiefs_of_Staff-Joint_Targeting_31_January_2013.pdf ("If the attack is directed against dual-use objects that are legitimate military targets but also serve a legitimate civilian need (e.g., electrical power or telecommunications), then this factor must be carefully balanced against the military benefits when making a proportionality determination"); Isable Robinson & Ellen Nohle, *Proportionality and Precautions in Attack: The Reverberating Effects of Using Explosive Weapons in Populated Areas*, 98 Int'l Rev. Red Cross 107, 132 (2016). This is also the view of Sassoli & Cameron, *supra* note 4, at 67.

19. AP-I, *supra* note 1, art. 52(3).

20. See discussion in Chapter 12, notes 28–34 and accompanying text.

21. AP-I, *supra* note 1, art. 51(4). The prohibition on indiscriminate attacks is part of the principle of distinction (*Legality of the Threat or Use of Nuclear Weapons*, Advisory Opinion, I.C.J. 8, 587, paras. 78–79 (1996) "The cardinal principles contained in the texts constituting the fabric of humanitarian law are the following. The first is aimed at the protection of the civilian population and civilian objects and establishes the distinction between combatants and non-combatants; States must never make civilians the object of attack and must consequently never use weapons that are incapable of distinguishing between civilian and military targets"); see also: *Constitutional Case No. C-291/07*, The Plenary Chamber of Colombia's Constitutional Court, 84–86 (Apr. 25, 2007) (cited in Int'l Comm. of the Red Cross, *Customary IHL, "Practice Relating to Rule 11. Indiscriminate Attacks," available at:* ihl-databases.icrc.org/customary-ihl/eng/docs/v2_rul_rule11) ("The principle of distinction is complex and encompasses a number

intentionally direct attacks at civilians or civilian objects, but remain indifferent to the effect of that attack on civilians.[22]

Customary international law mirrors the definition of indiscriminate attacks contained in article 51 of AP-I:[23]

> (4) Indiscriminate attacks are prohibited. Indiscriminate attacks are:
> a) those which are not directed at a specific military objective;
> b) those which employ a method or means of combat which cannot be directed at a specific military objective; or
> c) those which employ a method or means of combat the effects of which cannot be limited as required by this Protocol;
> and consequently, in each such case, are of a nature to strike military objectives and civilians or civilian objects without distinction.
>
> (5) Among others, the following types of attacks are to be considered as indiscriminate:
>
> a) an attack by bombardment by any methods or means which treats as a single military objective a number of clearly separated and distinct military objectives located in a city, town, village or other area containing a similar concentration of civilians or civilian objects;
> b) an attack which may be expected to cause incidental loss of civilian life, injury to civilians, damage to civilian objects, or a combination thereof, which would be excessive in relation to the concrete and direct military advantage anticipated.

One example of an indiscriminate attack can be found in the ICTY judgment in the *Martić* case. The Trial Court held that firing non-guided rockets with cluster munitions at the rockets' maximum range (50 km) at a densely populated civilian area was indiscriminate, due to the high dispersion of the munitions when launched from that range.[24]

of treaty and customary norms applicable in internal armed conflicts, in addition to, in many cases, enjoying *ius cogens* status. These rules [include] . . . the prohibition against indiscriminate attacks").

22. Dinstein, *supra* note 2, at 127. Indiscriminate attacks can be referred to as "attacks which strike civilians or civilian objects and military objectives without distinction." See: Prosecutor v. Galić, ICTY Trials Chamber, IT-98-29, *Judgment*, para. 57 (Dec. 5, 2003).

23. Jean-Marie Henckaerts & Louise Doswald-Beck, Customary International Humanitarian Law, Vol 1: Rules, rules 11–13 (2005).

24. Prosecutor v. Martić, ICTY Trial Chamber I, IT-95-11-T, *Judgment*, para. 463 (June 12, 2007); Dinstein, *supra* note 2, at 128.

One apparent connection between proportionality and indiscriminate attacks is that proportionality is a type of indiscriminate attack as described in article 51(5)(b) of AP-I. In fact, in several ICTY cases that found violations of proportionality, the court's discussion used proportionality as a proxy to show that the principle of distinction had been violated. In the *Blaskić* case, for example, the Trial Chamber held that the "vigorous" use of heavy weaponry to capture villages that were mostly occupied by civilians was disproportionate. This was deduced from the fact that most of the casualties had been civilians, rather than military personnel.[25] This decision seems to revolve less around allegations of the proportionality of the attack, and more as an attempt to prove that the attacks were aimed at civilians and were thus indiscriminate and in violation of the principle of distinction.[26] This also seems to be the situation in more recent cases such as the *Prlić* case[27] and the *Karadzic* case.[28] In these cases, the disproportionate nature of the attacks was used as *evidence* that the attack was indiscriminate.

A different connection between the two prohibitions of indiscriminate and disproportionate attacks relates to articles 51(4) and 51(5)(a) of AP-I in a specific context, and has come to the forefront of discourse in recent years: the use of explosive weapons in populated areas.

Warfare conducted in populated areas is likely to include attacks in which it is difficult or impossible to discriminate between civilian and military objectives. Conflicts in these areas thus often result in extensive harm to civilians and damage

25. Prosecutor v. Blaskić, ICTY Trial Chamber, IT-95-14-T, *Judgment*, paras. 507, 512, 651 (Mar. 3, 2000); Amichai Cohen, Proportionality in Modern Asymmetrical Wars, 22–23 (2010); Dinstein, *supra* note 2, at 131–32.

26. Cohen, Proportionality in Modern Asymmetrical Wars, *supra* note 25, at 23.

27. In *Prlic*, the Trial Chamber examined the heavy shelling of East Mostar, which had resulted in the killing and wounding of many people, mostly civilians. The Trial Chamber held that the attacks, which did not properly discriminate between military objectives and civilian objects, caused excessive harm to the civilian population in relation to the anticipated military advantage (Prosecutor v. Prlić, ICTY Trial Chamber III, IT-04-74-T, *Judgment*, Vol. II, para. 1018; Vol. III, paras. 1684–86 (May 9, 2013) (see also Vol. II, paras. 994–1018)). Recently, the Appeals Chamber criticized the Trial Chamber's finding on this matter, as the Trial Chamber had found that the damage was disproportionate without having determined the military advantage from the attack "and as such erred in law by failing to provide a reasoned opinion." Prosecutor v. Prlić, ICTY Appeals Chamber, IT-04-74-A, *Judgment*, Vol. I, para. 561 (Nov. 29, 2017).

28. In *Karadzić*, the ICTY Trial Chamber examined the shelling of Sarajevo between the end of the month of May and early June 1992, and held that the shelling of the city, particularly certain neighborhoods therein, was disproportionate. The Trial Chamber decided that although attacks against the city may have been launched by the SRK (Sarajevo-Romanija Corps) in response to Bosnian Muslim attacks from within the city, the attacks against the city as a whole, using various weapons and types of artillery, were indiscriminate and disproportionate. This finding was also based on statements preceding the attack according to which "Sarajevo will shake," made by commanders, who were aware of the civilian nature of the city (Prosecutor v. Karadzić, ICTY Trials Chamber, IT-95-5/18-T, *Judgment*, paras. 4052–55, 4497–4502 (Mar. 24, 2016) (see also paras. 4018–4055)).

to civilian objects. Consider for example a missile strike against a house in which a group of soldiers is taking shelter. The soldiers are lawful targets, and the house in which they're sheltering, normally a civilian object, is now a military target due to its use, and therefore it can also be targeted. However, if the missile strike damages a neighboring house, the attack might be considered both an indiscriminate attack and a disproportionate attack at the same time, depending on the circumstances: if the attack was directed at the military objective knowing that the neighboring house would also be directly hit, or if proper measures to protect the neighboring house were not taken, this might be considered an indiscriminate attack. If the number of civilian casualties in the neighboring house was excessive, this might be considered a disproportionate attack. This once again exhibits the close relation of the concepts in practice.

This type of situation was raised by the ICRC in its 2015 report, *International Humanitarian Law and the Challenges of Contemporary Armed Conflicts*.[29] Because contemporary hostilities are increasingly conducted in populated areas, the ICRC discussed the challenges faced in armed conflict regarding the use of explosive weapons in populated areas. Citing the high toll on the civilian population from such means of combat, the ICRC voiced the view that the use of explosive weapons in these areas could be both indiscriminate and disproportionate, and is likely to violate the prohibition on indiscriminate and disproportionate attacks. Naturally, it should be emphasized that this view of the ICRC relates to the use of such weapons in civilian surroundings. If the only foreseeable impact of the use of an explosive weapon is on a military target—such as in an attack on a military target in the desert—then such use cannot be regarded as indiscriminate or disproportionate.

The ICRC defines explosive weapons as "weapons that injure or damage by means of explosive force." The ICRC is concerned that these weapons may have "a 'wide impact area'—or 'wide-area effects'—when used in populated areas,"[30] either due to the large destructive radius of the individual weapon used, delivery systems that lack accuracy (such as mortars or artillery), or weapon systems that deliver multiple munitions over wide areas (such as multiple rocket-launcher systems).[31]

The ICRC's position is that

> explosive weapons with a wide impact area should not be used in densely populated areas due to the significant likelihood of indiscriminate effects,

29. Int'l Comm. of the Red Cross, *32nd International Conference of the Red Cross and Red Crescent: International Humanitarian Law and the Challenges of Contemporary Armed Conflicts*, 31–32 (Oct. 2015) [ICRC Challenges Report]. The issue was also raised in the Int'l Comm. of the Red Cross, *31st International Conference of the Red Cross and Red Crescent: International Humanitarian Law and the Challenges of Contemporary Armed Conflicts* (Oct. 2011).

30. *Id.*, at 49.

31. *Id.*, at 49. For an example of weapons which deliver multiple munitions over wide areas, see *supra* note 24 and the accompanying text.

> meaning that their use against military objectives located in populated areas is likely to fall foul of the IHL rules prohibiting indiscriminate and disproportionate attacks.[32]

This is due to the ICRC's assessment of the high likelihood of causing extensive harm to civilians and civilian objects, or to civilian infrastructure, which could have a long-term impact on the well-being of the civilian population.[33] While the ICRC is aware that a wide range of factors can alter a weapon's effects—such as the type of warhead, fuse, delivery system, range, and timing of the attack—its view is that explosive weapons with a wide impact should not be used in populated areas, due to their indiscriminate effects.[34]

Regarding the question of proportionality, the ICRC reviews a host of effects that could be caused by the use of explosive weapons in populated areas. These include not only the direct injury and death of civilians, but also the "reverberating effects" of the attacks within populated areas: displacement due to the loss of housing when homes are attacked; disruption of medical services when hospitals are attacked or power grids damaged; long-lasting harm to civilian infrastructure; and the possible spread of disease. It is the view of the ICRC that such reverberating effects should be included as part of the proportionality analysis as long as they are foreseeable, and that it is questionable whether such effects are adequately factored in by military commanders when assessing the proportionality of an attack.[35]

Several issues arising from the ICRC's position merit careful examination before adopting a prohibition on the use of explosive weapons in populated areas.

First, the ICRC's report examines in detail the effects of the use of explosive weapons on the civilian population, yet does not carry out a corresponding examination of the military necessity requiring the use of these weapons in populated areas. Such necessity could include, for example, the need to support ground troops, or to target enemy combatants and emplacements from a distance. Second, the report does not address concerns regarding the use of civilians as human shields by a party to an armed conflict. Creating a general prohibition on the use of certain munitions or weapons in populated areas would give an additional incentive to parties to the conflict to conduct their hostilities from within populated areas in order to gain extra protection from attack by limiting the arsenal of weapons that the opposing party could use in the conflict.

Third, as mentioned in the ICRC's report, a number of factors affect the extent of collateral harm caused by using explosive weapons in populated areas. If

32. *Id.*, at 49.

33. *Id.*, at 48.

34. *Id.*, at 50–51.

35. *Id.*, at 52. For a discussion regarding whether reverberating effects should be included in the proportionality assessment, see Chapter 5.

belligerent parties take proper precautions when choosing the means and methods of attack, then the extent of harm to civilians from attacks would be limited, and there will be no justification to limit the use of such weapon systems. Some might claim that a blanket prohibition would shift the balance between military necessity and humanity too far, by too severely restricting the belligerent parties.

Finally, it is unclear whether limiting the use of explosive weapons in populated areas will indeed achieve the worthy goal of significantly reducing the primary and secondary suffering and harm to the civilian population. Even if the ICRC's interpretation were to be accepted, this may still not cause the cessation of hostilities in populated areas, or even the cessation of harm to civilians within those areas. It is safe to assume that states would still pursue the same military goals by employing other means and methods of combat whose effects might not reduce the harm suffered by civilians.[36]

For example, one can examine a situation in which State B's soldiers are fighting against State A's troops from within a populated area, while State A's troops are outside the populated area. If State A intends to target State B's soldiers, it would presumably not be deterred from its plans simply because of the prohibition against using explosive weapons in a populated area. State A would seek alternative means and methods of targeting State B's soldiers, for example, by conducting house-to-house operations within the populated area with its infantry units. This operation would have to be conducted without covering artillery fire, which is a type of explosive weapon. However, the human cost to the lives of State A's soldiers from such an operation could be significant.[37] Such an operation would arguably also cause a lot of damage to the civilian infrastructure due to the house-to-house combat. Soldiers could still use certain explosive weapons or other forms of firepower, such as grenades, rifles, and smaller munitions explosives, whose effects are more limited than artillery, in order to destroy specific houses or buildings that are military objectives. While the extent of harm might be less than that resulting from the use of "explosive weapons" as defined by the ICRC, combat would still presumably cause severe harm to civilian infrastructure. As long as State B chooses to deploy its soldiers within or near homes, schools, hospitals, and high-rise buildings, and chooses to use civilian infrastructure for military purposes, then dual-use targets such as electricity grids and bridges would become permissible targets, and the resulting harm to civilians can unfortunately be expected to be extensive.

36. For example, the use of ground forces to carry out operations against terrorists might not necessarily result in fewer civilian casualties than targeted killings by air strike. Amichai Cohen & Tal Mimran, *Response: Shiri Krebs, 'Don't Ask, Don't Tell' Secrecy, Security, and Oversight of Targeted Killing Operations*, *in* DON'T ASK, DON'T TELL: SECRECY, SECURITY AND OVERSIGHT OF TARGETED KILLING OPERATIONS, 75, 99, 106 (Aug. 2015), *available at:* en.idi.org.il/media/4244/don-t_ask_don-t_tell.pdf.

37. For a discussion regarding the extent to which a state may endanger the lives of the civilians of the opposing belligerent party in order to protect its own soldiers, see Chapter 6.

## Protection of Cultural Property

The 1954 Hague Convention for the Protection of Cultural Property in the Event of Armed Conflict accords special protection to cultural property which is defines as "moveable or unmovable property of great importance to the cultural heritage of every people."[38] The Convention includes several obligations and protections to the cultural property. Similarly, article 53 of AP-I forbids attacks directed against "historic monuments, works of art or places of worship which constitute the cultural or spiritual heritage of people."[39]

The 1999 Second Protocol to the Hague Convention[40] explicitly states the principle of proportionality. Article 7 declares that all state parties to the protocol shall.

> c. refrain from deciding to launch any attack which may be expected to cause incidental damage to cultural property protected under Article 4 of the Convention which would be excessive in relation to the concrete and direct military advantage anticipated; and
> d. cancel or suspend an attack if it becomes apparent:
>    i. that the objective is cultural property protected under Article 4 of the Convention
>    ii. that the attack may be expected to cause incidental damage to cultural property protected under Article 4 of the Convention which would be excessive in relation to the concrete and direct military advantage anticipated.

States that are party to the protocol[41] therefore have a full obligation to include cultural property in their proportionality analysis. It does not seem, however, that this is considered part of customary law, and hence states that are not parties to the second protocol have no such obligation.

The real question is whether cultural objects should be treated differently from any other objects. We believe so, for two reasons.

First, cultural objects should be given more weight than regular civilian objects in proportionality analysis[42] as states are under a special obligation to refrain from attacking such objects if at all possible, even if a legitimate military purpose would have justified attacking a "regular" civilian object.

38. Hague Convention for the Protection of Cultural Property in the Event of Armed Conflict, May 14, 1954, art. 1, 249 U.N.T.S 358.

39. AP-I *supra* note 1, art. 53.

40. Second Optional Protocol to the 1954 Hague Convention for the Protection of Cultural Property in the Event of Armed Conflict, Mar. 26, 1999, 2252 U.N.T.S. 172.

41. According to the ICRC, there are 82 state parties at the time of writing.

42. DoD Manual *supra* note 18, para. 5.12.1.1.

Second, even according to the opinion that dual-use objects are no longer civilian objects for the purpose of applying the principle of proportionality, the situation may be different with regard to cultural objects. A cultural object or building has an intrinsic cultural value that supersedes its civilian nature. That value endures even if it is being used for military purposes, thereby rendering it a legitimate military objective. For example, an ancient fortress may be used for military purposes, but the party attacking it should take into account its historical and cultural nature when considering whether or not to destroy it.

The opposing view holds some weight, however, as under article 6(a) of the 1999 Second Protocol to the Hague Convention, when cultural property is used as a military objective, the special protection is waived.

# PART III

# Understanding Proportionality

This part of the book presents our view of proportionality using novel perspectives not often taken in discussions on this subject. We suggest that looking at procedures—both of the decision-maker and of the military and civilian authorities, before and after the attack—is an important element of proportionality. We discuss the procedures that commanders should follow, and the possible investigative mechanisms available to the state.

# 11

# The Vagueness of Proportionality

When considering the term "proportionality," most people intuitively assume that there is a quantitative value that can be attached to it. In this chapter, we question this assumption from two different points of view. First, we discuss the findings of two Israeli researchers which indicate that there actually is no agreement on a specific numerical formula among IHL experts or military officers. Second, we present the work of Boaz Ganor which attempts to create such a formula, and we critically evaluate this attempt.

## A. EXPERIMENTAL MEANINGS OF PROPORTIONALITY

As we have shown throughout this book, there are various disagreements regarding the principle of proportionality. In addition to theoretical disagreements, there also seems to be no explicit agreement as to how to apply the proportionality equation practically in real-life situations. No numerical weight is provided anywhere for each of the different variables.

Whether or not the uncertainty surrounding the principle of proportionality should be cause for concern has to do with the question whether some shared understanding exists as to how the term is applied in practice. If military officers and academics share a reasonably similar interpretation of the term as it is applied to concrete cases, resolving the academic differences may not be so important.

Until recently, this issue has not been tested in any scientific manner. We could analyze how the principle was applied in a particular case, but no basis existed for assuming how other military officers or experts might have behaved under similar circumstances.

In a recent paper, Daniel Statman and several colleagues attempt to remedy this deficiency.[1] In their research, they presented hypothetical scenarios to academic experts in IHL and military officers and asked them to apply the principle of proportionality to them. They then compared the responses with those of laypersons responding to the same scenarios.

1. Daniel Statman et al., *Unreliable Protection: An Experimental Study of Experts' In-Bello Proportionality Decisions*, 31 EJIL 429 (2020).

*Proportionality in International Humanitarian Law.* Amichai Cohen & David Zlotogorski, Oxford University Press.
 DOI: 10.1093/oso/9780197556726.003.0011

For example, in the case of an attack on an important military command base, experts and lay persons were asked what number of unintended civilian deaths, inflicted as collateral damage, would cause them to consider the attack a violation of the principle of proportionality.

The authors discussed the results of their survey from three angles as related to the understanding of the principle of proportionality: First, they assess whether the results were sensitive to the military value of the target—that is, whether respondents allowed for more civilian collateral damage for a more important military target. Second, they assessed the convergence of the different responses—whether professionals in the field had some shared understanding of the value of collateral damage allowed when attacking a specific military target. Third, they examined the robustness of the results—that is, whether the results were affected by biases.

The study found that military professionals and academic experts did indeed display greater sensitivity than laypersons in ascribing weight to varying military targets, as they allowed for more civilian collateral damage in cases involving more important military targets.

However, regarding the second point of discussion, no convergence was observed among any of the experts themselves, nor between them and other groups (professional soldiers and academics, experts from different countries). In the words of the authors: "Experts and officers did not reach reasonable convergence levels on the maximum number of civilian lives that may be risked in the scenarios presented to them."

In addition, the authors found that the responses of military professionals and academic experts were subject to biases. This result is, of course, worrying. As noted by the authors:

> The results of this research carry important implications for the ethics and laws of armed conflict. First, the apparent inability of expersts . . . to consistently determine the application of *in bello* proportionality implies that the protection of civilians during warfare is unreliable, even when warring parties attempt to abide by the proportionality principle. The protection of civilians may be insufficient in some cases, and, in others, the risk to civilians may overly restrict legitimate military plans. Second, the apparent inability of experts to reliably determine the correct application of *in bello* proportionality casts serious doubt over such *ex post* judgments. Given that the distribution of experts' proportionality judgments appears as an aggregation of mere guesses, *ex-post* approvals as well as condemnations of military actions are often unwarranted.[2]

Indeed, if even military officers serving in the same army cannot reach a shared answer regarding the application of the principle, what does this principle mean?

2. *Id.*, at 452.

One possible answer to this question is that proportionality is so context based that no uniform application is possible; every case of proportionality is different. When presented with a particular scenario in the survey, every respondent subconsciously assumed several factors from their own experience. Thus, the results of the survey were not really that different; they merely reflected the different life experiences of the respondents. There is some support for this assumption in the survey itself. Israeli field officers, most of them with combat experience in the West Bank or the Gaza Strip, gave answers that as a group were less divergent than the answers of other groups. This might mean that when asked about the application of proportionality, Israeli field officer respondents, who have similar experiences, assumed similar background circumstances regarding the scenarios based on their common experiences, and as a result, their answers were similar. Other respondents, such as US military officers, had very divergent combat experiences, and hence their responses diverged to a far greater extent

Then again, this might not be the reason for the similarity of the Israeli officers' responses. It might simply be that their shared combat experience was gained under the same command structure and standing orders, and hence they all applied the orders that they had been given to the questions they were asked.

## B. THE FORMULA OF PROPORTIONALITY

Could it be that the problem lies with insufficient knowledge, and that if soldiers and experts knew what proportionality was, they would be able to implement it?

The most elaborate attempt to create a formula for calculating proportionality was suggested by Professor Boaz Ganor.[3] The formula, it should be noted, is framed mostly toward the prevention of terrorist activity. Nevertheless, it provides insight into what elements the proportionality equation should include.

Ganor's basic insight is that the principle of proportionality can be presented mathematically in the following way:

$$P = Military\ Necessity(Advantage)/Expected\ Collateral\ Damage$$

where P represents a factor of proportionality.

For a given operation, if $P > 1$, then the operation is proportionate, whereas if $P < 1$, then it is disproportionate.

*Military necessity* is calculated as X*Y*Z, where:

- **X** represents the urgency of the situation. The situation is accorded a value from 1 to 10 according to its urgency, where 1 represents minimal potential urgency and 10 represents a ticking bomb situation.

3. Boaz Ganor, Global Alert: The Rationality of Modern Islamist Terrorism and the Challenge to the Liberal Democratic World, Chapter 3: The Proportionality Dilemma in Countering Terrorism (2015).

- Y represents the necessity of the operation. Ganor suggests that the value of Y is the difference between the number of casualties suffered by the attacking force in the operation under review, versus those caused by an alternative, riskier operation. Thus, if the options are to attack with ground forces and suffer 15 soldier casualties, or to attack by air, with no risk to the attacking side, then the value of Y is 15. Naturally, in more complex cases, quantifying this value would become impossible.
- Z represents the military advantage gained. In the classic scenario in which a terrorist attack is prevented, the value of Z is the number of lives saved as a result of having prevented the terrorist act.

*Expected collateral damage*: Ganor assumes that not all collateral damage is the same. He differentiates between the lives of innocent civilians, the number of which he suggests should be cubed ($n^3$); the lives of civilians who are voluntarily involved (such as voluntary human shields), which number he suggests should be squared ($n^2$); and the lives of combatants (n). This gives the greatest weight to the lives of civilians, followed by the lives of voluntary participants in hostilities, and finally, the lives of combatants.

In the case of a single attack undertaken to prevent a specific terrorist act, Ganor's formula is therefore:

$$P = \frac{X * Y * Z}{n^3 + n^2 + n}$$

Whenever P is larger than 1, the action is proportional. Whenever it is smaller than 1, the action is disproportional.

This formula is easier to conceptualize when lives are at stake. The military advantage gained from preventing a terrorist act is saving lives. The number of lives saved can be easily counted and translated into the value of the "anticipated military advantage" of the attack.

In some contexts, Ganor's formula is helpful in revealing the problematic nature of some of the claims mentioned earlier in this book. For example, Ganor's view is that strategic considerations, such as a lack of disruption to civilian life in the attacking state, should be taken into account as part of the military advantage. Hence, in cases where the attack is expected to prevent a specific terrorist attack, he adds another variable to the military advantage calculus, C, which is assigned a value between 1 (no interference with public life even if the attack is successful) and 50 (extreme interference with public life).

Thus, in cases where a specific terrorist attack is prevented by a targeted killing operation, Ganor's formula looks like this:

$$P = \frac{X * Y * Z * C}{n^3 + n^2 + n}$$

As a thought experiment, and what Ganor terms a "conceptual exercise" the formula is helpful, especially because it assists the decision-maker in taking into account all relevant variables. In addition, Ganor's innovative suggestion is that when assessing proportionality, we do not have to adopt a strict answer to many of the questions we raised. For example, Ganor assumes that proportionality should assign value to the lives of civilians directly participating in hostilities, and to combatants. Possibly, some forms of collateral damage are not ignored, but rather considered to be less important, and thus accorded a lesser value in the formula.[4]

However, it is doubtful whether the formula actually provides practical assistance. First, Ganor does attempt to translate his formula to also fit cases of attacks that are not intended to halt a specific terrorist activity. In these cases, the use of the formula becomes much less intuitive. When the military advantage to be attained is not the saving of civilian lives but something whose value cannot be so easily enumerated, such as the control of a specific area or the encircling of an enemy compound, then the formula offers very little assistance.

Second, it is hard to understand, and Ganor does not explain, what value should be accorded to non-lethal harm to civilians, or to damage to property or cultural objects.

Third, the use of the C variable actually highlights one of the dangers in using strategic considerations as part of the proportionality formula. If the value of C is 25, meaning that a medium interference in public life will be prevented if the terrorist attack is thwarted, the number of collateral damage justified in an attack to prevent the attack would be multiplied by 25. Apart from the apparent arbitrariness of the value of C and the ensuing result, it also highlights the fact that uninvolved civilians will bear the full burden of the fear caused by terrorism. This result does not seem to us to be in line with the correct application of the principle of proportionality, as it merely shifts the disruption of civilian life from on party to the conflict to civilians of the other party.

There is one important respect in which Ganor seems to deviate from the accepted interpretation of the principle of proportionality in IHL. Ganor uses the value of P = 1 as the dividing line between a proportionate and disproportionate response. In other words, if the collateral damage is even slightly greater than the military advantage, Ganor deems the operation to be disproportionate. This, however, is an incorrect application of the rule. Article 51 of Additional Protocol I expressly prohibits only acts in which the collateral damage is *excessive* compared

4. See our discussion of direct participation in hostilities (Chapter 8) and human shields (Chapter 9).

with the military advantage attained.[5] Ganor's formula does not seem to be a correct interpretation of international law at least in this regard.

## C. RULES OF THUMB

A different kind of attempt to inject some clarity into the concept of proportionality was undertaken by Newton and May.[6] Instead of trying to achieve a clear formula of proportionality, Newton and May suggest using "rules of thumb" in order to reduce the uncertainties of the application of proportionality.

Newton and May suggest four "rules of thumb" that should direct the decision regarding the proportionality of a specific activity: (a) *The Common Denominator Principle*—the attempt to find a common denominator of both parts of the equation. That is, translate military advantage to "how many lives would be saved" in order to compare it to the expected collateral damage to civilians; (b) *The Civilian Precautionary Principle*—only weighty military considerations can justify any harm to the lives of civilians; (c) *Unobserved Target Principle*—Indirect military fire on civilian areas should only be launched following express authority from an upper level of command; (d) *The Respect for Fellow Humans Principle*—the principle that enemy fighters are also human beings whose lives also deserve respect.[7]

We concur with most of these "rules of thumb." Other than the last, they reflect a fairly uncontroversial view of the principle of proportionality. We are not sure, however, that Newton and May have sufficiently specified how these "rules of thumb" should be applied. For example, the search for a common denominator is certainly a useful way of thinking about the problem of proportionality in the abstract. But commanders might find it extremely difficult to translate this "rule of thumb" into a workable point of reference. Even with modern technology and intelligence, it is very tricky to evaluate the actual damage that will be prevented by the elimination of a particular terrorist. Hence, at most, this prescription can only be of use as a directive to commanders to think about this question. The second "rule of thumb," *the civilian precautionary principle*, seems to us to reflect current practice, and possibly law, and is already embedded in military orders, at least in those issued by armed forces respecting IHL. The third rule, *the unobserved target principle*, seems to us to be extremely important, and, as will be shown in the next chapter, constitutes part of what we consider to be the procedural aspects of proportionality.

The fourth "rule of thumb," respect for the lives of soldiers, has already been discussed in earlier parts of this book.[8] We agree that, especially in

5. Protocol Additional to the Geneva Conventions of 12 August 1949, and Relating to the Protection of Victims of International Armed Conflicts (Protocol I), June 8, 1977, art. 51(5)(b), 57(2)(a)(iii), 1125 U.N.T.S. 3.

6. Michael Newton & Larry May, Proportionality in International Law 283–99 (2014).

7. *Id.*, at 285–87.

8. Chapter 1, note 16, and the accompanying text.

asymmetrical armed conflicts, the attacking party should also show consideration for the lives of enemy soldiers. We also think that, at some level, states should consider preserving the lives of their own soldiers when assessing the military advantage of the attack. These issues have been discussed throughout the present book, and especially in Chapter 6, when discussing force protection. Even so, it is worth emphasizing that this discussion turns out to be of little practical assistance in the actual application of the principle of proportionality.

## D. INHERENT VAGUENESS?

In addition to the rules of thumb detailed above, Newton and May also suggest a framework of thresholds, according to which the principle of proportionality is interpreted. As we explained in Chapter 3, Newton and May attempt to strike a different balance between IHL and HRL in the context of different kinds of conflicts.[9]

Newton and May's framework of thresholds does assist in resolving some doubts regarding the application of the principle of proportionality. For example, in targeted killing operations, unless intended to prevent a major imminent attack, Newton and May assume that collateral damage resulting in death is almost never allowed. Furthermore, Newton and May's framework provides a simple scale that can be used to draw comparisons between different types of conflicts and the legality of attacks within those conflicts.

Yet, even if we adopt Newton and May's framework, some major questions regarding the interpretation of the principle of proportionality remain. First, Newton and May do not provide guidelines for the application of proportionality in classic armed conflicts, or high-intensity armed conflicts between states and NSAs. Second, even where Newton and May do suggest clear limits to the application of proportionality, for example, targeted killing operations, their position is controversial, at least with regard to the law.

The reason for the divergence of opinion regarding proportionality might lie elsewhere. Perhaps the principle is inherently vague, and intentionally so. If no amount of knowledge, study, or experience will necessarily lead to the same results, perhaps the goal of the principle is not to achieve the same results across the board. The following chapter will address this issue, and argue that proportionality in IHL is not so much about the numbers, as about ensuring the undertaking of a process that weighs competing interests. The relative weighting to be used in any given case is intentionally left beyond the purview of the principle.

9. Newton & May, *supra* note 6. See our detailed discussion of the framework in Chapter 3, section C.

# 12

# Procedural Aspects of Proportionality

Article 51 of the First Additional Protocol to the Geneva Conventions provides a substantive definition of the principle of proportionality: An attack is prohibited if it is expected to cause collateral damage that is excessive compared with the expected military advantage. We have already explained in detail how states apply this general definition, as well as the main disagreements regarding its utilization.

However, as discussed, in previous chapters the substantive approach to proportionality in IHL does not always lead to clear answers. In fact, as mentioned in the previous chapters, in their empirical study, Sulitzeanu-Kenan and his colleagues even questioned the efficacy of the proportionality rule itself, in view of their findings.[1] Although we consider their position unwarranted, we do agree that the substantive definition does not provide satisfactory guidance regarding the proper application of the principle of proportionality.

In this chapter, we attempt to answer these difficulties. We suggest application of the principle of proportionality should focus on what we term the procedural aspects of the principle of proportionality—the precautions taken before an attack, the decision-making processes, and the institutions put in place in order to verify whether the rule of proportionality was properly applied.

With respect to proportionality, as in many other areas of international law, military practice and scholarship have advanced along different tracks.[2] While legal scholars were asking the substantive question regarding moral and quantitative aspects of proportionality, military lawyers were doing something completely different. Armed forces translated the principle of proportionality into a bureaucratic process, which has become an essential part of the way in which armies operationalize the principle of proportionality.

In the following two chapters we will describe how these procedures are ideally supposed to work, and what happens in practice. Due to the inherent difficulties in the substantive approach to proportionality, it would be wiser that procedures

1. Raanan Sulitzeanu-Kenan, Mordechai Kremnitzer & Sharon Alon, *Facts, Preferences, and Doctrine: An Empirical Analysis of Proportionality Judgment*, 50 L. & Soc'y Rev. 348 (2016).

2. David Luban, *Military Necessity and the Cultures of Military Law*, 26 Leiden J. Int'l L. 315 (2013).

*Proportionality in International Humanitarian Law.* Amichai Cohen & David Zlotogorski, Oxford University Press.
 DOI: 10.1093/oso/9780197556726.003.0012

be the subject on which lawyers should focus when evaluating a state's adherence to the principle of proportionality.

One introductory comment is required: the procedures we describe here were put in place by states in order to apply IHL in general, and did not necessarily apply to the principle of proportionality. Precautions, decision-making processes, and investigations are important to the application of all principles of IHL, and not only to cases of suspected violations of the principle of proportionality.

However, as we will show in the following chapters, because of the uncertainty surrounding the interpretation of many aspects of proportionality, specific procedures were developed explicitly in order to address its application.

## A. THE LEGAL BACKGROUND

The analysis of procedures in the application of proportionality begins with article 57 of AP-I, which discusses "precautions in attack."[3] This article requires the attacking force to evaluate not only the issue of proportionality, but also a much wider series of issues before embarking on an attack. It has to consider the possibility of advanced warning (article 57(2)(c)); it must use means and methods of warfare that cause the least damage to civilians (57(2)(a)(ii)); and military commanders have to select, from among multiple military objectives, those which are least harmful to civilians if those targets will give a similar military advantage (57)(3)).

3. Protocol Additional to the Geneva Conventions of August 12, 1949, and Relating to the Protection of Victims of International Armed Conflicts (Protocol I), June 8, 1977, art. 57, 1125 U.N.T.S. 3 [AP-I] states the following:

1. In the conduct of military operations, constant care shall be taken to spare the civilian population, civilians and civilian objects.
2. With respect to attacks, the following precautions shall be taken:
   (a) those who plan or decide upon an attack shall:
      (ii) take all feasible precautions in the choice of means and methods of attack with a view to avoiding, and in any event to minimizing, incidental loss of civilian life, injury to civilians and damage to civilian objects;
      (iii) refrain from deciding to launch any attack which may be expected to cause incidental loss of civilian life, injury to civilians, damage to civilian objects, or a combination thereof, which would be excessive in relation to the concrete and direct military advantage anticipated;
   (b) an attack shall be cancelled or suspended if it becomes apparent that the objective is not a military one or is subject to special protection or that the attack may be expected to cause incidental loss of civilian life, injury to civilians, damage to civilian objects, or a combination thereof, which would be excessive in relation to the concrete and direct military advantage anticipated;
   (c) effective advance warning shall be given of attacks which may affect the civilian population, unless circumstances do not permit.
3. When a choice is possible between several military objectives for obtaining a similar military advantage, the objective to be selected shall be that the attack on which may be expected to cause the least danger to civilian lives and to civilian objects.

Traditionally, article 57 was considered a tool for commanders in order to implement different facets of the prohibitions contained in earlier articles in AP-I. However, in current armed conflicts, and especially in planned operations such as targeted killings, article 57 has become a much more important norm. Armed forces that resort to targeted killings have come to consider it to be a blueprint for planning and executing an attack. In this approach, the main duty of the armed forces, and of military lawyers, is to undertake a series of bureaucratic tests and processes that take into account the existence of civilians.

The general principle of proportionality's analysis as it exists in constitutional and administrative law,[4] is sometimes divided into three different questions. The first concerns the rational connection between the legitimate aim and the action taken. In IHL, this is covered by the principle of necessity and the principle of distinction. The second question concerns necessity and asks: Is there a way to achieve the desired (legitimate) goal with less collateral damage? The third question (proportionality in the narrowest sense, or *strictu sensu*) relates to the balance between the desired result and the harm caused by the action. In IHL, this means balancing between the concrete and direct military advantage gained and the collateral damage inflicted. Most of the scholarship deals with the application of proportionality *strictu sensu*. However, the most important way in which proportionality makes a difference on the battlefield is by causing commanders to ask the first and second questions mentioned before: Will the concrete and direct military advantage in fact be achieved by the attack that also causes unintended harm to civilians? And is there a way to reduce the harm to civilians without cancelling the attack?

As we shall see, the emphasis placed on these questions in practice makes the difference between the second and third meanings of proportionality unclear.

## B. PROCEDURES

Contemporary armed conflicts are subject to decidedly heightened public awareness of civilian casualties. The media brings pictures of dead women and children into every home, and in so doing fosters public criticism not only of the specific operations in which civilians are harmed, but also of the overall military policy and strategy. This attention creates pressure on politicians and armed forces to avoid causing civilian casualties. It has also given rise to a phenomenon sometimes termed "the strategic corporal," the hypothetical non-commissioned officer whose actions in a remote part of the battlefield might create political and strategic problems for politicians and the high command.[5]

4. See Chapter 2.

5. Charles Krulak, *The Strategic Corporal: Leadership in the Three Block War*, THE MARINES MAGAZINE (1999), *available at*: http://www.au.af.mil/au/awc/awcgate/usmc/strategic_corporal.htm.

This problem seems to be especially acute in matters of proportionality, where the principle is vague. Moreover, Kasher and Kimhi found that individual soldiers interpret the meaning of the principle of proportionality based on their own personalities. A more aggressive person will tend to interpret the principle as allowing more firepower and more civilian collateral damage than someone who is less aggressive by nature.[6]

Naturally, this problem would be minimized if it were possible to train all soldiers to behave in ways that take into account all the strategic and political implications of their actions. Despite some attempts to attain this goal,[7] broadly speaking it has not proved realistic. Soldiers tend to take their own safety into account and to follow their instincts. They may have ideological or cultural biases that are not necessarily identical to those of their military or political superiors. In short, soldiers are like every other agent: they act to promote their own best interests which do not necessarily dovetail with those of their principals.[8]

One way to control soldiers' behavior is to create detailed procedures. Indeed, all bureaucracies adopt procedures precisely in order to control the way in which every bureaucrat within it operates. Procedures ensure, to at least some extent, that lower-level operatives enjoy only limited discretion, giving them only limited opportunities to deviate from the wishes and orders of the higher level in the organization—in the military case, the high command or the political echelon. However, military activity does not easily lend itself to control by procedure, especially during battles. The reasons are clear. Procedures are time-consuming, and battles require alacrity. Procedures are based on solid information and knowledge while winning battles is about innovation when confronted with uncertainties and the "fog of war." Procedures are universal and dogmatic whereas battles require flexibility and attention to the specific context.[9]

Yet the bureaucratic approach, we submit, is part of every armed activity. It is especially prevalent where there is a danger of causing civilian casualties. The context in which armed forces have used the most sophisticated approach toward procedures is that of targeted killing operations. The very essence of targeted killings is that they are preplanned, and thus they allow adequate time for the

6. Asa Kasher & Shaul Kimhi, *Moral Dilemmas in Military Situations: Proportionality Principle, Religiosity, Political Attitudes, and Authoritarian Personality* 27(3) J. Military Psychology 169 (2015).

7. See, e.g., Lynda Liddy, *The Strategic Corporal: Some Requirements in Training and Education* 11(2) The Australian Army J. 139 (2013), claiming that "the Australian Army must begin to foster a military culture that is aimed at preparing non-commissioned officers (NCOs) to become what has been described as 'strategic corporals.'"

8. For a full analysis, see Peter D. Feaver, Armed Servants: Agency, Oversight and Civil-Military Relations (2005).

9. Indeed, this is the reason armed forces adopt alternative modes of control. Such, for example, is the adoption of IHL, which serves as a mode of control. See: Eyal Benvenisti & Amichai Cohen, *War Is Governance: Explaining the Logic of the Laws of War from a Principal–Agent Perspective*, 112 Mich. L. Rev. 1363 (2014).

consideration of consequences. Such operations also require precise intelligence—specific knowledge regarding the whereabouts of the target—which further allows for the precise calibration of objectives at all levels of command. In short, targeted killings seem to offer the perfect arena in which modern armies can actually control the way in which operations take place by designing the procedures to be implemented in the course of such operations.

Given such considerations, it is not surprising that targeted killings have indeed become highly bureaucratized, especially concerning attention to civilian casualties. In a recent article, Gregory McNeal described the method by which the United States assesses collateral damage and the legality of targeted killings.[10] There is a strict evaluation of the possible damage to civilians, a requirement to gather information, and clear guidelines regarding who should be part of the decision-making process. There is also extensive use of scientific knowledge regarding the effects of different kinds of weapons, such as the radius of impact of different bombs or projectiles. All these considerations create a situation in which a very detailed set of procedures must be followed prior to launching a targeted killing operation. This policy has two basic goals: one is to limit the extent of civilians casualties as much as possible; the second is to assess the likelihood and number of civilian casualties, and to provide this information up the chain of command so that high-level military and political commanders can evaluate the potential consequences. For similar reasons to those applied by the US military, Israel also employs a heavily procedural process of defining targets and authorizing targeted killing operations.

But how is proportionality to be applied in practice? Who makes the decisions? What is the role of legal advisors? What is the proper procedure for assessing the proportionality of an attack? The following sections addresses these and other questions.

## C. THE SUITABLE DECISION-MAKER

Who is the agent most suitable for assessing the proportionality of an attack? Who should bear the responsibility if a wrong decision is made and a disproportionate attack is carried out? At what level should the decision about the proportionality of an be made: in the field, by the immediate commander or soldier who is on site and closest to the action; or at higher levels of command, where there is a better chance of being able to examine and assess the overarching military advantage that can be gained from the attack?

The international group of experts who authored the HPCR Manual on International Law Applicable to Air and Missile Warfare were of the opinion that proportionality is the obligation of "anyone with the ability and authority

10. Gregory S. McNeal, *Targeted Killing and Accountability*, 102 Georgetown L. J. 681 (2014).

to suspend, abort, or cancel an attack," even individual pilots.[11] Proportionality, according to this approach, is the purview of both the high command as well as soldiers in the field.

The problem with this approach is that if the broader definition of the "overall" military advantage of "the attack as a whole" is accepted as we argue in Chapter 4,[12] it is clearly preferable that the decision be made by higher-ranking members of the military.[13] This is, for example, the position of the United States, which states that responsibility lies with the commanders who wield authority over military operations, while combatants' responsibilities depend "on their role and assigned military duties in planning or conducting an attack."[14] As pointed out by Dinstein, the military advantage of an attack cannot always be apparent to the individual infantry soldiers or pilots in the field, as attacks are sometimes planned sequentially or as part of a wider tactical operation. Therefore, in his opinion, it would be incorrect to analyze proportionality based solely on one specific attack.[15] For example, attacks aimed at diverting the enemy from the main assault might appear to produce only a limited military advantage to those carrying them out, but, taken together with the other attacks that they enable, they can clearly attain a significant military advantage. In this manner, it has been suggested by Fenrick that it is unlikely that the proper level for assessing proportionality would be below the divisional level.[16] The drafting process of the Additional Protocols also suggests that it should be the higher echelons of command that assess the proportionality of attacks, rather than soldiers in the field.[17]

11. Program on Humanitarian Policy and Conflict Research (HPCR) at Harvard University, *Commentary on the HPCR Manual on International Law Applicable to Air and Missile Warfare* 94 (2010).

12. For a discussion of how the military advantage is analyzed, see Chapter 4, notes 205–34 and accompanying text.

13. Robert D. Sloane, *Puzzles of Proportion and the "Reasonable Military Commander": Reflections on the Law, Ethics, and Geopolitics of Proportionality*, 6 Harv. Nat'l Sec. J. 299, 313 (2015).

14. US Department of Defense, Law of War Manual, paras. 5.10.2–2.1 (2015, updated Dec. 2016) [DoD Manual]. The United States does, however, authorize pilots to suspend attacks if new information comes to light, though it makes clear that subordinates do not have the authority to second guess their commanders because they disagree with their decision or assessment. *Id.*, para. 5.11.4.

15. Yoram Dinstein, The Conduct of Hostilities under the Law of International Armed Conflict 134 (2nd ed., 2010).

16. W. J. Fenrick, *The Rule of Proportionality and Protocol I in Conventional Warfare*, 98 Mil. L. Rev. 91, 108 (1982). Interestingly, the divisional level is also the level at which the ICRC's Commentary on the First Additional Protocol envisaged legal advisors being permanently posted. Commentary on the Additional Protocols of 8 June 1977 to the Geneva Conventions of 12 August 1949, para. 3359 (ICRC, Yves Sandoz, Christophe Swinarki, & Bruno Zimmerman eds., 1987) [AP-I Commentary].

17. Fenrick, *Id.*, at 107–08.

An additional consideration that supports higher ranking commanders making the decision is that, in modern militaries, there are often situations in which higher levels of command have a more complete picture of the situation on the ground than soldiers in the heat of battle, and, thus, are better able to fully assess both the expected incidental harm to civilians and the military advantage.[18]

The two core approaches to determining the appropriate decision-maker both reflect attempts to find a balance between two conflicting interests: protecting civilians and military necessity.

On the one hand, the view that individual soldiers should be able to judge the proportionality of an attack is based on the idea that in combat situations it is often the case that the high command, who are not in the thick of the action, may not fully appreciate the risk and expected harm to civilian life. New facts may come to light in the course of an operation of which the commanders may not have been aware during the planning phase, and decisions regarding proportionality ought to be made based on the most up-to-date information. Civilian lives should not be forsaken merely because commanders had already made their assessment regarding an attack's proportionality before the attack unfolded. Even in today's technologically advanced battlefield, when commanders have access to real-time information from the front lines, this information might still be partial due to weather conditions, communications malfunctions, time constraints, or the challenge of managing a wider campaign. The front-line soldier or field officer might have access to more relevant information and be better able to assess proportionality in real time if the situation on the ground changes from that which was previously assessed.

On the other hand, those who support proportionality assessments being made by higher ranks seem to be guided by the fact that the operators in the field may not know all the operational and tactical ramifications of the attacks they are carrying out such as whether the attack is a diversion, or if other attacks rely on the first attack. This could also happen if the information regarding the nature of the target is highly classified, or if there are communication limitations and time constraints that do not permit transmission of the full operational picture. As a result, a crucial attack that could alter the course of the entire conflict may be

18. Schmitt and Merriam, for example, cite IDF personnel as cautioning "that the operations center often enjoys a better situational awareness of the target area than the pilot. Whereas the pilot is limited to onboard sensors and external feeds available in the aircraft, the operations center generally enjoys a refined and stable visual picture of the target area from RPA [remotely piloted aircraft (drone)] coverage and benefits from all-source intelligence fusion capability. Thus, unless a pilot personally observes indicators that raise doubt about the target, he or she is entitled to rely on the discretion of the operations center in executing the strike" (Michael N. Schmitt & John J. Merriam, *The Tyranny of Context: Israeli Targeting Practices in Legal Perspective*, 37 U. Pa. J. Int'l L. 53, 81 (2015)).

unnecessarily called off by front-line commanders due to the presence of, and risk to, a small number of civilians.[19]

Consider the following scenario: During World War II, Operation Fortitude was intended to deceive Nazi Germany into believing that the Allied invasion of Europe, Operation Overlord, would land elsewhere than on the beaches of Normandy. One of the decoy sites was Pas de Calais, where, in the months leading up to the invasion, numerous targets were bombed in order to shift Nazi Germany's attention away from Normandy to this decoy site.[20] The true landing site was highly classified, and although multitudes of people would ultimately participate in planning the assault, few of them actually knew where and when the true attack would take place.[21] Proportionality was not a norm during World War II. However, in a theoretical world in which proportionality *was* a legal norm during World War II, what would have happened if individual pilots, upon viewing their targets in Pas de Calais, had decided not to bomb them because they observed large concentrations of civilians below? What if they, contrary to the senior commanders that had approved the proportionality of the attacks, had decided that the expected civilian casualties did not warrant the attack? Their decision could have seemed justified to them, as they might not have known the true diversionary purpose of their attack. Ordinarily, destroying a railway crossing might not seem to justify significant civilian casualties. In this case, however, destroying that same target in order to safeguard the largest invasion in history might well have been justified. Otherwise, the success of the entire operation—the Allied invasion of France and Europe, which relied upon the successful deception—could have been jeopardized.

There are those who take a middle position. One of the authors of this book, for example, has written previously that "once an operation is underway, the primary responsibility for the review lies with the commander on the ground," though the expectations from him are lower due to the commander's lack of resources, such as intelligence, and time to plan.[22] Similarly, ICRC's *Commentary on AP-I* maintains that while the higher echelons have the primary responsibility for assessing the proportionality of an attack, subordinates also bear responsibility for the proportionality of attacks and must therefore be trained to determine whether the attacks in which they engage are proportionate.[23]

19. Contrast this to the oft-quoted Mishnaic and Talmudic quote: "Whoever destroys a soul, it is considered as if he destroyed an entire world. And whoever saves a life, it is considered as if he saved an entire world" (Mishnah Sanhedrin 4:5; Yerushalmi Talmud Sanhedrin 4:9).

20. See Chapter 4, notes 257–58 and the accompanying text.

21. Stephen E. Ambrose, D-Day June 6, 1944: The Climactic Battle of World War II 156 (1994).

22. Amichai Cohen, *The Principle of Proportionality in the Context of Operation Cast Lead: Institutional Perspectives*, 35 Rutgers L. Record 23, 33 (2009).

23. AP-I Commentary, *supra* note 16, para. 2197. Generally, IHL obligates commanders to facilitate the implementation of states' obligations. This requires commanders to "prevent and,

Kalshoven presents a similar view that the assessment of proportionality must be made by the higher echelons, but the lower echelons still bear responsibility and must follow certain guidelines. They must always obey the principle of distinction; assure that heavy weapons are not needlessly employed against military objectives; and most importantly, ascertain that "an attack is not carried out when no reasonable person could doubt the strictly limited military significance of the chosen target as compared to the severe damage the attack may be expected to cause among the civilian population." The unit must also be "thoroughly aware . . . of its basic obligation to spare the civilian population as much as possible."[24]

Stefan Oeter offers a similar position. In his opinion, officers and soldiers have to rely on the proportionality assessment made by their commanders, so long as the attack does not resemble "obvious war crimes such as deliberate indiscriminate attacks."[25] According to this view, soldiers and commanders in the field would have to assess the proportionality of an attack only if that attack was independently planned and carried out by them.[26]

An alternate solution to the question of who bears responsibility for assessing the proportionality of the attack synthesizes the two main different approaches, and could serve to bridge the gaps that occur in certain situations, primarily those in which soldiers in the field decide to abort attacks without knowing the full reason behind them.

This alternative solution would come into play in preplanned attacks or attacks that are handed down to soldiers or pilots by their commanders, and would involve what we term a "proportionality guideline." A proportionality guideline is an assessment tool given by senior commanders to the soldiers or pilots charged with carrying out an attack, along with the relevant targeting information. This guideline, which is based on the senior commanders' knowledge of the "attack as a whole," sets the upper limit of collateral damage that can be permitted in any given attack, based on the circumstances. It lets the soldiers and pilots know that the attack will remain proportionate as long as the expected collateral damage

where necessary, to suppress and to report to competent authorities breaches of the Conventions and of this Protocol" (AP-I, *supra* note 3, art. 87(1)). Furthermore, commanders are obligated to "ensure that members of the armed forces under their command are aware of their obligations" (AP-I, *supra* note 3, art. 87(2)). These obligations hold true even when, due to the developments of battle, commanders cannot exercise the required control over their troops. In those cases, a commander "must impose discipline to a sufficient degree, to enforce compliance with the rules of the Conventions and the Protocol, even when he may momentarily lose sight of his troops" (AP-I Commentary, *supra* note 16, para. 3550).

24. Frits Kalshoven & Liesbeth Zegveld, Constraints on the Waging of War: An Introduction to International Humanitarian Law 115 (4th ed., 2011).

25. Stefan Oeter, *Methods and Means of Combat, in* The Handbook of International Humanitarian Law, para. 460(2) (Terry Gill & Dieter Fleck eds., 2nd ed., 2008).

26. *Id.*

does not exceed the stated upper limit. These limits can be set as "high," "moderate," "limited," or in certain cases even as low as "no collateral damage."[27]

If it becomes apparent that the attack is expected to exceed the collateral damage permitted under the guideline, the attack must either be cancelled or suspended by the soldier in the field, or referred back to the commanders who issued the original proportionality guideline for reassessment based on the new information emerging from the field.[28] This would also seem to conform to the requirement of article 57(2)(b) of AP-I, which states:

> an attack shall be cancelled or suspended if it becomes apparent that the objective is not a military one or is subject to special protection or that the attack may be expected to cause incidental loss of civilian life, injury to civilians, damage to civilian objects, or a combination thereof, which would be excessive in relation to the concrete and direct military advantage anticipated.

The *Commentary on AP-I* explicitly states that this article is primarily directed at those executing the attacks, when their information is more accurate than that possessed by those who ordered or planned the attack—for example, due to their ability to visually assess the information in the field.[29]

In the example of the theoretical pilot in Operation Fortitude, although he might not know the reasons behind the assessments in the "proportionality guideline" provided by his commanders, the pilot would know that so long as the expected collateral damage did not exceed a "high" level, he could execute the attack. This would enable him to carry out a proportionate attack (though he may not understand why), and at the same time ensure that he could take into account new target-related information in the final moments before the attack.

This solution would enable soldiers to attack legitimate targets without calling back to base in cases in which circumstances change on the ground, so long as the attack remains within the upper limits of the proportionality guideline. Such a solution could also solve the problem posed by radio silence during crucial attacks.

Thus, using proportionality guidelines may provide a better balance between collateral damage and the need to achieve a military advantage, which can be better estimated by higher levels of command, while ensuring that those who pull the trigger can cancel or suspend attacks when real-time conditions in the field differ from those envisioned by their commanders.

27. Fleshing out these terms into numerical value is beyond the scope of this book. The conceptual suggestion is the essence.

28. Israel, for example, currently assesses proportionality in a manner that if significant new information emerges concerning the target, a reassessment of the proportionality of the attack must be carried out by all relevant officers involved in the targeting process, including the legal advisor (Schmitt & Merriam, *supra* note 18, at 79).

29. AP-I COMMENTARY, *supra* note 16, paras. 2220–21.

## Doubts

In combat situations, decisions are often shrouded in uncertainty. Therefore, proportionality assessments often are made when doubts exist regarding the correct application of the rule of proportionality. The first type of doubt is one in which the decision-maker is in doubt regarding the facts: Are the people around the target civilians or combatants? Are they voluntary or involuntary human shields?

AP-I article 50(1) of AP-I explicitly states: "In case of doubt whether a person is a civilian, that person shall be considered to be a civilian." Similarly, regarding civilian objects, article 52(3) states:

> In case of doubt whether an object which is normally dedicated to civilian purposes, such as a place of worship, a house or other dwelling or a school, is being used to make an effective contribution to military action, it shall be presumed not to be so used.

The decision-maker may of course continue to gather information regarding the targets and incidental damage until he or she is satisfied.[30] However, if doubt remains, then the assessment should be based on the obligation to consider all doubtful targets and incidental harms as if they are civilians.

It is unclear whether this article is of customary status, and if so, what the extent of the obligation might be.[31] The United States Department of Defense Law of War Manual, for example, expressly rejects the customary status of this presumption.[32] It does accept, however, that attacks may not be directed against civilians "based on merely hypothetical or speculative considerations" and that, in any case, determining whether a target is lawful or not is a task that must be carried out "in good faith based on the information available to them in light of the circumstances ruling at the time."[33]

The ICRC too, in its study of customary IHL, states that "the issue of how to classify an object in case of doubt is not entirely clear," and, "in case of doubt, a careful assessment has to be made under the conditions and restraints governing a particular situation as to whether there are sufficient indications to warrant an attack."[34] Even if the presumption in favor of civilian status is accepted as customary, the obligation's extent is unclear. It seems that at least some states believe

30. Emanuela-Chiara Gillard, Proportionality in the Conduct of Hostilities: The Incidental Harm Side of the Assessment 22 (Chatham House International Law Programme, 2018).

31. Michael N. Schmitt, *Targeting and International Humanitarian Law in Afghanistan, in* The War in Afghanistan: A Legal Analysis, 85 Int'l Law Stud. 307, 320 (2009).

32. DoD Manual, *supra* note 14, para. 5.4.3.2; Dinstein, *supra* note 15, at 98.

33. DoD Manual, *supra* note 14, para. 5.4.3.2.

34. Jean-Marie Henckaerts & Louise Doswald-Beck, Customary International Humanitarian Law, Vol. 1, rule 10 (2005) [Henckaerts & Doswald-Beck, ICRC Study].

that the presumption applies only when there is a serious doubt, or when there is no evidence to the contrary, and not in every case of doubt.[35]

Even if we agree that in cases of factual uncertainty there should be a presumption in favor of civilian status, there is still uncertainty with regard to two other possible situations: First, doubts regarding the evaluation of whether the incidental harm is excessive compared to the military advantage. And second, when a soldier who has been given orders has doubts regarding the facts or whether the attack would be considered "excessive."

In a recent post, Adil Haque claimed that in both cases, there is a duty not to attack.[36] First, Haque posits that when there is doubt regarding the evaluation of proportionality—that is, whether the incidental harm is excessive compared to the military advantage—the decision-maker should opt for restraint, and should not attack.

In our opinion, Haque's position is extremely problematic. Granted, a rule that requires restraint in case of doubt has many advantages, such as giving the commanders incentives to seek more intelligence, and counters commanders' natural desire to complete their mission and attack. However, these claims should not be pushed too far. The nature of the proportionality principle is that it requires balancing competing claims. In many cases, doubt is inherent in this balancing act, and yet commanders are required to decide. The principle of proportionality, as we have seen, is not about adhering to a numerical formula as no formula

35. Regarding the extent of the obligation, for example, it is the position of the United Kingdom that "in the practical application of the principle of civilian immunity and the rule of doubt, (a) commanders and others responsible for planning, deciding upon, or executing attacks necessarily have to reach decisions on the basis of their assessment of the information, from all sources, available to them at the relevant time, (b) it is only in cases of *substantial doubt*, after this assessment about the status of the individual in question, that the latter should be given the benefit of the doubt and treated as a civilian, and (c) the rule of doubt does not override the commander's duty to protect the safety of troops under his command or to preserve the military situation" (United Kingdom Ministry of Defence, Joint Service Publication 383, The Joint Service Manual of the Law of Armed Conflict, para. 5.3.4 (2004) (emphasis added)). In the *Galić* case, the ICTY Trial Chamber stated that "A widely accepted definition of military objectives is given by Article 52 of Additional Protocol I . . . In case of doubt as to whether an object which is normally dedicated to civilian purposes is being used to make an effective contribution to military action, it shall be presumed not to be so used. The Trial Chamber understands that such an object shall not be attacked *when it is not reasonable to believe*, in the circumstances of the person contemplating the attack, including the information available to the latter, that the object is being used to make an effective contribution to military action" (Prosecutor v. Galić, ICTY Trial Chamber, IT-98-29, *Judgment*, para. 51 (Dec. 5, 2003) (emphasis added)).

But see also the practice of many states as quoted in the ICRC's study of customary IHL, which supports the presumption in favor of civilian status in cases of doubt. Henckaerts & Doswald-Beck, ICRC Study *supra* note 34, vol. 2 (Practice) Rule 6 (c), *available at:* https://ihl-databases.icrc.org/customary-ihl/eng/docs/v2_rul_rule6_sectionc.

36. Adil A. Haque, *Proportionality and Doubt,* Just Security (Jan. 29, 2019), *available at:* https://www.justsecurity.org/62375/proportionality-doubt/.

exists, but rather about requiring military commanders to take precautions, and to avoid or minimize harm to the civilian population. The term "excessive" in AP-I, and the term "clearly excessive" in the Rome Statute, point in the opposite direction from Haque. Commanders should refrain from attacking based on their evaluation of the advantages and incidental damages. A commander who experiences no doubts when deciding to launch an attack in which civilians will be killed may not be driven to take all necessary precautions. Doubt, contrary to Haque's claim, is an essential part of the decision-making process, and lies at the root of the principle of proportionality.

Haque's second claim is that when the person executing the attack on the ground has doubts about whether or not to implement the attack, he should also choose not to attack.

We agree that when the soldier actually executing an attack discovers new information, which he assumes was not known to his commanders and which might affect the proportionality assessment, he must halt the attack. For example, according to this interpretation, if more civilians than expected appear near a military target, the pilot about to launch a bomb should rethink the proportionality of the attack. However, with regard to evaluations of excessiveness, we do not think that a soldier on the ground should be able to "reevaluate" the commands he is given in case of doubt. Certainly, a soldier is not allowed to follow a "manifestly unlawful" order. But the mere existence of doubt in the soldier's estimation is no indication that the command given is manifestly unlawful.

There are good military reasons for this conclusion, such as preserving the chain of command, and not requiring soldiers to be aware of all intelligence available to the high command. There is also a moral one. In our view, the principle of proportionality places the responsibility for implementing the principle on the shoulders of the commander. The commander has the necessary knowledge and responsibility to implement this principle. Asking soldiers to make these complex assessments would shift the responsibility from the commander to the soldier who does not possess the means to make these kinds of decisions and potentially allowing commanders to evade their responsibility. Knowing that their decisions will not be questioned by soldiers in the field places the responsibility squarely on the commander's shoulders.

## D. HOW MUCH INTELLIGENCE IS NECESSARY?[37]

> Intelligence assessments are necessarily based on incomplete information since only fragments of the true picture will be known.[38]

37. The authors wish to thank Dr. Asaf Lubin for his advice regarding this section.

38. McCann v. United Kingdom, E.Ct.H.R., App. No. 18984/91, paras. 189, 213 (1995) (Submission of the Government of the United Kingdom to the Grand Chamber). The court held that the United Kingdom failed in that they had not made "sufficient allowances for the possibility that their intelligence assessments might, in some respects at least, be erroneous," and that therefore, the recourse to the use of force was in violation of the state's Convention obligations.

> Many intelligence reports in war are contradictory; even more are false, and most are uncertain. (Carl von Clausewitz)[39]

What amount and quality of information does the law require commanders to have prior to making decisions regarding proportionality? The answer to this question is unclear. Being able to assess what information commanders *actually* had when making their decisions is highly unlikely, as "the planning and decision-making process of a commander is by definition secret and we will never know what he knew or what alternatives he had."[40]

This question does not exist in a void. There are cases in which the lack of information and intelligence was seen as a violation of international law.[41] One example of this can be found in the Report of the Special Investigatory Commission on the targeted killing of Salah Shehadeh, the commander of Hamas's military wing who was killed on July 22, 2002 in Gaza City.[42] The Shehadeh targeted killing operation unfortunately also killed 14 civilians, including Shehadeh's 15-year-old daughter, and the report concluded that the attack caused disproportionate collateral damage to civilians. The report stressed that it had not been known that the civilians would be in the target area, and the Commission declared that insufficient information had been gathered prior to the attack regarding the occupancy of houses in the vicinity of the target. Had proper intelligence been gathered—that is, had appropriate resources been allocated to examining the expected collateral damage—the attack might not have been undertaken.[43] This relates to the obligation to take precautions, which Israel, like the United States, views as part of the principle of proportionality, alongside the corollary obligation prohibiting attacks that would cause excessive harm to civilians.[44]

AP-I article 57(2)(a) obligates parties to armed conflicts to take "all feasible precautions" in order to determine the legality of their attacks, at least regarding the principle of distinction and the requirement to minimize incidental harm to civilians:[45]

39. W. Hays Parks, *Air War and the Law of War*, 32 Air Force L. Rev. 1, 181 (1990).

40. Marco Sassoli & Lindsey Cameron, *The Protection of Civilian Objects—Current State of Law and Issues de lege ferenda*, *in* The Law of Air Warfare: Contemporary Issues, 35, 71 (Natalino Ronzitti & Gabriella Venturini eds., 2006).

41. For an additional example, see *supra*, note 36.

42. See Chapter 5, notes 103–105 and the accompanying text.

43. *Report of the Special Investigatory Commission on the Targeted Killing of Salah Shehadeh* 77–81, 98–99 (Feb. 2011).

44. DoD Manual, *supra* note 14, para. 5.10.5.

45. An additional obligation to take precautions before an attack concerns the obligation to give effective warning to civilians (AP-I, *supra* note 3, art. 57(2)(c): "effective advance warning shall be given of attacks which may affect the civilian population, unless circumstances do not permit"). Though the obligation to give warning to the civilian population exists "unless circumstances do not permit," the Goldstone Report confused this element, incorrectly reading

> Those who plan or decide upon an attack shall: (i) do *everything feasible* to verify that the objectives to be attacked are neither civilians nor civilian objects and are not subject to special protection, but are military objectives within the meaning of paragraph 2 of Article 52 and that it is not prohibited by the provisions of this Protocol to attack them; (ii) take *all feasible* precautions in the choice of means and methods of attack with a view to avoiding, and in any event to minimizing, incidental loss of civilian life, injury to civilians and damage to civilian objects.[46]

The Committee to Review the NATO Bombing Campaign offered its position regarding the question of what is "feasible" in this context, requiring that "effective intelligence gathering systems" be employed, but giving commanders "some range of discretion" in deciding which resources should be used for this purpose:

> The obligation to do *everything feasible is high but not absolute.* A military commander must set up an *effective intelligence gathering system to collect and evaluate information* concerning potential targets. The commander must also direct his forces to use available technical means to properly identify targets during operations. *Both the commander and the aircrew actually engaged in operations must have some range of discretion to determine which available resources shall be used and how they shall be used.*[47]

In the *Targeted Killings* case, the Israeli HCJ stated:

> *Well established information* is needed before categorizing a civilian as [a combatant] . . . *Information which has been most thoroughly verified* is needed regarding the identity and activity of the civilian who is allegedly taking part in

this obligation as containing its own proportionality assessment: "The key limitation on the application of the rule is if the military advantage of surprise would be undermined by giving a warning. The same calculation of proportionality has to be made here as in other circumstances. The question is whether the injury or damage done to civilians or civilian objects by not giving a warning is excessive in relation to the advantage to be gained by the element of surprise for the particular operation. There may be other circumstances when a warning is simply not possible" (*Report of the United Nations Fact-Finding Mission on the Gaza Conflict*, U.N. Doc. A/HRC/12/48 para. 529 (Sep. 25, 2009) [The Goldstone Report]). As mentioned by Schmitt, the obligation to give warning prior to attack does not contain an obligation to do so if not giving a warning would cause excessive harm to civilians (Michael N. Schmitt, *Military Necessity and Humanity in International Humanitarian Law: Preserving the Delicate Balance*, 50 Va. J. Int'l L. 795, 827 (2010)).

46. AP-I, *supra* note 3, art. 57(2)(a)(i)–(ii) (emphasis added).

47. ICTY, Final Report to the Prosecutor by the Committee Established to Review the NATO Bombing Campaign Against the Federal Republic of Yugoslavia, para. 29 (2000) (emphasis added).

> the hostilities . . . In the case of doubt, careful verification is needed before an attack is made.[48]

However, these statements do not clarify what the terms "all feasible precautions" or "everything feasible" mean in practice and provide little guidance.

One view regarding the amount of information required, which is supported by certain state practice, is that when examining the proportionality of an attack after the fact, the proportionality assessment must be based on an objective standard: the information *reasonably* available at the relevant time.[49] This is also supported by the ICTY *Galić* case, in which the Trial Chamber noted that proportionality should be assessed by the standard of "a *reasonably well-informed* person in the circumstances of the actual perpetrator."[50]

According to the objective standard, the determination of what constitutes *reasonable* information to be gathered and assessed prior to an attack is context-specific. The more time the commander has for assessing the possible implications of the attack, the more information he is required to collect. For example, in a large-scale preplanned attack, an attacker would be required to gather all possible available information and subject the plan for the operation to an in-depth proportionality analysis. By contrast, under more time-sensitive conditions—for example, once an operation is already underway or when troops are under enemy fire—commanders can only be held to a lower standard, as time and resources are lacking, and it is not feasible to gather and analyze all of the information regarding the potential results of the attack. The commander making the decision can only do what can be reasonably expected of him in such a situation.[51] The question of what is reasonable in the *assessment* of the available information "will depend to some extent on the amount of information readily available, the staff at hand to deal with it, and whether that information raises questions that require further research of other sources of information."[52]

48. HCJ 769/02, Public Committee against Torture v. The State of Israel, PD 62(1) 507, para. 40 (2006) [Isr.] (emphasis added).

49. These states include Belgium, Canada, Germany, Ireland, New Zealand, Spain, the United Kingdom, and the United States; see Chapter 5, notes 139–46.

50. Galić, *supra* note 35, para. 58 (emphasis added). This quote, which discusses the standard under which tribunals should assess the decisions made by commanders ex post facto, is also instructive of the standard of information required for assessing proportionality—the information gathering must be "reasonable," so as to permit a commander to make decisions as a "reasonably well-informed person."

51. Cohen, *The Principle of Proportionality in the Context of Operation Cast Lead*, *supra* note 22, at 33.

52. A.P.V. Rogers, Law on the Battlefield 151 (3rd ed., 2012); Isable Robinson & Ellen Nohle, *Proportionality and Precautions in Attack: The Reverberating Effects of Using Explosive Weapons in Populated Areas*, 98 Int'l Rev. Red Cross 107, 136 (2016).

A different view supported by other states posits a subjective standard, requiring that proportionality assessments be based on the information that was available—*actually* available—at the relevant time.[53] While this position may help clarify how proportionality is to be assessed by tribunals or committees *after* the fact, it does little to clarify and guide practitioners with regard to how much and which information and intelligence should be gathered *before* an attack. It may help to recall that in assessing proportionality, the attacker must act "reasonably and in good faith."[54] This applies to the gathering of intelligence and feasible precautions, whose "interpretation will be a matter of common sense and good faith."[55]

A third position may offer a clearer view on this issue, while setting a relatively high standard: Information must continue to be gathered until doubts regarding the proportionality of the attack can be removed. One position in this regard requires commanders to

> employ *all means* of reconnaissance and intelligence available to them unless and until there is sufficient certainty of the military nature of a potential target for attack. As soon as there are no longer any *serious doubts* concerning . . . proportionality . . . the duty . . . is satisfied.[56]

An even higher threshold is set by the ICRC in its *Commentary on AP-I*, which states that targets should be identified "with great care," and "*in case of doubt, even if there is only slight doubt*, [commanders] must call for additional information and, if need be, give orders for further reconnaissance." Once gathered, the "evaluation of the information obtained must include a serious check of its accuracy, particularly as there is nothing to prevent the enemy from setting up fake military objectives or camouflaging the true ones."[57] According to the *Commentary*, states are obligated to take "the necessary identification measures in good time."[58] The

53. These include Australia, Austria, Ecuador, France, Israel, Italy, The Netherlands, and the U.S. See Chapter 5, notes 130–36; DoD Manual, *supra* note 14, para. 5.10.2.3. The Elements of Crimes of the Rome Statute seems to support this position as well. International Criminal Court, Elements of Crimes, 19 n.37 (2011) (requiring that the analysis of the crime of causing excessive incidental death be examined based on the "requisite information available to the perpetrator at the time").

54. Dinstein, *supra* note 15, at 133. The ICRC takes a similar view stating that "Putting these provisions into practice, or, for that matter, any others in Part IV, will require *complete good faith* on the part of the belligerents, as well as the desire to conform with the general principle of respect for the civilian population." AP-I Commentary, *supra* note 16, para. 1978 (emphasis added).

55. AP-I Commentary, *supra* note 16, para. 2198.

56. Oeter, *supra* note 25, para. 460(3).

57. AP-I Commentary, *supra* note 16, para. 2195.

58. *Id.*, para. 2198.

standard set by this position is high indeed, for, as Clausewitz wrote: "War is the realm of uncertainty."[59]

We believe that reasons of legal policy, necessitate adopting a scale regarding the duty to gather information. This seems to be reflected in some state practice. This scale can be described by using Newton and May's framework of thresholds, discussed in Chapter 3. The most important contexts in which states are expected to gather information are cases in which the state operates near a civilian population that it controls, or for which it is responsible. In the demonstrations near the Gaza border that began in 2018,[60] for example, Israeli soldiers were required not only to identify legitimate targets, but also to assess the number of civilians surrounding these targets, and the probability that they would be harmed by shooting at the legitimate targets. In targeted killing operations, the state is required to assess as much information as possible before an attack. Clearly, a lower scale of duty applies when a commander of a unit operating near civilians is under attack, and is expected to lead his troops to safety. An even lower scale applies when the states are involved in a battle, where no civilians are expected to be present.

## E. WARNINGS

An important part of protecting civilians from "becoming" collateral damage in an attack is the duty to warn civilians prior to that attack. This duty is clearly stated in article 57(c) of AP-I: "Effective advance warning shall be given of attacks which may affect the civilian population, unless circumstances do not permit." The duty to give advance warning also appears in the Hague Regulations,[61] and there are many historical examples of warnings that have been given prior to an attack.[62]

The goal of warning is simple—to alert the civilian population of the attack, and allow them to leave in order to save their lives. A warning is also an effective way for the attacking party to show that it indeed does not *intend* to target the civilian population.

There are two main forms of advanced warning that can be given: general and specific. A general warning is a message relayed by radio transmission, television, the internet, and so on, regarding the kinds of objectives that will be considered military objectives and attacked. A second form of warning is a specific warning given to residents of a particular building, warning that their building is about to be attacked because, for example, one of the apartments serves as a military command and control center.

59. Cited in Parks, *supra* note 39, at 181.

60. Described in Chapter 3, Section C.

61. The Hague Convention (IV) Respecting the Laws and Customs of War on Land, Annexed Regulations, 1907, art. 26, 205 C.T.S. 277: "The officer in command of an attacking force must, before commencing a bombardment, except in cases of assault, do all in his power to warn the authorities."

62. AP-I Commentary, *supra* note 16, at 686, para. 2222.

A warning should be effective—that is, it should allow the warned civilians enough time to evacuate the surroundings of the military object. Ideally, it should also direct the civilian population toward areas in which they will be safe. A warning that is not effective in this regard does not fulfil the obligation.

The main question regarding the interpretation of this paragraph in article 57(c) is the nature of the exception in the article—"unless circumstances do not permit." A flexible interpretation of this clause would mean that the attacking party would be able to bypass the general requirements. From the *Commentary to AP-I*, it seems that the exception relates specifically to surprise attacks, in which giving an advanced warning would make the attack itself ineffective.[63] This usually means that when the attack is directed against specific persons (such as in a targeted killing operation), no warning needs to be given. The standard adopted by the Israeli military advocate-general in his decisions regarding opening criminal investigations is that such a warning is not required if it would "thwart the purpose of the attack."[64] This standard seems to us to be correct.

A further interpretative issue is whether the use of the exception is subject to a proportionality assessment. The Goldstone Report read this exception to the requirement to give warning as containing its own proportionality assessment:

> The key limitation on the application of the rule is if the military advantage of surprise would be undermined by giving a warning. The same calculation of proportionality has to be made here as in other circumstances. The question is whether the injury or damage done to civilians or civilian objects by not giving a warning is excessive in relation to the advantage to be gained by the element of surprise for the particular operation. There may be other circumstances when a warning is simply not possible.[65]

Michael Schmitt, however, is of the view that the obligation to give warning prior to attack does not contain an obligation to carry out a proportionality assessment, even if not giving a warning would cause excessive harm to civilians.[66] Schmitt's view seems to us to be correct. There is no obligation to evaluate the harm that would be caused by not giving a warning.

This question relates to a larger issue concerning the effect of warnings on the proportionality assessment.

63. *Id.*, para. 2223.

64. IDF Military Advocate General, *Decisions of the IDF Military Advocate General Regarding Exceptional Incidents that Allegedly Occurred During Operation 'Protective Edge. Update No. 6*, 9, 10, 12 (Aug. 15, 2018), *available at:* https://mfa.gov.il/MFA/ForeignPolicy/IsraelGaza2014/Documents/Operation-Protective-Edge-MAG-Corps-Press-Release-Update-6-15-August-2018.pdf.

65. The Goldstone Report, *supra* note 45, para. 529.

66. Schmitt, *supra* note 45, at 827.

One view is that once an effective warning has been given, the civilian population that remains in the area should not be counted in the proportionality equation, since they chose not to follow the warning. According to this view, the civilian population that was able to respond to the warning (thus, excluding elderly people and people with disabilities who may not have been able to leave) but chose not to do so should be considered analogous to voluntary human shields, or even as direct participants.

A different view disconnects warnings from proportionality analysis. According to this view, an attacking party must give a warning, but those who stay are still civilians and are included in the proportionality analysis. Moreover, an attacking party certainly cannot simply "assume" that because an effective warning has been given, all those who remained behind are combatants, or are taking direct part in hostilities.

There are practical as well as utilitarian considerations that point toward accepting some form of trade-off between the use of effective warnings and flexibility in the use of proportionality. On a practical level, warnings will be more effective if the warning party believes that the use of warnings matters and that its warnings are being heeded. At the end of the day, effective warnings are not an end in and of themselves, but rather a means to lower civilian casualties. Civilians must take the warnings seriously, in order for the goal of lowering casualties to be achieved.

We believe that there is also a utilitarian logic for attacking parties here: if states that issue effective warnings were to be rewarded in some way, there would be a greater chance of more states using this method.

It seems to us, then, that there is a middle ground here. Certainly, the mere fact that a warning has been issued cannot serve as proof that all who choose to remain in the targeted area are combatants. Furthermore, those who stay behind should still be counted as civilians in the proportionality analysis. However, giving an advanced warning might lower the requirements regarding information gathering, or regarding the required level of proof the attacking party needs before deciding to attack.

## Roof Knocking

The practice of "roof knocking" has been used by Israeli forces in various conflicts in the Gaza Strip, particularly when attacking military objectives within civilian areas. One of the problems the IDF has faced is that, at times, either it was unable to warn inhabitants of specific targets about impending attacks, or its warnings went unheeded. The Israeli response was to use a form of warning shot, achieved by firing low-explosive projectiles at the building, sometimes directed at the corner of the rooftop. The shots were intended to signal to the civilians that an attack was imminent, and that it would have lethal potential. In many cases, the civilians did indeed vacate the military target following the roof knocking, and the IDF was able to complete the mission without causing civilian casualties.

Because the initial shot fired at the roof was sometimes lethal, some scholars criticized this method, arguing that it in itself constituted an attack against civilians.[67]

It seems to us that the roof-knocking tactic is the least harmful option in a very problematic situation. Granted, if the initial shot is directed at an uninvolved civilian with the intent to cause casualties and deter other civilians, then the tactic is a clear violation of the principle of distinction. However, the declared tactic is to direct the initial shot at a military target, knowing that civilians might be hurt, but with the ultimate goal of causing civilians to evacuate the premises. This seems to us to follow the basic requirements of the principle of proportionality.

## F. WHAT IS THE ROLE OF MILITARY LEGAL ADVISORS?

The role of legal advisors in the armed forces is detailed in AP-I article 82, which requires that:

> The High Contracting Parties at all times, and the Parties to the conflict in time of armed conflict, shall ensure that legal advisors are available, when necessary, to advise military commanders at the appropriate level on the application of the Conventions and this Protocol and on the appropriate instruction to be given to the armed forces on this subject.[68]

Initially, during the process of drafting this article, stronger wording was suggested. However, states appeared to be disinclined to accept the possibility that lawyers could impose stricter limits on their forces than would be imposed without oversight.[69] Today, the obligation to make legal advisors available, when necessary, to advise military commanders at the appropriate level on the application of IHL, represents customary international law.[70]

Over the past few decades, there has been growing discourse on the role of legal advisors in the implementation of IHL. As recently as the Vietnam War, American soldiers reportedly received little or no training in the laws of war, and the Judge Advocate General Department did not advise on operational matters. This has since changed, and currently the purview and role of military lawyers in the US military is the subject of extensive doctrine. This doctrine includes giving

67. See e.g., Hedi Viterbo, *Future-Oriented Measures*, *in* The ABC of the OPT: A Legal Lexicon of the Israeli Control over the Occupied Palestinian Territory 127 (Ben Naftali et al. Eds., Cambridge, 2018).

68. AP-I, *supra* note 3, art. 82.

69. Amichai Cohen, *Legal Operational Advice in the Israeli Defense Forces: The International Law Department and the Changing Nature of International Law*, 26 Conn. J. Int'l L. 367, 393 (2011); AP-I Commentary, *supra* note 16, art. 82.

70. Henckaerts & Doswald-Beck, ICRC Study, *supra* note 34, rule 141.

advice on varied matters, including operational plans, targets, and the treatment of detainees.[71]

The primary principle that governs the conduct of legal advisors is that their role is advisory.[72] They do not get to make the final decision for military commanders, who have the operational expertise. For example, within the IDF's military advocate-general (MAG), lawyers from the International Law Division (ILD) are given an advisory role that leaves the final decision on taking any course of action to the military commander.[73] The advisory role of military lawyers exists in US doctrine as well, and American commanders are even authorized to ignore the legal opinions of their advisors in extreme circumstances, in favor of crucial military needs.[74] The strictly advisory role of legal advisors seems to be changing, however. At least within the IDF, legal advisors are being brought into the decision-making process more than ever before, as military commanders seem to show reluctance to take action without an *ex ante* legal opinion authorizing operations. A slight shift away from a purely advisory role can also be seen in the reported reluctance of decision-makers to make decisions in defiance of legal opinions.[75] It currently appears that the legal opinions provided by the ILD with regard to preplanned attacks against military objects have obtained an almost binding nature. Formally, the final decision lies with the military commander, but it is very rare that a military commander will overrule the decision of a legal advisor.[76]

71. Cohen, *Legal Operational Advice in the Israeli Defense Forces*, *supra* note 69, at 393–94.

72. The second central Principle that governs the conduct of ILD lawyers is their independence. Independence means that the legal advice proffered is not based on the whims and wishes of the military commander. The independence of the ILD lawyers is further strengthened by the lawyers being placed outside of the chain of command, directly under the MAG's command, rather than under the commanders in the field. This does not imply that legal advisors are completely independent. The ILD lawyers work closely with the military commanders in command centers and are part of the military institution. As such, they are also affected by pressures to allow the military "to do its job" and complete its mission. Cohen, *supra* note 69, at 379, 382–83.

73. *Id.*, at 379.

74. *Id.*, at 380.

75. *Id.*, at 380–82.

76. The State of Israel, Ministry of Foreign Affairs, The 2014 Gaza Conflict: 7 July–26 August 2014: Factual and Legal Aspects, para. 245 (May 2015) ("This input includes a legal adviser's *binding* opinion regarding the legality of an attack, plus any stipulations for its execution . . . On the basis of all the professional opinions received, as well as any new information that becomes available, a senior commander may (i) approve the attack (where appropriate, subject to certain conditions), (ii) suspend the attack (for instance, because more information about potential collateral damage is necessary), or (iii) abort the attack altogether"); see also Schmitt & Merriam, *supra* note 18, at 86–87.

## G. CONCLUSION

Procedures are adopted in every bureaucracy in order to control the different operatives within it. The armed forces are no different. If anything, the armed forces possess more power than other governmental bureaucracies, and thus even more procedures are required to control them.[77] Our concern is different: Does this bureaucratic approach to the principle of proportionality protect civilians? Is the adoption of procedures an effective and relevant way to attain a balance between the necessities of war and the protection of human lives? We offer below, briefly, three sets of justifications for the procedural approach to proportionality: reasonableness, responsibility, and organizational culture.

### Creating a Zone of Reasonableness

One important effect of the use of procedures is to create a "zone of reasonableness." As we claimed earlier, the principle of proportionality cannot be interpreted to provide a precise number of civilian casualties that is not excessive. What it can and, and does do, is require that specific considerations be taken into account. It requires commanders to focus their attention, wherever possible, on the possibility that civilians are likely to be harmed. The commander is free to choose between various options, but all these options are presented within a general framework. The fact that the decision-maker takes civilian casualties into account is important. An acknowledgement of the need for a professional assessment of the military advantage in relation to civilian casualties itself assures that these will be taken into account, and not simply considered legitimate collateral damage.

### Responsibility and Control

Procedural and bureaucratic mechanisms create a visible hierarchy. It is clear who needs to make the decisions, and where the responsibility for those decisions lies. This issue lies at the heart of a general trend in current IHL to place responsibility for following IHL on policy makers, rather than on low-level soldiers. This trend is also evident in current international criminal law, which includes several sophisticated legal mechanisms intended to ensure that commanders will indeed face consequences for the actions of persons under their command.

Many of the procedures employed by armed forces in targeted killings are entirely in agreement with this general trend in IHL, since they concern the identity of the decision-maker. In both the United States and Israel, any chance that civilians might be killed requires moving the locus of decision-making up the chain of command, usually to the political level. This, too, improves the quality of assessment of the balance between military necessities and human lives. Moreover, the higher the level of decision-making, the higher the level of responsibility.

77. Amichai Cohen, *Guardians and Guards: The Israeli Supreme Court's Role in Matters of National Security*, *in* Civil Military Relations in Israel 171 (E. Rossman ed., 2014).

Responsibility for taking the lives of civilians should lie at the top. Political leaders and senior military commanders are the only persons who can decide on military policy, and it is they who should pay the price for decision-making failures.

## Organizational Culture

The requirement that decisions be reached in accordance with clear guidelines and procedures also ensures that more people are involved in the decision-making process. These participants, who are responsible for verifying that all procedures are followed, bureaucratize the use of military power. Since procedures consume time, this may mean that it will take longer to arrive at a decision. But the involvement of more participants means that a wider and more diverse range of opinions and interests will be reflected in the decision-making process. For example, some might be able to recall precedents from prior cases in the same country or abroad. Others could identify the effect of certain actions on media coverage, and integrate public opinion into the decision-making.

Lawyers constitute a unique sector, which is empowered by the emphasis on procedure. Because of their expertise in matters of procedure, the extensive use of procedures means that more lawyers will be involved in the process.[78] Lawyers, in turn, create even more pressure for adherence to bureaucratic processes. Clear bureaucratic processes allow lawyers to impose control over decision-making, leading to more transparent decision-making and greater uniformity between different cases. This also creates a paper trail that can be evaluated and investigated if anything goes wrong.[79]

It is therefore unsurprising that in targeted killing operations, where procedures are so important, lawyers play an extremely important role. They are attached to the armed forces, and are given a voice in major questions concerning the use of force.[80] Lawyers are involved in various stages of planning attacks; they point out difficulties as they arise; and propose alternative modes of action.[81]

To sum up: It is our view that using procedures represents the best understanding of the principle of proportionality. This use of procedures offers both a rational way to implement this principle, and the most effective way to protect the lives of civilians.

78. Regarding the role of lawyers in the US armed forces, see Jack L. Goldsmith, Power and Constraint: The Accountable Presidency after 9/11, Chapter 5 (NY, Norton & Co., 2012). On the expanding role of lawyers in the IDF, see: Alan Craig, International Legitimacy and the Politics of Security: The Strategic Deployment of Lawyers in the Israeli Military (2013); Schmitt & Merriam, *supra* note 18.

79. The rise of lawyers in armed forces is connected to the rise in investigations, which are one of the main roles of the lawyers in armed forces. See e.g., Goldsmith, *supra* note 78.

80. Cohen, *Legal Operational Advice in the Israeli Defense Forces*, *supra* note 69, at 367.

81. Goldsmith, *supra* note 78 (quoting military officers speaking of their units' lawyers as "consigliere").

13

# Judicial Review and Investigations

## A. INTRODUCTION

The analysis in this book has hitherto focused on how armed forces implement the principle of proportionality. In this penultimate chapter, we would like to devote some attention to the issue of judicial review over the application of the principle of proportionality, and to the investigation of its violations. We do not seek to address the general question of the role of courts (domestic or international) and criminal investigations with regard to IHL. Rather, we would like to make some brief comments regarding the specific role of courts and criminal investigations in applying the principle of proportionality. We begin with an exploration of the idea of *ex ante* review of the principle of proportionality, and move to the topics of *ex post* review, and criminal investigations.

## B. *EX ANTE* REVIEW

Articles 51(5)(b) and 57(2)(a)(iii) of the First Additional Protocol proscribe attacks that are *expected* to be cause excessive harm to civilians. Proportionality is therefore assessed *ex ante*. In any administrative matter, the executive branch, which includes the government and the military, is tasked with making decisions in real time based on the benefit of practical experience, which enables it to make better decisions than the other branches of government.

It is difficult to imagine judicial *ex ante* review for a military operation. But even if we were able to create a practical solution to this problem (such as in the FISA courts regarding eavesdropping),[1] *ex ante* judicial review would not be appropriate for applying the principle of proportionality. *Ex ante* administrative review by courts is usually limited due to the lack of expertise of courts in the specific subject matter. Even the most intrusive of administrative courts limit themselves to examining whether the decision of the administrative agency acts within

1. The Foreign Intelligence Surveillance Courts were established under the Foreign Intelligence Surveillance Act (FISA) (1978) 92 Stat. 1783. They have the authority to oversee requests by federal law enforcement and intelligence agencies for surveillance warrants against foreign spies inside the United States.

*Proportionality in International Humanitarian Law.* Amichai Cohen & David Zlotogorski, Oxford University Press.
 DOI: 10.1093/oso/9780197556726.003.0013

a "zone of reasonableness." In most cases, the administrative review is limited to the question of "whether the agency followed the correct procedures, possessed all of the relevant data, and held the appropriate hearings. In asking whether the agency's actions were reasonable, courts give deference to the substance of the agency's decision."[2]

In matters of national security, courts grant the executive branch much more leeway than in other government matters. Even the Israeli Supreme Court, perhaps the most intrusive of all judiciaries in matters of national security, has interfered *ex ante* in military matters only in very rare circumstances.[3] Courts are reluctant to examine military operations *ex ante* for fear that any delay in their assessment prior to an attack could delay operations, and they might bear responsibility for resulting damage. For these reasons, *ex ante* examination by the courts is unsuitable.[4]

Regarding IHL proportionality, the prospect of some kind of *ex ante* judicial review seems even less appropriate. As we saw, the principle of proportionality as usually interpreted has no widely agreed-upon substantive meaning. It is difficult to imagine that courts would be willing to intervene in a specific decision regarding the use of proportionality in IHL, even if one could come up with an institution that would be willing and able to submit to such a review. Due to the difficulty of second-guessing the substantive decisions made by commanders in the field, it has been suggested by one of the authors of this book that the most courts can do in examining proportionality is to scrutinize the procedural aspects of proportionality and the *decision-making process* of the commander.[5]

That there is very little chance of meaningful *ex ante* judicial review over proportionality does not necessarily mean that there can be *no* review. Proportionality in IHL authorizes the armed forces to make decisions regarding lives of innocent civilians, based on a balance between "good" and "evil," which is not objective in any sense. The armed forces may very well be the best evaluators of the concrete military advantage. Proportionality, however, also requires comparing this military advantage to the collateral damage that an attack would cause. As the Israeli Supreme Court president Aharon Barak famously noted in his seminal *Beit Sourik* judgment regarding the route of the Israeli West Bank barrier:

> The military commander is the expert regarding the military quality of the separation fence route. We are experts regarding its humanitarian aspects. The military commander determines where, on hill and plain, the separation fence

2. See Amichai Cohen, *The Principle of Proportionality in the Context of Operation Cast Lead: Institutional Perspectives*, 35 Rutgers L. Record 23, 32–33 (2009) (citations omitted).

3. Amichai Cohen & Stuart A. Cohen, Israel's National Security Law, chapter 6 (Routledge, 2012).

4. *Id.*, at 34.

5. *Id.*, at 33.

> will be erected. That is his expertise. We examine whether this route's harm to the local residents is proportional. That is our expertise.[6]

Justice Barak, naturally, referred to the court as the decision-maker in such matters. But logic does not necessarily direct us toward a judicial institution for the performance of an *ex ante* review. As we saw, judicial administrative review seems to be very problematic here. But Barak's general logic holds. The principle of proportionality in IHL is relevant to cases in which the armed forces are implicitly allowed to lethally attack innocent civilians. An unchecked application of this principle might undermine the entire structure of IHL, which is based on the protection of civilians. The importance of this issue, and the many uncertainties involved, would seem to require that an external institution should have some kind of *ex ante* oversight over the decisions of the armed forces.

In an attempt to deal with this lack of oversight of executive branch decisions, Ariel Zemach recently opined that the UN Security Council might form international advisory committees.[7] Such committees, suggests Zemach, acting under the umbrella of the Security Council, would offer states an interpretation of IHL tailored to their own situation, and provide immunity from international proceedings if the path offered by the committee is followed. Regardless of the feasibility of Zemach's suggestion, it suggests a movement toward external involvement in decisions on IHL matters.

Domestic institutions might be a more realistic option. One possible route is for the government to form a committee of experts to evaluate the legality (and morality) of all standing orders and rules of engagement, focusing on the application of the principle of proportionality. Because we support the view that proportionality is primarily about procedures, we believe that a review of procedures by an external committee would indeed be an effective tool for directing the armed forces as to how to implement the principle of proportionality.

## C. *EX POST* REVIEW: THE PROBLEM WITH THE CRIMINAL APPROACH

Whatever we think about *ex ante* review of the military action, it is clear that an *ex post* review, whether administrative or criminal, is the main tool available for implementation of the principle of proportionality. This form of review may incentivize commanders to properly assess and weigh the relevant considerations of proportionality in good faith.[8]

6. HCJ 2056/04, Beit Sourik Village Council v. The Government of Israel, 58(5) PD 807 (2004) [Isr.].

7. Ariel Zemach, *Indeterminacy in the Law of War*, 43 BROOK. J. INT'L L. 1 (2018).

8. One of the primary decisions that examined proportionality, the *Targeted Killings* case, also required attackers to assess the proportionality of the attack both prior to as well as subsequent to the attack (HCJ 769/02, Public Committee against Torture v. The State of Israel, PD 62(1) 507, para. 46, 54 (2006) [Isr.] [*Targeted Killings* Case]). Creating a double examination of

## Criminal Investigations

There is little question that states must investigate serious allegations of war crimes committed by individuals subject to their jurisdiction with a view to ascertaining the criminal responsibility of the suspected perpetrators. This rule is found in the grave breaches provisions of the Geneva Conventions.[9] It is also supported by the jurisprudence of human rights courts on violations of the right to life and of the prohibition against torture. This stipulates a second-order "effective remedy" obligation to respond through criminal investigation, and the prosecution of serious HRL violations by state agents as well as other perpetrators.[10]

Although the principle of proportionality is not mentioned in the Geneva Conventions, and hence does not form a part of the original definition of the grave breaches, it is clear that today's states have a duty to investigate and prosecute violations of the principle of proportionality. First, the definition of the grave breaches has been extended by AP-I to include violations of the principle of proportionality.[11] In addition, as we have seen throughout this book, the ICTY has consistently declared that a violation of the principle of proportionality is a war crime, and falls under the jurisdiction of the court.[12]

It is important to note that the grave breaches provisions of the Geneva Conventions entail much more than a duty to investigate and prosecute soldiers accused of committing war crimes. They also contain the following obligations: (1) to enact suitable criminal legislation;[13] (2) not to absolve perpetrators of grave

proportionality, one *ex ante* and the other *ex post*, guarantees that commanders shoulder their part of the responsibility for attacks and their consequences. A failure on the part of the decision-makers to make an effective *ex ante* assessment of an attack could be seen as recklessness on the part of the commanding officer. Furthermore, as article 28 of the Rome Statute criminalizes failures on the part of commanders to punish soldiers for violations, *ex post* investigations could create a strong incentive for commanders to order criminal prosecution of subordinates involved in attacks which were "clearly excessive" (Cohen, *supra* note 2, at 36–37; Rome Statute of the International Criminal Court, Jul. 17, 1998, art. 28, 2187 U.N.T.S. 90 (1998) [Rome Statute]).

9. Convention for the Amelioration of the Condition of the Wounded and Sick in Armed Forces in the Field, Aug. 12, 1949, art. 49, 75 U.N.T.S. 31 [GC-I]; Convention for the Amelioration of the Condition of Wounded, Sick and Shipwrecked Members of Armed Forces at Sea of Aug. 12, 1949, art. 50, 75 U.N.T.S. 85 [GC-II]; Convention Relative to the Treatment of Prisoners, Aug. 12, 1949, art. 129, 75 U.N.T.S. 135 [GC-III]; Convention Relative to the Protection of Civilian Persons in Time of War, Aug. 12, 1949, art. 146, 6 U.S.T. 3516, 75 U.N.T.S. 287 [GC-IV]; Protocol Additional to the Geneva Conventions of 12 August 1949, and Relating to the Protection of Victims of International Armed Conflicts (Protocol I), June 8, 1977, art. 85, 1125 U.N.T.S. 3 [AP-I].

10. See for example, Rodriguez v. Honduras, Inter-Am.Ct.H.R. (Ser. C) No. 4, para. 176 (1988).

11. AP-I, *supra* note 9, art. 85(3)(b).

12. E.g., Prosecutor v. Gotovina, ICTY Trial Chamber I, IT-06-90-T, *Judgment* (Apr. 15, 2011); Prosecutor v. Galić, ICTY Trial Chamber, IT-98-29, *Judgment* (Dec. 5, 2003).

13. GC-1, *supra* note 9, art. 49; GC-II, *supra* note 9, art. 50; GC-III, *supra* note 9, art. 129; GC-IV, *supra* note 9, art. 146; AP-I, *supra* note 9, art. 85(5).

breaches from legal responsibility;[14] and, most significantly, (3) to search and prosecute (or extradite) any individual—regardless of his or her nationality—who allegedly committed grave breaches.[15] Hence, the main effect of the grave breaches provisions appears to be the *internationalization* of war crimes, a process further enhanced by the inclusion of grave breaches provisions in the statutes of international criminal tribunals, including the International Criminal Court.[16]

## The Problem with Criminal Investigations

Criminal investigations of violations of war crimes are problematic for at least three reasons: (1) the lack of clear rules; (2) the use of legal advice; and (3) the general reluctance to prosecute, at both the national and international levels.

### Lack of Clear Rules

One problem confronting investigators and prosecutors endeavouring to apply criminal law to IHL violations involves the application of the principle of legality in situations of legal uncertainty. Although historically, IHL was associated with clear rules (reflecting to a considerable degree the combatants' self-interest),[17] the move from *rules* to *standards*[18] reduced legal certainty, and thus created serious problems for criminal enforcement—a process that assumes the existence of preexisting and well-defined legal prohibitions. As we have seen throughout this book, one of the best examples of this lack of clarity in IHL is the principle of proportionality. In its current form, holding a person responsible for a violation of the principle of proportionality runs counter to many of the basic requirements of criminal law.

### Legal Advice

Another important problem associated with the use of criminal law as a tool for suppressing violations of IHL is, perhaps paradoxically, the increased tendency of many militaries to resort to operational legal advice. Obtaining legal advice

14. *Id.*

15. *Id.*

16. Statute of the International Tribunal for the Prosecution of Persons Responsible for Serious Violations of International Humanitarian Law Committed in the Territory of the Former Yugoslavia since 1991, 25 May 1993, art. 2, U.N. Doc. S/RES/827; Statute of the International Criminal Tribunal for the Prosecution of Persons Responsible for Genocide and Other Serious Violations of International Humanitarian Law Committed in the Territory of Rwanda and Rwandan Citizens Responsible for Genocide and Other Such Violations Committed in the Territory of Neighbouring States, between 1 January 1994 and 31 December 1994, 8 Nov. 1994, art. 4, U.N. Doc. S/RES/955; Rome Statute, *supra* note 8, art. 8(2)(a).

17. Chris af Jochnik & Roger Normand, *The Legitimization of Violence: A Critical History of the Laws of War*, 35 Harv. J. Int'l L. (1994).

18. Amichai Cohen, *Rules and Standards in the Application of IHL*, 41 Isr. L. Rev. 41 (2008).

is mentioned in AP-I[19] and in the ICRC *Commentary to AP-I*. According to the *Commentary*, legal advisors should be available at the divisional level, or even at brigade level if the brigade operates independently.[20] Over time, the militaries of many states have developed operational legal advisory services for their respective armed forces, thus meeting to a large extent the standards identified in AP-I and the *Commentary*.[21]

There are several good reasons why armed forces should seek legal advice. Most obviously, the extensive reliance on legal advisors supports a culture of legality and internalizes international legal norms into the operations of the armed forces.[22] However, it may prove to be very problematic to prosecute commanders and other military personnel who follow the legal advice they receive, as basic principles of criminal law render it difficult to convict persons who followed the advice of their lawyers. Although legal advice cannot serve as a defence in circumstances where the violation of law was clear in nature,[23] the ambiguity of modern IHL norms renders it increasingly unlikely that clear violations would be committed in a manner exposing the service-member in question, or their lawyer, to criminal proceedings. Hence, operational legal advice may, in effect, shield the military service members who acted upon it from criminal responsibility.

This general claim is even clearer in the case of the principle of proportionality, which is ambiguous and requires further interpretation. It is expected that commanders would turn to legal advice especially when the rules are not clear. However, if the norm is so unclear as to allow a very broad range of legal opinions, it then becomes problematic to use criminal tools to investigate behavior under such circumstances.

19. AP- I, *supra* note 9, art. 82: "The High Contracting Parties at all times, and the Parties to the conflict in time of armed conflict, shall ensure that legal advisers are available, when necessary, to advise military commanders at the appropriate level on the application of the Conventions and this Protocol and on the appropriate instruction to be given to the armed forces on this subject."

20. This conforms to current American military doctrine; see Army Field Manual 27-100, 5–6 (1991).

21. Countries whose military manuals contain such obligations include Australia, Belgium, Cameroon, Canada, France, Germany, Hungary, Italy, Netherlands, Nigeria, Russia, Spain, Sweden, and the United States. Many of the states which have not joined the additional protocol have also declared that they possess this service—e.g., India, Sri Lanka, Turkey, and Israel. In fact, the ICRC Study on Customary International declared the existence of the legal advisors' service as customary in nature (Jean-Marie Henckaerts & Louise Doswald-Beck, Customary International Humanitarian Law, Vol. 1, 500 (2005) [ICRC Study].

22. Amichai Cohen, *Legal Operational Advice in the Israeli Defense Forces: The International Law Department and the Changing Nature of International Law*, 26 Conn. J. Int'l L. 367 (2011).

23. David Bowker, *Unwise Counsel; The War on Terrorism and the Criminal Mistreatment of Detainees in U.S. Custody*, *in* The Torture Debate in America 183 (KJ Greenberg ed., Cambridge, 2005).

## Criminal Investigations in Practice: Reluctance to Prosecute at the National Level

There is little question that states must investigate serious allegations of war crimes committed by individuals subject to their jurisdiction with a view to ascertaining the criminal responsibility of the suspected perpetrators. As mentioned before, this rule is found in the grave breaches provisions of the Geneva Conventions.[24] In operations where HRL should also be applied, the duty to investigate is supported by the jurisprudence of international human rights courts. These latter courts base the duty to investigate on violations of the right to life and the prohibition against torture, stipulating a second order "effective remedy" obligation to respond through criminal investigation and prosecution to serious IHRL violations by state agents as well as other perpetrators.[25]

The discussion of the duty to investigate violations is more explicit and detailed in HRL than in IHL. However, both legal scholars[26] and state practice[27] show that the principles of a proper investigation are quite similar in both branches of law, though their application in pure HRL cases may be stricter.

In its seminal *Isayeva* judgment,[28] the European Court of Human Rights laid down the basic principles of investigation under the European Convention of Human Rights, which in large parts mirrors the contents of other HRL instruments, such as the International Covenant on Civil and Political Rights. According to the Court, any investigation must incorporate the following criteria: independence, effectiveness, promptness, and some degree of public scrutiny. The Court refined these four criteria in its post-*Isayeva* jurisprudence,[29] including in the *Al Skeini* judgment.[30] Since the *Al Skeini* case dealt with events that took place in Iraq during that country's occupation by the US-UK-led coalition, in its judgment, the Court directly addressed the relationship between IHL and IHRL:[31]

24. GC-I, *supra* note 9, art. 49; GC-II, *supra* note 9, art. 50; GC-III, *supra* note 9; GC-IV, *supra* note 9, art. 146; AP-I, *supra* note 9, art. 85.

25. See e.g., Velasquez Rodriguez v. Honduras, Judgment of July 29, 1988, Inter-Am.Ct.H.R. (Ser. C) No. 4, para. 176 (1988).

26. Amichai Cohen & Yuval Shany, *Beyond the Grave Breaches Regime: The Duty to Investigate Alleged Violations of International Law Governing Armed Conflicts*, 14 Yearbook of International Humanitarian Law 37 (2012).

27. The Public Commission to Examine the Maritime Incident of 31 May, 2010, *Second Report: Israel's Mechanisms for Examining and Investigating Complaints and Claims of Violations of the Laws of Armed Conflict* (Feb. 2013), *available at:* https://www.gov.il/en/Departments/General/turkel_committee [The Turkel Commission Report].

28. Isayeva v. Russia, E.Ct.H.R., App. No. 57947-49/00, 836 (2005).

29. See e.g. Bazorkina v. Russia, E.Ct.H.R., App. No. 69481/01, para.117-119 (2006); Abuyeva v. Russia, E.Ct.H.R., App. No. 27065/05, para. 204-216 (2010).

30. Al Skeini v. U.K., E.Ct.H.R., App. No. 55721/07 ECHR (2011).

31. *Id.*, at para. 90-93.

> The Court has held that the procedural obligation under Article 2 continues to apply in difficult security conditions, including in a context of armed conflict . . . It is clear that where the death to be investigated under Article 2 occurs in circumstances of generalised violence, armed conflict or insurgency, obstacles may be placed in the way of investigators and, . . . concrete constraints may compel the use of less effective measures of investigation or may cause an investigation to be delayed. Nonetheless, the obligation under Article 2 to safeguard life entails that, even in difficult security conditions, all reasonable steps must be taken to ensure that an effective, independent investigation is conducted into alleged breaches of the right to life.[32]

International human rights courts have sometimes found that states have violated their duty to investigate.[33] The point, however, is that there is no national case we are aware of, in which a national court convicted a soldier or an officer of committing or ordering a disproportionate attack. Granted, national courts do not tend to convict the state's own soldiers, but in no case has an international tribunal criticized a domestic decision not to prosecute or convict in such cases.

In fact, it is difficult to find a national court case that even discussed the issue of proportionality, since indictments are almost never brought to court. Two examples of the very high threshold set by prosecutors for bringing cases are the German *Fuel Tankers* case, and the Israeli 2014 Operation Protective Edge investigations.

In the 2010 *Fuel Tankers* case, the Federal Prosecutor General at Germany's Federal Court of Justice investigated whether war crimes or other crimes under domestic law had been committed in the course of an airstrike that was ordered in September 2009 by a colonel of the German armed forces, acting as part of the international assistance force in Afghanistan. The strike was undertaken against two tankers that had been stolen by the Taliban near Kunduz, and resulted in the deaths of 91 civilians. In his detailed opinion, the Prosecutor General came to the conclusion that:

> Even if the killing of several dozen civilians would have had to be anticipated (which is assumed here for the sake of the argument), from a tactical-military perspective this would not have been out of proportion to the anticipated military advantages. The literature consistently points out that general criteria are not available for the assessment of specific proportionality because unlike legal goods, values and interests are juxtaposed which cannot be "balanced" . . . Therefore, considering the particular pressure at the moment when the decision had to be taken, an infringement is only to be assumed in cases of obvious excess where the commander ignored any considerations of

32. *Id.*, para. 164.

33. In addition to the above mentioned cases, see for example, Jaloud v. The Netherlands, E.Ct.H.R., App. No. 47708/08 (2014).

> proportionality and refrained from acting "honestly", "reasonably" and "competently" . . . This would apply to the destruction of an entire village with hundreds of civilian inhabitants in order to hit a single enemy fighter, but not if the objective was to destroy artillery positions in the village . . . There is no such obvious disproportionality in the present case. Both the destruction of the fuel tankers and the destruction of high-level Taliban had a military importance which is not to be underestimated, not least because of the thereby considerably reduced risk of attacks by the Taliban against own troops and civilians. There is thus no excess.[34]

The opinion of the German Federal Prosecutor General is exceptional, because it clearly states a claim that has been presented in detail in this book, but which is rarely admitted by lawyers: other than in very extreme cases, it is almost impossible to criminally convict for violations of IHL because of the inherent vagueness of the principles.

A slightly different approach was taken by the Israeli military advocate-general (MAG) regarding Operation Protective Edge, the Israeli military operation carried out in the Gaza Strip between July 8 and August 26, 2014. NGOs and Palestinians submitted hundreds of complaints claiming violations of IHL by the IDF during this operation. Operation Protective Edge was the first time that Israel extensively used the General Staff's Inquiry Body—an independent inquiry body, headed by a retired general, which was formed following the recommendations of the Turkel Commission.[35] In turn, the Turkel Commission was launched following several incidents in which the Israeli system of investigating suspicions of violations of IHL by IDF soldiers had been criticized by international bodies.[36] On the one hand, the Turkel Commission stressed the need for a full and independent investigation of credible claims against IDF soldiers. On the other hand, the Commission's position was that it is improper to launch criminal investigations based solely on accusations alleged by Palestinians, who have a clear incentive to submit baseless claims. Thus, the Turkel Commission recommended creating an independent inquiry body, which would perform a quick initial factual examination of claims, and provide a well-grounded factual basis on which the MAG would be able to decide whether to open a criminal investigation.

34. Federal Court of Justice, *Fuel Tankers case*, Federal Prosecutor General Decision (April 16, 2010). The translated decision is quoted in the IHL Database of Customary IHL, https://ihl-databases.icrc.org/customary-ihl/eng/docs/v2_rul_rule14#sectiona_vnaca.

35. The Turkel Commission Report, *supra* note 27.

36. The commission was formed after the Gaza flotilla incident of 2010. However, the real cause for its formation by the Israeli government was the criticism voiced against the Israeli system of investigation in the Goldstone Report published in September 2009. The commission was formed in June 2010, and issued the second part of its report, dealing with the investigation of suspicions of violations of IHL by IDF soldiers, in February 2013.

However, the direction in which the General Staff's Inquiry Body actually evolved was different from that originally envisioned by the Turkel Commission. Instead of providing an initial factual inquiry, the investigations of the Inquiry Body became lengthy and detailed. In one case, newspaper reports—probably based on information supplied by the members of the Body—referred to the inquiry as a "doctoral level thesis." The end result has been that the MAG now arrives at decisions on whether to open a criminal investigation based on inquiries that, in time and scope, are fairly similar to criminal investigations.[37]

The MAG has issued several "updates" regarding its decisions. In many of the cases included in these "updates," the MAG framed the issue as one of proportionality: the target was a military target and civilians were killed. In most of these cases, the MAG came to the conclusion that the presence of civilians in or around the target was not known to the IDF, and could not have been expected to be known. In those instances, the MAG took pains to stress that all the required steps were taken to collect intelligence, that the order was given by the proper authority, and that warnings were given where possible and relevant.[38]

### Criminal Investigations in Practice: Reluctance to Prosecute at International Level

That domestic courts, and prosecutors, do not use the principle of proportionality to pursue prosecutions does not necessarily mean that the principle is faulty. Instead, the problem may lie in the lack of enthusiasm of domestic institutions to prosecute. If this is the case, international courts might be more willing to use the principle of proportionality in criminal matters.

37. Amichai Cohen & Yuval Shany, *Israel's Military Advocate General Terminates "Black Friday" and Other Investigations: Initial Observations* (Aug. 27, 2018), *available at:* www.lawfareblog.com/israels-military-advocate-general-terminates-black-friday-and-other-investigations-initial.

38. E.g., in the case of the death of eight members of the Al- Najar family, who were killed in an Israeli air strike on their home, which the MAG decided constituted a military target as it also served as a Hamas command and control center. The MAG decision included the following typical statement: "After examining the factual findings and the material gathered by the General Staff's inquiry mechanism, the MAG found that the assault procedures were consistent with the provisions of Israeli law and the rules of international law. The decision to attack was made by the competent authorities, and the attack was directed against a clear military objective. The attack was consistent with the principle of proportionality, since at the time of the decision on the attack it was estimated that the extent of the collateral damage likely to result of the attack would not be excessive in relation to the military advantage that was expected to be received from it, and this assessment was not unreasonable under the circumstances. The attack was also carried out after precautions were taken to reduce the potential harm to civilians, with an emphasis on those housed in adjacent buildings. It was further found that it was not possible to pass on a warning prior to the attack to those who were in the building, as such a warning would have been expected to thwart the purpose of the attack. The actual harm to civilians who were not involved in the hostilities is a regrettable result, but it does not retroactively implicate the legality of the attack." [Our translation from the Hebrew original, included in the 4th MAG update regarding the Protective Edge investigation, June 11, 2015.]

Looking at the decisions of the ICTY reveals that, while the prosecution was willing to bring cases based on a violation of the principle of proportionality, the court was almost never willing to convict in these cases. The recent *Prlić* case offers a good example.

In *Prlić*, the Trial Chamber discussed a full-day bombardment of an "old bridge" in the city of Mostar, Bosnia by the Croatian Defence Council (HVO), the armed forces of the Croatian Bosnians. The bombardment took place in November 1993, during the later stages of the war in Bosnia, as part of the conflict between the HVO and the Army of the Republic of Bosnia and Herzegovina (ARBiH). The Trial Chamber held that the bridge was a legitimate military target, as the ARBiH used the road, but it was also the major route allowing the transfer of aid and supplies to Muslim residents in parts of Mostar.[39] The Trial Chamber concluded that the harm to civilians was excessive in relation to the military advantage attained by destroying the bridge, and hence that the attack was an unjustified destruction of the property. The Chamber did not explicitly mention the principle of proportionality,[40] but it is clear from its analysis that proportionality formed the basis of its decision. The court also mentioned that "the HVO command intended to destroy the Old Bridge of Mostar, thereby sapping the morale of the Muslim population of Mostar."[41]

In its judgment of November 27, 2017, the Appeals Chamber rejected the analysis of the Trial Chamber. It stated that it was clear that the bridge was a legitimate target. The Appeals Chamber also noted that the Trial Chamber did not specify the collateral damage to civilians, except for referring to "serious psychological harm" in general language.[42]

It is possible to explain the judgment in the *Prlić* case on the basis of its specific facts, in which no civilians were actually killed. However, in light of the decisions of the Appeals Chamber in the *Gotovina* case discussed earlier,[43] it seems that a pattern can be discerned here. The ICTY, much like domestic courts, finds it very

39. Prosecutor v. Prlić, ICTY Trial Chamber III, IT-04-74-T, *Judgment*, Vol. III, paras. 1581–83 (May 9, 2013) [Prlić Case].

40. Probably because the authority of the ICTY does not explicitly include violations of the principle of proportionality.

41. Prlić case, *supra* note 39, vol. 3 of the judgment of the Trial Chamber (May 2013), para. 1586. It is not clear whether the court mentioned the sapping of morale as its conclusion regarding the *real* intention of the HVO, or a general statement regarding the mental element of the HVO. If this was the real intention, then perhaps what the Trial Chamber meant to say is that the relevant legal analysis is that of violation of the principle of distinction, since the attack was directed at civilians. The Trial Chamber did not explain this in detail, and the appeals chamber ignored this statement altogether.

42. Prosecutor v. Prlić, ICTY Appeals Chamber, IT-04-74-A, *Judgment*, Vol. I, para. 411 (Nov. 29, 2017).

43. Prosecutor v. Gotovina, ICTY Appeals Chamber, IT-06-90-A, *Judgment*, para. 82 (Nov. 16, 2012).

hard to convict for violations of the principle of proportionality, except where it is clear that the disproportionate nature of the attack merely provides proof that the attacking party was, in fact, failing to apply the principle of distinction. Such, for example, is the decision of the Appeals Chamber in the *Galić* case, in which it stated that the Trial Chamber did not find any evidence of military activity in the specific area of bombardment.[44] In other cases, the ICTY Appeals Chamber explicitly stated that the real reason for the proportionality discussion was evidence of the violation of the principle of distinction.[45]

Our conclusion, therefore, is that even international courts and tribunals find it very difficult to convict for violating proportionality in cases where the discussion focuses solely on the balance between the value of a military target and the collateral damage to civilians.

## Should Criminal Prosecutions Be Forsaken?

As we have shown, there is ample evidence that prosecution is not the most effective way to effectively confront violations of the principle of proportionality. Below, we discuss alternatives to criminal prosecutions. At this stage, we would just like to highlight the fact that even if the criminal track is chosen, the emphasis should not be on prosecuting the particular soldiers who operated in violation of the principle of proportionality. A more effective approach, and one which is more in line with the nature of the principle of proportionality, is to use the doctrines of command responsibility[46] and precautionary obligations[47] as the basis for investigations and criminal proceedings.

### Command Responsibility

The concept of command responsibility, specified in AP-I articles 86 and 87 and now accepted, by and large, as part of customary international law, provides a general basis for the duty to investigate.[48] The command responsibility doctrine requires military commanders "to prevent and, where necessary, to suppress

44. E.g., ". . . For each of the scheduled incidents, the Trial Chamber carefully considered whether the civilian victims were the unintended victims of combat, and only reached a conclusion on the deliberateness of sniper targeting or the indiscriminate nature of shelling after determining that no reasonable possibility existed that the victims were mistaken for combatants or were unintentionally harmed by combat in their vicinity." Prosecutor v. Galić, ICTY Appeals Chamber, IT-98-29-A, *Judgment*, para. 235 (Nov. 30, 2006).

45. E.g., "The Trial Chamber's finding that disproportionate attacks "may" give rise to the inference of direct attacks on civilians is therefore a justified pronouncement on the evidentiary effects of certain findings, not a conflation of different crimes." Galić, Appeals Chamber, *Id.*, para. 133.

46. AP-I, *supra* note 9, art. 87, ICC Statute, *supra* note 16, art. 28.

47. E.g., AP-I, *supra* note 9, art. 57, 58.

48. Henckaerts & Doswald-Beck, ICRC Study *supra* note 21, Rule 153, at 558.

and to report to competent authorities breaches of the Conventions and of this Protocol."[49] Whereas considerable attention has been afforded in the legal literature and the case law of international criminal tribunals to the criminal law implications of dereliction on the part of commanders to prevent or punish war crimes (in particular, following the introduction of superior responsibility in article 28 of the ICC Statute),[50] far less attention has been given to the duty imposed on military commanders to investigate and prosecute in connection with violations not amounting to grave breaches For our purpose, it is clear that the broad duty to prevent and suppress—encompassing *all* breaches of the Geneva Conventions and AP-I—implies a concomitant obligation on the state party to conduct criminal or disciplinary investigations and prosecutions in appropriate cases.

Once a violation of the Convention or AP-I is expected to occur, or has already occurred, military commanders are required to take active steps to prevent and suppress the said violations. AP-I article 87(3) explicitly provides that the duty to suppress involves "where appropriate, to initiate disciplinary or penal action against violators thereof." In other words, with regard to violations of IHL that do not constitute grave breaches, military commanders are expected to resort to one of following responses: criminal measures, disciplinary measures, or—where appropriate—other measures not necessarily entailing individual responsibility; such measures are to be taken directly by the commander or by other competent authorities.[51]

In any event, investigating alleged violations is an integral part of the commander's duty to prevent and suppress. This is because investigating past violations will allow the commander to make an informed decision as to what would be, under the circumstances, the appropriate response to the alleged

49. AP I, *supra* note 9, art. 87(1).

50. Yuval Shany & Keren Michaeli, *The Case against Ariel Sharon: Revisiting the Doctrine of Command Responsibility*, 34 NYU J. Int'l L. & Politics 797 (2002); Yael Ronen, *Superior Responsibility of Civilian for International Crimes Committed in Civilian Settings*, 43 Vander. J. Transnat'l L. 313 (2010); Prosecutor v. Delalić ("Čelebići"), ICTY Appeals Chamber, IT-96-21-T, *Judgment*, paras. 54–104 (Feb. 20, 2001); Prosecutor v. Halilović, ICTY Appeals Chamber, IT-01-48-A, *Judgment* (Oct. 16, 2007).

51. See for example, Prosecutor v. Boškoski, ICTY Trial Chamber II, IT-04-82-T, *Judgment*, para. 418 (Jul. 10, 2008): "A superior's duty to punish the perpetrators of a crime may encompass an obligation to conduct an effective investigation with a view to establishing the facts. The obligation to investigate translates into an obligation on the part of the superior to take active steps to ensure that the perpetrators will be punished. To that end, the superior may exercise his own powers of sanction, or if he lacks such powers, report the perpetrators to the competent authorities. It has been held in the jurisprudence of the Tribunal that civilian superiors, who may lack the disciplinary or sanctioning powers of military commanders, may discharge their obligation to punish by reporting to the competent authorities whenever a crime has been committed if these reports are likely to trigger an investigation or initiate disciplinary or criminal proceedings."

violation;[52] such an investigation may also facilitate changes in the conduct of the military unit in question that would prevent future violations.

Because we view the principle of proportionality as procedural and institutional, we believe that the notion of command responsibility is especially important regarding investigations of possible violations of the principle. The whole notion of procedures as affecting the use of power assumes that commanders bear a responsibility to create and maintain these procedures and institutions.

### Precautionary Obligations

The broad duty to investigate violations can also be anchored in the precautionary obligations of the parties to the conflict. AP-I article 57(1) prescribes that "in the conduct of military operations, constant care shall be taken to spare the civilian population, civilians and civilian objects." In the same vein, article 57(2)(a)(ii) provides that the parties should "take all feasible precautions in the choice of means and methods of attack with a view to avoiding, and in any event to minimizing, incidental loss of civilian life, injury to civilians and damage to civilian objects."

Both obligations are closely related to the "least injurious means" prong of the proportionality test—that is, the requirement that parties select from among all possible measures, that might similarly advance their military goals, those measures that cause the least humanitarian harm. Investigation of past incidents in which harm has occurred is arguably part of the "constant care" that parties are expected to demonstrate in order to assess, on an ongoing basis, the proportionate nature of the means and methods of warfare they employ. In other words, monitoring the effects of military actions through investigation of possible violations arguably constitutes a "feasible precaution" against disproportionate harm.

## D. *EX POST* ASSESSMENT: AN ALTERNATIVE TO CRIMINAL TRIALS

One of the most important innovations of the *Targeted Killing* judgment handed down by Israel HCJ Justice Barak was the introduction of a requirement for an *ex post* examination of the application of the principle of proportionality whenever a civilian was killed.[53] Barak states that such an examination should be independent[54] and subject to judicial review.[55]

52. Commentary on the Additional Protocols of 8 June 1977 to the Geneva Conventions of 12 August 1949, para. 3560 (ICRC, Yves Sandoz, Christophe Swinarki, & Bruno Zimmerman eds., 1987): "[The commanders'] role obliges them to be constantly informed of the way in which their subordinates carry out the tasks entrusted them, and to take the necessary measures for this purpose."

53. *Targeted Killing* case, *supra* note 8, para. 40. Barak requires an examination whenever a civilian is killed, first of all to verify whether or not he or she was a direct participant in hostilities. Clearly, when *innocent* civilians are killed, such an examination is required (*Id.*, para 54).

54. *Id.*, para. 40.

55. *Id.*, para. 54.

It seems that according to Justice Barak, such an investigation should take place regardless of any credible claim of wrongdoing by the attacking party. The question here is not one of criminal responsibility, but rather of an assessment of how the principle of proportionality was applied. Justice Barak suggests that in appropriate circumstances, states should consider compensating civilian victims, apparently regardless of the question of whether the principle of proportionality was violated or not.[56]

This view is also supported by Henderson, who writes that states must conduct *ex post* reviews in order to assess the reliability of their planning methods, particularly as militaries often tend toward overambitiously assessing the advantage that will be gained from their planned bombing attacks.[57]

The United States takes a slightly different approach, stating that "reviews or investigations of incidents involving civilian casualties, *may be* appropriate in order to identify measures to mitigate the likelihood of future incidents of civilian casualties." The United States also called for the adoption of this procedure in "close call" situations. The purpose of such reviews and investigations is to learn and take appropriate action that will reduce the risk of similar incidents in the future.[58]

A more innovative approach would, we suggest, focus on alternative means of *ex post* review.

## The Non-Exclusive Nature of the Grave Breaches Regime under IHL

There is little doubt that states must investigate serious allegations of war crimes committed by individuals subject to their jurisdiction with a view to ascertaining the criminal responsibility of the suspected perpetrators. However, it seems that the Geneva Conventions go beyond the requirement for criminal investigations. The key word here is *suppression:* states are required not only to punish perpetrators of crimes, but also to see to it that similar crimes are not committed in the future.

All four grave breaches provisions contain the following language: "Each High Contracting Party shall take measures necessary for the *suppression* of all acts contrary to the provisions of the present Convention other than the grave breaches defined in the following Article."[59]

Thus, alongside the specific obligations to exercise criminal jurisdiction under the grave breaches regime, the Conventions introduce a general obligation of

56. *Id.*

57. Ian Henderson, The Contemporary Law of Targeting: Military Objectives, Proportionality and Precautions in Attack under Additional Protocol I 227 (2009).

58. US Department of Defense, Law of War Manual, para. 5.11.1 (2015, updated Dec. 2016) (emphasis added).

59. GC-I, *supra* note 9, art. 49; GC-II, *supra* note 9, art. 50; GC-III, *supra* note 9, art.129; GC-IV, *supra* note 9, art.146 (emphasis added).

taking measures necessary for suppression of other violations (in the original French text: *prendra les mesures nécessaires pour faire cesser les actes contraires aux dispositions de la présente Convention*).

In the same vein, AP-I article 86(1) provides that:

> The High Contracting Parties and the Parties to the conflict shall repress grave breaches, and take measures necessary to suppress *all other breaches*, of the Conventions or of this Protocol which result from a failure to act when under a duty to do so [emphasis added].

Although the duty to suppress other breaches under article 86(1) appears to be limited to omission-type violations, this must be understood in light of the duty imposed on military commanders in article 87 to prevent all violations of the Conventions and the Protocol by persons subject to their control.[60] Hence, the combination of articles 86 and 87 establishes a general duty to suppress all violations—certainly going far beyond the grave breaches regime.

The Israeli HCJ, which relies heavily on the principle of proportionality in its major decisions on IHL, has identified an obligation to investigate targeted killing operations, apparently in the context of a harm mitigation rationale:

> After an attack on a civilian suspected of taking an active part, at such time, in hostilities, a thorough investigation regarding the precision of the identification of the target and the circumstances of the attack upon him is to be performed (retroactively). That investigation must be independent . . . In appropriate cases it is appropriate to pay compensation as a result of harm caused to an innocent civilian.[61]

One possible non-criminal response to allegations or suspicions of violations of IHL, and especially allegations of violations of the principle of proportionality, can be found in the form of commissions of inquiry. Such commissions are composed of independent and impartial reviewers, and are authorized to ascertain the events leading up to the alleged violation and to issue policy and other recommendations. Such recommendations may lead to the revision of military practices and can include certain sanctions (such as demotion or dismissal of officers) or remedies (such as compensation to victims).[62] In certain cases, the

60. AP-I, *supra* note 9, art. 87(1) reads: "The High Contracting Parties and the Parties to the conflict shall require military commanders, with respect to members of the armed forces under their command and other persons under their control, to prevent and, where necessary, to suppress and to report to competent authorities breaches of the Conventions and of this Protocol."

61. *Targeted Killings* case, *supra* note 8, para. 40.

62. Yael Ronen, *Avoid or Compensate? Liability for Incidental Injury to Civilians Inflicted During Armed Conflict*, Brigade ("The Tagoba Report"), reform clarity in IHL is civilians on the other that soldiers strictly because of the society 42 VANDER. J. TRANSNAT'L L. 181 (2009).

factual record of commissions of inquiry may serve as the basis for follow-up legal proceedings, including criminal prosecution of suspected criminals. Arguably, some commissions—especially those composed of experts in military law and doctrine—are better placed than courts to review systemic problems involving IHL violations and to facilitate policy reforms.[63]

Recent examples of commissions of inquiry include the Somalia Commission appointed by the Government of Canada to investigate the misconduct of members of the Canadian Airborne Regiment at Belet Huen in South Central Somalia in 1993;[64] the inquiry conducted by the Dutch Institute for War Documentation into the responsibility of Netherlands forces for the Srebrenica massacre of 1995 in Bosnia and Herzegovina;[65] and The Iraq Historic Allegations Team (IHAT) set up by the British government to review and investigate allegations of abuse of Iraqi civilians by British armed forces personnel in Iraq during the period of 2003 to July 2009.[66]. In Israel, the state launched a special investigatory commission for an ad hoc review of the legality of the targeted killing of Salah Shehadeh in 2002,[67] and a committee, The Turkel Committee, was established in 2010 to review the legality of IDF operations against the Gaza Flotilla of 2009.[68] The United States has also resorted to commissions of inquiry to review the propriety of certain military or intelligence operations. Thus, a commission was established in the aftermath of the Abu Ghraib prison scandal;[69] another commission led by a former Secretary of Defense reviewed the entire detention operations of the United States;[70] and yet

63. The Israeli Supreme Court stressed this point. While rejecting a petition to open a criminal investigation into Israeli operations in the Gaza Strip in 2004, it noted that the Israeli system provides for alternative methods of investigation where, as in that case, criminal investigations are inappropriate. See HCJ 3292/07 Adallah v. Attorney General (Dec. 8, 2011) [Isr.]: "The petitioners before us ask for a criminal investigation to be conducted. In the circumstances before us, the tool of criminal investigation is inappropriate and does not properly respond to the problematic issues raised in this case, first and foremost for reasons based on the character of criminal law" (unofficial translation).

64. Report of the Somalia Commission of Inquiry (Canada, July 2, 1997), *available at:* https://nkitson.files.wordpress.com/2010/01/somalia-inquiry-report1.pdf.

65. http://www.srebrenica-project.com/index.php?option=com_content&view=article&id=140:niod-report&catid=12:2009-01-25-02-01-02.

66. https://www.gov.uk/government/groups/iraq-historic-allegations-team-ihat

67. Report of the Special Investigatory Commission on the Targeted Killing of Salah Shehadeh (Feb. 2011) [Strasberg-Cohen Report].

68. The Turkel Commission Report, *supra* note 27.

69. Article 15-6 Investigation of the 800th Military Police Brigade ("The Tagoba Report") (June 2004), *available at:* http://hrlibrary.umn.edu/OathBetrayed/Taguba-Report.pdf.

70. Final Report of the Independent Panel to Review the DOD Detention (August, 2004), *available at:* https://www.hsdl.org/?abstract&did=449289 [The Schlesinger Report].

another committee reviewed the responsibility of lawyers who authorized aggressive interrogation techniques.[71]

It seems to us that in cases of allegations regarding possible violations of the principle of proportionality, independent commissions would be especially fruitful, for two main reasons.

First, as we have seen, criminal investigations, and certainly criminal indictments, are very rare when allegations of violations of the principle of proportionality are involved. Indeed, using only criminal investigations might be counterproductive because, in most cases, no criminal charges would be brought, leading laypeople to assume that no violation had taken place. There is a need, especially in matters of proportionality, to use an institution that is able to pinpoint violations, without necessarily leading to criminal charges against wrongdoers.

Second, proportionality, as we have explained the term, involves procedures and precautions. These require the application of institutional, rather than personal, responsibility. Criminal investigations would not necessarily assist in arriving at such institutional solutions. To this end, it is much better to have an independent and permanent review mechanism, which would be able to identify the institutional reasons for possible violations, and suggest corrections for these institutional flaws.

Although commissions of inquiry may meet the general requirements of a proper investigation, this form of response nevertheless remains open to several objections. One key concern is that governments may manipulate the commission's mandate or composition in order to deflect responsibility or avoid it altogether. Hence, a critical assessment of the effectiveness and independence of each commission is warranted.

One possible way to guard against the threat of governmental manipulation of the composition of inquiry commissions may be to entrust their investigative tasks to permanent investigative bodies that would operate beside, or as part of, national humanitarian law commissions[72] or human rights institutions.[73] The structure of such permanent humanitarian law commissions (HLCs) should

71. The Office of Professional Responsibility, *Investigation into the Office of Legal Counsel's Memoranda Concerning Issues Related to the Central Intelligence Agency's use of "Enhanced Interrogation Techniques" on Suspected Terrorists* (July 29, 2009), *available at:* https://www.hsdl.org/?abstract&did=28555.

72. National Humanitarian Law Committees (NHLCs) now exist in 93 countries. Their functions vary from country to country, but frequently extend to: monitoring decisions taken by national security agencies; coordinating between different government agencies regarding the implementation of IHL; disseminating IHL material; proposing legislation that conforms with IHL; and reviewing international treaties and developments. For a description of NHLCs, see: http://www.icrc.org/eng/war-and-law/ihl-domestic-law/natrional-committees/index.jsp.

73. National Human Rights Institutions (NHRIs) or Commissions currently operate in more than a hundred countries. Their precise powers and functions vary in different states. In some places, they adjudicate complaints against the executive and its various agencies regarding violations of human rights, including at times violations committed by the military (as in the case of Uganda). See Lee Wetzel, *Post Conflict National Human Rights Institutions: Emerging Models from Northern Ireland and Bosnia& Herzegovina*, 13 COLUM. J. EURO. L. 427 (2007).

conform, as much as possible, to the Paris Principles governing the operation of national human rights institutions,[74] which call *inter alia* for independence, adequate resources, and representation of civil society.

Note that the permanency of HLCs addresses not only several independence and impartiality concerns, but also some effectiveness concerns: over time, permanent investigative bodies can accumulate considerable expertise in handling problems relating to IHL and HRL compliance in military operations. In addition, the establishment of a permanent HLC may signal greater commitment on the part of the state in question to international law[75]—which may in turn have reputational dividends, as well as decreasing the prospects of intervention by international judicial bodies in that state's military investigation system.

If established, an HLC could monitor the propriety of criminal or disciplinary investigations conducted by the military; but, more importantly, it could also engage in policy review—that is, it could review *ex post* whether a specific policy or operation was conducted in accordance with international law, and issue recommendations for future military actions. Such recommendations may help clarify for the military some of the more complex norms it is required to implement. HLC reports may also lead to the award of compensation by law or *ex gratia* payments to individuals harmed in military operations.[76] In order to fulfil these functions, HLCs need to be invested with genuine investigative powers, such as the power to require witnesses to appear before them, to obtain any document they seek, and to gather information *in situ*.

One important advantage of maintaining a permanent HLC concerns the aforementioned tension between the military need for secrecy and the principle of public scrutiny. By entrusting an independent commission with powers of monitoring and investigating military operations and inquiries, some degree of accountability and transparency is maintained; at the same time, the commission would be expected to protect the confidentiality of sensitive intelligence and testimonies. So, unlike courts, permanent HLCs would be able to deal with systemic issues—not just individual cases—and to do so in a more flexible and, at times, more confidential manner. Still, courts ought to retain the power to monitor the propriety of the commissions and their operations.[77]

74. Principles relating to the Status of National Institutions (The Paris Principles), Dec. 20, 1993, G.A. Res. 48/134.

75. For the importance of signaling the effectiveness of international law obligations, see Andrew T. Guzman, How International Law Works 58–59 (2008).

76. For a general call for compensation in all collateral damage cases, see Ronen, *supra* note 62.

77. The Ali Mousa decision, issued by the UK High Court of Justice in Dec. 2010, exercises this precise function with relation to the IHAT. In its decision, the court reviewed the independence and impartiality of the IHAT, which it declared to be sufficiently independent. *Ali Zaki Mousa v. Secretary of Defence* [2010] EWHC 3304 [U.K.].

## E. THE SALEH SHEHADEH TARGETED KILLING

As an illustration of our claim that procedures have become the main focal point of the legal analysis of targeted killings, and of *ex post* investigations, we will focus on one particular case: the targeted killing of Saleh Shehadeh by the Israel Defence Forces (IDF) in 2002. This case was extensively documented in the report of a special investigatory commission, the Strasberg-Cohen Commission.[78]

As detailed earlier in this book, the targeted killing operation of Saleh Shehadeh, the commander of Hamas's military wing, resulted in 14 civilian deaths.

Initially, the IDF refused to open an official investigation into the incident. However, in 2003, a petition to investigate was submitted to the Israeli Supreme Court (in its capacity as the High Court of Justice—a court with authority to review all governmental activities in Israel). In late 2006, while the petition was under consideration, the court published its landmark judgment in the *Targeted Killings* case, in which it ruled that targeted killings are not prohibited by IHL, provided they follow certain specific conditions.[79] In 2008, under pressure from the court,[80] the government opted to form a commission to investigate the Shehadeh killing. Headed by a retired Supreme Court justice, Tova Strasberg-Cohen, the commission submitted its report in February 2011.

The Strasberg-Cohen Commission concluded that, although some mistakes were made in the process leading up to the Shehadeh operation, there was no need for a criminal investigation. The Commission detailed the process that took place, and indicated the mistakes that were made. For our purposes, the most important element of the Commission's work was the general framework it specified for future decision-making in targeted killing operations.

First, the Commission interpreted the *Targeted Killings* judgment[81] to set out the following requirements for a targeted killing operation:

(a) The operation should take place only after the attacking party has gathered accurate and reliable information regarding the intended targets, if they are civilians who take direct part in the hostilities.
(b) The attacking party should take every feasible measure to attempt to secure the results with non-lethal weapons. All feasible efforts should especially be made to use less lethal measures.
(c) The principle of proportionality must be observed and the harm to uninvolved civilians must not be excessive.
(d) An investigatory committee should be established in order to investigate operations that result in exceptional outcomes.

78. Strasberg Cohen Report, *supra* note 67.

79. *Targeted Killings* Case, *supra* note 8.

80. HCJ 8794/03, Hass v. The Military Advocate General (Dec. 23, 2008) [Isr.].

81. *Id.*

In applying this normative framework to the specific case at hand, the Commission found that the Israeli security agencies responsible for the operation considered 13 civilian deaths to constitute a disproportionately high number. The Commission, however, concluded that there was no criminal responsibility, since the main failure in the operation was a mistaken intelligence assessment. Nevertheless, the Commission considered the mistake to have been avoidable. This was because the intelligence-gathering operation conducted by the Israeli Security Agency (ISA) focused principally on finding Shehadeh and on choosing the correct operational timetable for the action; insufficient attention was paid to gathering intelligence regarding the possibility of civilian casualties.

The Commission's recommendations are telling. After a general remark that Israel is committed to the principle of proportionality, and a recommendation that all security forces continuously be made aware of this commitment, the Commission did not specify what this principle actually means. Rather, its recommendations were principally concerned with procedural requirements as to how decisions regarding targeted killings (including proportionality assessments) should be made. Thus, the Commission suggested that all decisions in matters of targeted killings should be recorded (recommendations 9 and 10); that final decisions should be taken by the political echelon, and be made only in writing (recommendation 13); that disagreements between the heads of the security services, especially regarding harm to civilians, be brought before the political echelon (recommendations 14 and 15); that the prime minister and the minister of defence should reach a decision only after consulting with the IDF chief of staff and the head of the ISA (recommendation 16); that lawyers should be more involved in decision-making regarding targeted killings, and that any disagreement that they may have with the recommendations of the professional echelon should be brought to the attention of the political echelon (recommendation 17).

All these recommendations lead to a specific conclusion—that in targeted killings, the main concern is the procedure that should be followed. This is an important and integral part of the decision-making process, rather than its result.

The inability shown in this case of determining the specific number of deaths considered disproportionate is not unique. It is a natural result of the problems associated with the proportionality formulae as described earlier. The Commission's procedural recommendations are consistent with existing practice in a fundamental way: they reflect the tendency to frame proportionality as a set of procedural requirements.

Naturally, there are cases in which the principle of proportionality is clearly violated. In these cases, it is, of course, the duty of the relevant lawyers to alert the decision-makers to this violation. In fact, in these clear-cut cases, any decision-maker conducting a *bona fide* assessment of the situation would usually not need legal advice in order to understand the gravity of the situation. The lawyers' role becomes more significant in those grey areas in which a proportionality analysis does not yield clear results. But even in these cases, it is not the job of the lawyers to provide the commander with a specific number of "acceptable" civilian losses. In fact, the lawyer has no specific number to give. Rather, the lawyers' main contribution will be to stipulate procedures that will ensure that the decision-makers take civilian casualties into account.

# 14

# The Future of Proportionality

In modern armed conflicts, the principle of proportionality has become an extremely important part of IHL. Both states and non-state actors, which comprise a growing proportion of the parties to armed conflicts, act from within civilian populations. This means that the main question that the principle of proportionality was designed to deal with—namely, the balance between military advantage and collateral civilian damage—is becoming perhaps the central question in the application of IHL.

Despite its rising importance in modern IHL, the principle is notoriously difficult to implement, as we have seen throughout this book. There are disagreements over even the most basic questions of interpretation; there are practical problems regarding its actual application to specific situations; and there is an inherent ambiguity as to what factors form part of the balancing equation—which is the basic tenet of the principle.

In this book, we have tried to provide an overview of these issues, and where relevant, have offered our opinions. Moreover, as we have stressed throughout, and in light of the aforementioned difficulties, we support a procedural interpretation of the principle of proportionality. Such an interpretation—which emphasizes the procedural aspects of taking precautions in attacks over conducting a mathematical assessment of their results—could, in our view, provide a better mechanism for implementing the principle of proportionality. Perhaps more importantly, it provides a more realistic route to educating members of the armed forces as to how the principle of proportionality should be implemented in practice. Such procedures and precautions should include clear directives regarding the proper persons authorized to make decisions, the requirements for planning and intelligence gathering, and the requirement for advance warnings.

Naturally, this emphasis on precautions is intended to achieve the most important goal of proportionality: protecting civilian life during armed conflict. In addition, we believe that a procedural approach also resonates with the interest of states to apply proportionality. This approach makes it easier for decision-makers to control the behavior of the soldiers and officers actually executing the attacks. Because we believe that the "control" conception of IHL provides the best explanation for the interest of states in the application of IHL, it is imperative to adopt an

*Proportionality in International Humanitarian Law.* Amichai Cohen & David Zlotogorski, Oxford University Press.
 DOI: 10.1093/oso/9780197556726.003.0014

interpretation that coincides with this interest of states, and that thereby improves the chances of the principle of proportionality being properly implemented.

## A. ON THE FUTURE OF PROPORTIONALITY

This book has mostly focused on the way proportionality is, or should be, implemented in current armed conflicts. Rapid technological developments, both on and off the battlefield, are changing the way in which armed conflicts are, and will be, fought. Without straying too far into the realm of prophecy, in this final chapter we wish to sketch several areas in which we believe future developments may well necessitate further development in the understanding of the principle of proportionality. While a full discussion of all these possible developments lies outside the framework of this book, we hope that the present study will contribute to this discussion.

### Image-Fare

Armed conflicts are increasingly being judged by the way they are perceived, rather than the facts and actual events on the ground. The ability of victims of armed conflicts to disseminate information from the battlefield itself means that armed forces find it much more difficult to explain their position in the international arena. Social media and networks have very limited filters for verifying or controlling such information, and images of armed conflict travel quickly around the globe. An image of a single child victim of an attack may serve to change international perceptions of "good" and "bad" in a conflict.[1]

Another characteristic of modern forms of disseminating information is that social networks do not provide a meaningful forum for complex discussions. The inherent culture of short, rapid responses; and the echo chamber effect, have contributed to the growing public trend of taking unambiguous and simplistic positions. These characteristics of modern public discourse are not well suited to discussions of the principle of proportionality. Even if the public accepts the idea that enemy civilians should be protected or that military necessity can at times justify collateral harm to civilians, the delicate balancing required by proportionality is not well served by current –and, most likely, future – forms of public discussion.

In this context, it is worth asking whether armed forces will be able to create a culture of proportionality that is detached from public discussions about these issues. Even if this is possible, this can raise further questions about the justification for the armed forces in a democracy to have a culture of proportionality that is very different from civilian conceptions.

1. Ami Ayalon, Elad Popovich, & Moran Yarchi, *From Warfare to Imagefare: How States Should Manage Asymmetric Conflicts With Extensive Media Coverage*, 28(2) Terrorism & Political Violence 254 (2016).

## Cyber Warfare and Proportionality

In the not-so-distant future, armed conflicts will at least partly take the form of "cyber operations," in which the force used is not kinetic. There is as yet no agreed-upon definition of cyber warfare, but a useful provisional definition is that cyber warfare involves the use or targeting of computers, networks, and online control systems in the context of an armed conflict.

There is very little regulation of cyber warfare as defined here, and because cyber wars have not yet been conducted, at least openly, it is a question whether customary international law exists. In light of this lacuna, a group of experts in international law of war came together in 2013,[2] and again in 2017,[3] to create the Tallinn Manual, which represents the best effort to date to adapt the traditional laws of armed conflict to cyber operations.

A broad evaluation of the Tallinn Manual lies beyond the scope of this book. Suffice it to say that the approach taken by the Manual is that the traditional rules and concepts of IHL can be adapted to cyber warfare. For example, the Tallinn Manual defines a "cyber attack" as "a cyber operation . . . that is reasonably expected to cause injury or death to persons or damage or destruction to objects."[4] This definition is parallel to the general definition for the term "attacks" in IHL.[5] However, the Manual is also sensitive to the fact that persons can be injured as a direct result of an attack on a computer system that will cause the failure of some mechanism essential to the survival of human beings, such as a cyber attack on water purification systems resulting in infected water being supplied to the civilian population.

In the same manner, the definition of the rule of proportionality in the Tallinn Manual is quite similar to its general definition in IHL.[6] The Manual's commentary emphasizes that the nature of an attack as a "cyber attack" does not change the fact that the rule is relevant only when civilians are injured or killed? or civilian objects are destroyed. An example given by the Manual is an attack on the Global Positioning System (GPS), which confers a military advantage because of the military application of the GPS, but may also cause severe damage and injuries to civilians.[7] Apart from these adaptations, however, it seems that

2. Tallinn Manual 2.0 on the International Law Applicable to Cyber Operations 473 (Michael N. Schmitt ed., 2017) [Tallinn Manual 2.0].

3. *Id.*, at 226.

4. *Id.*, rule 92, at 413.

5. Protocol Additional to the Geneva Conventions of 12 August 1949, and Relating to the Protection of Victims of International Armed Conflicts (Protocol I), June 8, 1977, art. 49(1), 1125 U.N.T.S. 3 [AP-I].

6. "Rule 113 – Proportionality: A cyber-attack that may be expected to cause incidental loss of civilian life, injury to civilians, damage to civilian objects or a combination thereof, which would be excessive in relation to the concrete and direct military advantage, is prohibited" (Tallinn Manual 2.0, 2, at 470).

7. *Id.*, at 471.

the discussion of the rule of proportionality in the Tallinn Manual does not reflect the idiosyncrasies of cyber operations, but rather reflects a general approach to the correct interpretation of the principle of proportionality in IHL. Indeed, throughout this book we have cited the Tallinn Manual with regard to several issues that are not necessarily related to cyber operations.

There is one case in which the Manual does present what it considers to be a relevant difference, though we are not sure that this is justified. The Manual claims that the issue of uncertainty is especially relevant in cyber operations, since their effects cannot reliably be determined.[8] It is not clear what the basis for this claim is, and why the results of cyber operations are seen as harder to estimate than other indirect consequences of the use of force. At any rate, most of the experts cited in the Manual seem to believe that the degree of uncertainty is irrelevant, and that the perceived change in circumstances has no effect on the law.

However, the basic premises underlying this approach seem to raise important questions. Cyber operations are different not only in context and circumstances, but may completely alter the nature of war. A state deprived of a reliable online infrastructure could conceivably become totally incapable of functioning during armed conflicts. Critical infrastructures, such as power, water supply, sewage treatment, telecommunications, medical services, and others could be completely crippled. Hence, an attack on the cyber infrastructure might become the most important objective in armed conflicts. The damage to civilian life, even if no physical injury is caused, would be immense. In coming years, it will be increasingly difficult to imagine life without cyber technologies.

## Autonomous Weapons and Proportionality

As is evident to anyone following recent developments in warfare, states are already adopting fighting technologies that involve more autonomous weapon systems. Even now, many targeted killing operations are carried out by drones, operated from afar, albeit controlled by human operators. Furthermore, more and more highly sophisticated automated systems are being developed. These systems can now gather information on their own, with the human operator just issuing the final command. More highly developed systems can operate completely autonomously, with the human operator able to halt the operation only if deemed necessary.[9] In the future, all battlefield action might possibly—and perhaps even

8. *Id.*, at 475.

9. Jeroen van den Boogaard defines autonomous weapons systems in the following way: "The defining characteristic of autonomous weapons systems is the use of artificial intelligence software that provides the weapons system with a certain level of autonomy. As such, an autonomous system is a system that is capable of operating without direct human control or supervision in dynamic, unstructured, open environments based on feedback information from a variety of sensors." Jeroen Van den Boogaard, *Proportionality and Autonomous Weapons Systems*, 6(2) Journal of Int'l Human. Leg. Stud. 247 (2015).

probably—be based on autonomous weapons.[10] This is the so-called "man out of the loop" system, in which once a system is deployed, no human action or decision is required or even possible in the actual use of lethal force.[11]

From the point of view of IHL in general, and the principle of proportionality in particular, there is much to say in favor of the use of autonomous weapon systems informed by artificial intelligence. Computers and autonomous weapons hold the promise of being able to implement proportionality in a better way than is currently possible. Current developments in the field of computing show how quickly and accurately computers can gather information on a scale that far exceeds human capacities. Autonomous systems can be programmed to take into account more variables, to gather more information, and to implement stricter procedures. Ideally, whatever we consider the essence of the principle of proportionality to be, autonomous weapons will be able to implement it with more accuracy than a human soldier can. Furthermore, if an agreement could be reached regarding a formula for the application of the principle of proportionality, it would then be possible to develop an algorithm allowing the principle to be uniformly applied in practice. If states were to agree to use such algorithms, this could solve one of the major criticisms of proportionality, namely, that it is an area rife with ambiguity and uncertainty. Using such uniform systems, therefore, would have clear advantages.[12]

However, as with every new weapons system, it is important to evaluate whether autonomous systems create new challenges for the implementation and enforcement of IHL.[13] In the context of this book, the question is whether a fully autonomous weapons system may be programmed to follow the principle of proportionality. Several arguments have been made against the use of autonomous systems.

The first of these arguments is empirical. There are those who claim that technology will never develop to a level where a computer may take all possibilities into account and make correct decisions in battlefield situations.[14] They argue that the issue is simply too complex for a suitable algorithm to be created. However, while it may be true that current technology is not sufficiently advanced to offer a solution, we do not believe it is correct to assume that ultimately computers will not be able to gather information to the same extent that humans can. The ability of computers to operate in complex situations is evident in many areas of

10. On the development of such weapon systems, see Paul Scharre, Army of None: Autonomous Weapons and the Future of War (New York, 2018).

11. Yoram Dinstein, *Autonomous Weapons and International Humanitarian Law, in* Dehumanization of Lawfare 15, 18 (von Heinneg et al. eds., Springer, 2018).

12. Paul Scharre, Army of None: Autonomous Weapons and the Future of War 279–84 (New York, 2018); Yoram Dinstein, *Autonomous Weapons and International Humanitarian Law, in* Dehumanization of Lawfare 19 (von Heinneg et al. eds., Springer, 2018).

13. AP-I, *supra* note 5, art. 36.

14. Van den Boogaard, *supra* note 11, 261–64.

our lives, and the idea that computers will always be inferior to human decision-makers seems to us to be wrong.

The second claim, and one which should be taken more seriously, is that computerized decision-making robs the enemy of human dignity because no human is involved in the decision-making process.[15] Decisions about taking lives should be made by humans, it is claimed, not by computers.[16] Moreover, the application of IHL, and especially of the principle of proportionality, requires complex normative evaluations regarding the relative values of military advantages, human lives, the protection of soldiers, and so on. These are not decisions that can be made by machines.

As stated before, we see no reason to assume that computers cannot be programmed with enough information to enable them to make decisions in complex situations. Furthermore, it seems to us to be incorrect to think that a computer would in these cases act in a less consistent manner than a human decision-maker. Of course, if only a human may decide to take another human's life, then computers should not be given the power to make these decisions. But this categorical position is not universally accepted. For many, the real question is whether autonomous weapons systems will cause more harm – or less.

The third objection is that the development of autonomous weapons systems diminishes the disincentives for states to go to war. If people will no longer be killed in warfare, and only machines will be damaged or destroyed, then one of the most important political reasons for states to limit the recourse to armed conflict would disappear.

In their work on this subject, Anderson and Waxman convincingly explain why this argument should be rejected.[17] The idea that a weapon that reduces human suffering should be prohibited, because states would be more willing to go to war if their population will suffer less, distorts the logic of IHL. IHL has always rejected the traditional claim, made frequently by 19th-century Germany, that IHL is wrong because when parties operate under IHL, they are able to drag out the conflict, causing greater suffering to more people.

The fourth objection to autonomous weapons system comes from the world of cyber wars and hacking. Autonomous weapons, like every computer, can be broken into. If indeed wars will be fought between robots, the challenge will be how to protect them being hacked and taken over by hostile forces.

To us, it seems that there are three major claims that present a serious challenge to the ability of autonomous weapons systems to apply proportionality. These are the challenges of machine learning, human discretion, and responsibility.

15. Scharre, *supra* note 12.

16. *Id.*

17. Kenneth Anderson & Matthew Waxman, *Law and Ethics for Autonomous Weapons Systems* 17–19 (Hoover Institution, 2013).

**Machine Learning.** The idea that an autonomous weapons system could be "programmed" to include IHL rules runs counter to developments in the field of computing in recent years. Modern machine learning is based on the idea that computers can intuit patterns better than human beings. Using "big data," computers are able to identify patterns and achieve results without human programming. Currently, it is still possible for humans to intervene in machine learning and direct it. Soon enough, however, we might face a world in which machines learn how to operate from machines, with very little human involvement, if any. Moreover, machine learning based on big data is mostly about observing how the world operates. If most parties to armed conflicts *do not* respect IHL, it might become difficult to "teach" machines to ignore their behavior, and focus instead on some ideal world.

**Human Discretion.** In a recent chapter, Eyal Benvenisiti and Eliav Lieblich suggested that the main problem with autonomous weapons systems is their inability to use discretion in the application of general rules to the specific case.[18] Benvenisti and Lieblich claim that such a use of discretion cannot be achieved by an algorithm. This claim is especially relevant to the application of the principle of proportionality. Proportionality, as we saw throughout this book, is different from other principles of IHL in that procedures requiring discretion are part of the definition of principle. There is no single answer as to what constitutes excessive collateral damage to civilians relative to the concrete military advantage anticipated from an attack. As a way of dealing with this ambiguity, one of our main recommendations in this book has been to emphasize procedural requirements. These procedures mandate careful consideration and human intuition. It is not clear that computers would be capable of meeting the standards required.

**Responsibility.** IHL compliance is based on the idea that the responsibility for violations of IHL lies with a particular state or individual. This idea is easy enough to comprehend in the case of a soldier operating a rocket launcher. The soldier receives orders from a commanding officer, who is part of the chain of command of a state. If a violation of IHL occurs, responsibility lies with the state. If there is a grave breach of IHL, such as a violation of the principle of distinction, then it is the soldier who has violated IHL, and possibly the commanding officer, if the latter ordered the violation or could have prevented it.

But how does this chain of responsibility translate to an autonomous weapons system, in which the only, or major, human involvement was at the planning stage, by a programmer, who might even be from another country? Is the programmer criminally responsible for acts that might be carried out many years after his involvement ended? Is the state that bought the system responsible for reviewing

18. Eyal Benvenisti & Eliav Lieblich, *The Obligation to Exercise Discretion in Warfare: Why Autonomous Weapon Systems are Unlawful, in* Autonomous Weapons Systems: Law, Ethics, Policy 244 (Nehal Bhuta et al., eds., Cambridge University Press, 2016).

the compliance of the weapons system with IHL? And what if the purchasing country is poor and lacks the technical capabilities to perform such a review? Should less advanced countries be barred from buying complex weapon systems?

In our view, the existing answers to these questions are far from clear, and IHL lawyers still need to deepen their understanding of the interaction between IHL and autonomous weapons systems.

# Conclusion—A Way Forward?

In classic wars between two states, the main principle of IHL that protected civilians was the principle of distinction. The parties to the conflict were prohibited from directing their fire at civilians. The principle of proportionality was designed as a supplement to this rule, in order to resolve those relatively rare cases in which the effects of an attack on a military target cannot be separated from the civilian objective.

Today, the principle of proportionality plays a completely different role. In modern armed conflicts, at least some of the parties to the conflict pull civilians right into the battle. The use of human shields, combatants masquerading as civilians, and rockets shot from within populated areas, are all part of modern armed conflict. In fact, some parties to the conflict deliberately embed themselves within the civilian population in order to deter their adversaries from attacking.

It should come as no surprise that a principle initially designed to be of a relatively minor significance does not translate well when required to carry the heavy burden of being the most important principle of modern IHL. As we have seen in the first parts of this book, almost every issue relating to the correct application of proportionality gives rise to serious disagreement. States and armed forces need clarity regarding the rules they must apply. Under the best of circumstances, it is difficult to restrain fighting armed forces. The vaguer the norms that combatants are required to apply, the less likely they are to be implemented.[1]

Three different strategies have been proposed to confront this inherent vagueness. The first is the attempt to resolve all disagreements, and create a more crystallized application of proportionality. Such is the strategy adopted by Boaz Ganor, for example.[2] We believe that this strategy has not proven useful, and doubt whether it is feasible to expect all states to reach consensus regarding this issue.

The second strategy, presented by Newton and May, seeks to differentiate between different categories of armed conflicts, and clarifies how to apply proportionality in each category.[3] Undoubtedly, in cases such as targeted killing

1. Amichai Cohen, *Rules and Standards in the Application of IHL*, 41 Isr. L. Rev. 41 (2008).

2. Boaz Ganor, Global Alert: The Rationality of Modern Islamist Terrorism and the Challenge to the Liberal Democratic World (2015).

3. Michael Newton & Larry May, Proportionality in International Law (2014).

*Proportionality in International Humanitarian Law.* Amichai Cohen & David Zlotogorski, Oxford University Press.
 DOI: 10.1093/oso/9780197556726.003.0015

operations, Newton and May's framework does indeed provide clarity, allowing almost no collateral civilian casualties in such operations. But, as we discussed in Chapter 11, Newton and May's conclusions are arguable. Even if we accept their position, their suggestions only partially clarify how proportionality should be applied in cases of high intensity battles, such as Operation Protective Edge.

In Chapters 12 and 13 we propose a third strategy, namely, focussing on the "procedural" aspects of proportionality: precautions, information gathering, decision-making processes, and investigations. This strategy, we suggest, is the more useful one. It allows states to preserve their interests, while minimizing the collateral damage caused to civilians.

It is said that "Only the dead have seen the end of war."[4] This may be true, and yet, it is the task of the living to strive to mitigate the horrors of battle. With civilians now in the crosshairs of combat perhaps more than ever before, it is imperative to devise a clearer, more effective application of the principle of proportionality—a principle that can serve to minimize human suffering. Only time will tell if and which of these three strategies will rise to that task.

4. George Santayana, Soliloquies in England and Later Soliloquies 102 (1922).

# BIBLIOGRAPHY

## Books, Articles, and Book Chapters


Adjovi, Roland. 2013. "Introductory Note to United Nations Security Council Resolution 2093 on the Situation in Somalia." *International Legal Materials* 52 (5): p. 1185.

Alston, Philip. 2010. *Report of the Special Rapporteur on Extrajudicial, Summary or Arbitrary Executions*, UN Human Rights Council, A/HRC/14/24/Add.6.

Ambrose, Stephen E. 1994. *D-Day June 6, 1944: The Climactic Battle of World War II*. New York: Simon & Schuster.

Anderson, Kenneth and Matthew Waxman. 2013. *Law and Ethics for Autonomous Weapons Systems*. Stanford, CA: The Hoover Institution.

Aquinas, Thomas. 2002. "From Summa Theologiae." In *International Relations in Political Thought: Texts from the Ancient Greeks to the First World War*, edited by Chris Brown et al., p. 213. Cambridge: Cambridge University Press.

Ayalon, Ami, Elad Popovich, and Moran Yarchi. 2016. "From Warfare to Imagefare: How States Should Manage Asymmetric Conflicts with Extensive Media Coverage." *Terrorism and Political Violence* 28 (2): p. 254.

Bartels, Rogier. 2013. "Dealing with the Principle of Proportionality in Armed Conflict in Retrospect: The Application of the Principle in International Criminal Trials." *Israel Law Review* 46 (2): p. 271.

Bassiouni, Cherif M. 2008. "The New Wars and the Crisis of Compliance with the Law of Armed Conflict by Non-State Actors." *Journal of Criminal Law & Criminology* 98 (3): p. 711.

Beard, Jack M. 2009. "Law and War in the Virtual Era." *American Journal of International Law* 103 (3): p. 409.

Beevor, Anthony. 2012. *The Second World War*. Hachette: Weidenfeld & Nicolson.

Benbaji, Yitzhak and Daniel Statman 2019. *War by Agreement: A Contractarian Ethics of War*. Oxford: Oxford University Press.

Benvenisti, Eyal. 1999. "Exit and Voice in the Age of Globalization." *Michigan Law Review* 98: p. 167.

Benvenisti, Eyal. 2009. "Rethinking the Divide Between Jus ad Bellum and Jus in Bello in Warfare Against Nonstate Actors." *Yale Journal of International Law* 34 (2): p. 541.

Benvenisti, Eyal and Amichai Cohen. 2014. "War Is Governance: Explaining the Laws of War from a Principal–Agent Perspective." *Michigan Law Review* 112 (8): p. 1363.

Benvenisti, Eyal and Eliav Lieblich. 2016. "The Obligation to Exercise Discretion in Warfare: Why Autonomous Weapon Systems are Unlawful." In *Autonomous*

*Weapons Systems: Law, Ethics, Policy*, edited by Nehal Bhuta et al., p. 244. Cambridge: Cambridge University Press.

Blank, Laurie R. 2015. "Military Operations and Media Coverage: The Interplay of Law and Legitimacy." In *Routledge Handbook on Military Ethics*, edited by George Lucas, p. 348. London and New York: Routledge.

Blum, Gabriella. 2010. "The Dispensable Lives of Soldiers." *Journal of Legal Analysis* 2 (1): p. 115.

Blum, Gabriella. 2010. "The Laws of War and the "Lesser Evil." *Yale Journal of International Law* 35 (1): p. 1.

Blum, Gabriella. 2011. "On a Differential Law of War." *Harvard Journal of International Law* 52 (1): p. 164.

Bohrer, Ziv and Mark Osiel. 2013a. "Proportionality in Military Force at War's Multiple Levels: Averting Civilian Casualties vs. Safeguarding Soldiers." *Vanderbilt Journal of Transnational Law* 46 (3): p. 747.

Bohrer, Ziv and Mark Osiel. 2013b. "Proportionality in War: Protecting Soldiers from Enemy Captivity, and Israel's Operation Cast Lead—'The Soldiers are Everyone's Children.'" *South California Interdisciplinary Law Journal* 22 (2): p. 637.

Wan Den Boogaard, Jeroen. 2015. "Proportionality and Autonomous Weapons Systems." *Journal of International Human Legal Studies* 6 (2): p. 247.

Boothby, Bill. 2010. "'And for such Time as': The Time Dimension to Direct Participation in Hostilities." *New York University Journal of International Law and Policy* 42: p. 741.

Bowker, David. 2005. "Unwise Counsel: The War on Terrorism and the Criminal Mistreatment of Detainees in U.S. Custody." In *The Torture Debate in America*, edited by K.J. Greenberg, p. 183. New York: Cambridge University Press.

Boyle, Joseph M. 2006. "Towards Understanding the Principle of Double Effect." In *The Morality of War: Classical and Contemporary Readings*, edited by Larry May et al., p. 164. London: Pearson Education.

Brandon, Mark E. 2005. "War and the American Constitutional Order." In *The Constitution in Wartime: Beyond Alarmism and Complacency*, edited by Mark Tushnet, p. 11. Durham and London: Duke University Press.

Brown, Gary D. 2003. "Proportionality and Just War." *Journal of Military Ethics* 2 (3): p. 171.

Carlarne, Cinnamon P. et al. 2016. "International Climate Change Law: Mapping the Field." In *The Oxford Handbook on International Climate Change*, edited by Carlarne et al., p. 3. Oxford: Oxford University Press.

Chechko, Elena and Yuval Shany. 2018. "The Supreme Court of Israel Dismisses a Petition Against Gaza Rules of Engagement." *Lawfare Blog*. May 26. https://www.lawfareblog.com/supreme-court-israel-dismisses-petition-against-gaza-rules-engagement.

CNN. 2012. *Watching Israel's Missile Defense*. Nov. 20. security.blogs.cnn.com/2012/11/20/watching-israels-missile-defense/.

Cohen, Amichai. 2008. "Rules and Standards in the Application of IHL." *Israel Law Review* 41: p. 41.

Cohen, Amichai. 2009. "The Principle of Proportionality in the Context of Operation Cast Lead: Institutional Perspectives." *Rutgers Law Record* 35: p. 23.

Cohen, Amichai. 2010. "Proportionality in Modern Asymmetrical Wars." *Available at:* din-online.info/pdf/jc2.pdf.

Cohen, Amichai. 2011. "Legal Operational Advice in the Israeli Defense Forces: The International Law Department and the Changing Nature of International Law." *Connecticut Journal of International Law* 26 (2): p. 402.

Cohen, Amichai. 2014. "Guardians and Guards: The Israeli Supreme Court's Role in Matters of National Security." In *Civil Military Relations in Israel*, edited by E. Rossman, p. 171. Lanham, MD: Lexington Books.

Cohen, Amichai. 2018. "Analysis of Israel's Supreme Court Decision Allowing Lethal Force in Gaza." *Just Security*. May 27. https://www.justsecurity.org/57033/analysis-israels-supreme-court-decision-allowing-lethal-force-gaza/.

Cohen, Amichai and Stuart A. Cohen. 2012. *Israel's National Security Law*. London and New York: Routledge.

Cohen, Amichai and Tal Mimran. 2015 "Response: Shiri Krebs, 'Don't Ask, Don't Tell' Secrecy, Security, and Oversight of Targeted Killing Operations." In *Policy Paper 9E*, 75: 99. Aug. https://en.idi.org.il/publications/4291.

Cohen, Amichai and Yuval Shany. 2007. "A Development of Modest Proportions: The Application of the Principle of Proportionality in the Targeted Killings Case." *Journal of International Criminal Justice* 5: p. 310.

Cohen, Amichai and Yuval Shany. 2012. "Beyond the Grave Breaches Regime: The Duty to Investigate Alleged Violations of International Law Governing Armed Conflicts." *Yearbook of International Humanitarian Law* 14: p. 37.

Cohen, Amichai and Yuval Shany. 2015. "Contextualizing Proportionality Analysis? A Response to Schmitt and Merriam on Israel's Targeting Practices." *Just Security*. May 5. www.justsecurity.org/22786/contextualizing-proportionality-analysis-response-schmitt-merriam/.

Cohen, Amichai and Yuval Shany. 2018. "Israel's Military Advocate General Terminates 'Black Friday' and Other Investigations: Initial Observations." *Lawfare Blog*. Aug. 27. www.lawfareblog.com/israels-military-advocate-general-terminates-black-friday-and-other-investigations-initial.

Corn, Geoffrey S. 2017. "Transatlantic Workshop on International Law and Armed Conflict: Wounded and Sick, Proportionality, and Armaments." *Lawfare Blog*. Oct. 10. https://www.lawfareblog.com/transatlantic-workshop-international-law-and-armed-conflict-wounded-and-sick-proportionality-and.

Corn, Geoffrey and Andrew Culliver. 2017. "Wounded Combatants, Military Medical Personnel, and the Dilemma of Collateral Risk." *Georgia Journal of International & Comparative Law* 45: p. 445.

Craig, Alan. 2013. *International Legitimacy and the Politics of Security: The Strategic Deployment of Lawyers in the Israeli Military*. Lanham, MD: Lexington Books.

Criddle, Evan J. and Evan Fox-Decent. 2012. "Human Rights, Emergencies, and the Rule of Law." *Human Rights Quarterly* 34: p. 39.

Devereaux, Ryan. 2015. "Manhunting in the Hindu-Kush: Civilian Casualties and Strategic Failures in America's Longest War." *The Intercept*. Oct. 15. https://theintercept.com/drone-papers/manhunting-in-the-hindu-kush/.

Dinstein, Yoram. 2003. "Unlawful Combatancy." In *International Law and the War on Terror*, edited by Fred L. Borch and Paul S. Wilson, p. 151. Newport, RI: US Naval War College.

Dinstein, Yoram. 2004. *The Conduct of Hostilities under the Law of International Armed Conflict*. 1st ed. Cambridge: Cambridge University Press.

Dinstein, Yoram. 2010. *The Conduct of Hostilities under the Law of International Armed Conflict*. 2nd ed. Cambridge: Cambridge University Press.

Dinstein, Yoram. 2011. *War, Aggression and Self-Defence*. 5th ed. Cambridge: Cambridge University Press.

Dinstein, Yoram. 2014. *Non-International Armed Conflicts in International Law*. Cambridge: Cambridge University Press.

Dinstein, Yoram. 2014. "Remarks: Interpretive Complexity and the International Humanitarian Law Principle of Proportionality." *American Society of International Law Proceedings* 108: p. 82.

Dinstein, Yoram. 2016. *The Conduct of Hostilities under the Law of International Armed Conflict*. 3rd ed. Cambridge: Cambridge University Press.

Dinstein, Yoram. 2018. "Autonomous Weapons and International Humanitarian Law." In *Dehumanization of Lawfare*, edited by Heintschel Von Heinneg et al., p. 15. Berlin: Springer.

Dormann, Knut. 2003. "The Legal Situation of 'Unlawful/Unprivileged Combatants.'" *International Review of the Red Cross* 85 (849): p. 45.

Droege, Cordula. 2007. "The Interplay between International Humanitarian Law and International Human Rights Law in Situations of Armed Conflict." *Israel Law Review* 40 (2): p. 310.

Droege, Cordula. 2012. "Get Off My Cloud: Cyber Warfare, International Humanitarian Law, and the Protection of Civilians." *International Review of the Red Cross* 94 (886): p. 533.

Erlanger, Steven. 2014. "A Growing Arsenal of Homegrown Rockets Encounters Israel's Iron Dome." *New York Times*. July 9. https://www.nytimes.com/2014/07/10/world/middleeast/israel-gaza-missiles-iron-dome.html.

Feaver, Peter D. 2003. *Armed Servants: Agency, Oversight, and Civil-Military Relations*. Cambridge, MA: Harvard University Press.

Fenrick, W.J. 1982. "The Rule of Proportionality and Protocol I in Conventional Warfare." *Military Law Review* 98: p. 91.

Fenrick, William J. 2009. "Applying IHL Targeting Rules to Practical Situations: Proportionality and Military Objectives." *Windsor Yearbook of Access to Justice* 27: p. 271.

Franck, Thomas M. 2008. "On Proportionality of Countermeasures in International Law." *American Journal of International Law* 102 (4): p. 715.

Friedrich, Jorg. 2008. *The Fire: The Bombing of Germany 1940–1945*. New York: Columbia University Press.

Ganor, Boaz. 2015. *Global Alert: The Rationality of Modern Islamist Terrorism and the Challenge to the Liberal Democratic World*. New York: Columbia University Press.

Gardam, Judith G. 1993. "Proportionality and Force in International Law." *American Journal of International Law* 87 (3): p. 391.

Gardam, Judith. 2004. *Necessity, Proportionality and the Use of Force by States*. Cambridge: Cambridge University Press.

Gillard, Emanuela-Chiara. 2018. "Proportionality in the Conduct of Hostilities: The Incidental Harm Side of the Assessment." *Chatham House International Law Programme*. https://www.chathamhouse.org/sites/default/files/publications/research/2018-12-10-proportionality-conduct-hostilities-incidental-harm-gillard-final.pdf.

Gillespie, Alexander. 2011. *A History of the Laws of War: Volume 2, The Customs and Laws of War with Regards to Civilians in Times of Conflict*. Oxford: Hart Publishing.

Goldsmith, Jack L. 2012. *Power and Constraint: The Accountable Presidency after 9/11*. New York: Norton & Co.

Goldsmith, Jack L. and Eric A. Posner. 2005. *The Limits of International Law.* Oxford: Oxford University Press.

Goodman, Ryan. 2013. "The Power to Kill or Capture Enemy Combatants." *European Journal of International Law* 24: p. 819.

Greenwood, Christopher. 2002. "Legal Issues Regarding Explosive Remnants of War." *Group of Government Experts of States Parties to the Convention on Prohibitions or Restrictions on the Use of Certain Conventional Weapons.* U.N. Doc. CCW/GGE/I/WP.10 (2002).

Von der Groeben, Constantin. 2010. *German Federal Prosecutor Terminates Investigation Against German Soldiers With Respect to NATO Air Strike in Afghanistan, EJIL: Talk!* Apr. 29. https://www.ejiltalk.org/german-federal-prosecutor-terminates-investigation-against-german-soldiers-with-respect-to-nato-air-strike-in-afghanistan/#:~:text=April%2029%2C%202010-,German%20Federal%20Prosecutor%20Terminates%20Investigation%20Against%20German%20Soldiers%20With,NATO%20Air%20Strike%20in%20Afghanistan&text=Constantin%20von%20der%20Groeben%20is%20a%20Ph.

Guzman, Andrew T. 2008. *How International Law Works*. Cambridge: Cambridge University Press.

Haque, Adil A. 2019. "Proportionality and Doubt." *Just Security*. Jan. 29. https://www.justsecurity.org/62375/proportionality-doubt/.

Harari, Yuval Noah. 2017. *Homos Deus: A Brief History of Tomorrow*. London. Harvill Secker.

Hartman, Joan F. 1985. "Working Paper for the Committee of Experts on the Article 4 Derogation Provision." *Human Rights Quarterly* 7: p. 89.

Hashim, Ahmed S. 2006. *Insurgency and Counter-insurgency in Iraq*. Ithaca, NY: Cornell University Press.

Von Heinegg, Wolff Heintschel and Peter Dreist. 2010. "The 2009 Kunduz Air Attack: The Decision of the Federal Prosecutor-General on the Dismissal of Criminal Proceedings against Members of the German Armed Forces." *German Year Book of International Law* 53: p. 833.

Henckaerts, Jean-Marie and Louise Doswald-Beck. 2005. *Customary International Humanitarian Law*. Cambridge: Cambridge University Press.

Henderson, Ian. 2009. *The Contemporary Law of Targeting: Military Objectives, Proportionality and Precautions in Attack under Additional Protocol I.* Leiden: Martinus Nijhoff Publishers.

Herzberg, Anne and Gerald M. Steinberg. 2012. "IHL 2.0: Is There a Role for Social Media in Monitoring and Enforcement?" *Israel Law Review* 45: p. 493.

Higgins, Rosalyn. 1994. *Problems and Process: International Law and How We Use It.* Oxford: Oxford University Press.

International Committee of the Red Cross. 1987. *Commentary on the Additional Protocols of 8 June 1977 to the Geneva Conventions of 12 August 1949*, edited by Yves Sandoz, Christophe Swinarki, and Bruno Zimmerman. Geneva: Martinus Nihoff Publishers.

International Committee of the Red Cross. 2016. *Commentary on the First Geneva Convention (I) for the Amelioration of the Condition of the Wounded and Sick in the Field*. 2nd ed.

International Committee of the Red Cross. 2017. *Commentary on the Second Geneva Convention: Convention (II) for the Amelioration of the Condition of the Wounded, Sick and Shipwrecked Members of Armed Forces at Sea*. 2nd ed. ihl-databases.icrc.org/applic/ihl/ihl.nsf/Comment.xsp?action=openDocument&documentId=1A35EE65211A18AEC12581150044243A.

International Committee of the Red Cross. 2018. *The Principle of Proportionality in the Rules Governing the Conduct of Hostilities Under International Humanitarian Law, International Expert Meeting June 22–23, 2016, Quebec*. Univesité Laval and the International Committee of the Red Cross.

Ipsen, Knut. 2013. "Combatants and Non-Combatants." In *The Handbook of International Humanitarian Law*, edited by Dieter Fleck, p. 80. 3rd ed. Oxford: Oxford University Press.

Jankowski, Paul. 2014. *Verdun: The Longest Battle of the Great War*. Oxford: Oxford University Press.

Jochnik, Chris af and Roger Normand 1994. "The Legitimization of Violence: A Critical History of the Laws of War." *Harvard Journal of International Law* 35 (2): pp. 49–95, 387.

Joseph, Sarah et al. 2004. *The International Covenant on Civil and Political Rights: Cases, Materials, and Commentary*. Oxford: Oxford University Press.

Judah, Tim. 2008. *Kosovo: What Everyone Needs to Know*. Oxford: Oxford University Press.

Kalshoven, Frits. 1992. Remarks by Frits Kalshoven, *American Society of International Law Proceedings* 86: p. 40.

Kalshoven, Frits and Liesbeth Zegveld. 2011. *Constraints on the Waging of War: An Introduction to International Humanitarian Law*. 4th ed. Cambridge: Cambridge University Press.

Kasher, Asa and Shaul Kimhi. 2015. "Moral Dilemmas in Military Situations: Proportionality Principle, Religiosity, Political Attitudes, and Authoritarian Personality." *Journal of Military Psychology* 27 (3): p.169.

Kasher, Asa and Amos Yadlin. 2005. "Military Ethics of Fighting Terror: An Israeli Perspective." *Journal of Military Ethics* 4 (1): p. 3.

Kasher, Asa and Amos Yadlin. 2009. "Israel & the Rules of War: An Exchange." *The New York Review of Books*. June 11. www.nybooks.com/articles/2009/06/11/israel-the-rules-of-war-an-exchange/.

Kleffner, Jan. 2018. "Military Collaterals and Ius in Bello Proportionality." *Israel Year Book of Human Rights* 48: p. 43.

Kretzmer, David. 2013. "The Inherent Right to Self Defence and Proportionality in Jus Ad Bellum." *European Journal of International Law* 24: p. 235.

Krulak, Charles. 1999. "The Strategic Corporal: Leadership in the Three Block War." *The Marines Magazine*. http://www.au.af.mil/au/awc/awcgate/usmc/strategic_corporal.htm.

Lederman, Marty. 2016. "A Quick Response to John Merriam on Proportionality and Military Medical Personnel." *Just Security*. July 9. https://www.justsecurity.org/31909/quick-response-john-merriam-proportionality-military-medical-personnel/.

Lefkowitz, David. 2008. "Collateral Damage." In *War: Essays in Political Philosophy*, edited by Larry May, p. 145. Cambridge: Cambridge University Press.

Liddy, Lynda. 2013. "The Strategic Corporal: Some Requirements in Training and Education." *The Australian Army Journal* 11 (2): p. 139.

Lieblich, Eliav. 2018. "Collectivizing Threat: An Analysis of Israel's Legal Claims for Resort to Force on the Gaza Border." *Just Security*. May 16. https://www.justsecurity.org/56346/collectivizing-threat-analysis-israels-legal-claims-resort-force-gaza-border/.

Lillich, Richard B. 1985. "The Paris Minimum Standards of Human Rights Norms in a State of Emergency." *American Journal of International Law* 79 (4): p. 1072.

Luban, David. 2013. "Military Necessity and the Cultures of Military Law." *Leiden Journal of International Law* 26 (2): p. 315.

Lubell, Noam and Cohen, Amichai. 2020 "Strategic Proportionality: Limitations on the Use of Force in Modern Armed Conflicts." *International Law Studies* 96: p. 159.

Malkasian, Carter. 2007. "The First Battle for Fallujah, in War." In *Iraq: Planning and Execution*, edited by T.G. Mahnken and T.A. Keaney, p. 163. London and New York: Routledge.

May, Larry. 2007. *War Crimes and Just War*. New York: Cambridge University Press.

McCubbins, Mathew D. et al. 1989. "Structure and Process, Politics and Policy: Administrative Arrangements and the Political Control of Agencies." *Virginia Law Review* 75 (2): p. 431.

McCubbins, Mathew D. et al. 1999. "The Political Origins of the Administrative Procedure Act." *Journal of Law Economics and Organization* 15 (1): p. 180.

McCubbins, Mathew D., Roger G. Noll, and Barry R. Weingast. 1987. "Administrative Procedures as Instruments of Political Control." *Journal of Law Economics and Organization* 3: p. 243.

McNeal, Gregory S. 2014. "Targeted Killing and Accountability." *Georgetown Law Journal* 102 (1): p. 681.

Melzer, Nils. 2009. *Interpretative Guidance on the Notion of Direct Participation in Hostilities Under International Humanitarian Law*. Geneva: International Committee of the Red Cross.

Melzer, Nils. 2009. *Targeted Killing in International Law*. Oxford: Oxford University Press.

Meron, Theodor. 2000. "The Martens Clause, Principles of Humanity, and Dictates of Public Conscience." *American Journal of International Law* 94 (1): p. 78.

Merriam, John. 2016. "Must Military Medical and Religious Personnel Be Accounted for in a Proportionality Analysis?" *Just Security*. July 8. www.justsecurity.org/31905/military-medical-religious-personnel-accounted-proportionality-analysis/.

Meyerstein, Ariel. 2002. "Case Study: The Israeli Strike Against Hamas Leader Salah Shehadeh." *Crimes of War*. Sept. 19. http://www.crimesofwar.org/print/onnews/Shehadeh-print.html.

Milanovic, Marko. 2011. "Norm Conflicts, International Humanitarian Law, and Human Rights." In *International Humanitarian Law and International Human Rights Law*, edited by Orna Ban-Naftali, p. 95. Oxford: Oxford University Press.

Milanovic, Marko and Vidan Hadzi-Vidanovic. 2013. "A Taxonomy of Armed Conflict." In *Research Handbook on International Conflict and Security Law*, edited by Nigel D. White and Christian Henderson, p. 256. Cheltenham, UK: Edward Edgar Publishing.

Montefiore, Simon Sebag. 2011. *Jerusalem: The Biography*. New York: Alfred A. Knopf.

Morrow, James D. 2007. "When Do States Follow the Laws of War?" *American Political Science Review* 101: p. 559.

Morrow, James. 2014. *Order within Anarchy: The Laws of War as an International Institution*. New York: Cambridge University Press.

Newton, Michael and Larry May. 2014. *Proportionality in International Law*. New York: Oxford University Press.

Oeter, Stefan. 2008. "Methods and Means of Combat." In *The Handbook of International Humanitarian Law*, edited by Terry Gill and Dieter Fleck, p. 119. 2nd ed. Oxford: Oxford University Press.

O'Keefe, Roger. 2013. "Protection of Cultural Property." In *The Handbook of International Humanitarian Law*, edited by Dieter Fleck, p. 425. 3rd ed. Oxford: Oxford University Press.

Orend, Brian. 2013. *The Morality of War*. 2nd ed. Peterborough, ON: Broadview Press.

Parks, W. Hays. 1990. "Air War and the Law of War." *Air Force Law Review* 32 (1): p. 1.

Parks, W. Hays. 2007. "Asymmetries and the Identification of Legitimate Military Objectives." In *International Humanitarian Law Facing New Challenges*, edited by Wolff H. von Heinegg, p. 65. Berlin: Springer.

Paulus, Andreas and Mindia Vashakmadze. "Asymmetrical War and the Notion of Armed Conflict—A Tentative Conceptualization." *International Review of the Red Cross* 873 (91): p. 95.

Peters, Anne. 2016. "Global Animal Law: What Is It, and Why We Need It." *Transnational Environmental Law* 5 (1): p. 9.

Petit, Phillip. 1991. "Consequentialism." In *A Companion to Ethics*, edited by Peter Singer. Oxford: Blackwell.

Pictet, Jean. 1985. *Development and Principles of International Humanitarian Law*. Dodrecht: Martinus Nijhoff Publishers.

Pomson, Ori & Yonatan Horwitz. 2015. "Humanitarian Intervention and the Clean Hands Doctrine in International Law." *Israel Law Review* 48 (2): p. 219.

Posner, Eric A. 2003. "Centennial Tribute Essay, A Theory of the Laws of War." *University of Chicago Law Review* 70: p. 297.

Posner, Eric A. 2012. "Human Rights, the Laws of War, and Reciprocity." *Law & Ethics of Human Rights* 6 (2): p. 147.

Posner, Eric A. and Alan O. Sykes. 2013. *Economic Foundations of International Law*. Cambridge, MA: Belknap Press of Harvard University Press.

Program on Humanitarian Policy and Conflict Research at Harvard University. 2010. *Commentary on the HPCR Manual on International Law Applicable to Air and Missile Warfare*.

RAFAEL, Advanced Defense Systems Ltd. 2012. *Iron Dome*. www.rafael.co.il/Marketing/186-1530-en/Marketing.aspx.

Richmond Barak, Daphne and Eyal Feinberg. 2016. "The Irony of the Iron Dome: Intelligent Defense Systems, Law, and Security." *Harvard National Security Journal* 7: p. 469.

Roberts, Adam. 2008. "The Equal Application of the Law of War: A Principle under Pressure." *International Review of the Red Cross* 90 (872): p. 931.

Robinson, Isable and Ellen Nohle. 2016. "Proportionality and Precautions in Attack: The Reverberating Effects of Using Explosive Weapons in Populated Areas." *International Review of the Red Cross* 98 (1): p. 107.

Rogers, A.P.V. 2000. "Zero-Casualty Warfare." *International Review of the Red Cross* 82 (837): p. 165. www.icrc.org/eng/resources/documents/article/other/57jqcu.htm.

Rogers, A.P.V. 2004. *Law on the Battlefield*. 2nd ed. Huntington, NY: Juris Publishing.

Rogers, A.P.V. 2007. "The Principle of Proportionality." In *The Legitimate Use of Military Force: The Just War Tradition and the Customary Law of Armed Conflict*, edited by Howard M. Hensel, p. 189. Huntington, NY: Routledge.

Rogers, A.P.V. 2012. *Law on the Battlefield*. 3rd ed. Manchester and New York: Manchester University Press.

Ronen, Yaël. 2009. "Avoid or Compensate? Liability for Incidental Injury to Civilians Inflicted During Armed Conflict." *Vanderbilt Journal of Transnational Law* 42 (1): p. 181.

Ronen, Yaël. 2010. "Superior Responsibility of Civilian for International Crimes Committed in Civilian Settings." *Vanderbilt Journal of Transnational Law* 43 (2): p. 313.

Rozenzweig, Ido. "Rethinking the Basic Principles of IHL and Their Application to Combatants' Lives" (draft article, on file with authors).

Rubinstein, Amnon and Yaniv Roznai. 2011. "Human Shields in Modern Armed Conflicts: The Need for a Proportionate Proportionality." *Stanford Law & Policy Review 22* (1): p. 93.

Sassoli, Marco and Lindsey Cameron. 2006. "The Protection of Civilian Objects—Current State of Law and Issues de Lege Ferenda." In *The Law of Air Warfare: Contemporary Issues*, edited by Natalino Ronzitti and Gabriella Venturini, p. 35. Utrecht: Eleven International Publishing.

Sassoli, Marco et al. 2011. *How Does Law Protect in War?* Vol. 1. 3rd ed. Geneva: International Committee of the Red Cross.

Savage, Charlie. 2015. *Power Wars: Inside Obama's Post-9/11 Presidency*. New York: Little, Brown & Co.

Shaw, Malcolm N. 2008. *International Law*. 6th ed. Cambridge: Cambridge University Press.

Scharre, Paul. 2018. *Army of None: Autonomous Weapons and the Future of War*. New York: W. W. Norton & Company.

Schmitt, Michael N. 1999. "The Principle of Discrimination in 21 Century Warfare." *Yale Human Rights & Development Law Journal* 2 (1): p. 143.

Schmitt, Michael N. 2008. "Asymmetrical Warfare and International Humanitarian Law." *Air Force Law Review* 62 (1): p. 33.

Schmitt, Michael N. 2009. "Human Shields in International Humanitarian Law." *Columbia Journal of Transnational Law* 47 (2): p. 292.

Schmitt, Michael N. 2009. "Targeting and International Humanitarian Law in Afghanistan." In *The War in Afghanistan: A Legal Analysis, International Law Studies* 85 (1): p. 307.

Schmitt, Michael N. 2010. "Military Necessity and Humanity in International Humanitarian Law: Preserving the Delicate Balance." *Virginia Journal of International Law* 50 (4): p. 795.

Schmitt, Michael N. 2010. "Deconstructing Direct Participation in Hostilities: The Constitutive Elements." *New York University Journal of International Law and Policy* 42 (3): p. 697.

Schmitt, Michael. 2010. "The Interpretive Guidance on the Notion of Direct Participation in Hostilities: A Critical Analysis." *Harvard National Security Journal* 1 (1): p. 6.

Schmitt, Michael N. 2012. *Essays on Law and War at the Fault Lines*. The Hague: T.M.C. Asser Press.

Schmitt, Michael N. 2013. "Wound, Capture, or Kill: A Reply to Ryan Goodman's 'The Power to Kill or Capture Enemy Combatants.'" *European Journal of International Law* 24 (3): p. 855.

Schmitt, Michael. 2015. "The Relationship Between Context and Proportionality: A Reply to Cohen and Shany." *Just Security*. May 11. www.justsecurity.org/22948/response-cohen-shany/.

Schmitt, Michael and John Merriam. 2015. "A Legal and Operational Assessment of Israel's Targeting Practices." *Just Security*. Apr. 24. www.justsecurity.org/22392/legal-operational-assessment-israels-targeting-practices/.

Schmitt, Michael N. and John J. Merriam. 2015. "The Tyranny of Context: Israeli Targeting Practices in Legal Perspective." *University of Pennsylvania Journal of International Law* 37 (1): p. 53.

Schwartz, Yishai. 2015. "Defining Anticipated Military Advantage: The Importance of Certainty." *Lawfare Blog*. May 22. www.lawfareblog.com/defining-anticipated-military-advantage-importance-certainty

Shany, Yuval. 2009. *The Principle of Proportionality under International Law*. Jerusalem: Israel Democracy Institute (Heb.).

Shany, Yuval and Keren Michaeli. 2002. "The Case against Ariel Sharon: Revisiting the Doctrine of Command Responsibility." *New York University Journal of International Law & Politics* 34: p. 797.

Shepsle, Kenneth A. and Mark S. Bonchek. 1997. *Analyzing Politics: Rationality, Behavior, and Institutions*. New York: W. W. Norton.

Shereshevsky, Yahli. 2019. "HCJ 3003/18 Yesh Din – Volunteers for Human Rights v. Chief of General Staff, Israel Defense Forces (IDF)." *American Journal of International Law* 113 (2): p. 361.

Sidgwick, Henry. 1891. *The Elements of Politics*. London: Macmillan & Co.

Sloane, Robert D. 2009. "The Cost of Conflation: Preserving the Dualism of Jus in Bello and Jus ad Bellum in the Contemporary Law of War." *Yale Journal of International Law* 24: p. 47.

Sloane, Robert D. 2015. "Puzzles of Proportion and the 'Reasonable Military Commander': Reflections on the Law, Ethics, and Geopolitics of Proportionality." *Harvard National Security Journal* 6: p. 299.

Smith, Rupert. 2005. *The Utility of Force: The Art of War in the Modern World*. London: Allen Lane.

Solis, Gary. 2010. *The Law of Armed Conflict: International Humanitarian Law in War*. New York: Cambridge University Press.

Solis, Gary D. 2016. *The Law of Armed Conflict: International Humanitarian Law in War*. 2nd ed. New York: Cambridge University Press.

Statman, Daniel et al. 2020. "Unreliable Protection: An Experimental Study of Experts' In-Bello Proportionality Decisions." *The European Journal of International Law* 31 (2): 429.

Sulitzeanu-Kenan, Raanan, Mordechai Kremnitzer, and Sharon Alon. 2016. "Facts, Preferences, and Doctrine: An Empirical Analysis of Proportionality Judgment." *Law and Society Review* 50: p. 348.

*Tallinn Manual 2.0 on the International Law Applicable to Cyber Operations.* 2017. Edited by Michael N. Schmitt. New York: Cambridge University Press.

Totten, Mark. 2007. "Using Force First: Moral Tradition and the Case for Revision." *Stanford Journal of International Law* 43 (1): 95.

Viterbo, Hedi. 2018. "Future-Oriented Measures." In *The ABC of the OPT: A Legal Lexicon of the Israeli Control over the Occupied Palestinian Territory*, edited by Orna Ben Naftali et al., p. 127. Cambridge and New York: Cambridge University Press.

Voeneky, Silja. 2013. "Implementation and Enforcement of International Humanitarian Law." In *The Handbook of International Humanitarian Law*, edited by Dieter Fleck, p. 647. 3rd ed. Oxford: Oxford University Press.

Walzer, Michael. 2006. *Just and Unjust Wars.* 4th ed. New York: Basic Books.

Walzer, Michael and Avishai Margalit. 2009. "Israel: Civilians & Combatants." *The New York Review of Books.* May 14. www.nybooks.com/articles/2009/05/14/israel-civilians-combatants/.

Watson, Alan. 1998. *The Digest of Justinian, Volume 1*, edited and translated by Alan Watson, p. 291. Philadelphia: University of Pennsylvania Press.

Wetzel, Lee. 2007. "Post Conflict National Human Rights Institutions: Emerging Models from Northern Ireland and Bosnia & Herzegovina." *Columbia Journal of European Law* 13 (2): p. 427.

Wright, Jason D. 2012. "Excessive" Ambiguity: Analysing and Refining the Proportionality Standard." *International Review of the Red Cross* 94 (886): p. 819.

Zemach, Ariel. 2018. "Indeterminacy in the Law of War." *Brooklyn Journal of International Law* 43 (1): p. 1.

Zimmerman, Andreas. 2007. "The Second Lebanon War: Jus ad Bellum, Jus in Bello and the Issue of Proportionality." *Max Planck Yearbook of United Nations Law* 11 (1): p. 99.

Zlotogorski, David. 2013. "Derogation from the Obligations under the Refugee Convention in Times of Emergency in Israel." *HaMishpat Online: Human Rights* 18 (1): p. 25 (Heb.).

## International Reports and Statements

Human Rights Committee. 2001. *General Comment 29*, U.N. Doc. CCPR/C/21/Rev.1/Add.11.

Human Rights Committee. 2004. *General Comment 31*, U.N. Doc. CCPR/C/21/Rev.1/Add.13.

Human Rights Committee. 2013. *Consideration of Reports Submitted by States Parties under Article 40 of the Covenant Pursuant to the Optional Reporting Procedure: Fourth periodic reports of states parties due in 2013—Israel.* Oct, 14.

Human Rights Committee. 2018. *General Comment No. 36 (2018) on article 6 of the International Covenant on Civil and Political Rights, on the Right to Life.* Oct. 31. www.tbinternet.ohchr.org/Treaties/CCPR/Shared%20Documents/1_Global/CCPR_C_GC_36_8785_E.pdf.

International Committee of the Red Cross. 1956. *Draft Rules for the Limitation of the Dangers Incurred by the Civilian Population in Time of War.* ihl-databases.icrc.org/

applic/ihl/ihl.nsf/Article.xsp?action=openDocument&documentId=5968DF93FC478018C12563CD0051D111.

International Committee of the Red Cross. 2015. *32nd International Conference of the Red Cross and Red Crescent: International Humanitarian Law and the Challenges of Contemporary Armed Conflicts.*

International Criminal Court. 2011. *Elements of Crimes.* The International Criminal Court.

International Criminal Tribunal for the former Yugoslavia. 2000. *Final Report to the Prosecutor by the Committee Established to Review the NATO Bombing Campaign Against the Federal Republic of Yugoslavia.* http://www.icty.org/en/press/final-report-prosecutor-committee-established-review-nato-bombing-campaign-against-federal.

*Report of the Detailed Findings of the Independent Commission of Inquiry Established Pursuant to Human Rights Council Resolution.* U.N. Doc. A/HRC/29/CRP.4. June 23. https://www.ohchr.org/en/hrbodies/hrc/coigazaconflict/pages/reportcoigaza.aspx.

United Nations Human Rights Council. 2009. *Report of the United Nations Fact-Finding Mission on the Gaza Conflict,* U.NOTE Doc. A/HRC/12/48. Sept. 25.

## State Ratifications and Observations of International Treaties

Australia, *Statement on Ratification of AP-I,* June 21, 1991, 1642 U.N.T.S. 473, *available at:* ihl-databases.icrc.org/applic/ihl/ihl.nsf/Notification.xsp?action=openDocument&documentId=10312B4E9047086EC1256402003FB253.

Austria, *Statement on Ratification of AP-I,* Aug. 13, 1982, 1289 U.N.T.S. 303, *available at:* ihl-databases.icrc.org/applic/ihl/ihl.nsf/Notification.xsp?action=openDocument&documentId=C5CD201B43C3E56AC1256402003FB262.

Belgium, *Statement on Ratification of AP-I,* May 20, 1986, 1435 U.N.T.S. 367, *available at:* ihl-databases.icrc.org/applic/ihl/ihl.nsf/Notification.xsp?action=openDocument&documentId=EA2560B9B790488EC1256402003FB2BC [Belgium, *Statement on Ratification of AP-I*].

Canada, *Statement on Ratification of AP-I,* Nov. 20, 1990, 1591 U.N.T.S. 462, *available at:* ihl-databases.icrc.org/applic/ihl/ihl.nsf/Notification.xsp?action=openDocument&documentId=172FFEC04ADC80F2C1256402003FB314..

France, *Statement on Ratification of AP-I,* Apr. 11, 2001, *available at:* ihl-databases.icrc.org/applic/ihl/ihl.nsf/Notification.xsp?action=openDocument&documentId=D8041036B40EBC44C1256A34004897B2 [France, *Statement on Ratification of AP-I*].

Germany, *Statement on Ratification of AP-I,* Feb. 14, 1991, 1607 U.N.T.S. 526, *available at:* ihl-databases.icrc.org/applic/ihl/ihl.nsf/Notification.xsp?action=openDocument&documentId=3F4D8706B6B7EA40C1256402003FB3C7.

Ireland, *Statement on Ratification of AP-I,* May 5, 1999, 2073 U.N.T.S. 28, *available at:* ihl-databases.icrc.org/applic/ihl/ihl.nsf/Notification.xsp?action=openDocument&documentId=27BBCD34A4918BFBC1256402003FB43A.

Italy, *Statement on Ratification of AP-I,* Feb. 27, 1986, 1425 U.N.T.S. 438, *available at:* ihl-databases.icrc.org/applic/ihl/ihl.nsf/Notification.xsp?action=openDocument&documentId=E2F248CE54CF09B5C1256402003FB443 [Italy, *Statement on Ratification of AP-I*].

Netherlands, *Statement on Ratification of AP-I,* Jun. 26, 1987, 1477 U.N.T.S. 300, *available at:* ihl-databases.icrc.org/applic/ihl/ihl.nsf/Notification.xsp?action=openDocument&documentId=E6EF925C67966E90C1256402003FB532.

New Zealand, *Statement on Ratification of AP-I,* Feb. 8, 1988, 1499 U.N.T.S. 358, *available at:* ihl-databases.icrc.org/applic/ihl/ihl.nsf/Notification.xsp?action=openDocument&documentId=8FEC3861203ABE21C1256402003FB53B.

Spain, *Statement on Ratification of AP-I,* Apr. 21, 1989, 1537 U.N.T.S. 390, *available at:* ihl-databases.icrc.org/applic/ihl/ihl.nsf/Notification.xsp?action=openDocument&documentId=FC622F31C9E2236EC1256402003FB660.

United Kingdom of Great Britain and Northern Ireland, *Reservation*, July 2, 2002, *available at:* ihl-databases.icrc.org/applic/ihl/ihl.nsf/Notification.xsp?action=openDocument&documentId=0A9E03F0F2EE757CC1256402003FB6D2.

U.S., *Statement on Consent to Be Bound by CCW Protocol III on Incendiary Weapons*, Jan. 21, 2009, 2562 U.N.T.S. 36.

## State Reports and Publications

### Israel

The State of Israel, Ministry of Foreign Affairs. 2009. *The Operation in Gaza 27 December 2008–18 January 2009: Factual and Legal Aspects.*

*Report of the Special Investigatory Commission on the Targeted Killing of Salah Shehadeh.* Feb. 2011. www.pmo.gov.il/SiteCollectionDocuments/PMO/32communication/spokemes/reportshchade.pdf.

IDF Military Advocate General. 2018. *Decisions of the IDF Military Advocate General Regarding Exceptional Incidents that Allegedly Occurred During Operation 'Protective Edge. Update No. 6.* Aug. 15. https://mfa.gov.il/MFA/ForeignPolicy/IsraelGaza2014/Documents/Operation-Protective-Edge-MAG-Corps-Press-Release-Update-6-15-August-2018.pdf.

The Public Commission to Examine the Maritime Incident of 31 May 2010. 2013. *Second Report: Israel's Mechanisms for Examining and Investigating Complaints and Claims of Violations of the Laws of Armed Conflict.* https://www.gov.il/en/Departments/General/turkel_committee.

### United Kingdom

United Kingdom Ministry of Defence. 2004. *Joint Service Publication 383, The Joint Service Manual of the Law of Armed Conflict*. Shirvenham, UK: The Joint Doctrine & Concepts Centre.

### United States

US Department of Defense. 2014. *Law of War Manual U.S. Army Field Manual 3-24 Insurgencies and Countering Insurgencies.*

US Department of Defense. 2016. *Law of War Manual* (Updated Dec. 2016.)

US Procedures for Approving Direct Action against Terrorist Targets Located Outside the United States and Areas of Active Hostilities. 2013. May 22. https://www.justice.gov/oip/foia-library/procedures_for_approving_direct_action_against_terrorist_targets/download.

Headquarters, Department of the Army. 2014. *Field Manual 3-24/MCWP 3-33.5, Insurgencies and Countering Insurgencies*. June 2. Washington, D.C. fas.org/irp/doddir/army/fm3-24.pdf.

U.S. Joint Chiefs of Staff. 2013. *Joint Targeting, Joint Publication 3–60*. Jan. 31. www.cfr.org/content/publications/attachments/Joint_Chiefs_of_Staff-Joint_Targeting_31_January_2013.pdf.

*Article 15-6 Investigation of the 800th Military Police Brigade ("The Tagoba Report")*. 2004. http://hrlibrary.umn.edu/OathBetrayed/Taguba-Report.pdf.

Final Report of the Independent Panel to Review the DOD Detention. Aug. 2004. https://www.hsdl.org/?abstract&did=449289

The Office of Professional Responsibility. 2009. *Investigation into the Office of Legal Counsel's Memoranda Concerning Issues Related to the Central Intelligence Agency's Use of "Enhanced Interrogation Techniques" on Suspected Terrorists*. July 29. https://www.hsdl.org/?abstract&did=28555.

The White House. 2013. "Remarks by the President at the National Defense University." May 23. https://obamawhitehouse.archives.gov/the-press-office/2013/05/23/remarks-president-national-defense-university.

# INDEX

*For the benefit of digital users, indexed terms that span two pages (e.g., 52–53) may, on occasion, appear on only one of those pages.*

www.ingramcontent.com/pod-product-compliance
Lightning Source LLC
LaVergne TN
LVHW011819200926
848484LV00005B/1250

* 9 7 8 0 1 9 7 5 5 6 7 2 6 *